AF712269

ARROVIAN AGGREGATION MODELS

THEORY AND DECISION LIBRARY

General Editors: W. Leinfellner (*Vienna*) and G. Eberlein (*Munich*)

Series A: Philosophy and Methodology of the Social Sciences

Series B: Mathematical and Statistical Methods

Series C: Game Theory, Mathematical Programming and Operations Research

SERIES B: MATHEMATICAL AND STATISTICAL METHODS

VOLUME 39

Editor: H. J. Skala (Paderborn); *Assistant Editor*: M. Kraft (Paderborn); *Editorial Board:* J. Aczél (Waterloo, Ont.), G. Bamberg (Augsburg), H. Drygas (Kassel), W. Eichhorn (Karlsruhe), P. Fishburn (Murray Hill, N.J.), D. Fraser (Toronto), W. Janko (Vienna), P. de Jong (Vancouver), T. Kariya (Tokyo), M. Machina (La Jolla, Calif.), A. Rapoport (Toronto), M. Richter (Kaiserslautern), B. K. Sinha (Cattonsville, Md.), D. A. Sprott (Waterloo, Ont.), P. Suppes (Stanford, Calif.), H. Theil (St. Augustine, Fla.), E. Trillas (Madrid), L. A. Zadeh (Berkeley, Calif.).

Scope: The series focuses on the application of methods and ideas of logic, mathematics and statistics to the social sciences. In particular, formal treatment of social phenomena, the analysis of decision making, information theory and problems of inference will be central themes of this part of the library. Besides theoretical results, empirical investigations and the testing of theoretical models of real world problems will be subjects of interest. In addition to emphasizing interdisciplinary communication, the series will seek to support the rapid dissemination of recent results.

The titles published in this series are listed at the end of this volume.

FUAD ALESKEROV

Boğaziçi University, Bebek, Istanbul, Turkey
and
Russian Academy of Sciences, Institute of Control Sciences, Moscow, Russia

ARROVIAN AGGREGATION MODELS

KLUWER ACADEMIC PUBLISHERS
BOSTON / DORDRECHT / LONDON

A C.I.P. Catalogue record for this book is available from the Library of Congress.

ISBN 0-7923-8451-2

Published by Kluwer Academic Publishers,
P.O. Box 17, 3300 AA Dordrecht, The Netherlands.

Sold and distributed in North, Central and South America,
by Kluwer Academic Publishers,
101 Philip Drive, Norwell, MA 02061, U.S.A.

In all other countries, sold and distributed
by Kluwer Academic Publishers,
P.O. Box 322, 3300 AH Dordrecht, The Netherlands.

Printed on acid-free paper

All Rights Reserved
©1999 Kluwer Academic Publishers, Boston
No part of the material protected by this copyright notice may be reproduced or
utilized in any form or by any means, electronic or mechanical,
including photocopying, recording or by any information storage and
retrieval system, without written permission from the copyright owner

Printed in the Netherlands.

TO MY PARENTS

TABLE OF CONTENTS

FOREWORD

Aggregation of individual opinions into a social decision is a problem widely observed in everyday life. During centuries people tried to invent the 'best' aggregation rule. In 1951 young American scientist and future Nobel Prize winner Kenneth Arrow formulated the problem in an axiomatic way, i.e., he specified a set of axioms to which every reasonable aggregation rule seems has to satisfy, and obtained that these axioms are inconsistent. This result, often called Arrow's Paradox or General Impossibility Theorem, had become a corner stone of social choice theory, a vast and ever increasing scientific field. In contrast to the earlier stage in the development of the theory, these works focus on finding a solution to the problem within the framework of the axiomatic approach with modified or weakened conditions than those proposed by K.Arrow.

The main condition used by K.Arrow was his famous Independence of Irrelevant Alternatives. This very condition pre-defines the 'local' treatment of the alternatives (or pairs of alternatives, or sets of alternatives, etc.) in aggregation procedures. The counterparts of that condition are called in the monograph as Locality condition.

Remaining within the framework of the axiomatic approach and based on the consideration of local rules, the book investigates three formulations of the aggregation problem according to the form in which the individual opinions about the alternatives are defined, as well as to the form of desired social decision. In other words, we study three aggregation models. What is common between them is that in all models some analogue of Independence of Irrelevant Alternatives condition is used. That is why we call these models as Arrovian aggregation models.

Chapter 1 presents a general description of the problem of axiomatic synthesis of local rules, and introduces problem formulations for various versions of formalization of individual opinions and collective decision.

Chapter 2 formalizes precisely the notion of 'rationality' of individual opinions and social decision. Various types of binary relations (preferences) are introduced and investigated. The characteristic conditions (often called Expansion-Contraction Axioms) identifying different classes of choice functions are defined here, and the interrelations between them are established. Additionally, the choice functions rationalizable by numerical (utility) functions are described, and interrelations between them and the choice functions rationalizable via binary relations are determined.

Chapter 3 deals with the aggregation model for the case of individual opinions and social decisions formalized as binary relations. Two types of local rules which are called Social Decision Rules, or Social Decision Functions, are studied. The explicit forms of those rules are completely investigated. Rules restricted by rationality constraints, i.e., by constraints on domains and ranges of the rules, are studied as well.

Chapter 4 deals with Functional Aggregation Rules which transform into a social choice function individual opinions defined as choice functions. In doing so, rationalizability of those choice functions is not assumed, that is, consideration is in general given to the non-classical choice functions. The explicit form of these rules is obtained and rules which satisfy different rationality constraints — such as those generating social choice functions from different classes in the set of choice functions — are studied.

Chapter 5 considers another model - Social Choice Correspondences when the individual opinions are formalized as binary relations, and the collective decision is look for as a choice function. The explicit form of rules is studied enabling a proper mapping with and without additional rationality constraints on the social choice function. The obtained classes comprise rules such as the generalized Pareto rules. Several new classes of rules are introduced and analyzed.

Bibliography lists the major publications in the field of axiomatic synthesis of Arrovian aggregation models.

ACKNOWLEDGEMENTS

First of all I would like to mention my dear friend and teacher Professor Mark Aizerman who was most supportive until his death in 1992. Mark and I made the study of functional aggregation rules (which presented in Sections 4.1-4.8 of Chapter 4), and his comments and help were very valuable for my studies of other models presented here.

I would like to express my deep gratitude to Professors Kenneth Arrow, Salvador Barbera, Michel Le Breton, Charles Plott, Norman Schofield, and Amartya Sen for their permanent interest to and support of this work.

I would like to thank also several colleagues from Boğaziçi University (Istanbul, Turkey) – Professors Ahmet Alkan, Güven Alpay, Emre Alper, and Süleyman Özmucur. I am particularly grateful to Professors Hasan Ersel and Murat Sertel for their support.

I also thank my graduate students in Boğaziçi University who took my courses on Social Choice Theory during 1996 -1998, and made a lot of helpful suggestions and comments.

Mrs. Natalya Andryushina prepared first (Russian) version of this text. Dr. Rovshan Mustafaev and Mr. Boris Mazets made computerized versions of all drawings. Mr. Boris Mazets did a lot of work to prepare the text in LATEX. I am thankful to these colleagues, as well as to Kluwer Publishers and Mr. Allard Winterink personally for patience and help expressed during the preparation of the manuscript.

Finally, my thanks go to my wife Inna and daughter Sara who always reveal their love and encouragement.

Naturally, all shortcomings are of my solely responsibility.

This work had been partially supported by the grants of European Community (ACE-91-RO2 and INTAS Project "Measurement and Aggregation of Preferences"), Russian Foundation of Basic Research (95-01-00057A), and by NATO Fellowship Program 1995-1996. All this support is gratefully acknowledged.

1

AGGREGATION: A GENERAL DESCRIPTION

1.1 Introduction

Collective decision making on the basis of aggregation procedures (in particular, on basis of voting procedures) dates from antiquity. Plutarch tells in his ' Lives' about two rules used at the times of the legendary Spartan king and legislator Lycurgus (IX – VIII cc. B.C.). One rule was used, in modern terms, for electing to a club: 'And they say that a candidate for membership in one of these messes underwent the following ordeal. Each of the mess-mates took in his hand a bit of soft bread, and when a servant came along with a bowl upon his head, then they cast it into this without a word, like a ballot, leaving it just as it was if he approved of the candidate, but if he disapproved, squeezing it tight in his hand first. For the flattened piece of bread had the force of a perforated, or negative, ballot. And if one such is found in the bowl, the candidate is not admitted to the mess, because they wish all its members to be congenial[1]'. Only the members of a club participated in the election.

Another procedure was used for electing the 'Council of the Elders,' where all Spartan population took part: 'The election was made in the following manner. An assembly of the people having been convened, chosen men were shut up in a room near by so that they could neither see nor be seen, but only hear the shouts of the assembly. For as in other matters, so here, the cries of the assembly decided between competitors. These did not appear in the body, but each one was introduced separately, as the lot fell, and passed silently through the assembly. Then the secluded judges, who had writing-tablets with them, recorded in each case the loudness of the shouting, not knowing for whom it was given, but only that he was introduced first, second, or third, and so on. Whoever was greeted with the most and loudest shouting, him they declared elected[2]'.

The origin of aggregation theory traditionally dates back to the end of the XVIII-th century when two members of l'Académie Française, J.C.Borda and I.A.Condorcet proposed procedures of collective choice (see [65] , [84]). Furthermore, Condorcet constructed the following remarkable example demonstrating that the well-known majority rule could give rise to unsolvable paradoxes.

---

1 Plutarch's Lives in eleven volumes. Cambridge, Massachusets, Harvard University Press. First print 1914, reprinted 1928, 1948, 1959. v.1, p.239-241

2 Ibid., p.285

Let a group of three individuals (electors) evaluate three alternatives — x, y, and z. The first elector prefers x to y and y to z, (and hence x to z), which is designated conventionally as $x \succ y \succ z$. The preferences of the second and third electors are, respectively, $z \succ x \succ y$ and $y \succ z \succ x$. If we assume that one alternative is preferable to another for the group as a whole if it is preferred at least by two (simple majority) members, we obtain the following collective decision based on the individual preferences: $x \succ y \succ z \succ x$, that is, for the group x is better than y, y is better than z, and z is better than x.

This striking result (often referred to as *Condorcet Paradox* or *Paradox of Voting*) gave rise to numerous studies that continued till the middle of this century and were aimed at avoiding such paradoxes by using other, more sophisticated procedures. Among the scientists who proposed their own aggregation rules were, for example, Rev. C.L. Dodgson [99, 100] known better as Lewis Carroll, the author of "Alice's Adventures in Wonderland" and "Through the Looking-Glass and What Alice Found There," E.Nanson [203] , et al. However, examples were constructed for all of these procedures demonstrating occurrence of similar paradoxes. The reader interested in the background of voting theory is referred to the monographs of D.Black [48] , H.Nurmi [205] , and V.Vol'skiy and Z.Lezina [274] .

The next important milestone in the development of the aggregation theory as we wrote above was reached in 1951 when K.Arrow formulated the problem of aggregation in different terms and solved it. Disregarding any particular rule, he formulated some conditions to be satisfied by any reasonable aggregation procedure, and his attempt to describe explicitly a procedure meeting these conditions had led to an absolutely unexpected conclusion — the conditions proved to be incompatible.

In the next Sections we study some examples and present a general description of aggregation problem.

1.2 Analysis of examples

Aggregation theory studies the following model: a group of any finite number n of agents (individuals, voters) considers a finite set A of alternatives (these can be candidates, plans, projects, etc.). Within the framework of some constraints that are similar for everybody[3], the agents can formulate their own opinions about the alternatives to be selected. The problem is to 'process' the generally non-coinciding decisions of the agents into a single social decision meeting the same constraints, if any. Consideration can be given either to the deterministic or the probabilistic statement of the problem. Below, we discuss the deterministic one[4].

Analysis of not only some social processes where n can be regarded as sufficiently great, but also of collective decision making in 'small groups' such as boards, committees, meetings, etc., reduces to the models of this kind. We begin with two examples of aggregation rules.

3 The constraints can be exemplified by pointing out the number of options to be selected, etc.

4 For probabilistic re-formulation of aggregation models see, e.g., [39] .

Example 1. Let the collective decision is made by the '*k-majority*' rule if the number k $(1 \leq k \leq n)$ is fixed in advance, and that the decision is adopted by the group if at least k agents are for it. Various aggregation systems such as '*simple majority*' $(k = \lceil n/2 \rceil)$, '*qualified majority*' $(k = \lceil \alpha \cdot n \rceil$ where, for example, $\alpha = 2/3)$, '*unanimity*,' $(k = n)$ or '*One vote*' $(k = 1)$, are the special cases of the k-majority procedure. We note that the first procedure described by Plutarch is classified as that of Unanimity.

Example 2. Let us now consider that the collective decision is adopted according to *plurality rule*: the number of 'votes' for each alternative is counted, and those alternatives (possibly, several) for which the number of votes is maximal are selected (see the second procedure described by Plutarch, if every voter cried for only one candidate). One can directly see that for the case of two alternatives if abstention from expressing one's opinion is not permitted, the results of the k-majority rule and plurality rule coincide. Yet, for $|A| \geq 3$ the choice based on the k-majority rule may be empty, whereas the choice by plurality rule is always nonempty, but it may happen that more than half of agents disagree with the chosen alterative. Indeed, let the set A consists of the alternatives $\{x, y, z\}$, the number of agents be seven, the first two choose x, the next two, y, and the remaining three, z. According to the plurality rule, the alternative z will be chosen, although four of the seven agents are against it. If the k-majority rule with $k = \lceil n/2 \rceil = 4$, i.e. simple majority rule, is used, the choice will be empty.

These and other difficulties arising at use the two above mentioned rules have led to dozens of various procedures for social choice (see,e.g., [50, 72, 73, 104, 107, 165]), and the descriptions of new rules are still appearing in the literature (see, e.g., [241, 252]). However, as might be expected, it turned out that the 'best' procedure does not exists, and that each has its advantages and disadvantages. This gave rise to the problem of rules synthesis by defining a list of natural properties to be satisfied by the rule under study. It was first done by K.Arrow [27, 29] in his General Impossibility Theorem, which is formulated and studied in the next Section.

1.3 Arrow's General Impossibility Theorem

Although K.Arrow in his classic monograph [29] gave several versions of his *General Impossibility Theorem*, differing in conditions to which the rule transforming individual opinions to collective decision is to satisfy, we will consider in this section only one of the versions of that Theorem. Moreover, I consider here a more restricted model just to simplify readers' efforts to understand that classic result in this introductory Chapter. The problem is stated as follows. There are at least three individuals in the society, and the number of alternatives is not less than three. Individual opinion of an agent i is given as *linear order* P_i which can be represented as a graph of a very special type - transitive chain (Figure 1-1) and allows a simple interpretation of P_i as preference ('better than') relation. In this case any individual comparing two alternatives can state which one is better than the other. Individual opinions hence are represented as *profile*, i.e., as an ordered set $\vec{P} = (P_1, ..., P_n)$ of linear orders.

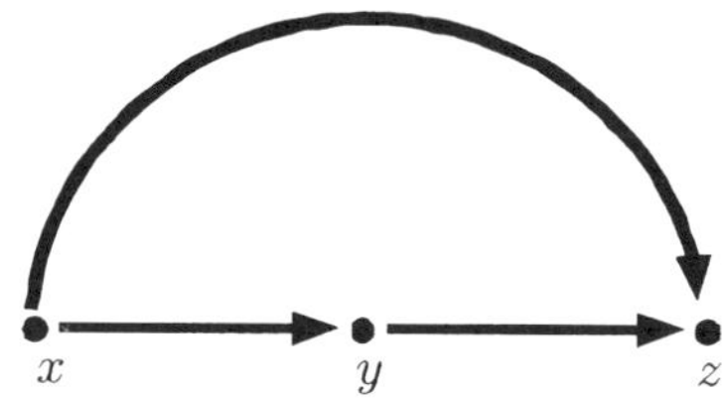

Figure 1-1

The first condition we can formulate following K.Arrow is the Condition of *Unrestricted Domain*:

(UD) Any linear order P_i is admissible as individual opinion.

Social decision in the model stated here is represented as a linear order P_i, i.e. for each pair of alternatives one alternative is socially preferred to the other. Hence, the rule in study is a function f defined on the n-tuples of individual linear orders; the range of f is the set of all linear orders, i.e., if $\mathcal{P}$ is the set of all linear orders, then $f : \mathcal{P}^n \to \mathcal{P}$.

Now let us define a *choice function* which is derived from collective decision P. Such function is called in [29] a *social welfare function*. This function $C(\cdot)$ for every non-empty subset X of the set A of alternatives defines the set of best alternatives in such a way that

$$C(X) = \{y \in X \mid \text{there is no } x \in X \text{ such that } xPy\}, \tag{1.1}$$

i.e., chooses on each X an undominated alternatives with respect to P. The function $C(\cdot)$ which can be derived as (1.1) from P is called *rationalizable by a binary relation* P.

The function $C(\cdot)$ derived from the linear order P shown at the Figure 1-1 is given in the Table 1-1. In this Table the values $C(\{x\})$ for each x are not shown which are assumed to be equal to the presented set, i.e. $C(\{x\}) = x$.

Table 1-1

X	{x,y,z}	{x,y}	{x,z}	{y,z}
C(X)	{x}	{x}	{x}	{y}

Before stating the next condition by which the aggregation rule is restricted, let us define the *contraction* P/X of binary relation P defined on the set A on a non-empty subset $X \subseteq A$. Namely, $P/X = P \cap (X \times X)$.

We introduce now the main restriction on the function f (on aggregation rule), Arrow's famous Condition of *Independence of Irrelevant Alternatives*.

(IIA) Let two individual profiles $\vec{P}$ and $\vec{P'}$ be given, and let $C(\cdot)$ and $C'(\cdot)$ be corresponding social welfare functions. Let for a given X these profiles are such that $\forall i\ P_i/X = P_i^{'}/X$. Then $C(X) = C'(X)$.

Let us illustrate this condition (IIA). On Figure 1-2 two profiles $\vec{P} = \{P_1, P_2, P_3\}$ and $\vec{P'} = \{P_1^{'}, P_2^{'}, P_3^{'}\}$ are shown. On the set $X = \{x, y, z\}$ $P_i/X = P_i^{'}/X$ for all i. Indeed, $P_1/X = \{(x,y),(x,z),(y,z)\}$, and it is equal to $P_1^{'}$;

$$P_2/X = \{(y,x),(y,z),(x,z)\} = P_2'/X;$$

and

$$P_3/X = \{(z,x),(z,y),(x,y)\} = P_3'/X.$$

Then according to the IIA the social choices $C(\{x,y,z\})$ and $C^{'}(\{x,y,z\})$ are to coincide. Note that $P_2/\{w,z\} = \{(z,w)\} \neq P_2'/\{w,z\}$.
Otherwise speaking, according to IIA, social decision on X is made without taking into account irrelevant alternatives.

The next constraint is *Pareto Principle* .

(PP) If for all i xP_iy holds, then xPy,

i.e., interpreting P_i and P as 'better than' relations, this condition says that if for everybody x is better than y, then it is the case for the social decision as well.

The last condition which we impose on the function f is also a very natural one. It restricts f in such a way that no person is decisive over any pair of alternatives regardless of opinions of other members of a society. It was called by K.Arrow '*Non-dictatorship*' Condition.

(ND) There is no $i_0 \in N$ such that $xP_{i_0}y$ implies xPy.

These four conditions look very natural indeed and seem to be desirable for any aggregation rule to satisfy these conditions. The striking result obtained by K.Arrow however was of opposite spirit.

Theorem 1.1 *Conditions (UD), (IIA), (PP) and (ND) are inconsistent.*

Proof. I practically cite here the original proof of the Theorem ([29] , p.98-100) modified it to the framework stated above[5].
A set of individuals V is called *decisive set* for x against y if x is socially chosen when every individual in V prefers x to y and every individual not in V prefers y to x. The proof falls into two parts. It is first shown that if an individual is decisive

[5] In Chapter 3 another proof of the Theorem will be given.

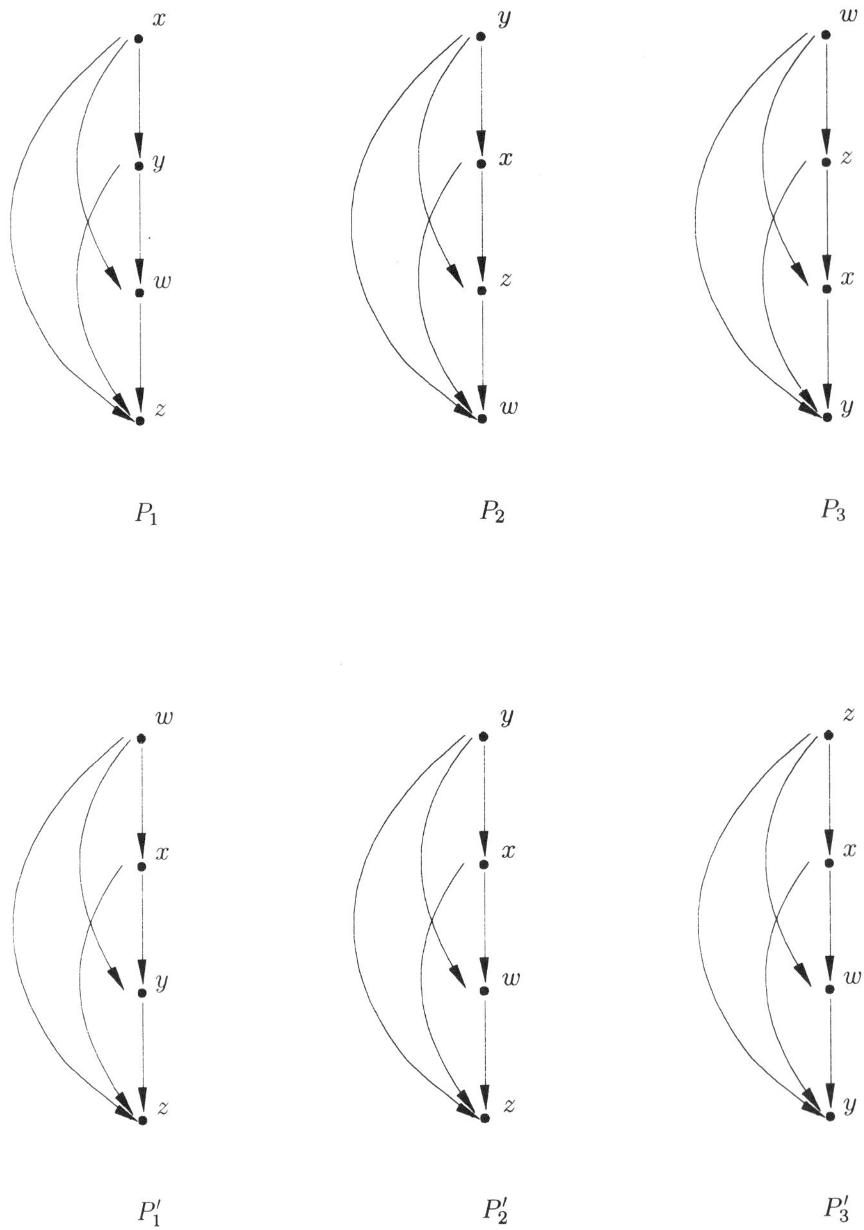

Figure 1-2

for some pair of alternatives, then he is a dictator, which is excluded by Condition ND; the impossibility theorem itself then follows very easily from the first result and Pareto Principle. We distinguish one individual, called I, and introduce the following notations for statements about the social welfare function:
(1) $x\ \bar{D}\ y$ means that x is socially preferred to y whenever I prefers x to y, regardless of the orderings of other individuals;
(2) xDy means that x is socially preferred to y if individual I prefers x to y and all other individuals have the opposite preference.
This notation is only legitimate because of Condition IIA, which assures us that the choice between x and y depends only on the preferences of all individuals concerning those two alternatives. Note that the statement, $x\ \bar{D}\ y$, implies xDy and that xDy is the same as the assertion that I is a decisive set for x against y. Suppose then that xDy holds for some x and y. We will first suppose that there are three alternatives altogether. Let the third alternative be z. Suppose I orders the alternatives, x, y, z in descending order, whereas all other individuals prefer y to both x and z, but may have any preferences as between the last two. Then I prefers x to y, whereas all others prefer y to x; from (2), this means that xPy. All individuals prefer y to z; by Condition PP, yPz. Then by transitivity, xPz; but then this holds whenever $xP_I z$, regardless of the orderings of other individuals. In symbols,
(3) xDy implies $x\ \bar{D}\ z$. Again suppose xDy, but now suppose that I orders the alternatives, z, x, y, whereas all other individuals prefer both z and y to x. By a similar argument, xPy and zPx, so that zPy.
(4) xDy implies $z\ \bar{D}\ y$. Interchanging y and z in (4) yields
(5) xDz implies $y\ \bar{D}\ z$. Replacing x by y, y by z, and z by x in (3) yields
(6) yDz implies $y\ \bar{D}\ x$.
Since $x\ \bar{D}\ z$ implies xDz, and $y\ \bar{D}\ z$ implies yDz, we can, by chaining the implications (3), (5), and (6), deduce
(7) xDy implies $y\ \bar{D}\ x$. If we interchange x and y in (3), (4), and (7), we arrive at the respective implications yDx implies $y\ \bar{D}\ z$, yDx implies $z\ \bar{D}\ x$, yDx implies $x\ \bar{D}\ y$, and these can each be chained with the implication (7) to yield
(8) xDy implies $y\ \bar{D}\ z$, $z\ \bar{D}\ x$, and $x\ \bar{D}\ y$. Implications (3), (4), (7), and (8) together can be summarized as saying
(9) If xDy, then $u\ \bar{D}\ v$ holds for every ordered pair u,v from the three alternatives x, y, and z; i.e., individual I is a dictator for the three alternatives.
Because of Condition UD, we can extend this result to any number of alternatives. Suppose aDb holds, and let x and y be any pair of alternatives. If x and y are the same as a and b, either in the same or in the reverse order, we add a third alternative c to a and b; then we can apply (9) to the triple a, b, c and deduce $x\ \bar{D}\ y$ by letting $u = x$, $v = y$. If exactly one of x and y is distinct from a and b, add it to a and b to form a triple to which again (9) is applicable. Finally, if both x and y arc distinct from a and b, two steps are needed. First, add x to a and b, and deduce from (9) that $a\ \bar{D}\ x$ and therefore aDx. Then, again applying (9) to the triple a, x, y, we find that $x\ \bar{D}\ y$. Thus, aDb for some a and b implies that $x\ \bar{D}\ y$ for all x and y, i.e., individual I is a dictator. From the Condition ND it can be concluded that

(10) xDy cannot hold for any individual I and any pair x, y.
The remainder of the proof is now an appropriate adaptation of the Paradox of Voting. By Condition PP, there is at least one decisive set for any ordered pair,x, y, namely, the set of all individuals. Among all sets of individuals which are decisive for some pairwise choice, pick one such that no other is smaller; by (10) it must contain at least two individuals. Let V be the chosen set, and let the ordered pair for which it is decisive be x, y. Divide V into two parts, V_1, which contains only a single individual, and V_2, which contains all the rest. Let V_3 be the set of individuals not in V. Consider now the case where the preference order of V_1 is x, y, z, that of all members of V_2 is z, x, y, and that of all members of V_3 is y, z, x.
Since V is decisive for x against y, and all members of V prefer x to y while all others have the opposite preference, xPy. On the other hand, it is impossible that society prefers z to y since that would require that V_2 be decisive on this issue; this is impossible since V_2 has fewer members than V, which, by construction, has as few members as a decisive set can have. Hence, yPz, and, since xPy, society must prefer x to z. But then the single member of V_1 would be decisive, and we have shown that to be impossible. Thus the contradiction is established. ■

One can re-formulate Theorem in the following way.

Theorem 1.2 *Conditions (UD), (IIA) and (PP) together satisfy iff the aggregation rule is a dictatorial one.*

The result stated by these theorems is often called *Arrow's Paradox*. One of the possible interpretations of this paradox is as follows. If everybody in the society is rational in the sense that she can "rank" all alternatives, then for the social decision to be rational in this very sense there is only one possibility, namely, social linear order must be defined by some dictator. Naturally, we impose two other constraints on aggregation function f - IIA and PP. This result created an overwhelming number of publications and discussions and can be considered as a corner-stone of modern social choice theory. The careful look on the conditions stated above as well as on the framework itself shows the ways along which this model can be elaborated and developed. Different possible ways to extend the framework of the arrovian model are discussed at the next sections.

1.4 Individual opinion: a formalization

The problem of aggregation cannot be formulated in precise terms until the notion of 'individual opinion' is formalized. For example, in Arrow's General Impossibility Theorem individual opinions have been represented as linear orders. The individual opinions can be described either by indicating some relations[6] between the alternatives from A (either between their subsets, or between subsets of alternatives and individual

[6] The concept of relations is based on preference of one alternative to another, on similarity or difference between alternatives, etc.

alternatives), or by indicating the alternatives selected by the agent from each non-empty subset $X \subseteq A$. Traditionally, the first approach formalizes the agent's opinion about alternatives as a *binary relation* P on the set A, i.e., $P \subseteq A \times A$. The second approach to describing agents' opinions consists in indicating directly the subset $Y \subseteq X$ chosen from each non-empty X from A. The set of all pairs $\{(X, Y)\}$ defines a *choice function* denoted by $C(\cdot)$ in what follows. Both approaches are interrelated by a *choice rule* π, explaining how the chosen alternatives $Y \subseteq X$ are distinguished in X using the contraction of the binary relation P on the set X, P/X. The rule π is exemplified by, e.g., selection of undominated alternatives if P is binary relation between alternatives, etc.

We introduce three spaces (sets) for consideration — the space $\mathcal{B}$ of the binary relations P, the space $\mathcal{C}$ of the choice functions $C(X)$, and the space Π of the choice rules (Figure1-3).

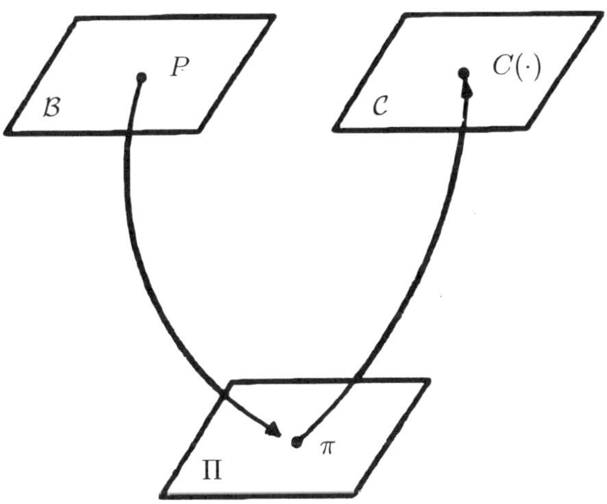

Figure 1-3

When the 'point' P in $\mathcal{B}$ and π in Π are chosen, the 'point' $C(\cdot)$ in $\mathcal{C}$ is fixed as well. Now, the question 'How a particular i-th agent makes choice?' can be answered in two ways — either one can indicate the relation P and the rule π used (for example, 'the agent chooses undominated alternatives with respect to P'), or describe somehow her choice function $C(\cdot)$ (for example, as a table 'given X – chosen Y' for all $X \subseteq A$). The introduction of the notions 'binary relation,' 'choice rule,' and 'choice function' translates the descriptive approach to the notion of reasonable, motivated choice (choice of a certain type, e.g., type $\mathcal{D}$) into the problem of formal description of some domains $\mathcal{B}_{\mathcal{D}}$, $\Pi_{\mathcal{D}}$ and $\mathcal{C}_{\mathcal{D}}$, respectively, to which must belong the relation P, the rule π, or the function $C(\cdot)$. Theory of choice introduces its own language for description of the domains $\mathcal{B}_{\mathcal{D}}$, $\Pi_{\mathcal{D}}$, and $\mathcal{C}_{\mathcal{D}}$.

The domains $\mathcal{B}_{\mathcal{D}}$ are defined by listing the properties of a permissible class of relations. For example, the domain $\mathcal{B}_{\mathcal{D}}$ consists of all acyclic binary relations, all transitive binary relations, etc. In the space of choice functions the domains $\mathcal{C}_{\mathcal{D}}$ are defined by listing their characteristic properties reflecting each aspects of the logic of external, I/O description of the agent's choice. This logic dwells on the concept of changes occurring in the choice with variation (narrowing or widening) of the presentation X. Without going into details (see Chapter 2), we only mention here that X' and X can be related by the *Heredity Condition* **H** (Sen's $\boldsymbol{\alpha}$) as

$$\forall X', X \subseteq A : X' \subseteq X \Longrightarrow C(X') \supseteq C(X) \bigcap X'.$$

The theory of choice still has no standard ways of isolating the domains $\Pi_{\mathcal{D}}$ in the space Π. Therefore, either a particular rule π, or a rule with "free parameters" is defined[7].

Remark 1. Another approach to formalization of individual's opinion is to represent it through one criterion (utility function) or a family of criteria. A choice rule in the first case defines a set of alternatives on which the criterion has extremal, e.g., maximal values. In the latter case different choice rules are used, e.g., Pareto rule. In the framework considered here which goes back to the monograph by K.Arrow and his followers, two main assumptions are used. First, the set of alternatives is assumed to be finite. Second, a criterion (criteria) is supposed to be defined in ordinal scale, i.e., up to an arbitrary monotonic transformation. This means that only the information which criterial value is greater than the other is taken into account regardless of absolute values of the criterial estimations themselves. Under these assumptions such 'criterial' formalization as it will be shown in Chapter 2 is equivalent to a representation of individual opinion in the form of binary relation of some special type.

Remark 2. In some cases a choice function which represents individual opinion can be defined not on all possible subsets X of A but on somehow restricted family of subsets. This approach is mainly used in mathematical economics where the family of subsets is defined according to budget constraints or more generally as family of convex subsets of A. In what follows we will consider the case where choice function is defined on the family $\mathcal{A}$ of all non-empty subsets of A, i.e., $\mathcal{A} = 2^A \setminus \{\emptyset\}$ and

$$C(\cdot) : \mathcal{A} \to 2^A \text{ and } C(X) \subseteq X \text{ for all } X \in \mathcal{A}.$$

In some special cases we will consider a choice function to be single - valued, i.e.

$$C(\cdot) : \mathcal{A} \longrightarrow A.$$

The set (space) of all choice functions on A will be denoted hereafter as $\mathcal{C}_A$, or simply as $\mathcal{C}$. Generally, we do not restrict a choice function to be non-empty, i.e., we admit $C(X) = \emptyset$ for some[8] X. The subspace of $\mathcal{C}$ which consists of all non-empty choice

[7] For example, the choice of the best r alternatives from X (for $card(X) > r$) by a linear order (parameter r).

[8] The fact that for some X $C(X) = \emptyset$ can be interpreted as refusal from choice.

functions will be denoted as $\mathcal{C}^+$. Finally, the subspace of $\mathcal{C}^+$ which contains all single-valued choice functions will be denoted as $\widehat{\mathcal{C}}$.
Now, everything required to formulate the problem of synthesis of aggregation rules is available.

1.5 Aggregation: the synthesis problem

We study three different formulations of the problem of synthesis of aggregation rules. Consideration of the aggregation rule as an operator mapping n individual opinions into a single social decision is what there is in common between them. The difference between them lies in the definition of what is regarded as the agents' opinion and the social decision — a binary relation or a choice function. To describe these formulations, we introduce three sets of rules denoted as Π_I, Π_{II}, and Π_{III} (Figure 1-4). Their elements are denoted as π_I, π_{II}, and π_{III}, respectively[9].
Let us denote as N the set of all agents, $N = \{1, ..., n\}$, and let us denote the n binary relations $P_1, \ldots, P_n$ of the agents, the profile, as $\{P_i\}_{i \in N}$ or $\vec{P}$. Similarly, the n choice functions $C_1(\cdot), \ldots, C_n(\cdot)$ are denoted as $\{C_i(\cdot)\}_{i \in N}$ or $\vec{C}$. The operator $\pi_I \in \Pi_I$ maps a profile $\{P_i\}$ into one binary relation P:

$$\pi_I : \{P_i\} \longrightarrow P.$$

Such operator will be called hereafter following the tradition of social choice theory as *Social Decision Rule*, or *Social Decision Function*.

In contrast to the operator π_I, the definition of the rule π_{II} makes no use at all of the notion of binary relation. The operator $\pi_{II} \in \Pi_{II}$ maps the functional profile $\{C_i(\cdot)\}$ into the social choice function $C(\cdot)$:

$$\pi_{II} : \{C_i(\cdot)\} \longrightarrow C(\cdot),$$

that is, directly maps the agents' choice into the collective choice and it is the social choice rule in the precise sense of this term.
This rule will be called as *Functional Aggregation Rule.*

The above two rules (Examples 1 and 2) may be regarded as examples of the rule π_{II}.

Finally, the rule π_{III} is defined as an extension of the notion of choice rule π introduced for description of individual choice; π_{III} is assumed to be a choice rule applicable not only to an individual binary relation, but also to the profile $\{P_i\}_{i \in N}$ considered as a whole, and mapping it into the social choice function

$$\pi_{III} : \{P_i\} \times \mathcal{A} \longrightarrow C(\cdot).$$

[9] In the literature there is no statement of the problem formalizing the agents' opinions as choice functions and looking for the social decision as an element of the space $\mathcal{B}$. This is due to the fact that, assuming representation of the individual' opinion in such a general form as choice functions, it would be senseless to look for a social decision in an 'intermediate' form such as binary relation.

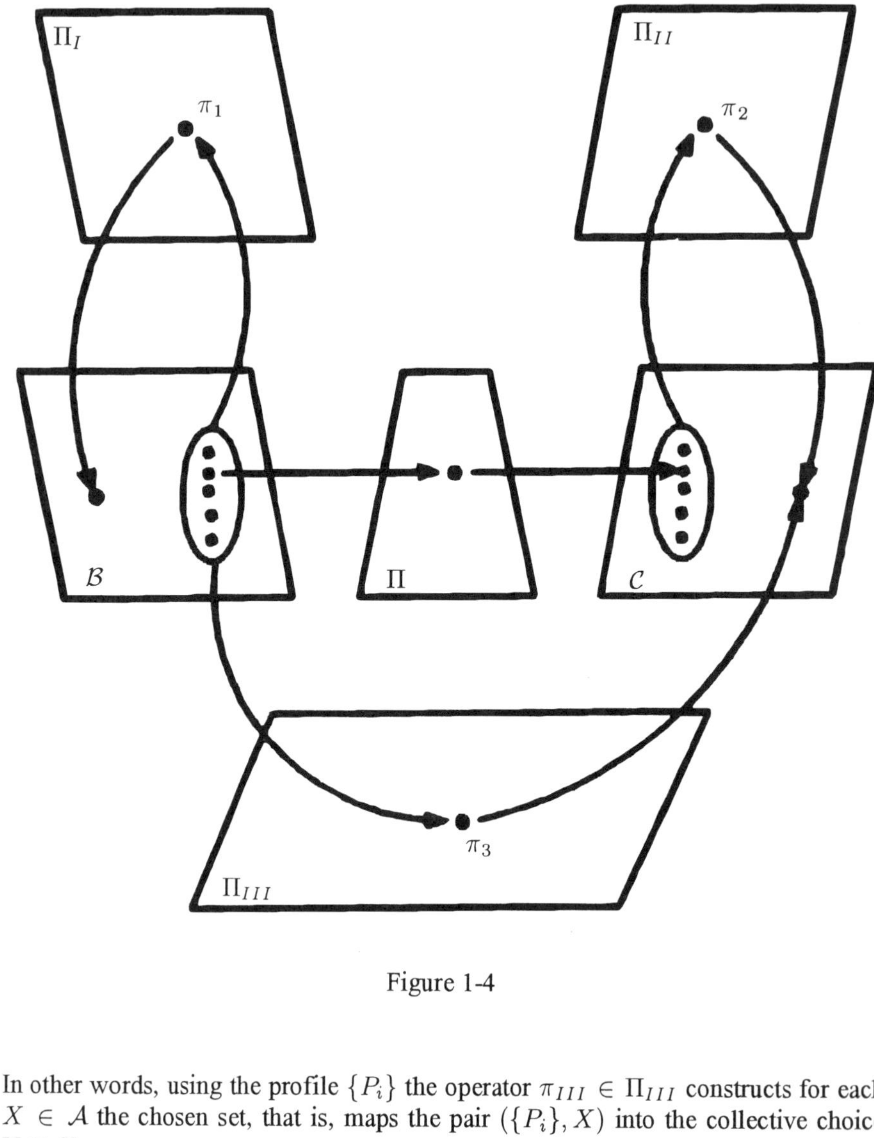

Figure 1-4

In other words, using the profile $\{P_i\}$ the operator $\pi_{III} \in \Pi_{III}$ constructs for each $X \in \mathcal{A}$ the chosen set, that is, maps the pair $(\{P_i\}, X)$ into the collective choice $Y \subseteq X$.
This rule following the tradition of social choice theory will be called *Social Choice Correspondence*.

In all three cases consideration is given to the classes of rules π_I, π_{II}, and π_{III} satisfying some set of additional conditions formulated for them in a similar manner.

The main condition is that of locality. We assume hereafter that the spaces Π_I, Π_{II} and Π_{III} comprise, respectively, only the local rules. Let us explain the locality condition for Π_I (for social decision functions) via example. The local operator π_I decides whether xPy is true for the social decision P depending only on whether xP_iy is true or not for each of individual binary relations. Stated differently, when deciding whether xPy is true, the information about the agents' opinion about other ordered pairs of alternatives is disregarded[10]. For example, for the unanimity rule, the social binary relation P is assumed to contain xPy if and only if xP_iy for all agents $(i = 1, ..., n)$.

For the space Π_{II}, i.e., for functional aggregation rules, the locality condition is introduced in a different manner: the local rule π_{II} 'decides' to include or not the alternative $y \in X$ into the social choice only relying upon the information that the agents include this alternative y into their choice, this decision being independent of the agents' attitude toward other alternatives from $X \setminus \{y\}$, or, all the more so, other alternatives from A and other subsets X'. For example, the k-majority rule is local: to make decision about inclusion of x into the collective choice from X one needs only to know how many agents include x into their choice $(x \in Y_i = C_i(X))$. Contrastively, the plurality rule from Example 2, is not local — to make decision about including x into the social choice, it is not enough to know how many agents include x into their choices, agents' decisions about all other alternatives from X are required as well.

Few definitions of locality can be found in the literature for the Social Choice Correspondences - rules from Π_{III}. For example, if individual binary relations are linear orders, the rule π_{III}, which includes an alternative y into the choice from X, is called local if y is a 'top element' in linear orders of agents.

The mainstream of publications devoted to synthesis of aggregation rules deals with local operators. So, we include the locality requirement into the definition of the spaces Π_I, Π_{II}, and Π_{III}, specifying each time this notion in precise terms. In what follows, we will only deal with the spaces of local rules!

In any of such spaces, domains of local rules can be distinguished according to some additional conditions, which are usually called *normative conditions*. We denote these domains by Π_{IT}, Π_{IIT} and Π_{IIIT}, respectively. In all of the three spaces, the T-type domains are introduced in a similar manner: several conditions (characteristic properties of the operators) are formulated each isolating a domain in Π_i. Further, a typical example of a collection of three normative conditions is presented for the operators from Π_I:

1. *Pareto Principle.* If all agents hold that xP_iy, the collective binary relation must include xPy.
2. *Neutrality.* Using the individual relations, the rule determines the social binary relation between any pair of alternatives in the same manner, that is, does not intentionally distinguish in advance some pairs of alternatives. Neutrality is violated if, for example, the male and female candidates require different numbers of votes to be elected.
3. *Anonimity* (Symmetry). The rule is neutral with respect to the agents, that is, impartially takes into account the opinion of any of them.

For example, the anonymous rule must disregard the official positions of agents, and assign all agents the same number of votes. Within the framework of the model under

[10] Chapter 3 discusses two locality conditions for the rules from Π_I.

consideration, all these conditions seem equally obligatory for any reasonable aggregation rule. Each condition distinguishes a domain in the corresponding space Π_i. This enables one to determine the classes to which the reasonable aggregation rule *a fortiori* seem belonging.

It was assumed above that the profile $\{P_i\}$ or $\{C_i(\cdot)\}$ may consist of any binary relations or choice functions, and no additional constraints on the form of collective decisions P or $C(\cdot)$ were imposed. Let us consider now another way of identifying the operator classes Π_{iS} $(i = I, II, III)$. It was mentioned already which reasons lead to isolation of the domains $\mathcal{B}_S$ in $\mathcal{B}$ (for example, any acyclic binary relations, etc.) and $\mathcal{C}_S$ in the space of choice functions $\mathcal{C}$ (for example, $\mathcal{C}_S$ comprises functions satisfying the Heredity condition **H**). If one assumes that all agents hold to their P_i or $C_i(\cdot)$ from those classes, it is only natural to require that the social decision P or $C(\cdot)$ be from the same classes, because only in this case the collective decision satisfies the same requirements of 'reasonableness' as for the individual agents. We call the constraints of this kind *rationality constraints*.

The rationality constraints lead to the restriction of the *domain* and *range* of the aggregation rule. Hence, the domain of the rules π_I and π_{III} is $\mathcal{B}^n = \mathcal{B} \times \mathcal{B} \times ... \times \mathcal{B}$ unless we do not restrict it somehow, otherwise it is denoted as Q_d^n. Analogously, for a rule π_{II} the domain in the unrestricted case is $\mathcal{C}^n = \mathcal{C} \times \mathcal{C} \times ... \times \mathcal{C}$. In all these cases we denote the domain of a rule π_i $(i = I, II, III)$ as Q_d^n, and call Q_d the *domain of definition* of π_i. For brevity, we will very often call Q_d as domain of π_i specifying explicitly the difference between Q_d and Q_d^n when necessary.

Thus, for the rules π_I, the classes of the space $\mathcal{B}$ are the domains and ranges Q_d and Q_r; for the operators π_{II}, the domains Q_d and Q_r are the classes of the space $\mathcal{C}$; and for the procedures π_{III}, the sets Q_d and Q_r satisfy the conditions $Q_d \subseteq \mathcal{B}$ and $Q_r \subseteq \mathcal{C}$. For the rules of the first and second types, the domains Q_d and Q_r are always assumed to be related by $Q_d \subseteq Q_r$, that is, the opinions permissible as individual ones are also permitted as social decisions. Obviously, the corresponding mapping

$$Q_d^n \rightarrow Q_r$$

cannot be performed by any operators π_I, π_{II} and π_{III}. Therefore, the operator classes S_i consisting of the rules which perform a given mapping are naturally separated in the spaces Π_i.

Let us suppose now that some class S_i is given and in the corresponding space Π_i an other class T_i is fixed containing rules which satisfy, for instance, Pareto Principle, Neutrality and Anonymity conditions. These classes S_i and T_i can coincide, be embedded, intersect, or be disjoint.

Now, we formulate the problem of synthesis of aggregation rules: for each of separate classes S_i and T_i find the explicit form of rules which belong to these classes and study which rules fill the intersection of different classes S_i and T_i. This situation for the space Π_I is shown at Figure 1-5. On this Figure the intersection of the classes S and T contains some rule π_I which transforms profiles $\overrightarrow{P} \in Q_d^n$ to social binary relations belonging to $Q_r = Q_d$.

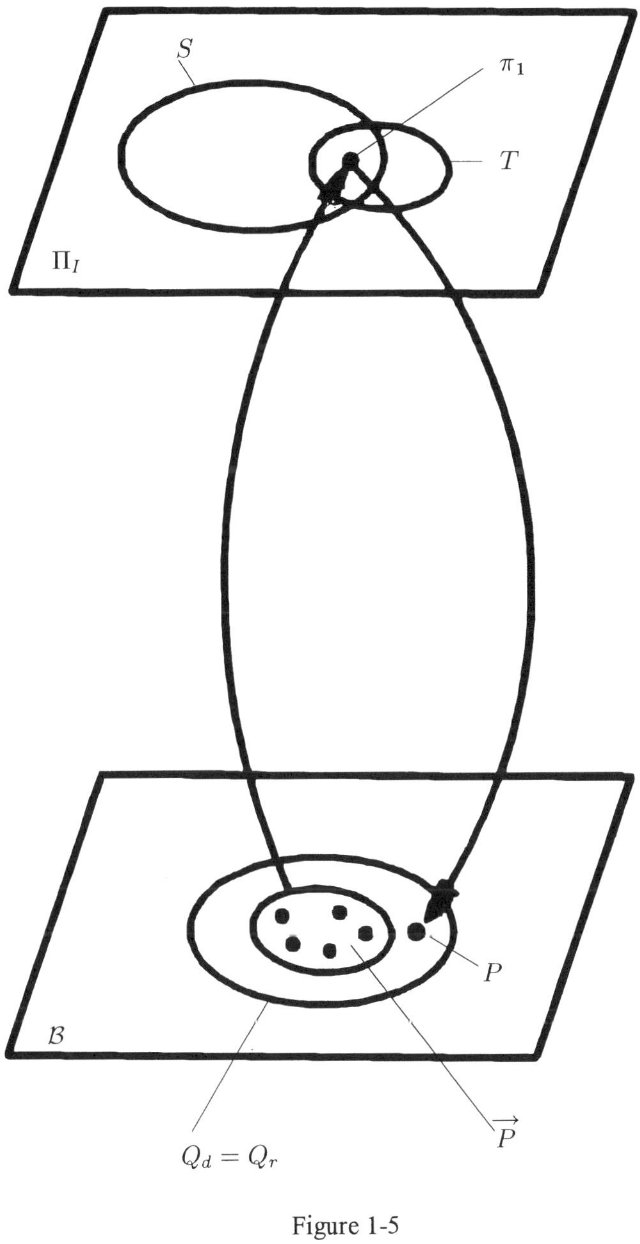

Figure 1-5

In this terminology Arrow's General Impossibility Theorem can be understood as follows. Let us denote the class isolating by rationality constraints Q_d=Q_r=$\mathcal{P}$ where $\mathcal{P}$

is the set of all linear orders on A, as S. Furthermore let us denote the class of rules which satisfy Pareto Principle and Non-Dictatorship conditions[11] as T. Then Arrow's Theorem states that the intersection of S and T is empty. The other formulation of Arrow's Theorem (Theorem 2 from the Section 1.3) is as follows: let us denote now the class of rules which satisfy Pareto Principle as T. Then the intersection of S and T contains only dictatorial rules.

The problem for the operator spaces Π_I, Π_{II} and Π_{III} will be discussed below in Chapters 3–5.

1.6 Concluding remarks and guide to the literature

Remark 1. I would like to emphasize that not all aggregation models are covered by the approach considered here. There are wide classes of rules which use some intermediate information to construct a social decision. This intermediate information can be majority relation and on this way several rules were invented (see, e.g., [21, 85, 124, 164, 225]). Such information can be obtained in the form of criterion, e.g., sum of scores, which is used in plurality rule, inverse Borda rule, etc. Moreover there are multi-step rules such as Coombs' procedure, Nanson's rule, etc. (see, e.g., [21,205]). In what follows we study one-step procedures which satisfy some analog of Arrow's Independence of Irrelevant Alternatives, i.e., locality condition depending on in which form the individual opinions and social decision are presented. Then, the main attention is attracted to study of rules and their representation from subclasses which are isolated by some natural normative conditions and rationality constraints. However, it turns out that even in these cases which seem to be very specific ones because very few rules are local, it is possible to obtain very interesting rules. Moreover, a locality condition allows to construct in some sense complete theory which for non-local cases is far of completeness.

Remark 2. The condition of Independence of Irrelevant Alternatives has been a subject of wide discussions in the literature. These discussions were concerned about how reasonable is IIA; the examples were constructed to show violation of that fundamental condition. Other papers analyzed, in particular, how IIA and the properties of the social welfare function are connected in case when the latter is rationalizable by binary relation P. For corresponding publications the reader is referred to [10, 11, 26, 37, 49, 67, 68, 71, 77, 89, 107, 109, 137–140, 159, 167, 169, 174, 176, 177, 186, 204, 207, 209, 214, 224, 229, 235, 238, 243–246, 264, 269]

Arrow's proof of General Impossibility Theorem was given in [27, 29] ; in the second edition of the monograph 'Social Choice and Individual Values' by K.Arrow [29] one can already find several proofs of the Theorem. Different other proofs of General Impossibility Theorem were given in [40, 54, 56, 58, 169, 186, 238, 239] .

General view on the three different models of social choice presented above was first given in [5, 11]

---

[11] The Condition of Independence of Irrelevant Alternatives is already included in the definition of the space Π_{III}.

2

RATIONALITY OF INDIVIDUAL OPINIONS AND SOCIAL DECISIONS

2.1 Introduction

This Chapter extends the ideas deal with description of individual opinions and social decisions that were briefly presented in Chapter 1. Section 2.2 investigates various types of binary relations and defines the notion of pair-dominant, or rationalizable by a binary relation, choice. In this Section main types of binary relations used in social choice theory are defined - linear orders, weak orders, strict partial orders, and acyclic relations. Section 2.3 gives another well-known concept of choice, based on the 'extremization paradigm' — that of a choice function rationalizable by some numerical (utility) function, studies the classical unicriterial and multicriterial choice models. We study three different types of multicriteral models - Paretian, weak Paretian, and joint-extremal ones. The equivalence of Paretian and weak Paretian models is shown. Section 2.4 lists Expansion-Contraction Axioms (rationality conditions) for choice functions, and studies their mutual relations. The axioms of Heredity, Concordance, Outcast, Arrow's Choice Axiom in different versions, Choice Monotonicity, Choice Resolutness are studied. Section 2.5 establishes relations between the classes of rationalizable choice functions and the domains in the space of choice functions described in Section 2.4. The classical pair-dominant choice functions are shown to define a small, but important part of the models describing individual opinions and social decisions. Section 2.6 contains concluding remarks and gives a guide to the literature.

2.2 Binary relations

As was already mentioned in Chapter 1, representation of individual opinions and collective decision as binary relations is a way to formalize them. The literature on choice theory defines the form of the binary relations under consideration by some descriptive concepts such as the 'best' of two alternatives, which was formalized as the notion of 'preference.' The properties of the binary relations such as acyclicity, transitivity, etc., appear in a natural way in the course of this study.
The attempt to formalize the notion of preference leads to considering two different

(both in sense and use) basic relations — those of strict preference, P, and of nonstrict preference, R. The fact that two alternatives $x, y \in A$ are related by P is interpreted as 'the alternative x is preferred to y' or 'the alternative x is better than the alternative y.' The relation R between $x, y \in A$ can be interpreted either as 'x is not worse than y,' or 'x is at least as good as y.' Abstracting from the treatment of pair relations between alternatives in terms of preferences (see for more detail [6]), we consider those properties of binary relations that correspond to the generally accepted ideas of rationality.

A binary relation P is a subset of direct product $A \times A$, where A is a finite set of alternatives[12]. The *complement relation* $\overline{P}$ of P is a binary relation such that $\overline{P} = A \times A \setminus P$ or, equivalently, $\overline{P} = \{(x,y) \mid (x,y) \notin P\}$. The *inverse relation* P^{-1} for a given P is defined as $P^{-1} = \{(x,y) \mid (y,x) \in P\}$. The *identity relation* $\triangle$ is defined as $\triangle = \{(x,x) \mid x \in A\}$.

At Fig.2-1a the relation P is given, and at Figs.2-1b - 2-1c — the relations $\overline{P}$ and P^{-1}.
Let us now list the main properties of binary relations.
The relation P is called

- *reflexive,* if $\forall x \in A \ \ (x,x) \in P$;
- *irreflexive,* if $\forall x \in A \ \ (x,x) \notin P$;
- *acyclic,* if the graph P has no cycles of any length (in particular, pairs (x,x));
- *transitive,* if $\forall \ x, y, z \in A \ \ xPy$ and $yPz \Rightarrow xPz$;
- *negatively transitive,* if [13] $\forall x, y, z \in A \ \ x\overline{P}y$ and $y\overline{P}z \Longrightarrow x\overline{P}z$;
- *complete,* if $\forall x, y \in A \ \Rightarrow (x,y) \in P$ or $(y,x) \in P$;
- *connected,* if $\forall x, y \in A \ \ x \neq y \Rightarrow (x,y) \in P$ or $(y,x) \in P$;
- *antisymmetric,* if $\forall x, y \in A \ \ (x,y) \in P$ and $(y,x) \in P \Rightarrow x = y$;
- *asymmetric,* if $\forall x, y \in A \ \ xPy \Rightarrow y\overline{P}x$;
- *symmetric,,* if $\forall x, y \in A \ \ xPy \Rightarrow yPx$.

Remark. The *composition* $P \circ Q$ of two given binary relations P and Q is a binary relation such that

$$P \circ Q = \{(x,y) \mid \exists \, z \in A \text{ such that } xPz \text{ and } zQy\}$$

Composition of a binary relation with itself $P \circ P$ is usually denoted as P^2. This operation is associative and hence can be extended on any number of components.
Using the composition of relations one can check that any binary relations P defined above is

- reflexive, if $\triangle \subseteq P$;
- irreflexive, if $P \subseteq A \times A \setminus \triangle$;
- acyclic, if the binary relation $\bigcup_{i=1}^{\infty} P^i$ is irreflexive;

---

[12] Any binary relation can be conveniently represented by the oriented graph where the vertices correspond to the alternatives from A, and the oriented arc going from the vertex x to the vertex y corresponds to the pair (x, y) in P. When discussing the properties of binary relations, we will often make use of graphs and the graph terminology. The graph corresponding to the binary relation P will be denoted by the same character.

[13] Sometimes, an equivalent condition $\forall x, y, z \in A \ \ xPy \Rightarrow xPz$ or zPy is used instead of the negative transitivity condition.

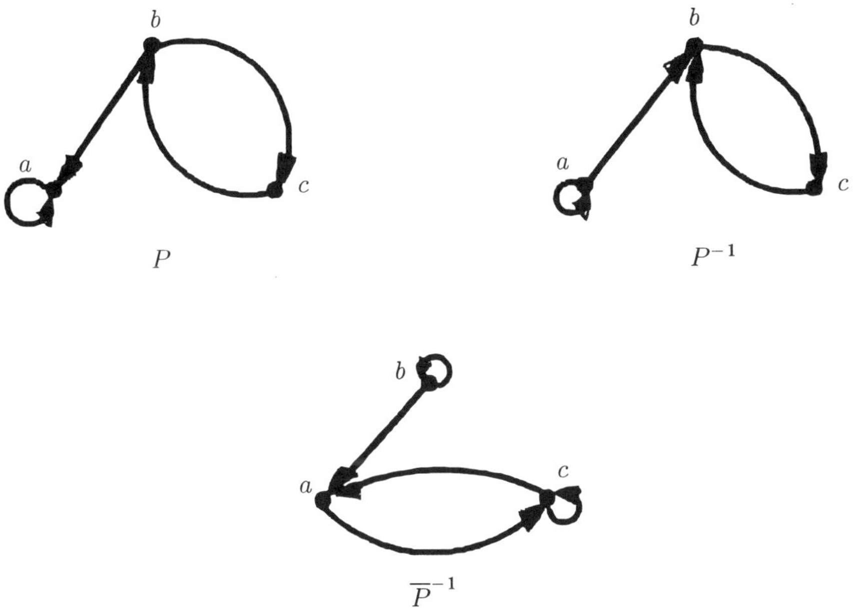

Figure 2-1

- transitive, if $P^2 \subseteq P$;
- negatively transitive, if $\overline{P}^2 \subseteq \overline{P}$;
- complete, $P \cup P^{-1} = A \times A$;
- connected, if $\overline{\triangle} \subseteq P \cup P^{-1}$;
- antisymmetric, if $P \cap P^{-1} \subseteq \triangle$;
- asymmetric, if $P \cap P^{-1} = \emptyset$;
- symmetric, $P = P^{-1}$.

Consider now those binary relations which are mainly used in social choice theory and which are derived from the relations given above.

An irreflexive transitive relation P is called *strict partial order*, and an irreflexive, transitive and negatively transitive one is called *weak order*. A weak order which is connected is called a *linear order*. An irreflexive connected binary relation is called a *tournament*. One can easily check that transitive *tournament* is a linear order.

Remark. All of the introduced above classes of binary relations to an extent correspond to the notion of 'preference.' Let us consider now the relation P satisfying the conditions of irreflexivity, symmetricity, and transitivity. Relations of this kind are called *equivalence* relations. Fig. 2-2 shows an example of equivalence relation. Let P be a binary relation. Using it, one can construct an indifference relation $I_P = A^2 \setminus (P \bigcup P^{-1})$. Then, it can be proved that I_P is an equivalence relation iff P is a weak order.

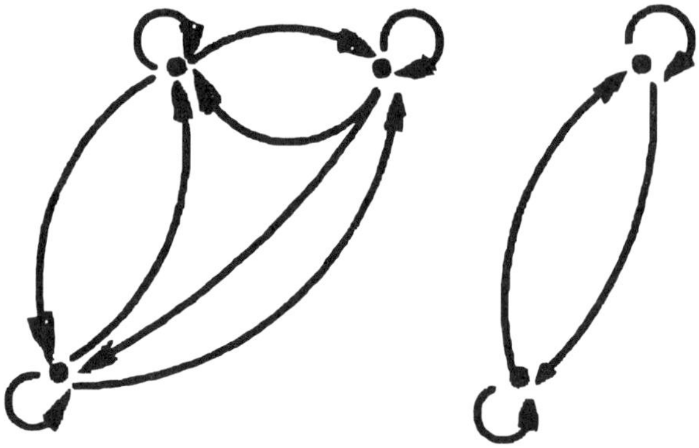

Figure 2-2

For a weak order, the graph P is structured as follows: all vertices (alternatives from A) can be decomposed into disjoint ordered (enumerated) subsets ('layers'), where no arc exists between the vertices of the same layer, and from each vertex arcs go to all vertices of the 'lower' layers (see the example in Fig.2-3 showing for simplicity the case of only three layers containing two vertices each).

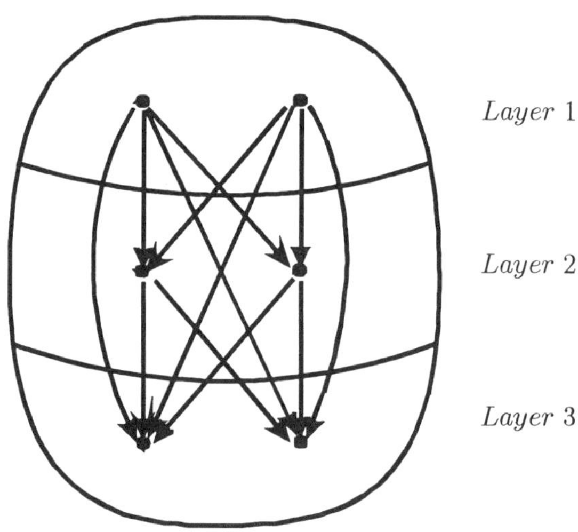

Figure 2-3

If each layer has only one vertex in a graph of this kind, this graph is called transitive chain, and its corresponding relation P is a linear order. We will often (particularly, in examples and proofs) represent linear orders using the sign $\succ$, e.g., as $x \succ y \succ z$.

Denote the class of linear orders by $\mathcal{LO}$, of weak order, by $\mathcal{WO}$, of acyclic relations, by $\mathcal{AR}$, of strict partial orders, by $\mathcal{SPO}$. The interrelations between the classes follow immediately from their definitions.

$$\mathcal{LO} \subset \mathcal{WO} \subset \mathcal{SPO} \subset \mathcal{AR};$$

The use of binary relations in the classical theory dwells upon the presumption of pair-dominance: in a presented set X, that alternative is chosen which does not 'fail" the pairwise comparisons with other alternatives from X; in other words, if it is undominated alternative in the set X with respect to the relation P. Hence,

$$C(X) = \{y \in X | \rceil \exists x \in X \; : \; xPy\} \tag{2.1}$$

This notion of the chosen alternative which passes through pairwise comparisons can be defined in a different form, if the relation under study is reflexive:

$$C(X) = \{y \in X | \forall x \in X \; : \; yRx\}, \tag{2.2}$$

i.e. y dominates all alternatives in X with respect to R.

Let a choice function $C(\cdot)$ be given. If for a given choice function $C(\cdot)$ there exists binary relation P (respectively, R) such that $C(\cdot)$ can be represented in a form (2.1) (or, (2.2)) then $C(\cdot)$ is said to be *rationalizable* by P (by R). A choice function $C(\cdot)$ rationalizable by some binary relation will be called hereafter *pair-dominant choice function*.

We conclude this section by a remark about the possibility of empty choice.

Remark. Along with the assumption of pair-dominance, the classical models of choice were augmented by the assumption of non-empty choice, which resulted immediately in acyclicity of the relation P in (2.1). Indeed, if P contains some cycle on the vertices, say, $X = \{x_1, ..., x_l\}$, then using the rule (2.1) on this set X, one immediately obtains $C(X) = \emptyset$. Under the assumption of empty choice, the same choice function can be rationalized by two different binary relations. Indeed, let us consider the relations P' and P'' shown in Fig.2-4.

One can readily see that the choice functions $C'(\cdot)$ and $C''(\cdot)$ constructed according to rule (2.1) coincide on them. The occurring ambiguity in this case can be eliminated by introducing relation P^*, which can be called *equivalent extension* of the original relation P and is constructed as follows. Let P be a binary relation. We construct its equivalent extension P^* so that $P^* = P \cup \{(x,y) | (y,y) \in P\}$. In other words, if P contains a pair of the form (y,y), then P is completed by all the pairs of the form $(x,y), x \in A$. The choice functions rationalizable via P and P^* are related in the following way.

Theorem 2.1 *Let P be a binary relation, P^* be its equivalent extension, $C_P(\cdot)$ be*

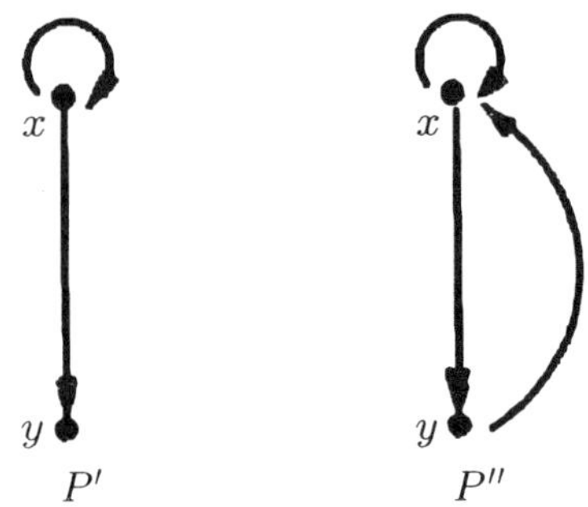

Figure 2-4

the pair-dominant choice function on P*, and* $C_{P^*}(\cdot)$ *be pair-dominant choice function on* P^**. Then,* $\forall X \in \mathcal{A}\ C_P(X) = C_{P^*}(X)$.

Proof. Since $P \subseteq P^*$, $C_P(\cdot) \supseteq C_{P^*}(\cdot)$ holds. Show that $C_P(\cdot) \subseteq C_{P^*}(\cdot)$. Suppose on the contrary that there exists X and x such that $x \in C_P(X)$ and $x \notin C_{P^*}(X)$. This means that there is some y such that yP^*x but $(y, x) \notin P$. According to the construction of P^*, yP^*x iff $(x, x) \in P$, hence $x \notin C_P(X)$. ■

2.3 Criterial model of choice

We have considered above a model of choice dwelling on the presumption of pair-dominance. Another model of choice, which is based on the 'extremization paradigm,' seems to go back to the monograph by V.Pareto [210] . It assumes that on A there is a quality (value, utility) criterion, and the choice on $X \subseteq A$,comprises the alternatives with extreme, by this criterion, values. Let us discuss the model in formal terms. A *criterion* $u(\cdot)$ is assumed to be defined on A so that a criterial estimate $u(x)$ corresponds to each $x \in A$. The criterion $u(\cdot)$ will be assumed below for the sake of definiteness is required to maximize. The rule of choice is written as

$$C(X) = \{y \in X | \rceil \exists x \in X : u(x) > u(y)\}. \tag{2.3}$$

or, equivalently, as

$$C(X) = \{y \in X | \forall x \in X : u(y) \geq u(x)\}$$

A function $C(\cdot)$ representable in the form (2.3) is referred to as *rationalizable by the criterion* $u(\cdot)$ or *unicriterial* choice function. We will often denote such function as $\langle u(\cdot), (2.3)\rangle$.

Theorem 2.2 *The class of unicriterial choice functions* $\{\langle u(\cdot), (2.3)\rangle\}$ *coincides with the class of pair-dominant choice functions* $\{\langle P, (2.1)\rangle\}$ *for* P *being weak order re-*

lations. The subclass of the unicriterial choice functions under the constraint $\forall x, y$ $x \neq y \Rightarrow u(x) \neq u(y)$ *coincides with the class of pair-dominant choice functions for* P *being linear orders.*

Proof. Let unicriterial choice function $\langle u, (2.3)\rangle$ be defined. Let us construct the relation P in the following way

$$xPy \Longleftrightarrow u(x) > u(y).$$

Obviously this relation is acyclic, transitive and negatively transitive, i.e., P is a weak order. The fact that the choice on each X by unicriterial choice function coincides with pair-dominant choice by making use of P follows from the definition of P.
Let now a weak order P be given. Construct by P the partition of A in the following way:

$$A_1 = \{y \in A \mid \rceil \exists x \in A \text{ such that } xPy\},$$

$$A_2 = \{y \in A \setminus A_1 \mid \rceil \exists x \in A \setminus A_1 \text{ such that } xPy\},$$

$$\dots$$

$$A_t = \{y \in A \setminus \bigcup_{j=1}^{t-1} A_j \mid \rceil \exists x \in A \setminus \bigcup_{j=1}^{t-1} A_j \text{ such that } xPy\}.$$

The system of sets $\{A_1, \dots, A_t\}$ is finite (by virtue of the finiteness of A) and is a partition of A. It is obvious that for any $x, y, z \in A_i$ $(i = 1, ..., t)$ $x\overline{P}y\overline{P}z$ holds. Consider now x and y such that $x \in A_i$, $y \in A_j$, and $i < j$. Let us show that xPy. Indeed, if $x\overline{P}y$, then $\exists z \in A_i$ such that zPy. Then by the condition $(\forall x, y, z\ zPy \Rightarrow xPy$ or $zPx)$, which is equivalent to the negative transitivity condition, either zPx and then $x \notin A_i$, or xPy. Let us construct a function $u(\cdot)$ such that for any $x \in A_i$, $i = 1, ..., t$, $u(x) = t - i + 1$.Then choice by u according to the rule (2.3) on any X coincides with the choice by P according to the rule (2.1).
The second statement of the theorem is obvious, because in the case $\forall x, y$ $x \neq y$ $u(x) \neq u(y)$ the constructed relation P is connected, i.e., P is a linear order. On the other hand, if P is a linear order then each element A_i of the partition $\{A_i\}$ consists of only one element. ■

Let us study now choice functions rationalizable via vector of criteria rather than a unique criterion. Formally, a vector of n criteria $u_1(\cdot), \dots, u_n(\cdot)$ is assumed to be given, a vector of criterial estimates $\vec{u}\,(x)$ is assigned to each alternative $x \in A$, and the rule of choice extends the notion of extremizational rule for one criterion. There are several rules of this type, of which one, the Pareto rule, is accepted unconditionally by all researchers:

$$C(X) = \{y \in X \mid \rceil \exists x \in X \text{ such that } (\forall i\ u_i(x) \geq u_i(y)$$

$$\text{and } \exists i_0 \text{ such that } u_{i_0}(x) > u_{i_0}(y))\} \quad (2.4)$$

The corresponding choice function will be called the *Paretian* choice function. The weak version of this rule is written as follows:

$$C(X) = \{y \in X \mid \rceil \exists x \in X \text{ such that } \forall i \; u_i(x) > u_i(y)\}, \quad (2.5)$$

and the corresponding choice function will be called as *weak Paretian* one.

We demonstrate via example the difference between Paretian and weak Paretian choice functions. Fig.2-5 shows in the two-criteria space the estimates of alternatives from the set $A = \{x_1, \ldots, x_{12}\}$. On this set Paretian choice is equal to $\{x_3, x_4, x_5\}$, and weak paretian one is equal to $\{x_1, \ldots, x_7\}$.

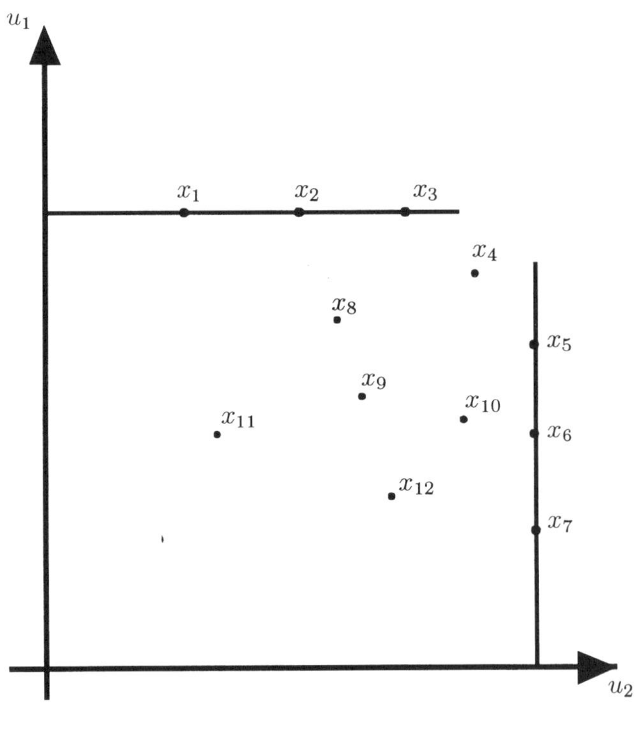

Figure 2-5

Theorem 2.3 establishes the interrelations between the classes of Paretian and weak Paretian choice functions, as well as between these classes of functions and the class of pair-dominant choice functions.

Theorem 2.3 *The classes of Paretian and weak Paretian choice functions coincide. The class of Paretian choice functions coincides with the class of pair-dominant choice functions with the relations P in the definition of the latter being strict partial orders.*

Before we prove the theorem, let us explain its statement. The coincidence of the two classes of functions means the following: for any choice function $C(\cdot)$ rationalizble by a set of criteria $\overrightarrow{u}$ using the rule (2.4) there exists a set of criteria $\overrightarrow{v}$ such that a choice function $\widetilde{C}(\cdot)$ rationalizable via a set $\overrightarrow{v}$ using the rule (2.5) is equal to $C(\cdot)$. Naturally, the inverse statement is also true: for a choice function $\widetilde{C}(\cdot)$ rationalizble by $\overrightarrow{v}$ with (2.5) there exists a set $\overrightarrow{u}$ such that the choice function $C(\cdot)$ rationalizable via a set $\overrightarrow{u}$ and (2.4) is equal to $\widetilde{C}(\cdot)$. Note that the number of functions in the sets $\overrightarrow{u}$ and $\overrightarrow{v}$ may be different.

Proof. Let a vector $\vec{u}$ be given on A. Denote as $C_{wP}(\cdot)$ and $C_P(\cdot)$ the weak Paretian and Paretian choice functions defined on $\vec{u}$ via the rules (2.5) and (2.4), respectively. By the definition of those rules it follows immediately that $C_P(\cdot) \subseteq C_{wP}(\cdot)$. Let us note here that if functions $u_i(\cdot)$ are strict, then, by definition of rules (2.4) and (2.5), these two choice functions coincide.
Let us construct now the binary relation P as follows:

$$xPy \Longleftrightarrow \forall i \in N \;\; u_i(x) \geq u_i(y) \text{ and } \exists i_0 \text{ such that } u_{i_0}(x) > u_{i_0}(y).$$

It is obvious that P is irreflexive and transitive, i.e., P is a strict partial order. Define a pair-dominant choice function $C_{PD}(\cdot)$ on P via the rule (2.1). Then $C_{wP}(\cdot) \subseteq C_{PD}(\cdot)$. Indeed, if $y \in C_{wP}(\cdot)$ then $\overline{\exists} x \in X$ such that ($\forall i \in N \; u_i(x) \geq u_i(y)$ and $\exists i_0$ such that $u_{i_0}(x) > u_{i_0}(y)$). But in this case according to the construction of P, $\overline{\exists} x \in X$ such that xPy. Hence, $y \in C_{PD}(\cdot)$.
Let now a choice function $C_{PD}(\cdot)$ be given rationalizable by a strict partial order P. Construct the set $\vec{u}$ and the choice function $C_P(\cdot)$ rationalizable by this $\vec{u}$. To do this we use two theorems by Szpilrajn (see, e.g., [105, 265]). First Szpilrajn's theorem states that for any strict partial order P there exists a linear order P' such that $P \subseteq P'$. That linear order is called a *linear extension* of P. According to the second Szpilrajn's theorem any strict partial order P is equal to the intersection of all its linear extensions, i.e.,

$$P = \bigcap_i P'_i, \; P'_i \supseteq P \text{ for all } i \in N,$$

N being here the set of indices of all linear extensions of P.
Let now $\{P'_i\}$ be the set of all linear extensions of a given P. Define the set $\{u_i(\cdot)\}_{i \in N}$ as follows:

$$u_i(x) > u_i(y) \Longleftrightarrow xP'_iy.$$

Since P'_i is a linear order, for any x and y such that $x \neq y$ we have $u_i(x) \neq u_i(y)$. On $\vec{u}$ define a choice function $C_P(\cdot)$ via the rule (2.5). Let us show that $C_{PD}(\cdot) \subseteq$

$C_P(\cdot)$. Indeed, let $y \in C_{PD}(X)$ for some X. Then $\overline{\exists} x \in X$ such that xPy. Since $P = \cap_i P'_i$, then if there exist P'_i such that $x\ P'_i y$, then there must exist P'_j such that $yP'_j x$, because otherwise it follows that $xP'_i y$ for all i, i.e., xPy. Now, according to the construction of $\{u_i\}$ we obtain that if for some i $u_i(x) > u_i(y)$ holds, then for some j $u_j(y) > u_j(x)$, i.e., $y \in C_P(X)$. Thus, the following inclusions have been obtained

$$C_P(\cdot) \subseteq C_{wP}(\cdot) \subseteq C_{PD}(\cdot) \subseteq C_P(\cdot)$$

which proves the theorem ■

Due to this result we will consider hereafter only weak Paretian functions and briefly call them Paretian choice functions.

Another way for the choice function to be rationalizable via vector of criteria was introduced in [7] , and is called *joint-extremal* choice. It is defined by an n-tuple of criteria $\vec{\varphi}$ and the following choice rule

$$C(X) = \{y \in X | \exists i \in N \text{ such that } \forall x \in X : u_i(y) \geq u_i(x)\},$$

that is, this rule chooses alternatives that are extremal at least by one criterion. Since, according to Pareto rule, these extremal alternatives also are included into the Paretian choice, the choice $C_P(\cdot)$ and the joint-extremal choice $C_{je}(\cdot)$ on the same set of criteria are related as follows: $\forall X \subseteq A$

$$C_{je}(X) \subseteq C_P(X).$$

2.4 Expansion-Contraction Axioms

A traditional way of postulating rational properties of choice consists in indicating how the chosen set $Y = C(X)$ varies under different 'deformations' of the set X. Below, we present the properties called *Expansion-Contraction Axioms* that will be used in this monograph. The most common rationality condition is that of *non-empty choice*, that is,

$$C(X) \neq \emptyset \text{ for all } X \in A.$$

It is worth mentioning that before 1977, the publications which did not presume non-emptiness of choice, were scarce. In what follows, we consider the cases of empty and non-empty choice. The empty choice may be treated as 'refusal' to make choice when considering individual opinions and as impossibility of making social decision in case of social choice.

Another rationality condition consists in that the choice on any X does not coincide with the entire X, which is called *choice resoluteness*.

We formalize this condition as

$$\forall X : |X| > 1 \Rightarrow C(X) \subset X.$$

Sometimes, consideration is given to the *weak resoluteness* condition, namely,

$$C(A) \subset A$$

that is, the resoluteness of choice on the entire A.

Several other axioms below are of wide use in social choice theory.

Definition 2.1 The function $C(\cdot)$ will be said to satisfy the *Heredity condition* (denoted by **H**), if

$$X' \subseteq X \Rightarrow C(X') \supseteq C(X) \cap X'$$

for all $X, X' \in A$.

It is as follows: if a set is contracted by eliminating some alternatives, the alternatives chosen in the original set and remaining in the contracted one do get into the choice (Fig.2-6). This condition implies that the world champions in some sport competition are among the national champions, or that the goods selected from an assortment providing wide opportunities for comparison and choice, all the more so will be selected from a narrower assortment. In these terms, the condition **H** only seems the natural requirement to reasonable choice. We note that the condition **H** does not rule out the possibility that the choice from the contracted set X' also includes the alternatives that did not get into the choice from the extended set X, and particularly if $X' \bigcap C(X) = \emptyset$, then condition **H** imposes no constraints on $C(X')$.

Now we make the condition **H** stronger.

Definition 2.2 The function $C(\cdot)$ will be said to satisfy the Strict Hereditycondition or *Arrow's Choice Axiom* (denoted by **ACA**) if the following two independent conditions

$$X' \subseteq X \Longrightarrow \begin{cases} \text{if } C(X) = \emptyset, \text{ then } C(X') = \emptyset; \\ \text{if } C(X) \cap X' \neq \emptyset, \text{ then } C(X') = C(X) \cap X', \end{cases}$$

are simultaneously satisfied for all $X, X' \in A$.

If the choice is not empty for all X, that is, if only the functions from the subspace C^+ are considered, only the second line remains in condition **ACA**. Condition **ACA** demands that all alternatives chosen from X and remaining in the contracted set X' and only them be selected from X' (Fig.2-7). This condition in no way limits the choice from X' if $C(X) \neq \emptyset$, but $X' \bigcap C(X) = \emptyset$.

In terms of illustrative examples given above Condition **ACA** means that:

— if there are world champions, they and only they are recognized as the best in a national team;

— if the contracted assortment includes the goods chosen from the extended one, these goods and only they will be selected from the contracted assortment.

One can see from these examples to what extent Condition **ACA** is stronger than **H**.

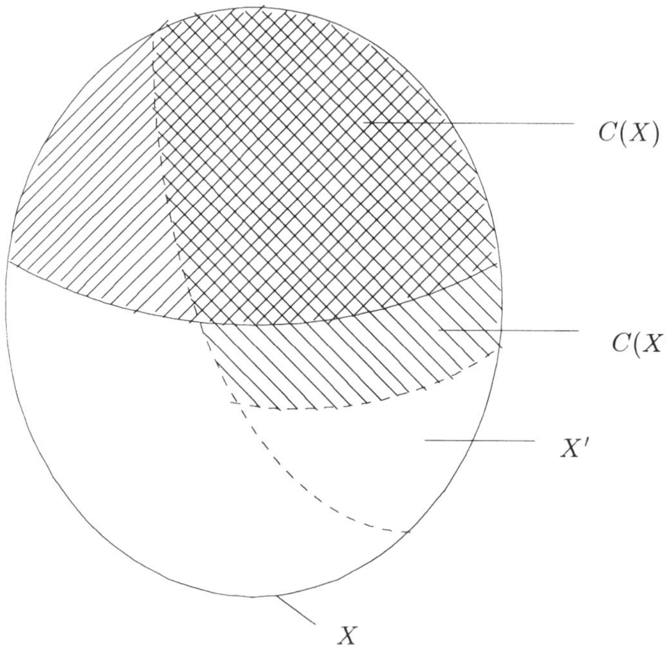

Figure 2-6

Definition 2.3 The function $C(\cdot)$ satisfies the *Concordance condition* (denoted by C) if

$$X = X' \bigcup X'' \Longrightarrow C(X) \supseteq C(X') \bigcap C(X'')$$

for all $X', X'' \in A$.

The condition **C** requires that all alternatives chosen simultaneously from the sets X' and X'' be included into the choice if their union $X = X' \bigcup X''$ is presented (Fig.2-8). Needless to say that the choice from $X = X' \bigcup X''$ may have alternatives that are out of choice at separate presentations of X' and X'' even if they are presented both in X' and X'' (all the more so if they are present in only one of these sets).
In the above examples:
— the sportsmen who are included in both teams and are the champions in both of them are the champions of the united team;
— if the goods are chosen by the customer from two different assortments, they are chosen if the combined assortment is presented.

Definition 2.4 The function $C(\cdot)$ satisfies the condition of Independence of *Outcast*

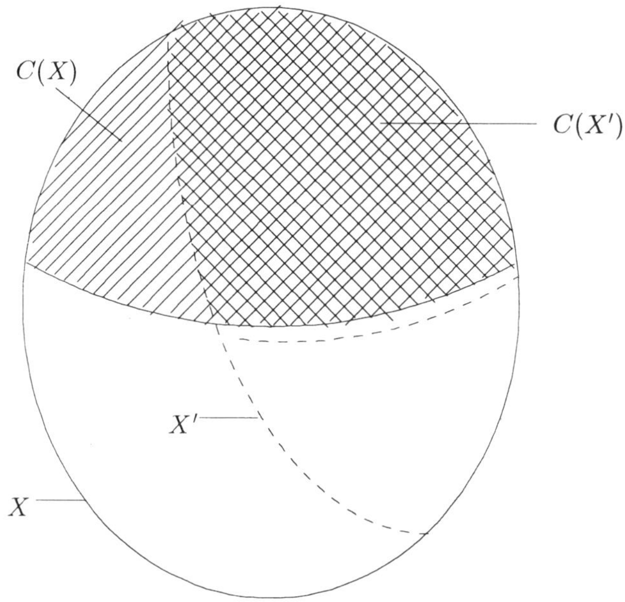

Figure 2-7

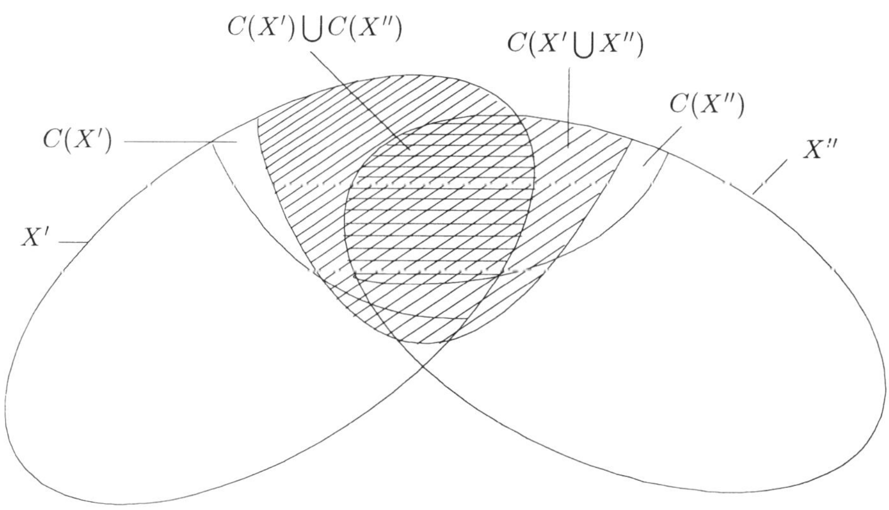

Figure 2-8

Alternatives (denoted by **O**) if for all $X, X', X'' \in A$

$$C(X) \subseteq X' \subseteq X \Longrightarrow C(X') = C(X),$$

or, equivalently,

$$X'' \subseteq X \setminus C(X) \Longrightarrow C(X \setminus X'') = C(X)$$

.

Condition **O** is satisfied by those choice functions where contraction of X by outcasting some or even all alternatives not chosen from the initial set X does not change the choice (Fig.2-9).

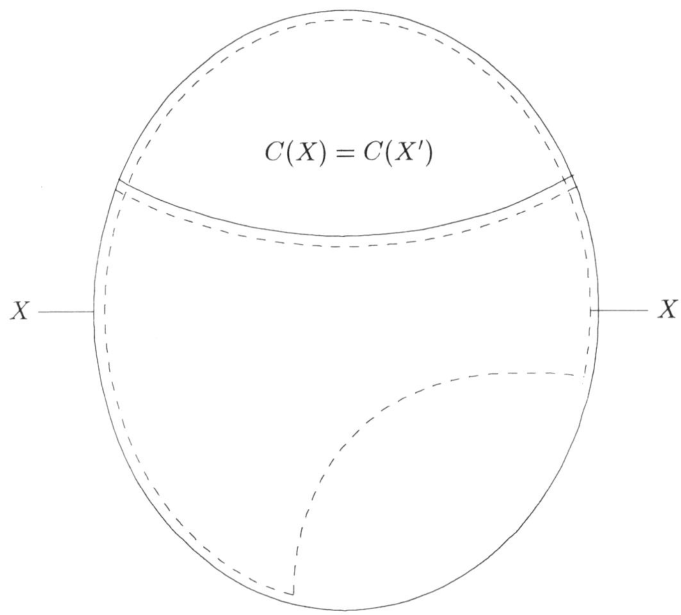

Figure 2-9

In terms of descriptive examples:
— outcasting from the team some (or even all) sportsmen who are not champions does not change the list of champions;
— outcasting from the assortment some (or all) goods that were not chosen by the customer leaves the list of chosen goods unchanged.

We will use also the equivalent formulation of the condition **O** (see [6]): condition **O** is equivalent to the conjunction of the following two conditions:

$$1)\ x \in C(X),\ z \notin C(X) \Rightarrow x \in C(X \setminus \{z\});$$
$$2)\ y \notin C(X), z \notin C(X) \Rightarrow y \notin C(X \setminus \{z\}).$$

Each of the axioms (**H**, **ACA**, **C**, and **O**) distinguishes in the space $\mathcal{C}$ a domain comprising all the choice functions satisfying the corresponding condition. Below, these domains will be denoted by the same notations **H**, **ACA**, **C**, and **O** as their corresponding characteristic properties.

The overline denoting negation ($\overline{\mathbf{H}}$, $\overline{\mathbf{ACA}}$, $\overline{\mathbf{C}}$, and $\overline{\mathbf{O}}$) will also mean that the corresponding axiom is not satisfied, so that $\overline{\mathbf{H}}$, $\overline{\mathbf{ACA}}$, $\overline{\mathbf{C}}$, and $\overline{\mathbf{O}}$ denote the domains comprising all choice functions for which the corresponding property is not satisfied. In these terms, the intersections

$$a)\mathbf{H} \cap \mathbf{C} \cap \mathbf{O};\ b)\overline{\mathbf{H}} \cap \mathbf{C} \cap \mathbf{O};\ c)\overline{\mathbf{H}} \cap \overline{\mathbf{C}} \cap \mathbf{O},\ \text{etc.},$$

denote the domains of the space $\mathcal{C}$ comprising a) all functions satisfying simultaneously Conditions **H**, **C**, and **O**; b) all functions satisfying Conditions **C** and **O**, but not satisfying **H**; c) all functions satisfying Condition **O**, but not satisfying **H** and **C**, etc.

Altogether there are eight possible combinations of the three axioms **H**, **C**, and **O** and their negations, which gives rise to the questions of how these eight domains are located in the space $\mathcal{C}$, and how the domain **ACA** is located with respect to them. Similar questions can be posed for the subspaces $\mathcal{C}^+$ and $\widehat{\mathcal{C}}$. They are answered by the following theorem.

Theorem 2.4 *a) In the space $\mathcal{C}$ the properties* **H**, **C** *and* **O** *are independent, that is, all eight domains*

$$\mathbf{H} \cap \mathbf{C} \cap \mathbf{O};\ \overline{\mathbf{H}} \cap \mathbf{C} \cap \mathbf{O}, \ldots, \overline{\mathbf{H}} \cap \overline{\mathbf{C}} \cap \overline{\mathbf{O}}$$

are not empty.

b) The property **ACA** *is stronger than each of the properties* **H**, **C** *and* **O**, *that is, the domain* **ACA** *lies strictly within the intersection* $\mathbf{H} \cap \mathbf{C} \cap \mathbf{O}$.

c) In the subspace $\mathcal{C}^+$ the domains **H**, **C**, **O**, *and* **ACA** *are related in the same way as in $\mathcal{C}$.*

d) In the subspace $\widehat{\mathcal{C}}$ the domains **H**, **ACA**, *and* **O** *coincide, thus, making up the domain* $\mathbf{H} - \mathbf{O} - \mathbf{ACA}$ *located strictly within the domain* **C**, *i.e.,* $\mathbf{H} - \mathbf{O} - \mathbf{ACA} \subset \mathbf{C}$.

The statement of Theorem 2.4 is illustrated by Figs.2-10a), b), c) associated, respectively, with the spaces $\mathcal{C}, \mathcal{C}^+$, and $\widehat{\mathcal{C}}$.

Proof. We will prove only the statements b) and d) of the theorem since the statements a) and c) can be easily checked directly by constructing the examples[14].

[14] The complete proof of this theorem is given in [6]

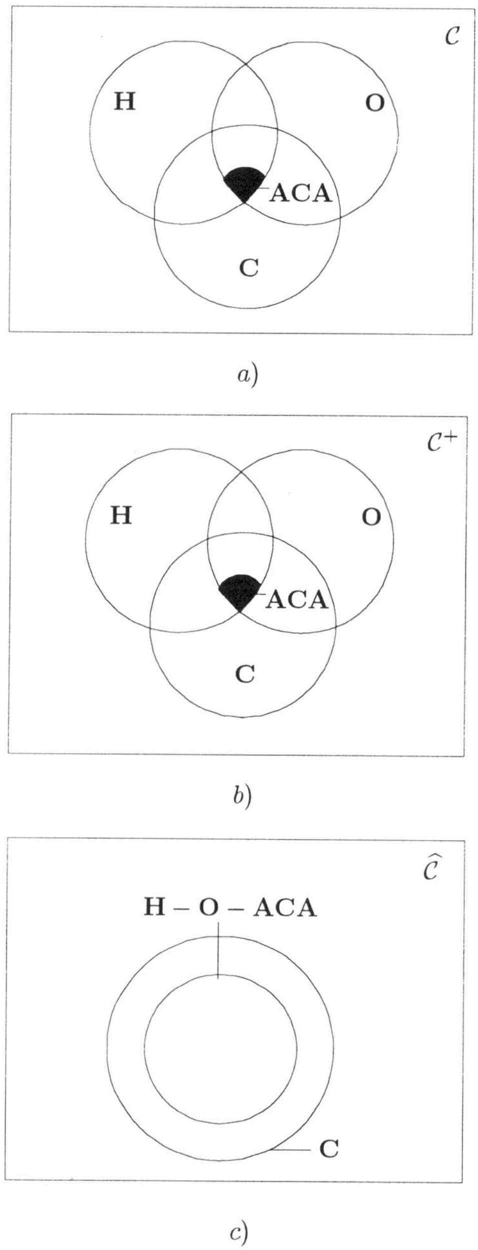
$\mathcal{C}$
H
O
ACA
C
a)
$\mathcal{C}^+$
H
O
ACA
C
b)
$\widehat{\mathcal{C}}$
H – O – ACA
C
c)

Figure 2-10

The fact that functions satisfying $\mathbf{ACA}$ also satisfy $\mathbf{H}$ is evident from the definition of $\mathbf{ACA}$. If $\mathbf{ACA}$ is satisfied, $\mathbf{O}$ is satisfied as well. Indeed, if $C(X) = \emptyset$, the choice on any subsets of X is empty according to $\mathbf{ACA}$, i.e. $\mathbf{O}$ is satisfied. Consider the set $X' : C(X) \subseteq X'$ for $C(X) \neq \emptyset$. According to $\mathbf{ACA}$, $C(X') = C(X) \bigcap X' = C(X)$, which coincides with $\mathbf{O}$.
Show that $\mathbf{C}$ is satisfied. Let $y \in C(X') \bigcap C(X'')$. Demonstrate that $y \in C(X' \bigcup X'')$. Let, on the contrary, $y \notin C(X' \bigcup X'')$. Consider the following two cases:
Case c_1). Let $C(X' \bigcup X'') = \emptyset$. Then $C(X') = C(X'') = \emptyset$ according to $\mathbf{ACA}$, which contradicts the assumption.
Case c_2). Let $x \in C(X' \bigcup X'')$. If $x \in X'$ (similarly, if $x \in X''$), since $C(X') = C(X' \bigcup X'') \bigcap X'$, $y \notin C(X')$ according to $\mathbf{ACA}$. This contradiction proves the assertion of the theorem in what concerns $\mathbf{ACA}$, i.e. $\mathbf{ACA} \subseteq \mathbf{H} \cap \mathbf{C} \cap \mathbf{O}$. The fact that this inclusion is strict can be checked via an example.
Prove the last assertion of the theorem. In $\widehat{C}$ the assertions $\mathbf{ACA} \Rightarrow \mathbf{H}$, $\mathbf{ACA} \Rightarrow \mathbf{O}$, and $\mathbf{ACA} \Rightarrow \mathbf{C}$ follow from the corresponding facts in C. Prove that a) $\mathbf{H} \Rightarrow \mathbf{ACA}$, and b) $\mathbf{O} \Rightarrow \mathbf{ACA}$.
Let $\mathbf{H}$ be satisfied. Consider the function $C(\cdot) \in \mathbf{H}$ and an arbitrary $X \in A$. Let $C(X) = \{x\}$. Then, $C(X') = \{x\}$ for any X' such that $x \in X' \subset X$, that is $C(X') = \{x\}$, which coincides with the formulation of $\mathbf{ACA}$.
Let $\mathbf{O}$ be satisfied. Consider the function $C(\cdot) \in \mathbf{O}$ and some $X \in A$. Let $C(X) = \{x\}$. Then, $C(X') = \{x\}$ for X' such that $C(X) \subseteq X' \subseteq X$, that is $C(X') = X' \bigcap C(X)$, which again coincides with the formulation of $\mathbf{ACA}$ ■

Now we generalize Conditions $\mathbf{H}$ and $\mathbf{C}$. We require that these conditions be satisfied only on two-element sets X. Then, the condition $\mathbf{H}$ is written as

$$C(X) \subseteq \bigcap_{y \in X} C(\{x, y\}),$$

and condition $\mathbf{C}$ as

$$\bigcap_{y \in X} C(\{x, y\}) \subseteq C(X).$$

These axioms were called in [7] *inverse Condorcet condition* and *direct Condorcet condition*, respectively, and designated as $\mathbf{Con}^-$ and $\mathbf{Con}^+$. Joint satisfaction of these conditions is called the *Condorcet Principle* and designated as $\mathbf{PC}$.

Theorem 2.5 *The domain of functions satisfying the Condorcet principle coincides with the domain distinguished by the conjunction of the conditions* $\mathbf{H}$ *and* $\mathbf{C}$, *i.e.*, $\mathbf{PC} = \mathbf{H} \cap \mathbf{C}$.

Proof. As follows from the inclusions $\mathbf{C} \subset \mathbf{Con}^+$ and $\mathbf{H} \subset \mathbf{Con}^-$, the functions satisfying simultaneously $\mathbf{H}$ and $\mathbf{C}$ satisfy Condorcet Principle as well.
Let us show that the conditions $\mathbf{H}$ and $\mathbf{C}$ are satisfied for $C(\cdot) \in \mathbf{Con}^+ \bigcap \mathbf{Con}^-$. First, check satisfaction of $\mathbf{C}$. Consider two sets, X' and X'' $(X' \bigcup X'' = X)$ and prove that $x \in C(X' \bigcup X'')$ if $x \in C(X')$ and $x \in C(X'')$.

As follows from the condition $\mathbf{Con}^-$, $\forall y' \in X' \quad x \in C(\{x, y'\})$ and $\forall y'' \in X''$ $x \in C(\{x, y''\})$ and therefore, $\forall y \in X \quad x \in C(\{x, y\})$. Thus, $x, \in C(X)$ follows from satisfaction of $\mathbf{Con}^+$.
Prove that $\mathbf{H}$ is satisfied. Indeed, if $x \in C(X)$, then $\forall y \in X \quad x \in C(\{x, y\})$ by virtue of $\mathbf{Con}^-$, and $\forall X' \subset X \quad x \in C(X')$ by virtue of $\mathbf{Con}^+$ ∎

Besides the rationality conditions **H**, **C**, **O** and **ACA**, other axioms are discussed in the literature. We will cite some of them and establish their interrelations with **H**, **C** and **O**.

Definition 2.5 The choice function satisfies the *Choice Monotonicity* condition (denoted by **CM**) if $C(X') \subseteq C(X)$ holds for every X, X' such that $X' \subseteq X$.

As follows immediately from its definition, Choice Monotonicity condition and condition **H** are dual, that is, if the function $C(\cdot)$ satisfies **H**, the function $\overline{C}(X) = X \backslash C(X)$ satisfies **CM**, and vice versa.
Below, we introduce another condition of rationality.

Definition 2.6 The choice function will be said to satisfy *Arrow's Choice Axiom in strong version* (denoted by $\mathbf{ACA}^*$) if there exists a non-empty subset A^* of the set A such that $\forall X \in A$

$$C(X) = X \cap A^*.$$

This condition is related to other conditions introduced above by the following theorem.

Theorem 2.6 *The class of choice functions satisfying the condition of strong constancy is strictly embedded into the class* **ACA**, *and the functions of this class are defined by the conjunction of the Choice Monotonicity and Heredity axioms, i.e.,* $\mathbf{ACA}^* = \mathbf{H} \cap \mathbf{CM} \subset \mathbf{ACA}$.

Proof. The fact that any function which satisfies $\mathbf{ACA}^*$ also obeys **ACA** is evident. One can directly check that $\mathbf{ACA}^* \subseteq \mathbf{H} \cap \mathbf{CM}$. Let us prove the inverse statement. Let $A^* = C(A)$. Then due to the condition **H** we have $C(X) \supseteq A^* \cap X$. Due to the condition **CM** we have $C(X) \subseteq A^*$ and $C(X) \cap X = C(X) \subseteq A^* \cap X$. From this inclusions follow $C(X) = X \cap A^*$ ∎

Remark. In the case of non-empty choice the Choice Monotonicity condition defines a single 'point' in the space of choice functions — the function $C(X) \equiv X$ for all $X \in A$. Indeed, since in this case $C(\{x\}) = \{x\}$ for any x and in virtue of Condition **CM**, $x \in C(X)$ for all x and X such that $x \in X \in A$, that is, $C(X) = X$. Similarly, Condition $\mathbf{ACA}^*$ defines the same function, because the set A^* must coincide with the set A for non-empty choice.

2.5 Relations between the classes of choice functions

Now we establish mutual relations between the classes of choice functions introduced in Sections 2.2 and 2.3, and the classes of choice functions distinguished by the corresponding Expansion-Contraction Axioms introduced in Section 2.4.

Theorem 2.7 *The class of pair-dominant choice functions rationalizable by arbitrary binary relations coincides with the domain* $\mathbf{PC} = \mathbf{H} \cap \mathbf{C}$ *in the space* $\mathcal{C}$.

Proof. Let $\mathcal{C}_{PD}$ denotes the class of pair dominant choice functions.
Let us prove first the inclusion $\mathbf{H} \bigcap \mathbf{C} = \mathbf{PC} \subseteq \mathcal{C}_{PD}$. Let the choice function $C(\cdot)$ $\in \mathbf{PC}$ be given. Condorcet principle implies that

$$x \in C(X) \text{ if and only if } x \in \bigcap_{y \in X} C(\{x, y\})$$

Then let us construct the relation P in such a way that

$$xPy \text{ if and only if } x \in C(\{x, y\}),$$

and define the choice function $C'(\cdot)$ on P via the rule (2.1). Show that $C(\cdot) \subseteq C'(\cdot)$. Indeed, since $x \in C(X)$ then $x \in \bigcap_{y \in X} C(\{x, y\})$. According to the construction of P this means that $\overline{\exists} y \in X$ such that yPx, i.e., $x \in C'(X)$.
Prove now that $\mathcal{C}_{PD} \subseteq \mathbf{H} \bigcap \mathbf{C}$. Let function $C(\cdot) \in \mathcal{C}_{PD}$ be defined. First show that $C(\cdot) \in \mathbf{H}$. Assume the contrary: for some X and $x \in C(X)$ there exists $X' \subset X$ such that $x \in X'$ and $x \notin C(X')$. This implies that $\exists y \in X'$ is such that yPx. However, $y \in X$, and thus $x \notin C(X)$ according to the rule (2.1). This contradiction proves that $C(\cdot) \in \mathbf{H}$.
Now, demonstrate that $C(\cdot) \in \mathbf{C}$. Let $x \in C(X')$ and $x \in C(X'')$. As follows from $x \in C(X')$, there is no $y \in X'$ such that yPx. As follows from $x \in C(X'')$, there is no $y \in X''$ such that yPx. Then, there is no y in $X = X' \bigcup X''$ such that yPx and $x \in C(X)$, that is C is obeyed ■

The following theorem considers the case of non-empty choice, and the results then are extended to the case of empty choice.

Theorem 2.8 *(generalized Sen's Theorem)*
a) The class of pair-dominant choice functions rationalizable by an acyclic binary relations coincides with the domain $\mathbf{H} \cap \mathbf{C}$ *in the space* $\mathcal{C}^+$ *of nonempty choice functions;*
b) the class of pair-dominant functions on strict partial order coincides with the domain $\mathbf{H} \cap \mathbf{C} \cap \mathbf{O}$ *in the space* $\mathcal{C}^+$;
c) the class of pair-dominant functions on weak order coincides with the domain $\mathbf{ACA}$ *in the space* $\mathcal{C}^+$; *and*
d) the class of pair-dominant functions on linear orders coincides with the domain $\mathbf{ACA}$ *in the space* $\widehat{\mathcal{C}}$ *of single valued choice functions.*

Proof. The statement a) of the theorem follows immediately from Theorem 2.7 taking into account that for non-empty choice the relation P must not have cycles.

Let us prove statement b). Construct the relation P according to the given function $C(\cdot) \in \mathbf{H} \cap \mathbf{C} \cap \mathbf{O}$ as we did it in the proof of Theorem 2.7. The acyclicity of P follows from the statement a). Let us prove that P is transitive. Suppose on the contrary, that there exist x, y, and z such that $xPyPz$ but $x\overline{P}z$. Then consider $X = \{x, y, z\}$. The chosen alternatives according to the function $C(\cdot)$ will be $C(X) = \{x\}$. Exclude from X the alternative y which is not chosen and then $C(X \setminus \{y\}) = \{x, z\}$, i.e. the condition $\mathbf{O}$ is violated. The fact that a choice function on some strict partial order P satisfies the conditions $\mathbf{H} \cap \mathbf{C} \cap \mathbf{O}$ can be checked directly.

c). According to the statement b) and due to the fact that $\mathbf{ACA} \subset \mathbf{H} \cap \mathbf{C} \cap \mathbf{O}$ the constructed relation P should be at least strict partial order. Show now that P is negatively transitive. Let us use an equivalent condition $\forall x, y, z\ xPy \Rightarrow xPz$ or zPy. Suppose this condition is violated, i.e., $\exists x, y, z$ such that xPy and $x\overline{P}z$ and $z\overline{P}y$. Then $C(\{x, y, z\}) = \{x, z\}$ and $C(\{z, y\}) = \{z, y\}$, which violates the condition $\mathbf{ACA}$. The fact that the function rationalizable by weak order satisfies $\mathbf{ACA}$ can be checked directly.

d) Now statement d) follows directly from c) taking into account the fact that the choice on the linear order by the rule (2.1) is always single valued due to the connectedness of linear order ■

Theorems 2.2, 2.3, and 2.8 lead to the following

Corollary 2.1 *a) The class of multicriterial paretian choice functions coincides with the domain* $\mathbf{H} \cap \mathbf{C} \cap \mathbf{O}$ *in the space* $\mathcal{C}^+$;
b) the class of unicriterial choice functions coincides with the domain $\mathbf{ACA}$ *in* $\mathcal{C}^+$; *and*
c) the class of choice functions rationalized via strict criteria (that is, such that $u(x) \neq u(y)$ *for any* $x, y \in A$*) coincides with the domain* $\mathbf{ACA}$ *in* $\widehat{\mathcal{C}}$.

The previous Section discussed the function of joint-extremal choice. We determine the domain of functions generated by this choice rule. Introduce into consideration a new characteristic condition proposed for the first time by C.Plott [220] .

Definition 2.7 The choice function $C(\cdot)$ is called a *path–independent (or Plott's) function* if it satisfies the following condition

$$\forall X_1, X_2 \in A \quad C(X_1 \bigcup X_2) = C(C(X_1) \bigcup C(X_2)). \tag{2.6}$$

If (2.6) is violated, one could find in X two subsets such that if one presents them separately, makes choice from them and uses the union of chosen alternatives as the next presentation, the result might differ from what is obtained at single presentation of the initial set X. This condition rules out such a possibility.

The path independence axiom isolates a set of choice functions, that is a domain in $\mathcal{C}$. It will be called the domain of path–independent (**PI**) functions or the domain of Plott's functions.

Let us determine now the relation between the Plott's functions domain and the fundamental domains **H**, **C** and **O** in the choice function space.

Theorem 2.9 *The domain of functions satisfying the path-independence condition coincides in* $\mathcal{C}$ *with the intersection of* **H** *and* **O**.

Proof. First we prove the following

Lemma 2.1 *The domain in* $\mathcal{C}$ *isolated by the following condition*

$$\forall X_1, X_2 \in A \quad C(X_1 \bigcup X_2) = C(C(X_1) \bigcup X_2) \tag{2.7}$$

coincides with that isolated by (2.6), that is coincides with the domain of path–independent functions.

Proof of Lemma. Let the condition (2.7) be satisfied. We demonstrate that (2.6) is satisfied as well. Double application of (2.7) results in $\forall X_1, X_2 \in A \; C(X_1 \bigcup X_2) = C(X_2 \bigcup C(X_1)) = C(C(X_2) \bigcup C(X_1))$.
Inversely, let (2.6) be satisfied. Demonstrate that (2.7) is satisfied. First, note that if a function $C(\cdot)$ satisfies (2.6), $\forall X \subseteq A \quad C(C(X)) = C(X)$ (it suffices to assume in (2.6) that $X_1 = X_2 = X$). Then, $\forall X_1, X_2 \subseteq A$

$$C(X_1 \bigcup X_2) = C(C(X_1) \bigcup C(X_2)) = C(C(X_1) \bigcup C(C(X_2))),$$

and application of (2.6) to the correct expression in this equality gives

$$C(C(X_1) \bigcup C(C(X_2))) = C(X_1 \bigcup C(X_2)),$$

that is, (2.7) is satisfied. Lemma is proved.
Let now function $C(\cdot)$ satisfy the **PI** condition. Show that it satisfies **H** and **O**. Consider arbitrary sets X and $X_1 \subseteq X$. Denote $X \backslash X_1$ by X_2. Then, according to **PI** condition

$$C(X) = C(X_1 \bigcup X_2) = C(C(X_1) \bigcup C(X_2)) \subseteq C(X_1) \bigcup C(X_2)$$

and

$$X_1 \bigcap C(X) \subseteq X_1 \bigcap (C(X_1) \bigcup C(X_2)) =$$

$$[X_1 \bigcap C(X_2)] \bigcup [X_1 \bigcap C(X_1)] = C(X_1),$$

because $X_1 \bigcap C(X_2) = \emptyset$ by virtue of $X_1 \bigcap X_2 = \emptyset$. Thus, $C(X_1) \supseteq C(X) \bigcap X_1$, which proves that **H** is satisfied.
Let now $X' \subseteq X \backslash C(X)$. Denote $X_1 = X \backslash X'$. One can write $X = X \bigcup X_1$. Making use of (2.7) and previous Lemma, obtain

$$C(X) = C(C(X) \bigcup X_1) = C(X_1),$$

because $C(X) \subseteq X_1$. This proves that **O** is satisfied.
Let now $C(\cdot) \in \mathbf{H} \bigcap \mathbf{O}$. Demonstrate that it satisfies **PI**. Consider arbitrary sets X, X_1 and X_2 such that $X_1 \bigcup X_2 = X$. In compliance with the condition **H**, $C(X_1) \supseteq C(X) \bigcap X_1$ and $C(X_2) \supseteq C(X) \bigcap X_2$. So, $C(X_1) \bigcup C(X_2) \supseteq C(X) \bigcap (X_1 \bigcup X_2) = C(X)$, but in this case $C(X_1) \bigcup C(X_2) = X \backslash X'$ where $X' \subseteq X \backslash C(X)$. Using now the condition **O**, obtain: $C(C(X_1) \bigcup C(X_2)) = C(X \backslash X') = C(X)$ which proves that **PI** is satisfied ■

In the following theorem the domain is fixed which is filled by the choice functions rationalizable by the vector of criteria and the rule of joint-extremal choice.

Theorem 2.10 *The class of joint-extremal choice functions coincides in $\mathcal{C}$ with the domain* $\mathbf{H} \cap \mathbf{O}$.

Proof ([194]). Consider first the case of non-empty choice and prove two lemmas.

Lemma 2.2 *Let $A = \{x_1, \ldots, x_m\}$ and a function $C(\cdot) \in \mathbf{H}$ be defined. Let $\widetilde{C}(\cdot)$ be the choice function rationalizable by a linear order P such that $x_1 P x_2 P \ldots P x_m$. Then, the condition*

$$\forall X \;\; \widetilde{C}(X) \subseteq C(X) \tag{2.8}$$

is satisfied if and only if

$$x_1 \in C(A), x_2 \in C(A \backslash \{x_1\}), \ldots, x_m \in C\left(A \backslash \bigcup_{j=1}^{m-1} \{x_j\}\right) \tag{2.9}$$

Proof. Prove that (2.9) follows from (2.8). To this end, it suffices to assume that $X = A$, which results in $x_1 \in C(A)$; then, $X = A \backslash \{x_1\}$, which gives $x_2 \in C(A \backslash \{x_1\})$, etc.
Inversely, let $C(\cdot) \in \mathbf{H}$ and let (2.9) holds. Consider an arbitrary $X \in A$. Let $\widetilde{C}(X) = \{x_j\}$. Then, $X \subseteq A \backslash \{x_1, \ldots, x_{j-1}\} = X'$ and $C(X) \supseteq C(X') \bigcap X$ according to **H**. Since by assumption $x_j \in C(X') \bigcap X$, then $x_j \in C(X)$ and, therefore, $\widetilde{C}(X) \subseteq C(X)$.
Lemma is proved.

Lemma 2.3 *Any function $C(\cdot)$ from the domain $\mathbf{H} \bigcap \mathbf{O}$ in $\mathcal{C}^+$ is representable as*

$$C(X) = \bigcup_i \widetilde{C}_i(X) \textit{ for all } X, \tag{2.10}$$

where $\widetilde{C}_i(\cdot)$ is the choice function rationalizable by linear order P_i.

Proof. Consider arbitrary $X \in A$ and $x \in C(X)$. Show that a linear order $P_i = P(X, x)$ can be constructed such that the corresponding function $\widetilde{C}_i(\cdot)$ satisfies (2.8)

and $\widetilde{C}_i(X) = \{x\}$. Having determined such functions $\widetilde{C}_i(\cdot)$ for all $X \in A$ and $x \in C(X)$, obtain then that (2.10) holds.
Define now each relation $P_i = P(X, x)$ in the form of $x_1 P x_2 P \dots P x_m$ choosing the sequence $x_1, \dots, x_m$ so that it satisfies (2.9). To this end, consider $C(A)$. If $C(A) \subseteq X$, obtain $C(A) = C(X)$ in compliance with **O**, and assume that $x_1 = x$, the remaining terms of the sequence being determined arbitrarily from (2.9).
If $C(A) \not\subseteq X$, determine $x_1 \in C(A) \backslash X_1$ and to determine x_2 (as well as $x_i, 3 \leq i \leq m$), repeat the procedure, only replacing A by $A \backslash \{x_1\}$ $\left(A \backslash \cup_{j=1}^{i} \{x_j\}\right)$. The alternative x by construction has lower number in the sequence $x_1, \dots, x_m$ than other alternatives from X and thus $\widetilde{C}(X) = \{x\}$. $\widetilde{C}_i(\cdot)$ satisfies (2.8) by virtue of Lemma 2.2. Lemma 2.3 is proved.

Now, we prove the theorem. Consider the general case of $\mathbf{H} \bigcap \mathbf{O}$, that is admit also empty choice. The set A due to the condition **O** is decomposable into two parts by the choice function from this domain so that $A_1 \bigcap A_2 = \emptyset$, $A_1 \bigcup A_2 = A; \forall X \in A_1 \quad C(X) \neq \emptyset$ and $\forall X \in A_2 \quad C(X) = \emptyset$. In fact, assume that $A_2 = \cup_x Z_x$ where Z_x is all the subsets of A where choice is empty. Then, $\forall X \subseteq A_2 \quad X = \cup_x (X \bigcap Z_x)$. From **O**, $\forall x \; C(X \bigcap Z_x) = \emptyset$ and therefore, $C(X) = \emptyset$ from **H**. For the set $A_1 = A \backslash A_2$, the condition $\forall X \in A_1 \quad C(X) \neq \emptyset$ is satisfied by construction of A_2.
Now the above proof for the non–empty case is extended to that under consideration where empty choice is admitted, the set A_1 being regarded as A. Let us construct for each choice function $\widetilde{C}_i(\cdot)$ the criterion u_i on A_1 according to the corresponding relation P_i in such a way that

$$u_i(x) > u_i(y) \Longleftrightarrow x P_i y,$$

and extend it on A_2 using the 'label' function $\Psi(\cdot)$. It is obvious that the constructed vector of criteria with the joint extremal rule defines the choice function under study. The fact that any choice function rationalizable by vector of criteria and joint-extremal rule satisfies the conditions $\mathbf{H} \cap \mathbf{O}$ can be checked directly ■

The joint-extremal choice functions, thus, do not satisfy the Condorcet principle, although it looks very reasonable.

Now we address the functions that admit empty choice. Turning now to the functions from the domain $\mathbf{H} \cap \mathbf{C} \cap \mathbf{O}$, one can see that if the condition **O** is satisfied, the form of the binary relations that admit empty choice when using the pair dominant rule (2.1) is pre-defined. Namely, if this condition is satisfied and the choice on a set $X \in A$ is empty, the choice on any $X' \subseteq X$ is empty as well.

In [6] the notion was introduced of *two-level binary relation* P of a given form — P is referred to as the two-level relation if the set A is a union of two sets A_1 and A_2, here $A_1 \cup A_2 = A$ and $A_1 \cap A_2 = \emptyset$. The contraction of P to A_1 is the relation of a given form — weak order, for example; the contraction of P to A_2 features $\forall x \in A_2 (x, x) \in P$, and $(x, y) \notin P$ takes place for any $x, y \in A$ such that $x \in A_2, y \in A_1$. Thus, one can introduce the notions of two-level linear, weak, and partial orders. It is precisely these relations that define the classical pair-dominant choice functions admitting empty choice, and we obtain the following obvious result

Theorem 2.11 *The class of pair dominant functions on the two-level a) partial orders, and b) weak orders coincides with the domain in C distinguished, respectively, by the following conditions: a)* $\mathbf{H} \cap \mathbf{C} \cap \mathbf{O}$, *and b)* $\mathbf{ACA}$.

The difference between Theorems 2.8 and 2.11 is in that such an insignificant extension of the binary relations enables one to describe the domains in the space C (that is, admitting empty choice), the domains being described by the same Expansion-Contraction Axioms as for the non-empty choice. We make this construction of two-level relations somewhat stronger. Let us consider a relation P such that the contraction of P to A_1 is an empty relation. The graph in Fig.2-11 exemplifies such a relation. We refer to such relations P as trivial weak orders.

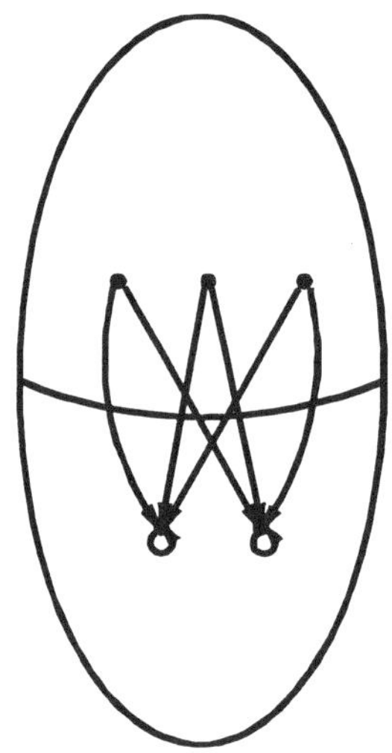

Figure 2-11

The following statement is also obvious

Theorem 2.12 *The class of pair dominant choice functions on the trivial weak orders coincides with the domain* $\mathbf{ACA}^*$ *in the space* C.

Directing now our attention to the criterial choice functions which admit an empty choice we note that the corresponding criteria can be constructed as follows: the set A is again decomposed into the sets A_1 and A_2, and the alternatives from A_2 carry 'labels' — the attributes indicating that they are to be always rejected from choice. For example, in addition to the criterion $u(\cdot)$, a function $\Psi(\cdot)$ is defined such that $\forall x \in A_1\ \Psi(x) = 1$, $\forall x \in A_2\ \Psi(x) = 0$, and the choice rule for the unicriterial case is as follows:

$$C(X) = \{y \in X | \Psi(y) = 1 \text{ and } (\rceil \exists x \in X : u(x) > u(y))\}$$

Using these choice representation, one can obtain an analogue of the Corollary 2.1.

Chapters 3 and 4 of [6] describe completely in which form the choice functions from the domains **H**, **C**, and **O** separately are rationalizable. It turns out that if the logic of dominant choice is preserved and the Condorcet principle (as well as the presumption of pair-dominance that follows from it) is rejected, one has to introduce constructions more complicated than binary relations — namely, the hyper-relations where, for instance, the alternative $x \in X$ can be dominated by the set $X' \in \mathcal{A}$. Such a situation is exemplified by the joint-extremal choice functions as in the following example. Let us discuss the estimates of alternatives in the two-criterial space (u_1, u_2) shown in Fig.2-12.

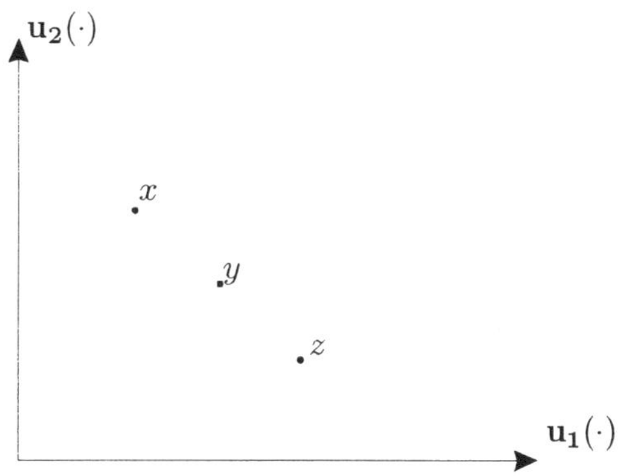

Figure 2-12

In the pair presentations all alternatives are chosen, and if the positive Condorcet condition were obeyed, the choice on the entire A coincide with the set A. However, $C(A) = \{x, z\}$, and this fact can be regarded as domination of the alternative y by the set $\{x, z\}$, although y is not dominated separately by x and z. This situation can not be described under the framework of classic rationality which is based as it was mentioned above on the presumption of pair dominance. However, below we will consider voting models based on binary relations rather than on such general and abstract formal construction as hiper-relations.

2.6 Concluding remarks and guide to the literature

Remark 1. Let us summarize the results obtained in this Chapter for the case of space

C^+, i.e., for the case of non-empty choice. Fig.2-13 represents these results on Venn diagramm constructed for domains isolated by conditions **H**, **C**, **O**, and **ACA**. As it is obviously seen, results of rational choice theory cover the class **H**$\cap$ **C** and its subclasses **H**$\cap$ **C**$\cap$ **O** and **ACA**. For all these classes Fig.2-13 shows corresponding binary relations and criterial models via which the choice functions from these classes are rationalizable.

Remark 2. The classic theory of choice assumes that the individual chooses the best alternative by maximizing some utility function or weak order. The traditional pair-dominant paradigm was the subject of active discussion in [7, 34, 94, 133, 144, 145, 234]

In [268] an experimental confirmation for the violation of the classical rationality in description of individual opinions is provided. The analysis of the foundations of rational choice theory attracted a special attention of scientists during last two decades. The different opinions are expressed in the literature. One of them are cited below.

'It may be that we are witnessing a curious phenomenon in which rational choice theories are fortified in every discipline by reference to their alleged success elsewhere, when a more global view of things would reveal the emperor to be, if not entirely naked, somewhat scantily clad' ([134]).

R.D.Luce proposed [168] a less limited version of rational behavior requiring maximization within a discrimination threshold — the chosen alternative is regarded as equivalent to another one if the difference between them does not exceed the threshold. If re-write in terminology accepted in this book, the corresponding choice function will be as follows

$$C(X) = \{y \in X \mid \overline{\exists} x \in X \text{ such that } u(x) - u(y) > \varepsilon\}.$$

It has been studied in [1] (see, also, [6, 16]) the properties of corresponding functions $C(\cdot)$ under different definitions of ε, namely, when ε depends on the set X and/or comparable alternatives x and y.

Remark 3. Another area of study is related to analysis of 'non-local' models of the tournament type. As was demonstrated in [273] , it may happen that the choice model which is represented by a set of criteria and the (not pair-dominant) rule counting the "victories" of one alternative over another and choosing that with the maximal number of scores, satisfies none of the above rationality conditions **H**, **C**, or **O**. This paper discusses other conditions of rationality for the functions generated by the tournament choice (see, also, [23, 24]).

The models of multicriterial choice and its properties were the subject of study in several books (see, e.g., [46, 170]).

In above study of pair-dominant choice we used binary relations P in 'strict' version, which satisfy irreflexivity conditon. For the use of binary relations, which are reflexive, in choice models readers refer to [28] , [143] , [241] , [243] , [244] , [247] ,[263] ,[264] . The study about equivalency of choice models on irreflexive and reflexive binary relations is given in [7, 143] (see also [6]).

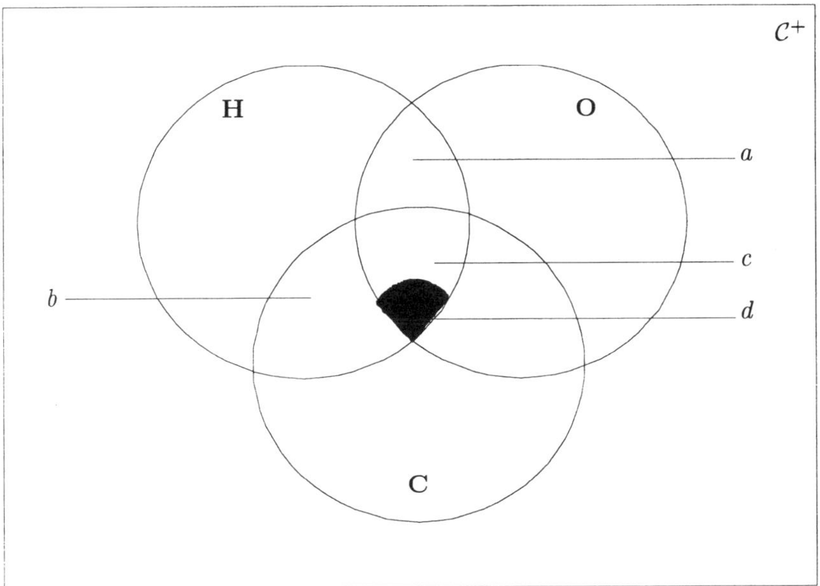

Figure 2-13:a) - joint-extremal choice functions; b) - pair-dominant functions on acyclic relations; c) - pair-dominant functions on strict partial orders, Paretian choice functions; d) - pair-dominant functions on weak orders, unicriterial functions

The axiom **H** was introduced first in [80] , (Postulate 4), and was used in choice theory in many publications (see, [28] (Axiom 2), [243] (Condition α), and other authors. This form of the condition **ACA** was introduced in [80] (Postulate 6) and is also known as a form of the 'strong axiom of revealed preferences' by P.Samuelson, the Axiom $C4$ by K.Arrow ([28]). Condition **C** is Postulate 10 by H.Chernoff or the condition γ by A.Sen. This condition **O** is not widely used in the publications on the theory of choice, although its appearance dates from H.Chernoff ([80] , Postulate 5), see also Axiom 2 by A.Sen. In [194] this axiom was called Aizerman's Condition. Condition CM was first introduced in [8] . The condition of path independence was first introduced by C.Plott [220] , and was studied in many papers on social choice theory (see, e.g., [7,36,51,115,147,151,171]).
The condition **ACA*** was introduced and studied in [8, 9] . Condition of choice resoluteness seems to have been first formally studied in [223] .
Crucial impact in using Expansion-Contraction Axioms in choice theory is due to A.Sen (see [243–247]). The rejection of classical pair-dominant paradigm is mainly due to works by A.Sen [243,244] . First attempts to formalize non-classical approach to choice was made by M.Aizerman, N.Zavalishin, and E.Pyatnitski [8,9] . M.Aizerman

and A.Malishevski [7] first used hyper-relations in non-classical models of choice (see, also, [6]). For further studies the reader is referred to [172,204] .
The second statement of Theorem 2.3 is due to [206] .. Theorem 2.4 was first given (without proof) in [7] . For its complete proof and a detailed study of Conditions **H**, **C**, **O**, and **ACA** the reader refers to [6] . Theorem 2.6 was proved in [8] .
For the case of non-empty choice, Theorem 2.8 was proved in [243] , statement c) - in [28] , for an arbitrary case in [6] , which also proves Corollary 2.1. Theorem 2.8 was proved in [220] . Theorem 2.9 was stated in [7] , its proof here is due to [192] ; the other proof can be found in [6] .

3

SOCIAL DECISION FUNCTIONS

3.1 Introduction

In this Chapter we consider aggregation rules which transform individual binary relations (agents' preferences) into social binary relations (social preferences). Such rules were called in Chapter 1 as Social Decision Functions (briefly, SDFs).
Chapter 3 consists of two parts. The first one which includes Sections 3.2-3.10 deals with strongly local rules. These rules make the decision about the inclusion of a pair (x, y) into the social binary relation P depending only on the information about inclusion of this very pair (x, y) in agents' preferences[15] P_i. On the other hand, local SDFs in general form make a social decision about a pair (x, y) taking into account an information about the pair (y, x) in agents' preferences as well. Otherwise speaking, in strongly local rules we check only 'direct' opinions of agents, whereas in local rules the 'opposite' opinion (about (y, x)) is also taken into account[16]. Local SDFs are studied in Sections 3.11-3.15.

Using these two definitions of locality we consider in this Chapter similar problems for strongly local and local Social Decision Functions. Section 3.2 introduces the notion of strongly local SDFs, and give the representation of those rules in terms of winning coalitions and boolean functions of boolean variables. Section 3.3 lists a set of normative conditions, and defines the important subclass in the set of all strongly local SDFs - the Central Class, the rules from which satisfy Non-imposition, Monotonicity and Neutrality conditions. Section 3.4 studies the representation of the rules from the Central Class. This Class contains federation rules and its particular forms: olygarchy, sindicate, dictator, and k-majority. In Section 3.5 the rules restricted by main rationality constraints are studied, those constraints being acyclicity, transitivity and connectedness of individual and social binary relations. In Section 3.6 we compare the classes of rules restricted by rationality constraints with the subclasses of the Central Class. Section 3.7 gives another proof of Arrow's General Impossibility Theorem. In Section 3.8 the ranges of the rules under study are considered to be some new classes of binary relations. We introduce and consider l-acyclic binary relations, single-source relations, interval orders, and semi-orders. Then we establish the representation of those rules and compare the classes of the rules thus obtained with the subclasses of the Central Class. In Section 3.9 the problem of aggregation of equivalence relations via strongly

[15] The condition of strong locality is called in the literature as Strong Binariness.

[16] Locality condition is called Binariness.

local SDFs is considered. Section 3.10 states and extends famous result in aggregation theory concerning non-monotonic strongly local rules - Wilson's Theorem about anti-dictatorship.

Section 3.11 introduces the notion of local SDFs, and gives a representation of these rules in terms of boolean functions of three-valued logic variables and via pairs of winning-loosing coalitions. Sections 3.12-3.15 just extend the corresponding notions and results for strongly local rules given in Sections 3.3-3.6. The final Section of Chapter 3 (Section 3.16) contains concluding remarks and guide to the literature.

3.2 Strong locality

Let us first briefly remind the framework of the model. Each agent i from the set $N = \{1, ..., n\}$, $2 \leq n < \infty$, defines her opinion about the alternatives from the finite set $A = \{x_1, ..., x_m\}$, $m \geq 3$, in the form of binary relation P_i. An aggregation rule F transforms a profile of agents' preferences $\{P_i\}$ (denoted also as $\vec{P}$) into a social binary relation P. A rule $F \in \Pi_I$ is assumed to be defined on the n-tuple $Q_d^n = Q_d \times ... \times Q_d$, $Q_d \subseteq \mathcal{B}$, where $\mathcal{B}$ is the set of all binary relations on A. Thus, the domain of F is n-tuple $Q_d \times ... \times Q_d$. The set Q_d itself will be called the domain of definition of F. The range of F is a set Q_r, $Q_r \subseteq \mathcal{B}$. Until Section 3.5 Q_d and Q_r are not restricted, i.e., $Q_d = Q_r = \mathcal{B}$.

Let $V(x, y; \vec{P})$ be the set of agents which in the profile $\vec{P}$ include the pair (x, y) into their binary relation P_i, i.e.,

$$V(x, y; \vec{P}) = \{i \in N \mid xP_iy\}.$$

Definition 3.1 A Social Decision Function F is said to satisfy *strong locality* condition if for any pair (x, y) and any two profiles $\vec{P}$ and $\vec{P'}$ such that $V(x, y; \vec{P}) = V(x, y; \vec{P'})$ the following holds

$$(x, y) \in P \Longleftrightarrow (x, y) \in P',$$

where $P = F(\vec{P})$, and $P' = F(\vec{P'})$.

In words, strong locality condition restricts a SDF in such a way that the information about 'irrelevant' pairs (y, x), (x, z), (z, w), etc., does not matter in decision making about the inclusion of a pair (x, y) into a social binary relation P. Hence, the condition of strong locality is a counterpart of the Independence of Irrelevant Alternatives.

The set (space) of all strongly local Social Decision Functions F will be denoted as Π_I^s.

Let us consider another definition of strong locality. Let $l_i(x, y)$ be a boolean (two-valued) variable such that

$$l_i(x,y) = \begin{cases} 1, \text{ if } xP_iy, \\ 0, \text{ else.} \end{cases}$$

Then the strong locality of F is equivalent to the existence of *boolean function* $f(x,y)$ such that

$$f(x,y;\,\overrightarrow{l}) = \begin{cases} 1, \text{ if } xPy, \\ 0, \text{ else.} \end{cases}$$

On the other hand, a strongly local rule can be represented via a set of winning coalitions in the following manner. Let us call a coalition and denote as $\omega^{(x,y)}$ a subset of the set of agents N, i.e., $\omega^{(x,y)} \subseteq N$. The totality of coalitions $\omega^{(x,y)}$ will be denoted as $\Omega(x,y)$. The set $\{\Omega(x,y)\}_{(x,y)}$ defined for all $(x,y) \in A \times A$ will be called the list of coalitions (briefly, list).
Some list $\{\Omega(x,y)\}_{(x,y)}$ be given, let us define the rule ψ such that

$$xPy \Leftrightarrow V(x,y;\overrightarrow{P}) \in \Omega(x,y). \tag{3.1}$$

The class of all rules ψ under all possible $\{\Omega(x,y)\}_{(x,y)}$ is denoted as Ψ. The following theorem holds

Theorem 3.1 *The classes Π_l^s and Ψ coincide.*

Proof. Let a local rule F be given. Construct $\Omega(x,y)$ for each (x,y) as follows: for any profile $\overrightarrow{P}$ if $(x,y) \in F(\overrightarrow{P})$, then include $V(x,y;\overrightarrow{P})$ to $\Omega(x,y)$. Via the lists $\{\Omega(x,y)\}_{(x,y)}$ and (3.1) we obtain the aggregation rule ψ. Show that $F = \psi$. Let $(x,y) \in F(\overrightarrow{P})$. Then by construction of $\Omega(x,y)$, $(x,y) \in \psi(\overrightarrow{P})$. Let $(x,y) \notin F(\overrightarrow{P})$ and suppose $(x,y) \in \psi(\overrightarrow{P})$. The there exists a profile $\overrightarrow{P'}$ such that $V(x,y;\overrightarrow{P}) = V(x,y;\overrightarrow{P'})$ and $V(x,y;\overrightarrow{P'}) \in \Omega(x,y)$. But then, by locality of F, $(x,y) \in F(\overrightarrow{P})$. It is evident that any rule ψ defined via $\{\Omega(x,y)\}_{(x,y)}$ and (3.1) is local. ■

Theorem 3.1 states that any strongly local SDF F can be represented via the list $\{\Omega(x,y)\}_{(x,y)}$ and the rule (3.1). The group $\omega^{(x,y)} \in \Omega(x,y)$ is *winning coalition* in the following sense: the members of $\omega^{(x,y)}$ are able to enforce the decision about the inclusion (x,y) in P by including (x,y) in their P_i even though other agents j from $N \setminus \omega^{(x,y)}$ have a different opinion, say, yP_jx, or yI_jx, where I_j is the indifference relation for P_j.
The representation of a rule via a set of lists $\{\Omega(x,y)\}_{(x,y)}$ and the rule (3.1) will be called hereafter as Ω- (or *list*) *representation* of the rule F.

Remark 1. Let us consider a *game in normal form* $\Gamma = \langle 2^N, v\rangle$, where 2^N is the set of all subsets of N, including the empty set, and v is a *payoff function*, $v : 2^N \to \mathcal{R}_+$ such that $v(\emptyset) = 0$.

The game Γ is called a *simple game* if $\forall\omega \subseteq N$ either $v(\omega) = 0$ or $v(\omega) = 1$. Coalitions ω for which $v(\omega) = 1$ are called winning coalitions, and all other coalitions are called loosing ones. From the definition of strongly local rule F in terms of logic functions it is obvious that the list Ω for F contains all winning coalitions, and strong locality condition of F is equivalent to the existence of a simple game Γ.
Note that we do not restrict v to be superadditive:

$$\forall\omega,\ \omega' \in 2^N \text{ such that } \omega \cap \omega' = \emptyset \Rightarrow v(\omega \cup \omega') \geq v(\omega) + v(\omega'),$$

which is the usual constraint on v in game theory.

Remark 2. The main theorem of boolean logic states that any boolean function f can be written explicitly in disjunctive normal form as[17]

$$f(x, y; \vec{l}\,) = \bigvee_{\omega \in \Omega(x,y)} \bigwedge_{i \in \omega} l_i^{\omega}(x, y),$$

where $\Omega(x, y) = \{\omega_1^{(x,y)}, ..., \omega_{q(x,y)}^{(x,y)}\}$ is a collection of $q(x, y)$ coalitions varying with (x, y), and

$$l_i^{\omega}(x, y) = \begin{cases} l_i(x, y), & \text{if } i \in \omega, \\ \mid l_i(x, y) - 1 \mid, & \text{else.} \end{cases}$$

Alternatively, according to the theorem, f can be written explicitly in conjunctive normal form as

$$f(x, y; \vec{l}\,) = \bigwedge_{\varepsilon \in E(x,y)} \bigvee_{i \in \varepsilon} l_i^{\varepsilon}(x, y),$$

where $E(x, y) = \{\varepsilon_1^{(x,y)}, ..., \varepsilon_{p(x,y)}^{(x,y)}\}$ and l_i^{ε} is defined in the same fashion as before. If $f(x, y)$ is represented in disjunctive normal form (DNF) ([183]), the list $\Omega(x, y)$ will consist for $(x, y) \in A$, of the coalitions $\omega^{(x,y)}$ corresponding to the terms of DNF (i.e., conjunctions of variables l_i or their negations $\bar{l}_i$, $i = 1, \ldots, N$, in it). In doing so, each group $\omega^{(x,y)}$ is composed of the indices of variables that are involved positively (i.e., as l_i and not as $\bar{l}_i$) into the given term.

Similarly, consideration can be given to representation of $f(x, y)$ in the conjunctive normal form (CNF), and another list $E(x, y)$ can be constructed. This list consists of groups $\varepsilon^{(x,y)}$ corresponding to the terms of a given CNF, each group as before consisting of indices j belonging to the positively involved (into the corresponding term) variables l_j. Using this dual list $E(x, y)$, one can define dual list representation for the original rule F:

$$(x, y) \notin P \Leftrightarrow (\exists\varepsilon^{(x,y)} \in E(x, y) \ : \ V(x, y; \vec{P}) = N \backslash \varepsilon^{(x,y)}).$$

[17] The operations $\bigvee$ and $\bigwedge$ are boolean addition and multiplication, respectively, defined by $l_i \bigvee l_j = 1$ if $l_i + l_j \geq 1$ and $l_i \bigvee l_j = 0$ otherwise, and $l_i \bigwedge l_j = 1$ if $l_i + l_j = 2$ and $l_i \bigwedge l_j = 0$ otherwise.

3.3 Normative conditions

In this Section we introduce a number of normative conditions. A particular SDF F may posesses any of these properties, but not necessarily so. In parenthesis after each condition the restriction on the list $\Omega(x, y)$ of a rule F which satisfies that condition is given.

(NI). *Non-Imposition* Condition. In literature this condition is often called *Sovereignty* condition but we will always use the word 'Non_Imposition'. This condition is in fact a conjunction of the following two conditions.
(NI^+). *Positive Non-Imposition*: For each pair $x, y \in A$ there is a profile $\{P_i\}$ such that $(x, y) \in P = F(\{P_i\})$.
[$\forall x, y \in A$, $\Omega(x, y) \neq \emptyset$. This condition guarantees that any collection $\Omega(x, y)$ contains at least one group (which may be empty!)]

(NI^-). *Negative Non-Imposition*: For each pair $x, y \in A$ there is a profile $\{P_i\}$ such that $(x, y) \notin P = F(\{P_i\})$.
[$\forall x, y \in A$, $\Omega(x, y) \neq 2^N$. By this condition, the pair (x, y) does not belong to the relation P, regardless of the profile $\{P_i\}$; this would not be the case if $\Omega(x, y) = 2^N$.]
If conditions NI^+ and NI^- are simultaneously satisfied, then the presence or the absence of any pair $(x, y) \in P$ depends on the profile $\{P_i\}$ and is not determined a priori by the rule F.

(M). *Monotonicity*: For the profile $\{P_i\}$, let $(x, y) \in P = F(\{P_i\})$. Replace the profile $\{P_i\}$ with the profile $\{P_i'\}$ so that for all i such that $(x, y) \in P_i$ we now have $(x, y) \in P_i'$, but for some j for which in the 'old' profile $(x, y) \notin P_j$, we may now have in the new profile $(x, y) \in P_j'$. Then $(x, y) \in P' = F(\{P_i'\})$.
Formal statement of the monotonicity condition: $\forall x, y$ if $V(x, y, \{P_i\}) \subseteq V(x, y, \{P_i'\})$ and $(x, y) \in P = F(\{P_i\})$, then $(x, y) \in P' = F(\{P_i'\})$.
[If $\omega \in \Omega(x, y)$, then $\forall \widetilde{\omega} : \omega \subseteq \widetilde{\omega} \subseteq N \Rightarrow \widetilde{\omega} \in \Omega(x, y)$. Monotonicity Condition stipulates that for any coalition from the set $\Omega(x, y)$, all its supersets also belong to $\Omega(x, y)$.]

(Ne). *Neutrality*: If for all $i \in N$, $xP_iy \Leftrightarrow vP_iw$, then $xPy \Leftrightarrow vPw$. This condition guarantees that the presence of a pair in P is determined by 'identical' pairs in $\{P_i\}$ in the same way for all pairs of alternatives.
[$\forall x, y, v, w \in A$, $\Omega(x, y) = \Omega(v, w) = \Omega$. By condition Ne, all the lists $\Omega(x, y)$ are the same, i.e., $\Omega = \{\omega_1, \omega_2, ..., \omega_q\}$]

(An). *Anonymity*: $F(P_1, ...P_n) = F(P_{\eta(1)}, ...P_{\eta(n)})$, where η is an arbitrary one-to-one mapping of N onto N. This condition guarantees that the social binary relation P is invariant to voters' re-enumeration, and is determined only by the unordered collection of their preferences.

[Let η be a one-to-one mapping of N onto N and let $\eta(\Omega(x,y)) = \Omega'(x,y)$ be a collection of groups for the pair (x,y) obtained from $\Omega(x,y)$ by applying the mapping η. Then $\Omega(x,y) = \Omega'(x,y)$. Condition An implies that two collections of groups $\Omega'(x,y)$ and $\Omega(x,y)$ for the pair (x,y) which differ only by numbering in N necessarily coincide]
The rules which satisfy Anonymity Condition can be independently described by the following condition:
For any $x,y \in A$, if a list $\Omega(x,y)$ contains a group ω with $|\omega| = k$ (where $0 \leq k \leq n$), then all the groups ω' with $|\omega'| = k$ are also included in $\Omega(x,y)$.

(U^+). *Positive Unanimity*: if for every $i \in N$, xP_iy, then xPy, i.e., if every agent considers x is more preferable than y, then it is the case for social decision as well.
[$\forall(x,y)$ $N \in \Omega(x,y)$, i.e., the set of all agents (grand coalition) N belongs to every list $\Omega(x,y)$]

(U^-). *Negative Unanimity*: if for every $i \in N$, $(x,y) \notin P_i$, then $(x,y) \notin P$, i.e., if every agent considers x is not more preferable than y, then it is the case for social decision as well.
[$\forall(x,y)$ $\emptyset \notin \Omega(x,y)$, i.e., the empty set does not belong to a list $\Omega(x,y)$]
Each of these properties determines a special class in the space of all local SDFs.
Let us introduce now four special rules:
Constant rule $\mathbf{1}$: $\forall\ \vec{P}$, $F(\vec{P}) = A \times A$, i.e., independently of a profile $\vec{P}$ the social decision contains always all pairs (x,y) for all x, $y \in A$;
Constant rule $\mathbf{0}$: $\forall\ \vec{P}$, $F(\vec{P}) = \emptyset$, i.e., independently of a profile $\vec{P}$ the social decision contains no pairs (x,y);
$\mathcal{U}$: *Unanimity* rule. For any profile $\vec{P}$,

$$P = \bigcap_{i \in N} P_i,$$

i.e., the social decision contains the unanimous decision of all the members of the set N;
$\mathcal{V}$: 'At least one vote for' rule (briefly, *One vote rule*). For any profile $\vec{P}$,

$$P = \bigcup_{i \in N} P_i,$$

i.e., the social decision contains the decisions of each member of the set N.

We define now three important subclasses in the space of all strongly local rules.

Definition 3.2 A class of rules satisfying the conditions

$$\text{(a) } (NI^+) \cap (NI^-) \cap (M),$$

$$(b)\ (NI^+) \cap (NI^-) \cap (M) \cap (Ne),$$

and

$$(c)\ (NI^+) \cap (NI^-) \cap (M) \cap (Ne) \cap (An),$$

will be referred to respectively, as, (a) *Basic*, (b) *Central*, and (c) *Symmetrically Central Class in* Π_I^s.

Denote these Classes by Λ^{Bas}, Λ^C, and Λ^{SC}, respectively.
The next topic of our analysis in this Section is the relationship between classes of rules satisfying conditions (NI^+)– (U^-). In what follows, such relationships between the classes of rules are shown by geometrical figures in the space of all strongly local rules (via Venn diagrams). The various regions in these diagrams ('images' of different classes) will be denoted by the same letters and called by the same names as the conditions defining the corresponding classes of rules[18].

Theorem 3.2 *The relative position of the classes* $(NI^+) - (U^-)$ *in the space* Π_I^s *is shown on Figure* 3-1.

Proof. There are a total of 64 conjunctions of conditions NI^+,...,Ne, U^+ and U^- and their negations. The following relations hold. Some of them are obvious while others readily follow from the list representation of strongly local SDFs. The obvious relations are the following: a) $U^+ \Rightarrow NI^+$; b) $U^- \Rightarrow NI^-$; c) $\overline{NI^-} \cap Ne \Rightarrow M$; d) $\overline{NI^-} \cap Ne \Rightarrow U^+$; e) $\overline{NI^+} \cap Ne \Rightarrow U^-$; f) $\overline{NI^+} \cap Ne \Rightarrow M$.
Let us prove the following relations: g) $NI^+ \cap M \Rightarrow U^+$. From NI^+ we have $\forall x, y \in A \quad \Omega(x,y) \neq \emptyset$. From M follows that if $\omega' \in \Omega(x,y)$, then $\forall \tilde{\omega} : \omega' \subseteq \tilde{\omega} \subseteq N$, $\tilde{\omega} \in \Omega(x,y)$. Hence $N \in \Omega(x,y)$, i.e., U^+ holds ; h) $\overline{NI^+} \cap \overline{NI^-} \cap Ne = \emptyset$. From $\overline{NI^+}$ it follows that there are $x, y \in A$ such that $\Omega(x,y) = \emptyset$. By Ne, $\Omega(x,y) = \emptyset$ for all $x, y \in A$. By $\overline{NI^-}$, there are $x, y \in A$ such that $\Omega(x,y) = 2^N$, and by (Ne) $\Omega(x,y) = 2^N$ for all $x, y \in A$; i) $NI^- \cap M \Rightarrow U^-$. By M, if $\omega' \in \Omega(x,y)$, then $\forall \tilde{\omega} : \omega' \subseteq \tilde{\omega} \subseteq N$, $\tilde{\omega} \in \Omega(x,y)$. If $\emptyset \in \Omega(x,y)$, then by M $\Omega(x,y) = 2^N$ which contradicts NI^-.
The above properties a)-i) reduce the various 64 conjunctions of conditions NI^+,...,Ne, U^+ and U^- to 20 conjunctions. The reader can check by examples that all classes shown at Figure 3-1 are non-empty. Since we use those 20 non-empty conjunctions later, they are given below.
1) $\overline{NI^+} \cap \overline{NI^-} \cap \overline{M} \cap \overline{Ne} \cap \overline{U^+} \cap \overline{U^-}$;
2) $\overline{NI^+} \cap \overline{NI^-} \cap M \cap \overline{Ne} \cap \overline{U^+} \cap \overline{U^-}$;
3) $\overline{NI^+} \cap NI^- \cap \overline{M} \cap \overline{Ne} \cap \overline{U^+} \cap \overline{U^-}$;
4) $\overline{NI^+} \cap NI^- \cap \overline{M} \cap \overline{Ne} \cap \overline{U^+} \cap U^-$;
5) $\overline{NI^+} \cap NI^- \cap M \cap \overline{Ne} \cap \overline{U^+} \cap U^-$;
6) $\overline{NI^+} \cap NI^- \cap M \cap Ne \cap \overline{U^+} \cap U^-$;
7) $NI^+ \cap \overline{NI^-} \cap \overline{M} \cap \overline{Ne} \cap \overline{U^+} \cap \overline{U^-}$;

18 To avoid misunderstanding, note that the shape and the size of the different regions in this and the following diagrams are absolutely arbitrary and are to be used only for illustrative purposes.

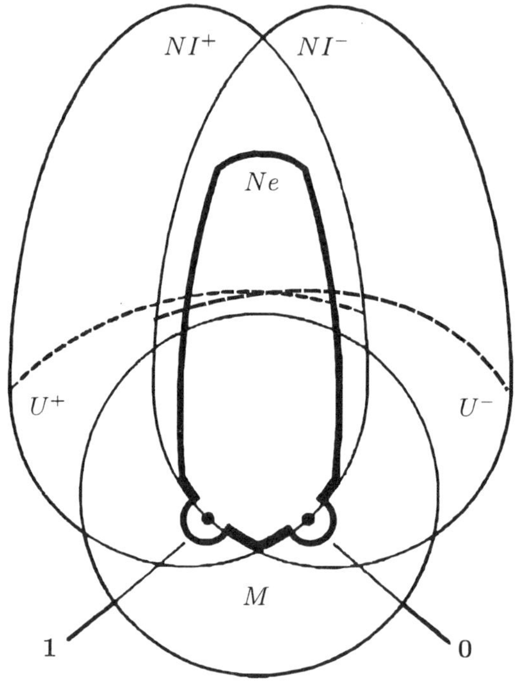

Figure 3-1

8) $NI^+ \cap \overline{NI^-} \cap \overline{M} \cap \overline{Ne} \cap U^+ \cap \overline{U^-}$;
9) $NI^+ \cap \overline{NI^-} \cap M \cap \overline{Ne} \cap U^+ \cap \overline{U^-}$;
10) $NI^+ \cap \overline{NI^-} \cap M \cap Ne \cap U^+ \cap \overline{U^-}$;
11) $NI^+ \cap NI^- \cap \overline{M} \cap \overline{Ne} \cap \overline{U^+} \cap \overline{U^-}$;
12) $NI^+ \cap NI^- \cap \overline{M} \cap \overline{Ne} \cap \overline{U^+} \cap U^-$;
13) $NI^+ \cap NI^- \cap \overline{M} \cap \overline{Ne} \cap U^+ \cap \overline{U^-}$;
14) $NI^+ \cap NI^- \cap \overline{M} \cap \overline{Ne} \cap U^+ \cap U^-$;
15) $NI^+ \cap NI^- \cap \overline{M} \cap Ne \cap \overline{U^+} \cap \overline{U^-}$;
16) $NI^+ \cap NI^- \cap \overline{M} \cap Ne \cap \overline{U^+} \cap U^-$;
17) $NI^+ \cap NI^- \cap \overline{M} \cap Ne \cap U^+ \cap \overline{U^-}$;
18) $NI^+ \cap NI^- \cap \overline{M} \cap Ne \cap U^+ \cap U^-$;
19) $NI^+ \cap NI^- \cap M \cap \overline{Ne} \cap U^+ \cap U^-$;
20) $NI^+ \cap NI^- \cap M \cap Ne \cap U^+ \cap U^-$.

Note that the conjunction 6) defines for all $\vec{P}$, $F(\vec{P}) = \emptyset$ (the constant rule **0**); the conjunction 10) defines $P = A \times A$ for all $\{P_i\}$ (the constant rule **1**) ■

Remark. Figure 3-1 does not show the class of rules defined by condition An. This class of rules has nonempty intersections with any of the classes NI^+ - Ne, U^+ and U^-.

We conclude this Section by introducing the notion of the Basic list for a given strongly local rule F from the Central Class Λ^C.

Definition 3.3 The set ω' will be said to dominate the set ω if the inclusion $\omega' \supset \omega$ holds.

Definition 3.4 Let us call a subset $\Omega^B = \{\omega\}$ from a given list Ω the *Basic list* for Ω if no ω from Ω^B dominates any other ω' from Ω^B.

One can see that the definition of the Basic list may be given not only for the rules from the Central Class, but also for any arbitrary list $\Omega(x, y)$. However it is only for the class of monotonic rules (condition M) the Basic list may be defined unambiguously as a set of elements of the list Ω minimal with respect to set inclusion, which are exactly those that form this Basic list. By virtue of this uniqueness we can study only the properties of Basic lists when considering Ω- representations of the SDFs from the Central Class.

3.4 Rules from Central Class

Since the rules from the Central Class satisfy Monotonicity Condition we define them via their Basic list Ω^B.

Definition 3.5 A rule $F \in \Lambda^C$ is called a *federation rule* if

$$\Omega^B = \{\omega_1, ..., \omega_r\}.$$

Note that due to the Non-Imposition conditions NI^+ and NI^-, $\{\emptyset\} \notin \Omega^B$ and $\Omega^B \neq \emptyset$. It can be easily checked that a social binary relation P is constructed by a federation rule as

$$P = \bigcup_{\omega \in \Omega^B} \bigcap_{i \in \omega} P_i,$$

for every profile $\vec{P}$, i.e., the set N of all agents is divided on groups ω, and social decision P is a unanimous decision of members from at least one group ω. The rule $\mathcal{U}$ is a special case of the federation rule which corresponds to $\Omega = \Omega^B = (N)$. The rule $\mathcal{V}$ is a special case of the federation rule as well which corresponds to $\Omega^B = (\{1\}, ..., \{n\})$.

The class of all federation rules will be denoted as $\Lambda^{\cup\cap}$.

The next rule will be introduced using a dual Basic list E^B.

Definition 3.6 A rule $F \in \Lambda^C$ is called the *representation rule* if

$$E^B = \{\varepsilon_1, ..., \varepsilon_s\}.$$

It can be directly checked that the social decision P is constructed by this rule as

$$P = \bigcap_{\varepsilon \in E^B} \bigcup_{i \in \varepsilon} P_i.$$

In words, the set N is divided into groups $\varepsilon_1, ..., \varepsilon_s$, and the social decision is the unanimous decision of agents taken by one from each group ε_j, $j = 1, ..., s$, i.e., it is the unanimous decision of representatives from each group ε_j. The rules $\mathcal{U}$ and V are special cases of the representation rule which correspond to $E^B = (\{1\}, ..., \{n\})$ and $E^B = (N)$, respectively.
Denote the class of all representation rules on N as $\Lambda^{\cap\cup}$.
Since the operations $\cup$ and $\cap$ are distributive, we obtain the following obvious result: $\Lambda^{\cup\cap} = \Lambda^{\cap\cup}$, i.e., the classes of federation and representation rules coincide.

Definition 3.7 A federation rule for which $\Omega^B = (\omega)$ is called an *oligarchy rule*.
A representation rule for which $E^B = (\varepsilon)$ is called a *syndicate rule*.
An oligarchy rule for which $\Omega^B = (\{i_0\})$ (respectively, $E^B = (\{i_0\})$) is called dictator rule, or, simply, *dictator*.

Immediately from the Definition 3.7 one can obtain that for the rules introduced the social decision is constructed via elements of a profile $\vec{P}$ in the following way:
- for oligarchy rule

$$P = \bigcap_{i \in \omega} P_i;$$

- for syndicate rule

$$P = \bigcup_{i \in \varepsilon} P_i;$$

- for dictator rule

$$P = P_{i_0}.$$

Otherwise speaking, the social decision made by an oligarchy rule coincide with the unanimous decision of the members of ω, and all other members of society can not influence the social decision. Social binary relation constructed by a syndicate rule contains all individual relation of the members of a group ε. The decision made by dictator rule coincide with that of some pre-determined agent - dictator i_0. Again, comparing the definitions of these rules with those of $\mathcal{U}$ and $\mathcal{V}$, one can see that Unanimity rule is an oligarchy rule with $\omega = N$; One vote rule is a syndicate rule with $\varepsilon = N$.
The classes of the oligarchy, syndicate and dictatorial rules will be denoted as $\Lambda^{\cap}$, $\Lambda^{\cup}$, Λ^d, respectively.
Let us study now the special case of a federation rule such that intersection of all ω's from Ω is not empty, i.e., $\emptyset \neq \omega_0 = \cap_{\omega \in \Omega} \omega$. If $\omega_0 \in \Omega$, then it is an oligarchy

rule. Consider the case when $\omega_0 \notin \Omega$. It is obvious that the agents from ω_0 have a veto-power: any agent from ω_0 can 'block' the inclusion of a pair (x, y) into social decision P, but even unanimous decision of the members of ω_0 is not sufficient for a pair (x, y) to be in P. It is necessary that the members from some group $\omega_i \backslash \omega_0$ support this decision. The rules of this kind are called *Veto-rules*. The class of veto-rules will be denoted as Λ^{VR}. Any oligarchy rule is a veto-rule, but in that particular case the agents from ω_0 do not need a support of any other agent - they can enforce the decision themselves, and other agents from $N \setminus \omega_0$ do not influence a social decision anyhow.

Definition 3.8 A federation rule is called a *k-majority* one (or *k-votes rule*) if

$$\Omega^B = \{\omega_1, ..., \omega_q\},$$

$$\forall i = 1, ..., q, \; card(\omega_i) = k, \; q = \binom{n}{k}.$$

It is obvious that for k-majority rule the social decision coincides with union of the unanimous decisions of each group consisting of at least k agents. In contrast to all rules defined before, where we can see how unequally agents can be treated by social decision function under study, in the latter case participants are 'distributed' over the coalitions ω uniformly.
The set of all k-majority rules will be denoted as Λ^{kM}.

Let us define now the subclass of Veto-rules - the *Collegium rules*. To this end, consider some one-to-one mapping η from N onto N with the following restriction: $\eta(\omega_0) = \omega_0$, where $\eta(\omega_0) = \{j \mid \eta^{-1}(j) \in \omega_0\}$. Then, a veto-rule which is invariant to all mappings η of such kind is called a collegium rule.

Example below explains the collegium rule.
Example. Let $N = \{1, ...5\}$, $\omega_0 = \cap_{\omega \in \Omega} \omega = \{1, 2\}$. Then veto-rule can be defined by, e.g., the following Basic list $\Omega^B = (\{1, 2, 3\}, \{1, 2, 4\})$. Possible four collegium rules in this case are defined by the following four basic lists:

$$\begin{aligned}
\Omega^B &= (\{1, 2\}), \\
\Omega^B &= (\{1, 2, 3\}, \{1, 2, 4\}, \{1, 2, 5\}), \\
\Omega^B &= (\{1, 2, 3, 4\}, \{1, 2, 3, 5\}, \{1, 2, 4, 5\}), \\
\Omega^B &= (\{1, 2, 3, 4, 5\}).
\end{aligned}$$

The first and last rules are the oligarchy ones, the last being the Unanimity rule, other two rules are collegium rules in a proper sense. Otherwise speaking, in veto-rules any coalition $\omega_i \in \Omega$ must contain the subgroup ω_0, and agents from $N \setminus \omega_0$ can be distributed over the groups from Ω unequally, even do not belong to any group ω_i in Ω. In contrast to the general case, in collegium rule agents from $N \setminus \omega_0$ belong to the coalitions ω_i in an equal way.
The set of all collegium rules will be denoted as Λ^{col}.

Remark 1. Collegium rule is used in the Security Council of the United Nations Organization, in which $card(N) = 15$, the group ω_0 consists of five permanent members (China, France, Great Britain, Russia, USA), and 11 other members are re-elected each year. The decision in the Security Council is made by simple majority (eight votes for) providing the unanimous approval of the decision by permanent members.

Remark 2. In Central Class Monotonicity condition holds, i.e.,

$$\forall \omega \in \Omega, \omega \subseteq \widetilde{\omega} \subseteq N \Rightarrow \widetilde{\omega} \in \Omega. \tag{3.2}$$

The structure of the set Ω for an oligarchy rule can be defined as

$$\forall \omega_1, \omega_2 \in \Omega \Rightarrow \omega_1 \cap \omega_2 \in \Omega. \tag{3.3}$$

The system of subsets of some universal set (in our case N) with the properties (3.2) and (3.3) is called *filter*.
For the dictatorial rule, we have an additional property:

$$\omega \in \Omega \Longleftrightarrow N \setminus \omega \notin \Omega. \tag{3.4}$$

Indeed, if $\omega \in \Omega$ and $N \setminus \omega \in \Omega$, then by (3.3) $\{\emptyset\} \in \Omega$, which due to the Monotonicity condition leads to $\Omega = 2^N$, contradicting the Non-Imposition condition (namely, NI^-). If neither ω nor $N \setminus \omega$ belong to Ω, and $\Omega^B = \{i_0\}$, then since all supersets of $\{i_0\}$ belong to Ω, i_0 belongs either to ω or to $N \setminus \omega$.
The system of sets which satisfies the properties (3.2) - (3.4) is called *ultrafilter*.
Finally, the system of sets which satisfies (3.2) and the property

$$\bigcap_{\omega \in \Omega} \omega \neq \emptyset,$$

is called in [76, 189] a *pre-filter*.

The relations between the classes of federation and representation rules and their subclasses introduced above are summarized in the following theorem, the statement of which is just a corollary from the definitions of the classes of the rules under study.

Theorem 3.3 *1) The Central Class in* Π_I^s *coincides with the class of federation rules; 2) The relations between the subclasses of the class of federation rules are as shown at Figure* 3-2.

3.5 Rationality constraints

Until now we did not restrict the domain of definition Q_d and the range Q_r of a social decision function F under study, i.e., they have been assumed to coincide with the set

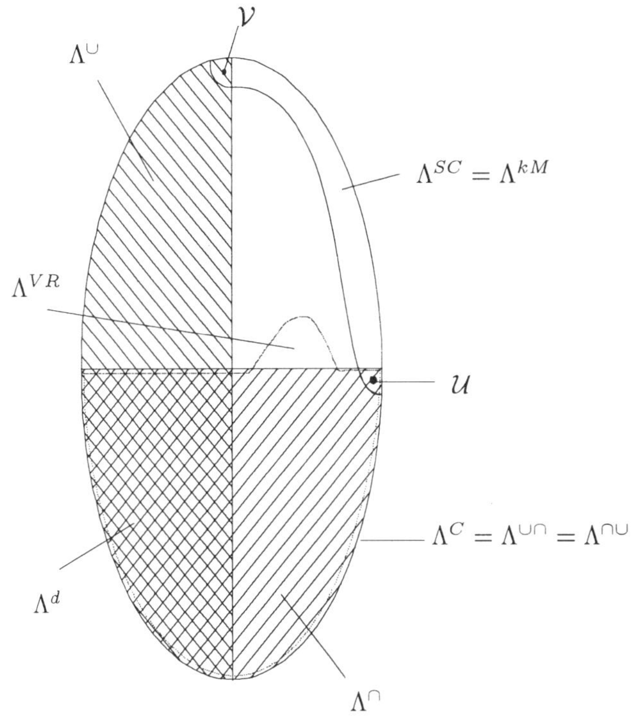

Figure 3-2

$\mathcal{B}$ of all binary relations on the set A. Let us consider the cases when Q_d and Q_r are somehow restricted.

Definition 3.9 The two classes Q_d and Q_r in $\mathcal{B}$ will be called closed with respect to a strongly local rule F if for any profile $\{P_i\}$ such that $\forall i\ P_i \in Q_d$ the following holds $F(\{P_i\}) \in Q_r$.
The two classes Q_d and Q_r in $\mathcal{B}$ will be called to be closed with respect to a class $\mathcal{F}$ of strongly local rules if for any rule $F \in \mathcal{F}$ and for any profile $\{P_i\}$ such that $\forall i$ $P_i \in Q_d$ the following holds $F(\{P_i\}) \in Q_r$.
The maximal in set-theoretic sense class of rules relative to which the classes Q_d and Q_r are closed will be called the *complete class of closedness* for a pair (Q_d, Q_r) and will be denoted as $\Lambda(Q_d, Q_r)$.

Let us consider now the classes $\Lambda(Q_d, Q_r)$ for different subsets $Q_d, Q_r \subset B$. Such classes as it was explained in Chapter 2, are defined with respect to some concepts of rationality of individual opinions and social decisions. Two most important concepts are expressed in terms of acyclicity and transitivity of the binary relations in question. In this Section we will consider as Q_d only one subclass of $\mathcal{B}$, that of linear orders

$\mathcal{LO}$. However, it turns out that this choice of Q_d is not too restrictive - the results are valid in a more general case. As the range of a rule F we study several different classes in $\mathcal{B}$. In this Section we consider Q_r to be the sets of acyclic relations ($\mathcal{AR}$), transitive relations ($\mathcal{T}$) and connected ones ($\mathcal{C}n$), as well as the sets of strict partial orders ($\mathcal{SPO}$) and linear orders ($\mathcal{LO}$).

On the other hand, we do not restrict the rules under study by some normative conditions, i.e., we consider only strongly local SDFs from corresponding classes $\Lambda(Q_d, Q_r)$. Let us introduce some constraints on the list Ω of a given rule F.

(ac) For any $x_1, x_2, ..., x_m$ and any ω_1,...,ω_m such that $m = card(A)$,

$$\omega_1 \in \Omega(x_1, x_2), ..., \omega_m \in \Omega(x_m, x_1)$$

the following relations hold:

$$\bigcup_{i=1}^{m} \omega_i \neq N \text{ or } \bigcap_{i=1}^{m} \omega_i \neq \emptyset;$$

(t) For any x_1, x_2, x_3 and any ω_1 and ω_2 such that $\omega_1 \in \Omega(x_1, x_2)$ and $\omega_2 \in \Omega(x_2, x_3)$ and for any $\widetilde{\omega}$ such that $\omega_1 \cap \omega_2 \subseteq \widetilde{\omega} \subseteq \omega_1 \cup \omega_2$, the following holds $\widetilde{\omega} \in \Omega(x_1, x_3)$;

(cn) For any $x_1, x_2, x_1 \neq x_2$, if $\omega \notin \Omega(x_1, x_2)$, then $N \setminus \omega \in \Omega(x_2, x_1)$.

Condition (ac) states that these chosen sets ω_1,...,ω_m either do not cover the set N or their intersection is not empty. Condition (t) defines that any $\widetilde{\omega}$ which is larger or equal to the intersection $\omega_1 \cap \omega_2$ and is a subset of the union of these two sets belongs to the list $\Omega(x_1, x_3)$. Finally, condition (cn) states that if some coalition ω does not belong to the list $\Omega(x_1, x_2)$, then its complement belongs to the list $\Omega(x_2, x_1)$.
The following theorem holds.

Theorem 3.4 *A strongly local social decision function F belong to the classes a) $\Lambda(\mathcal{LO},\mathcal{AR})$; b) $\Lambda(\mathcal{LO},\mathcal{T})$; and c) $\Lambda(\mathcal{LO},\mathcal{C}n)$ if and only if the list Ω of F satisfies the conditions a) (ac); b) (t); and c) (cn), respectively.*

Proof. a) Let $Q_d = \mathcal{LO}$, and suppose that P does not contain cycles of length m and shorter, m being the number of elements in A. Show that the condition (ac) holds. Assume on the contrary that there are ω_1,...,ω_m such that $\omega_1 \in \Omega(x_1, x_2)$,...,$\omega_m \in \Omega(x_m, x_1)$ and $\bigcup_{i=1}^{m} \omega_i = N$ and $\bigcap_{i=1}^{m} \omega_i = \emptyset$. Consider first the case $m = 3$, and the profile shown below.

$i \in \overline{\omega}_1 \cap \omega_2 \cap \omega_3 : \quad x_2 \succ x_3 \succ x_1,$
$i \in \omega_1 \cap \overline{\omega}_2 \cap \omega_3 : \quad x_3 \succ x_1 \succ x_2,$
$i \in \omega_1 \cap \omega_2 \cap \overline{\omega}_3 : \quad x_1 \succ x_2 \succ x_3,$
$i \in \overline{\omega}_1 \cap \overline{\omega}_2 \cap \omega_3 : \quad x_3 \succ x_2 \succ x_1,$
$i \in \omega_1 \cap \overline{\omega}_2 \cap \overline{\omega}_3 : \quad x_1 \succ x_3 \succ x_2,$
$i \in \overline{\omega}_1 \cap \omega_2 \cap \overline{\omega}_3 : \quad x_2 \succ x_1 \succ x_3.$

It is easily seen that $(x_1 P_i x_2 \Leftrightarrow i \in \omega_1) \Rightarrow x_1 P x_2$; $(x_2 P_i x_3 \Leftrightarrow i \in \omega_2) \Rightarrow x_2 P x_3$; $(x_3 P_i x_1 \Leftrightarrow i \in \omega_3) \Rightarrow x_3 P x_1$, i.e., we obtain cycle $x_1 P x_2 P x_3 P x_1$. The logic of the proof remains valid for the case $m > 3$. Let I_l denotes that there is the pair

(x_l, x_{l+1}), $l = 1, ..., m$, $l_{m+1} \equiv l_1$, in the relation P, and $\overline{I_l}$ denotes that there is the pair (x_{l+1}, x_l). We can construct a linear order for any conjunction of the form $\overline{I}_1 \bigwedge I_2 \bigwedge ... \bigwedge I_m$,...,$I_1 \bigwedge I_2 \bigwedge ... \bigwedge \overline{I}_m$, $\overline{I}_1 \bigwedge \overline{I}_2 \bigwedge ... \bigwedge I_m$,..., with the exception of two conjunctions $\bigwedge_{i=1}^{m} I_i$ and $\bigwedge_{i=1}^{m} \overline{I}_i$. Indeed, a binary relation which corresponds to each conjunction is acyclic, and transitive closure of it is a linear order. Thus, we obtain the cycle of length m.
Conversely, let there exists a profile $\{P_i\}$, $P_i \in \mathcal{LO}$, $i = 1, ..., n$, and P contains the cycle of the length $p \leq m$, i.e., $x_1 P x_2 P ... P x_{p-1} P x_p P x_1$. Hence it follows that $V(x_1, x_2; \{P_i\}) \in \Omega(x_1, x_2), ..., V(x_p, x_1; \{P_i\}) \in \Omega(x_p, x_1)$. We will show that $\omega' = N \backslash (V(x_1, x_2; \{P_i\}) \cup ... \cup V(x_p, x_1; \{P_i\})) = \emptyset$. Assume that $i \in \omega'$ exists . Then, since $Q_d = \mathcal{LO}$, we have either $x_1 P_i x_2$ or $x_2 P_i x_1$. If $x_1 P_i x_2$, then $V(x_1, x_2; \{P_i\}) \cap \omega' \neq \emptyset$. Let $x_2 P_i x_1$. Then for x_3 , either $x_2 P_i x_3$ or $x_3 P_i x_1$. If $x_2 P_i x_3$ then $V(x_2, x_3; \{P_i\}) \cap \omega' \neq \emptyset$. Let $x_3 P_i x_1$. Continuing the argument, we come either at $x_{p-1} P_i x_p$ or at $x_p P_i x_1$. In the first case, $V(x_{p-1}, x_p; \{P_i\}) \cap \omega' \neq \emptyset$ and in the second , $V(x_p, x_1; \{P_i\}) \cap \omega' \neq \emptyset$. Hence, $\omega' = \emptyset$.
Consider $\omega'' = V(x_1, x_2; \{P_i\}) \cap ... \cap V(x_p, x_1; \{P_i\})$. Suppose that $i \in \omega''$ exists . Then $x_1 P_i x_2 P_i ... P_i x_p P_i x_1$, which contradicts the condition $P_i \in Q_d = \mathcal{LO}$.

b) Let $Q_d = \mathcal{LO}$ and for all $\vec{P}$ social decision $P \in \mathcal{T}$. Show that condition (t) holds. Assume the contrary, i.e., let $\exists\, \omega_1, \omega_2$ and ω' such that $\omega_1 \in \Omega(x_1, x_2)$, $\omega_2 \in \Omega(x_2, x_3)$, $\omega_1 \cap \omega_2 \subseteq \omega' \subseteq \omega_1 \cup \omega_2$, and $\omega' \notin \Omega(x_1, x_3)$. Construct the following profile $\vec{P}$:

$i \in \omega_1 \cap \omega_2 \cap \omega' : \quad x_1 \succ x_2 \succ x_3,$
$i \in \overline{\omega}_1 \cap \omega_2 \cap \omega' : \quad x_2 \succ x_1 \succ x_3,$
$i \in \omega_1 \cap \overline{\omega}_2 \cap \omega' : \quad x_1 \succ x_3 \succ x_2,$
$i \in \overline{\omega}_1 \cap \omega_2 \cap \overline{\omega'} : \quad x_2 \succ x_3 \succ x_1,$
$i \in \omega_1 \cap \overline{\omega}_2 \cap \overline{\omega'} : \quad x_3 \succ x_1 \succ x_2,$
$i \in \overline{\omega}_1 \cap \overline{\omega}_2 \cap \overline{\omega'} : \quad x_3 \succ x_2 \succ x_1.$

Then $V(x_1, x_2; \vec{P}) = \omega_1$. Since $\omega_1 \in \Omega(x_1, x_2)$ we obtain $x_1 P x_2$. Analogously, $V(x_2, x_3; \vec{P}) = \omega_2$, and $x_2 P x_3$. But $V(x_1, x_3; \vec{P}) = \omega'$ and since $\omega' \notin \Omega(x_1, x_3)$, we have $(x_1, x_3) \notin P$ which contradicts transitivity of P.
Let now there exists a profile $\vec{P}$ such that $x_1 P x_2 P x_3$, but $x_1 \overline{P} x_3$. Show that condition (t) is violated. Consider $V(x_1, x_2; \vec{P}) \in \Omega(x_1, x_2)$ and $V(x_2, x_3; \vec{P}) \in \Omega(x_2, x_3)$. Since $P_i \in \mathcal{LO}$ for all i, if $x_1 P_i x_2$, then $\forall x_3$ either $x_1 P_i x_3$ or $x_3 P_i x_2$. Thus, the minimal set ω' such that $\forall i \in \omega'$, $x_1 P_i x_3$ is the set $V(x_1, x_2; \vec{P}) \cap V(x_2, x_3; \vec{P})$ (the case $\omega' = \emptyset$ is allowed). Analogously, the maximal set ω'' such that $\forall i \in \omega''$, $x_1 P_i x_3$ is the set $V(x_1, x_2; \vec{P}) \cup V(x_2, x_3; \vec{P})$. Now, since transitivity of P breaks down, there exists $\widetilde{\omega}$ such that $\omega' \cap \omega'' \subseteq \widetilde{\omega} \subseteq \omega' \cup \omega''$ such that $\widetilde{\omega} \notin \Omega(x_1, x_3)$, i.e., the condition (t) is violated.
c) Asuume that condition (cn) does not hold, i.e. there is $\omega \subseteq N$ such that $\omega \notin \Omega(x, y)$ and $N \backslash \omega \notin \Omega(y, x)$. Consider the profile $\vec{P}$ such that $\forall i \in \omega$, $x P_i y$ holds, and $\forall i \in N \setminus \omega$, $y P_i x$ holds. Then $(x P_i y \Leftrightarrow i \in \omega)$ and $x \overline{P} y$. On the other hand, $(y P_i x \Leftrightarrow i \in N \backslash \omega)$ and also $y \overline{P} x$, i.e. $P \notin Cn$.

Now for fixed $x, y \in A$ and some $\{P_i\}$, let $x\overline{P}y$ and $y\overline{P}x$. Then $V(x,y;\{P_i\}) \notin \Omega(x,y)$ and $V(y,x;\{P_i\}) \notin \Omega(y,x)$. But by virtue of the inclusion $P_i \in \mathcal{LO} \subset \mathcal{C}n$, we have $V(x,y;\{P_i) \cup V(y,x;\{P_i\}) = N$. This violates condition (cn) ■

Remark 1. It can be easily checked (just by following the proof of above theorem) that the statements a) and b) of the Theorem 3.4 can be extended for the case $\mathcal{WO} \subseteq Q_d \subseteq Q_r$ for corresponding Q_r [3] . In those cases the conditions (ac) and (t) should be re-written in the following form:
(ac) For any ω_1,...,ω_m such that $m = card(A)$, $\omega_1 \in \Omega(x_1, x_2)$,...,$\omega_m \in \Omega(x_m, x_1)$ the following relations hold:

$$\bigcap_{i=1}^{m} \omega_i \neq \emptyset;$$

(t) For any ω_1 and ω_2 such that $\omega_1 \in \Omega(x_1, x_2)$ and $\omega_2 \in \Omega(x_2, x_3)$ and for any $\widetilde{\omega}$ such that $\omega_1 \cap \omega_2 \subseteq \widetilde{\omega} \subseteq N$, we have $\widetilde{\omega} \in \Omega(x_1, x_3)$.
Analogously, the statement c) can be extended to the case when $Q_d = \mathcal{C}n$.

Remark 2. From the proof of Theorem 3.4, one can obtain that F belongs to the complete class of closedness $\Lambda(\mathcal{LO},\mathcal{SPO})$ if and only if the list Ω for F satisfies the conditions (ac) and (t) simultaneously. Analogously, F$\in \Lambda(\mathcal{LO},\mathcal{LO})$ if and only if Ω satisfies (ac), (t), and (cn).

Consider now the properties $(ac) - (cn)$ of the list Ω in the Central Class. For this case those properties are re-written as
(ac^C) For any ω_1,...,ω_m such that $m = card(A)$, ω_1,...,$\omega_m \in \Omega$ the following relations hold:

$$\bigcup_{i=1}^{m} \omega_i \neq N \text{ or } \bigcap_{i=1}^{m} \omega_i \neq \emptyset;$$

(t^C) For any ω_1 and ω_2 such that $\omega_1, \omega_2 \in \Omega$ and for any $\widetilde{\omega}$ such that $\omega_1 \cap \omega_2 \subseteq \widetilde{\omega} \subseteq N$, we have $\widetilde{\omega} \in \Omega$;
(cn^C) If $\omega \notin \Omega$, then $N \setminus \omega \in \Omega$.

We use these properties in the next Section where we compare the class of federation rules and its subclasses with the rules from the intersections $\Lambda(\mathcal{AR}) \cap \Lambda^C$, ..., $\Lambda(\mathcal{C}n) \cap \Lambda^C$.

Let us consider now very important statements about the connection of rationality constraints with the Neutrality and Monotonicity conditions. They will be formulated as the following lemmas.

Lemma 3.1 $\Lambda(\mathcal{LO},\mathcal{T}) \cap \Lambda^{NI^+} \subset \Lambda^{Ne}$*, i.e., any rule, which satisfies positive Non-Imposition and transform individual linear orders into social transitive binary relations, obeys Neutrality condition as well.*

Proof. Let $\omega_1 \in \Omega(x, y)$ and $\omega_2 \in \Omega(y, z)$. Consider the following profile:

$i \in \omega_1 \cap \omega_2 : \quad x \succ y \succ z,$
$i \in \overline{\omega}_1 \cap \omega_2 : \quad y \succ z \succ x,$
$i \in \omega_1 \cap \overline{\omega}_2 : \quad x \succ z \succ y,$
$i \in \overline{\omega}_1 \cap \overline{\omega}_2 : \quad z \succ y \succ x.$
Then, $(i \in \omega_1 \Leftrightarrow (x,y) \in P_i) \Rightarrow (x,y) \in P$; $(i \in \omega_2 \Leftrightarrow (y,z) \in P_i) \Rightarrow (y,z) \in P$. For P to be transitive it should be $(x,z) \in P$. But $(x,z) \in P_i \Leftrightarrow i \in \omega_1$, i.e., $\omega_1 \in \Omega(x,z)$.
Let now $\omega_1 \in \Omega(x,z)$ and $\omega_2 \in \Omega(v,x)$. Consider the following profile:
$i \in \omega_1 \cap \omega_2 : \quad v \succ x \succ z,$
$i \in \overline{\omega}_1 \cap \omega_2 : \quad z \succ v \succ x,$
$i \in \omega_1 \cap \overline{\omega}_2 : \quad x \succ v \succ z,$
$i \in \overline{\omega}_1 \cap \overline{\omega}_2 : \quad z \succ x \succ v.$
Then, $(i \in \omega_1 \Leftrightarrow (x,z) \in P_i) \Rightarrow (x,z) \in P$; $(i \in \omega_2 \Leftrightarrow (v,x) \in P_i) \Rightarrow (v,x) \in P$. For P to be transitive it should be $(v,z) \in P$. But $(v,z) \in P_i \Leftrightarrow i \in \omega_1$, i.e., $\omega_1 \in \Omega(v,z)$. So, we have shown that $\forall \omega \in \Omega(x,y) \Rightarrow \omega \in \Omega(v,z)$ for any $(z,v) \in A \times A$, which means Neutrality of F. ■

From the proof of Lemma 3.1 immediately follows that the statement is valid for any Q_d such that $LO \subseteq Q_d \subseteq T$, i.e., the constraint on F to be transitive together with positive Non-Imposition guarantees the Neutrality of F even for wider classes of Q_d.

Lemma 3.2 $\Lambda(\mathcal{LO},\mathcal{T}) \cap \Lambda^{U^+} \subset \Lambda^M$, *i.e., any rule, which satisfies positive Unanimity and transform individual linear orders into social transitive binary relations, obeys Monotonicity condition as well.*

Proof. Since $\Lambda^{U^+} \subset \Lambda^{NI^+}$ we obtain that $\Lambda(\mathcal{LO},\mathcal{T}) \cap \Lambda^{U^+} \subset \Lambda^{Ne}$. Suppose $\omega \in \Omega$ and $\omega' \supset \omega$. Show that $\omega' \in \Omega$. To this end consider the following profile:
$i \in \omega \qquad x \succ y \succ z,$
$i \in \omega' \setminus \omega \quad y \succ x \succ z,$
$i \in N \setminus \omega' \quad y \succ z \succ x.$
Then $V(x,y;\vec{P}) = \omega$, hence xPy; $V(y,z;\vec{P}) = N$, and since $F \in \Lambda^{U^+}$, yPz. Since $F \in \Lambda(\mathcal{LO},\mathcal{T})$, we have xPz, but $V(x,z;\vec{P}) = \omega'$. Thus, $\omega' \in \Omega$. ■

Lemmas 3.1 and 3.2 imply the following corollary.

Corollary 3.1 $\Lambda(\mathcal{LO},\mathcal{T}) \cap \Lambda^{U^+} \subset \Lambda^M \cap \Lambda^{Ne}$.

It is worth reminding that we have restricted the domain of definition Q_d and the range Q_r of F in such a way that $Q_d \subset Q_r$, i.e., any relation admissible as individual opinion is admissible as social one.

Let us show at the end of this Section that a violation of that constraint turns out to be in some important cases inconsistent with Non-Imposition property of the rules under study. Just to give the reader the impression about that situation let us consider the case when $Q_d = \mathcal{AR}$ and $Q_r = \mathcal{T}$, i.e., that is the case when the classes Q_d and Q_r are intersected. To this end we consider the following example.

Example. Let $A = \{x, y, z\}$, $N = \{1, 2, 3\}$, and consider the profile $\vec{P}$ such that $\forall i \in N$ we have $x \succ y$ and $y \succ z$. Note that since individual opinions are represented by acyclic but not transitive binary relations, $x \succ z$ does not hold. In this case

$$V(x, y; \vec{P}) = V(y, z; \vec{P}) = N.$$

If the aggregation rule F under study belongs to the class $\Lambda^M \cap \Lambda^{NI^+}$, then for social decision xPy and yPz holds. But for P to be transitive it should be $\{\emptyset\} \in \Omega(x, z)$, and condition (M) implies $\Omega(x, z) = 2^N$, i.e. (NI^-) is violated.
This example is not rare exception - rather it can be shown that in all cases when Q_d is not a subset of Q_r, the violation of Non-Imposition condition can be obtained.

3.6 Comparing classes in Λ^C

Before turning to the comparison of aggregation rules classes, let us discuss conditions $NI^+, ..., Ne$ used to define the Central Class in the space Π_I^s.
When the Non-Impositon conditions NI^+ and NI^- are simultaneously satisfied, the decision concerning the presence or absence of any pair (x, y) in the relation P cannot be 'imposed' by the aggregation rule and is always determined with respect of agents' opinions, i.e. the profile $\{P_i\}$. The monotonicity condition M excludes situations in which the decision accepted by a certain number of voters can be rejected because of 'new' agents, who previously disagreed with the decision, now accept it. The Neutrality condition Ne guarantees that the decision accepted by the aggregation rule does not depend on the names of different alternatives. This condition excludes procedures in which a certain relationship between pairs of alternatives in P is established by means of different requirements for different pairs of alternatives.
All four conditions are quite natural, and the Central Class includes those procedures which satisfy these requirements.
The Anonymity condition An is no less natural than condition Ne. It identifies aggregation rules which operate equally with individuals (while condition Ne ensures equity of alternatives).

On the other hand, the rationality constraints introduced above seem to be quite reasonable as well. We discussed them in Chapter 2, but it is worth mentioning those arguments again. The acyclicity condition guarantees that choice made according pair-wise comparisons of alternatives will not be empty on any subset of the set A. Transitivity ensures that if an alternative x is preferred to y which in turn is preferred to z, then x is preferred to z. Finally, connectedness means that any two alternatives can be compared in terms of preferences. The conjunction of those rationality constraints lead to the isolation in the set $\mathcal{B}$ the set of strict partial orders and the set of linear orders.
Before we formulate the main results of this Section, let us introduce the notion of the rank of the set Ω.

Definition 3.10 The *rank* (or *Nakamura number*) of the list Ω is a natural number $\nu(\Omega)$ such that Ω contains $\nu(\Omega)$ sets intersection of which is empty, while the intersection of fewer sets from Ω is not empty. If $\bigcap_{\omega\in\Omega}\omega \neq \emptyset$, then by definition $\nu(\Omega) = \infty$.

Let us introduce next the subclass of the federation rules with the following property.

Definition 3.11 For a given set of alternatives A, we say that a federation rule F is *strong federation rule* if the rank of the list Ω of F is greater than m, where $m = card(A)$, i.e., $\nu(\Omega) > m$. The class of strong federation rules will be denoted as $\Lambda_m^{\cup\cap}$.

Theorem 3.5 *The intersection of the Central Class Λ^C with the complete class of closedness a) $\Lambda(\mathcal{LO}, \mathcal{AR})$; b) $\Lambda(\mathcal{LO}, \mathcal{SPO})$; c) $\Lambda(\mathcal{LO}, \mathcal{LO})$, coincides in case a) $\Lambda_m^{\cup\cap}$; b) $\Lambda^{\cap}$; and c) Λ^d.*

Proof. Statement a) is just a corollary from the statement a) of Theorem 3.4. b) From the condition (t^C) follows that the intersection of all ω's in Ω, i.e., $\omega_0 = \cap_{\omega\in\Omega}\omega$, belongs to Ω. Due to the conditions (NI) and (M) the set ω_0 is not empty. Hence $\Omega^B = (\omega_0)$, which coincides with the definition of the oligarcgy rule. c) Since linear order is transitive, we have that $\omega_0 = \cap_{\omega\in\Omega}\omega$ belongs to Ω and $\omega_0 \neq \emptyset$. Show that $card(\omega_0) = 1$. Indeed, let $card(\omega_0) > 1$. Without loss of generality suppose that $\omega_0 = \{i, j\}$, and $\{i\}, \{j\} \notin \Omega$. Then according to the condition (cn^C), $N \setminus \{i\} \in \Omega$, and due to the condition (t^C) we obtain $\omega_0 \cap (N \setminus \{i\}) = \{j\} \in \Omega$ ■

Thus, if individual opinions are given as linear orders and social binary relation is to be acyclic, then this can be done via the rule from the Central Class if and only if it is a strong federation rule. Note that in our previous definitions of the rules no parameter be presented. For strong federation rule it is not the case: for some set of alternatives A the rule can be strong, for some A - not. Consider, for example, the rule F with Ω^B such that

$$\Omega^B = (\{1, 2\}, \{1, 3\}, \{2, 3, 4\}).$$

Then for $m = 2$ F is strong federation rule, but for $m > 2$ it is not the case. When social binary relation is to be a strict partial order it can be constructed only by an oligarchic rule. Finally, the transformation from individual linear orders into social linear orders can be made via the rule from Λ^C if and only if it is a dictatorial rule. The statement a) of the Theorem 3.5 can be expressed in the equivalent form.

Theorem 3.6 *Let F be a federation rule, and Ω be its list. Then F constructs acyclic binary relations from individual linear orders if and only if $m < \nu(\Omega)$, where $m = card(A)$.*

The following corollary holds

Corollary 3.2 *Any Veto-rule constructs an acyclic social binary relation from individual linear orders.*

Proof. Since for any Veto rule we have $\emptyset \neq \omega_0 = \cap_{\omega\in\Omega}\omega$, the rank of Ω is $\nu(\Omega) = \infty$. Hence, the statement a) of the Theorem 3.5 holds for any m ■

Theorem 3.7 *Let $m \geq n$ and $F \in \Lambda^C \cap \Lambda(\mathcal{LO}, \mathcal{AR})$. Then F is a Veto-rule.*

Proof.Suppose that there is no i such that $i \in \omega$ for every $\omega \in \Omega$. Consider all coalitions $\omega_{-i} \in \Omega$ such that $i \notin \omega_{-i}$ for all $i \in N$. Then intersection of n such coalitions is empty, so $\nu(\Omega) \leq n$. Since $n \leq m$, we obtain $\nu(\Omega) \leq m$ which due to Theorem 3.6 contradicts acyclicity of P ■

Theorem 3.7 states that if the number of alternatives is greater or equal to the number of agents, and we would like the social decision to be an acyclic binary relation, then under arbitrary profiles of individual linear orders it can be done only by Veto-rule.

Let us apply the results stated by the Theorem 3.5 to the Symmetrically Central Class. Since according to Theorem 3.2 Symmetrically Central Class coincides with the class of k-majority rules we give the corresponding result below in terms of those rules.

Theorem 3.8 *a) A rule F belongs to the intersection of the class of k-majority rules Λ^{kM} with the complete class of closedness $\Lambda(\mathcal{LO}, \mathcal{AR})$ if and only if $m < \left\lceil \frac{n}{n-k} \right\rceil$, where $m = card(A)$, $n = card(N)$, and $\lceil x \rceil$ denotes the smallest integer greater than or equal to x;*
b) A rule F belongs to the intersection of the class of k-majority rules Λ^{kM} with the complete class of closedness $\Lambda(\mathcal{LO}, \mathcal{SPO})$ if and only if it is the Unanimity rule $\mathcal{U}$, i.e., n-majority rule;
c) There is no rule F which belongs to the intersection of the Symmetrically Central Class Λ^C with the complete class of closedness $\Lambda(\mathcal{LO}, \mathcal{LO})$.

Proof. a) Let us show that for a k-majority rule the rank of the list Ω is equal to $\nu(\Omega) = \left\lceil \frac{n}{n-k} \right\rceil$. Indeed, Ω contains p coalitions of the size k with empty intersection if and only if there exist p coalitions of the size $n-k$ the union of which is equal to N, i.e.,

$$\cap_{i=1}^{p}\omega_i = \emptyset,\ card(\omega_i) = k \Leftrightarrow$$

$$\Leftrightarrow \cup_{i=1}^{p}\omega_i' = N,\ card(\omega_i') = n-k.$$

This implies that $p(n-k) \geq n \Leftrightarrow p \geq \left\lceil \frac{n}{n-k} \right\rceil$.

Statements b) and c) follow from Theorem 3.2: b) follows from $\Lambda^{kM} \cap \Lambda^{\cap} = \mathcal{U}$; c) follows from $\Lambda^{kM} \cap \Lambda^{d} = \emptyset$ ■

Five remarks relating to Theorems 3.5-3.8 are in order:

Remark 1. As follows from the remark after Theorem 3.4 the statements a) and b) of Theorems 3.5 and 3.8 can be extended for the cases $\mathcal{LO} \subseteq Q_d \subseteq Q_r = \mathcal{AR}$ and $\mathcal{LO} \subseteq Q_d \subseteq Q_r = \mathcal{T}$, respectively.

Remark 2. Analogously, as follows from Lemma 3.1 the statements b) of Theorems 3.5 and 3.8 can be extended for the case when instead of Monotonicity and Neutrality the only normative condition is needed - that of Positive Unanimity. Otherwise speaking, we can re-formulate those statements in the following form:

$$\Lambda(\mathcal{LO}, \mathcal{SPO}) \cap \Lambda^{U^+} = \Lambda^{\cap},$$

and

$$\Lambda(\mathcal{LO}, \mathcal{SPO}) \cap \Lambda^{U^+} \cap \Lambda^{An} = \mathcal{U}.$$

Remark 3. Let us exclude from the set of all strict partial orders the empty relation $P = \emptyset$. Then the statements b) of Theorems 3.5 and 3.8 are not valid yet - in the first case we obtain the class Λ^d, and in the second case the intersection $\Lambda(\mathcal{LO}, \mathcal{SPO})$ with Λ^{SC} is empty. Indeed, since the rule in the first case is an oligarchical one, then if any two members of the group ω has 'opposite' preferences, then the social decision is $P = \emptyset$. Thus, the case with oligarchy rule in a certain sense is 'non-robust' - removal of a single binary relation from the class of strict partial orders replaces the oligarchy rule with dictatorial one. The case with a dictatorship, on the other hand, is robust - small deformations of the class preserve the existence of a dictator.

Remark 4. The Unanmity rule, which is the only rule in the intersection $\Lambda(\mathcal{LO}, \mathcal{SPO}) \cap \Lambda^{SC}$ is of little interest, since it generates empty or 'poor' social binary relations.

Remark 5. It is easy to show that $m < \left\lceil \frac{n}{n-k} \right\rceil \Leftrightarrow k > n\frac{m-1}{m}$. If $m = 10$, then to guarantee the acyclicity of P by k-majority rule k should be greater than $k > 0.9n$. In case of 100 agents, an admissible rule is 91-majority, or 92-majority, etc. The extreme case is n-majority (Unanimity) rule, which as we already know leads to very poor or even empty social binary relations P.

3.7 Arrow's General Impossibility Theorem

In Chapter 1 we studied a version of Arrow's General Impossibility Theorem for the case $Q_d = Q_r = \mathcal{LO}$, and we repeated the original proof by K.Arrow. Below we consider the statement of Arrow's Theorem for the domain of definition Q_d and the range Q_r of strongly local SDFs being equal to the set of all complete[19], transitive and negatively transitive[20] binary relations. The relation with those properties is often

[19] A relation R is complete if $\forall x, y$ either xRy or yRx.

[20] A relation R is negatively transitive if $x\overline{R}y\overline{R}z \Rightarrow x\overline{R}z$.

called *complete pre-order*. The class of all complete pre-orders on A will be denoted as $\mathcal{CP}$.
If I_R denotes the indifference relation for R, i.e.,

$$I_R = R \cap R^{-1},$$

where $R^{-1} = \{(x,y) \mid (y,x) \in R\}$, then the asymmetric part of R is denoted as P, i.e., $P = R \setminus I_R$. It is easy to check that for a complete pre-order I_R is the equivalence relation, i.e., reflexive, symmetric, and transitive binary relation, and P is a weak order.

Let us formulate now Arrow's conditions.
Unrestricted domain (UD): $Q_d = \mathcal{CP}$;
Non-imposition (NI): $\forall (x,y)\, \exists \overrightarrow{R}, \overrightarrow{R'}$ such that $(x,y) \in F(\overrightarrow{R})$ and $(x,y) \notin F(\overrightarrow{R'})$;
Monotonicity (M): xRy, $V(x,y;\overrightarrow{R}) \subseteq V(x,y;\overrightarrow{R'}) \Rightarrow xR'y$;
Non-dictatorship (ND): there is no $i \in N$ such that for any $\overrightarrow{R}$, $F(\overrightarrow{R}) = R_i$.

Theorem 3.9 *Let $card(A) \geq 3$ and $Q_r = \mathcal{CP}$. Then there is no F which satisfies conditions UD, NI, M and ND.*

We will not prove this Theorem but rather obtain its proof as a corollary of Theorem 3.4 and Lemmas 3.1 and 3.2. It is easy to check that the statement of Lemma 3.1 remains valid for Q_d being arbitrary subclass of the class of transitive binary relations which includes the class $\mathcal{CP}$. Hence, from Lemma 3.1 we obtain

$$\Lambda(\mathcal{CP},\mathcal{CP}) \cap \Lambda^{NI^+} \Rightarrow \Lambda^{Ne},$$

i.e., the corresponding rule F is defined by unique list Ω. Again, it is easy to check that the statements b) and c) of Theorem 3.4 remain valid for $Q_d = \mathcal{CP}$ (see also Remark after Theorem 3.4), i.e.,

$$F \in \Lambda(\mathcal{CP},\mathcal{T}) \text{ if and only if } \Omega \text{ for } F \text{ satisfies condition } (t),$$

and

$$F \in \Lambda(\mathcal{CP},\mathcal{C}n) \text{ if and only if } \Omega \text{ satisfies } (cn).$$

Thus, F obeys NI, M, and Ne, i.e., $F \in \Lambda^C$. Now just repeating the proof of the statements b) and c) of Theorem 3.5 we obtain $F \in \Lambda^d$, which contradicts the condition ND.

In words, if the number of alternatives is not less than 3, individuals are rationale in a sense that they can express their opinion about alternatives in the form of complete pre-order, and a social decision is to be a complete pre-order as well, then there is no strongly local non-dictatorial social decision function which satisfies positive and negative Non-Imposition, and Monotonicity conditions. If we omit in the statement of Theorem 3.9 the requirement of negative Non-Imposition, then the rule F under study can be constant rule 1 as well.

Consider now the case when $card(A) = 2$. It can be interpreted as the existence of only two special alternatives, say, $A = \{yes$ (adopt the bill), no (reject it)$\}$. Agents have to make a decision about the bill, and agent's preference can be $yes \succ no$, $no \succ yes$, or she can be indifferent to these two alternatives, i.e., $yes \sim no$. Then it can be directly checked that any non-imposed, neutral and monotonic rule, i.e., any rule from the Central Class, belong to the class $\Lambda(\mathcal{CP},\mathcal{CP})$, i.e., satisfies the conditions of Arrow's Theorem. In particular, it is k-majority rule, which satisfies additionally Anonymity condition. Thus, for this case there is very reasonable rule satisfying all properties which seem to be quite natural for voting systems. We will discuss the analogous result later in this Chapter.

3.8 Rationality constraints: further results

In this Section we extend the notion of acyclicity to that of l-acyclicity, and introduce a new subclass of acyclic binary relations, that of 'single-source' binary relations. We shall study as well some subclasses of the class of strict partial orders, namely, semi-orders and interval orders. These classes of binary relations will be considered as the domain of definition Q_d and the range Q_r of strongly local rules.

3.8.1 l-Acyclic relations

Let us begin with the definition of l-acyclicity.

Definition 3.12 A binary relation P will be said to be *l-acyclic* if P does not contain cycles of the lenth l and shorter, l being some integer such that $l > 0$.

It is obvions that for $l \geq m$, m being the number of alternatives, l-acyclicity of P just means that P is acyclic, so l-acyclicity is a weakened version of acyclicity. If acyclicity of P is considered to be too rectrictive in a sense that individual can make correct evaluations about the relations between alternatives only on small subsets of A (of a cardinality l and less), then l-acyclicity can be considered as a proper substitute to the acyclicity condition.

Let us denote the class of all l-acyclic binary relations as $l\mathcal{AR}$. Introduce now the following property on the list Ω of a given social decision function F.

(lac) Let $p \geq 2$ be given. For any s $(2 \leq s \leq p)$ and for any $\omega_1, ..., \omega_s$ such that $\omega_1 \in \Omega(x_1, x_2)$, $\omega_2 \in \Omega(x_2, x_3)$, ..., $\omega_p \in \Omega(x_p, x_1)$ the following holds

$$\bigcap_{i=1}^{s} \omega_i \neq \emptyset\,.$$

Theorem 3.10 *A local rule F belongs to class $\Lambda(l\mathcal{AR},l\mathcal{AR})$, i.e. transforms the profiles from the domain $(l\mathcal{AR})^n$ to the range $Q_r = l\mathcal{AR}$, if and only if the list Ω of a rule F satisfies the condition (lac).*

Proof. Let the condition (lac) holds. Show that $F \in \Lambda(l\mathcal{AR},l\mathcal{AR})$. Assume on the contrary that there exists a profile $\vec{P}$ such that $\forall i\ P_i \in l\mathcal{AR}$, but $P = F(\vec{P}) \notin l\mathcal{AR}$, i.e., there are $x_1, ..., x_s$, $(s \leq l)$ such that $x_1 P x_2 P ... P x_s P x_1$. These means that

$$\begin{aligned} V(x_1, x_2; \vec{P}) &\in \Omega(x_1, x_2), \\ &\dots \\ V(x_s, x_1; \vec{P}) &\in \Omega(x_s, x_1). \end{aligned}$$

Consider the set

$$\omega' = V(x_1, x_2; \vec{P}) \cap ... \cap V(x_s, x_1; \vec{P})).$$

Suppose $\exists i \in \omega'$. Then $x_1 P_i x_2 P_i ... P_i x_s P_i x_1$, which contradicts l-acyclicity of P_i. Hence, $\omega' = \emptyset$, i.e., the condition (lac) is violated.
Let now $P_i, P \in l\mathcal{AR}$. Show that (lac) holds. Assume on the contrary that (lac) does not hold. Consider the case $l = 3$, and the profile shown below:
$i \in \overline{\omega}_1 \cap \omega_2 \cap \omega_3 : \quad P_i = \{(x_2, x_3), (x_3, x_1)\};$
$i \in \omega_1 \cap \overline{\omega}_2 \cap \omega_3 : \quad P_i = \{(x_1, x_2), (x_3, x_1)\};$
$i \in \omega_1 \cap \omega_2 \cap \overline{\omega}_3 : \quad P_i = \{(x_1, x_2), (x_2, x_3)\};$
$i \in \overline{\omega}_1 \cap \overline{\omega}_2 \cap \omega_3 : \quad P_i = \{(x_3, x_1)\};$
$i \in \overline{\omega}_1 \cap \omega_2 \cap \overline{\omega}_3 : \quad P_i = \{(x_2, x_3)\};$
$i \in \omega_1 \cap \overline{\omega}_2 \cap \overline{\omega}_3 : \quad P_i = \{(x_1, x_2)\};$
$i \in \overline{\omega}_1 \cap \overline{\omega}_2 \cap \overline{\omega}_3 : \quad P_i = \emptyset.$
Then it is easy to check that P contains the cycle $x_1 P x_2 P x_3 P x_1$, which contradicts the assumption $P \in l\mathcal{AR}$. The general case $l > 3$ can be proved in a similar way as in the proof of Theorem 3.4 with only exception that the case $\bigwedge_{i=1}^{m} I_i$ is allowed ■

Let us give example of the rule F which belongs to the intersection $\Lambda(l\mathcal{AR},l\mathcal{AR})$ with Symmetrically Central Class.
Example. Let $N = \{1, ..., 5\}$. Since any rule F from Λ^{SC} is a k-majority rule, the rule F under question is a k-majority rule. Let F be 4−majority rule, i.e. $\Omega^B = (\{1,2,3,4\}, \{1,2,3,5\}, \{1,2,4,5\}, \{1,3,4,5\}, \{2,3,4,5\})$. It is easy to check that all five ω's from Ω^B has empty intersection. However, the intersection of any four ω's is non-empty. Hence, according to the Theorem 3.10, F belongs to the class $\Lambda(l\mathcal{AR},l\mathcal{AR})$ with $l = 4$, i.e., for any profile the social binary relation does not contain cycles of the length 4 and less. On the other hand, there are profiles for which social binary relation P contains the cycle of the length 5.

3.8.2 Single-source relations

Consider now the next rationality constraint. We assume that both individual opinions and social decisions are represented as 'single-source' binary relations, which are a special kind of acyclic binary relations.

Definition 3.13 An acyclic relation P will be called a *single-source* binary relation if there exists $x \in A$ such that for any $y \in A$ there exist $z_{1,...,} z_l \in A$ such that $xPz_1Pz_2P...Pz_lPy$, and wPx for no $w \in A$.

Otherwise speaking, for any alternative y on the corresponding graph P there exists a path from x to y, and no directed arc goes from any other vertex of P to x. The example of single-source binary relation is given on the Figure 3-3. It is evident that any linear order is the single-source relation as well.

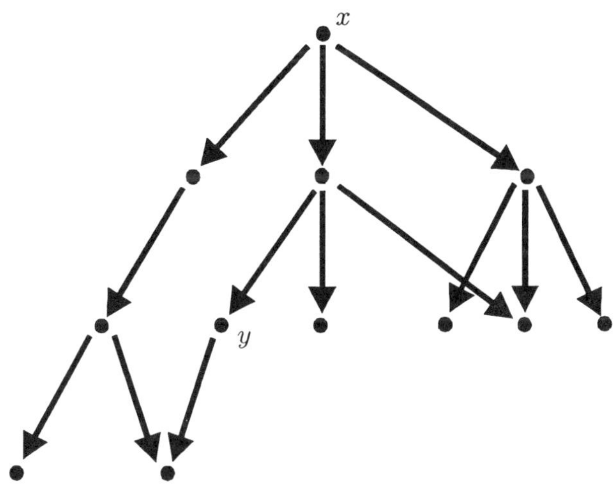

Figure 3-3

A single-source binary relation P can be interpreted as an ordinal counterpart of the representation of agents' preferences in the spatial model of voting. In that model the alternatives are assumed to be the vectors in R^n, any agent has her 'ideal' point (the most preferable alternative), and the far an alternative in question is from the ideal point of agent, the less preferable it is (see, e.g., [108, 178]).
A single-source relation P_i, representing the opinion of agent i, can be interpreted in the same way. Indeed, the source x can be treated as the ideal point, and the far is the alternative y from x (i.e., the longer is the path from x to y), the less preferable can be considered y. Let us denote the class of single-source binary relations on A as SS.
Suppose now that agents express their opinions about alternatives via single-source binary relations P_i, the source x_i possibly being different for each i. To which condition should satisfies a strongly local rule F to contruct the social single-source binary relation P, or, in other words, in which case F belongs to the class $\Lambda(SS,SS)$? The answer to this question is given by the next theorem.

Theorem 3.11 *A rule F belongs to the intersection of the class $\Lambda(SS,SS)$ with Λ^C if and only if it is the dictator rule, i.e.,*

$$\Lambda(SS, SS) \cap \Lambda^C = \Lambda^d.$$

Proof. We will first show that if $F \in \Lambda(SS,SS)$ then the condition Ne follows from conditions NI^+, NI^-, and M. Without loss of generality assume $m = 3$. Consider $\Omega(x, z)$ and $\Omega(x, y)$ and suppose that there exists $\omega \in \Omega(x, z)$ and $\omega \notin \Omega(x, y)$. Consider the profile $\{P_i\}$ shown below (here $\omega' \in \Omega(y, z)$).

$$\begin{array}{ll} i \in \omega \cap \omega' : & P_i = \{(x, y), (y, z), (x, z)\}; \\ i \in \omega \setminus \omega' : & P_i = \{(x, z), (z, y)\}; \\ i \in \omega' \setminus \omega : & P_i = \{(y, z), (z, x)\}; \\ i \in N \setminus (\omega \cup \omega') : & P_i = \{(z, y), (z, x)\}. \end{array}$$

Note that $(xP_iz \Leftrightarrow i \in \omega) \Rightarrow xPz$; $(yP_iz \Leftrightarrow i \in \omega') \Rightarrow yPz$. P is a single-source relation if yPx or xPy. But if yPx, then $V(y, x; \{P_i\}) = \emptyset \in \Omega(y, x)$ and given condition M this violates conditions NI^-. Therefore we have xPy. But $xP_iy \Leftrightarrow i \in \omega$, hence it follows that $\omega \in \Omega(x, y)$, i.e., $\Omega(x, z) \subseteq \Omega(x, y)$. We can similarly show that $\Omega(x, y) \subseteq \Omega(x, z)$, i.e., $\Omega(x, z) = \Omega(x, y)$. By the same way it can be proved that $\Omega(x, z) = \Omega(y, z)$, i.e., Neutrality of F. By Theorem 3.10, we have $\omega_0 = \bigcap_{j=1}^{m} \omega_i \neq \emptyset$ $(\omega_i \in \Omega)$. Take $i \in \omega_0$. If $\omega_0 = \{i\} \in \Omega$, then by M and Ne for $m > 2$ we obtain the required proposition. Let $\{i\} \notin \Omega$. Consider the profile $\{P_i\}$ such that $P_j = P_i^{-1} = \{(x, y) : yP_ix\}$, for all $j : j \neq i$ and $j \in \omega_l$, $i \in \omega_l$. For all the groups ω_k such that $i \notin \omega_k$ and for any l , $j \in \omega_k$, let $P_l = P_i$. Clearly, $P = \emptyset$, i.e., $P \notin SS$
■

Remark. As follows from the proof of Theorem 3.11 Neutrality of the rule under study is not pre-assumed in advance. Similarly to the case of transitive social relations it follows from rationality constraint.

3.8.3 Interval orders and semiorders

The result obtained by K.Arrow (Theorem 3.9) led to a search for other rationality constraints to obtain'positive' solution of aggregation problem in local case. And the natural question was 'Is there some class in between weak orders or linear orders (the corresponding aggregation rule in Λ^C is dictator one) and strict partial orders (with olygarchy rule), which can be generated via more interesting aggregation rules'? The answer to the question was found to be negative. To illustarate those results we study below the case when both Q_d and Q_r are the class of interval orders.

Definition 3.14 An irreflexive relation P which satisfies the following condition

$$\forall x, y, z, w \in A \; xPy \text{ and } zPw \Rightarrow xPw \text{ or } zPy,$$

is called *interval order*.

It is easy to check that an interval order P is transitive relation (just put in the definition of P $y = z$). Hence, any interval order is a strict partial order.
Interval orders have an interesting numerical representation which extends the representation for weak orders. For weak order P we obtained (see Chapter 2) the numerical representation via a utility function $u(\cdot)$ as follows

$$xPy \Leftrightarrow u(x) - u(y) > 0.$$

For an interval order P the numerical representation can be given in the following form

$$xPy \Leftrightarrow u(x) - u(y) > \varepsilon(y),$$

where $\varepsilon(y)$, $\varepsilon(y) \geq 0$, is some numerical function which represents 'an error' in evaluation of the utility of alternative.
Let us denote the class of all interval orders on A as $\mathcal{IO}$. The result obtained for aggregation of interval orders via strongly local rules is given below.

Theorem 3.12 $\Lambda(\mathcal{IO},\mathcal{IO}) \cap \Lambda^C = \Lambda^d$, *i.e., the pair* $(\mathcal{IO},\mathcal{IO})$ *is closed relative to the rule from the Central Class if and only if it is a dictator rule.*

Proof. The general condition for a rule to belong to the class $\Lambda(\mathcal{IO},\mathcal{IO})$ is the following one:

$$\forall \omega_1, \omega_2, \widetilde{\omega} \text{ such that } \omega_1 \in \Omega(x,y), \omega_2 \in \Omega(z,w),$$

$$\omega_1 \cap \omega_2 \subseteq \widetilde{\omega} \subseteq N \Rightarrow \widetilde{\omega} \in \Omega(x,w) \text{ or } \widetilde{\omega} \in \Omega(z,y).$$

An interval order is a strict partial order, hence, the rule in question belongs to some subclass of the oligarchy rules. Let ω be a coalition from the definition of oligarchic rule. Consider the following profile: for any i except one (say, j) let P_i be some interval order such that $\{(x,y),(z,w),(x,w)\} \subseteq P_i$, for agent j let $P_j \supseteq \{(x,y),(z,w),(z,y)\}$. Then the social decision P contains $\{(x,y),(z,w)\}$ but does not contain neither (x,w) nor (z,y), i.e., P is not an interval order ■

Moreover, in the proof of Theorem 3.12 there is no need to request in advance the Neutrality of the rule F under study. Due to Lemma 3.1, Neutrality of F follows from the transitivity of interval orders.

The result stated by Theorem 3.12 admits another interpretation. Since any interval order can be represented via utility function with error, even in this case when agent as well as social decision are permitted to be weakly rationale the corresponding aggregation rule is still the most restrictive - a dictatorial one.

Another interesting class of binary relations is the class of *semiorders*, which is a subclass of interval orders, satisfying additionally the semi-transitivity condition:

$$\forall x, y, z, w \in A \; xPy \text{ and } yPz \Rightarrow xPw \text{ or } wPz.$$

A relation from this class admits numerical representation via constant error function ε. However, a strongly local social decision function relative to which the class of semiorders is closed is also a dictatorial rule.

3.9 Aggregation of equivalences

An equivalentce relation introduced in Chapter 2 is a refxive, symmetric and transitive binary relation. In this section we consider the problem of aggregation of equivalences using strongly local social decision functions. The set of all equivalency relations will be denoted as $\mathfrak{Eq}$.

Aggregation of equivalences using simple majority rule seems was suggsted for the first time in [64] . In that monograph, the problem of clustering in some sense similar objects was considered. Each equivalency relation corresponds to the clustering obtained by some algorithm, and different algorithms can give different clusterings on the set A . Assuming n 'individual' clusterings being given, it was suggested then using simple majority rule to construct final ('social') clustering.

Consider the following example.

Example. Let $N = \{1, 2, 3\}$, $A = \{x, y, z\}$, and for any $i \in N$, $I_i \in \mathfrak{Eq}$; I_i being given below:

$$\begin{aligned} I_1 = &\quad \Delta \cup \{(x, y), (y, x)\}; \\ I_2 = &\quad \Delta \cup \{(x, y), (y, x), (x, z), (z, x), (y, z), (z, y)\}; \\ I_3 = &\quad \Delta \cup \{(x, z), (z, x)\}, \end{aligned}$$

where $\Delta = \{(x, x) \mid x \in A\}$.

We can construct the social relation I using simple majority (in this case 2-majority) rule. This I is shown below:

$$I = \Delta \cup \{(x, y), (y, x), (x, z), (z, x)\}.$$

It turns out that I is not the equivalency relation, since $zIxIy$ but $z\bar{I}y$. Thus simple majority rule transforms a profile of equivalency relations into a social relation which in general is not an equivalency relation.

Therefore, we formulate the problem as follows. Consider profiles from the set $(\mathfrak{Eq})^n$, where $\mathfrak{Eq}$ is a set of all equivalency relations on A; find the conditions under which a strongly local rule F transforms those profiles into a social equivalency relation, i.e., $Q_d = Q_r = \mathfrak{Eq}$.

Theorem 3.13 *A strongly local rule F belongs to $\Lambda(\mathfrak{Eq}, \mathfrak{Eq})$ if and only if the list Ω of F satisfies the following conditions*

$$a) \; \forall (x, x) \Rightarrow N \in \Omega(x, x);$$

$$b)\ \forall (x,y)\ \forall \omega, \omega \in \Omega(x,y) \Rightarrow \omega \in \Omega(y,x);$$

$$(t)\ \forall (x,y),(y,z),(x,z), \forall \omega_1, \omega_2, \widetilde{\omega}, \omega_1 \in \Omega(x,y),$$

$$\omega_2 \in \Omega(y,z), \omega_1 \cap \omega_2 \subseteq \widetilde{\omega} \subseteq N \Rightarrow \widetilde{\omega} \in \Omega(x,z).$$

Proof. Since individual binary relations are reflexive, then for social relation I to be reflexive it is necessary and sufficient that $N \in \Omega(x,x)$ for any x. Analogously, for I to be symmetric it must be $\omega \in \Omega(x,y) \Leftrightarrow \omega \in \Omega(y,x)$. To find the transitivity condition for I assume that $\omega_1 \in \Omega(x,y)$, $\omega_2 \in \Omega(y,z)$, but there is an ω such that $\omega_1 \cap \omega_2 \subseteq \omega \subseteq N$, which does not belong to $\Omega(x,z)$. Then consider the following profile:

$$\begin{array}{ll} i \in \omega_1 \cap \omega_2 \cap \omega: & I_i = \Delta \cup \{x \sim y, x \sim z, y \sim z\}; \\ i \in \overline{\omega}_1 \cap \overline{\omega}_2 \cap \omega: & I_i = \Delta \cup \{x \sim z\}; \\ i \in \overline{\omega}_1 \cap \omega_2 \cap \overline{\omega}: & I_i = \Delta \cup \{y \sim z\}; \\ i \in \omega_1 \cap \overline{\omega}_2 \cap \overline{\omega}: & I_i = \Delta \cup \{x \sim y\}, \end{array}$$

where $\Delta = \{(x,x) \mid x \in A\}$. Then $V(x,y;\ \overrightarrow{I}) = \omega_1$; $V(y,z;\ \overrightarrow{I}) = \omega_2$, and $V(x,z;\ \overrightarrow{I}) = \omega$. Hence, we obtain $xIyIz$, but $x\overline{I}z$.
Suppose now that condition (t) holds, but there exist a profile $\overrightarrow{I}$ such that $xIyIz$. Then $V(x,y;\ \overrightarrow{I}) \in \Omega(x,y)$; $V(y,z;\ \overrightarrow{I}) \in \Omega(y,z)$, and due to the transitivity of I_i, $i = 1,...,n$, the minimal set $V(x,z;\ \overrightarrow{I})$ is equal to $V(x,y;\ \overrightarrow{I}) \cap V(y,z;\ \overrightarrow{I})$. The maximal set $V(x,z;\ \overrightarrow{I})$ can be equal to N. Since condition (t) holds, xIz holds as well ■

Theorem 3.13 gives a general constraints on the list Ω for F to belong to $\Lambda(\mathfrak{Eq}, \mathfrak{Eq})$. It F satisfies positive Non-Imposition, then the result analogous to Lemma 3.1 holds, i.e.

$$F \in \Lambda(\mathfrak{Eq}, \mathfrak{Eq}) \cap \Lambda^{NI^+} \Rightarrow F \in \Lambda^{Ne}.$$

Moreover, due to the condition (t), F satisfies Monotonicity condition as well. So, a rule F in question belongs obviously to the class $\Lambda^C \cup \{\mathbf{0}\}$, i.e., F is either a rule from the Central Class or the constant rule $\mathbf{0}$. However, not any strongly local rule from Λ^C belongs to the class $\Lambda(\mathfrak{Eq}, \mathfrak{Eq})$ as it has been shown via the example above. Condition (t) gives an answer on the question which rules from Λ^C transforms individual equivalency relations into a social equivalency relations. Namely, due to the condition (t), $\emptyset \neq \omega_0 = \cap_{\omega \in \Omega} \omega$, and $\omega_0 \in \Omega$. But this is exactly the definition of an olygarchic rule.
So we obtain the following result.

Theorem 3.14 $\Lambda^{NI^+} \cap \Lambda(\mathfrak{Eq}, \mathfrak{Eq}) = \Lambda^{\cap} \cup \{\mathbf{0}\}$, *i.e., the class of rules which satisfy positive Non-Imposition and transform individual equivalency relations into a social equivalency relation coincide with the union of the class of oligarchic rules and constant rule* $\mathbf{0}$.

Since the rule 0 satisfies Anonimity condition and the intersection of oligarchic rules with the class Λ^{SC} consists of the only rule $\mathcal{U}$, we obtain the following corollary.

Corollary 3.3 $\Lambda^{NI^+} \cap \Lambda^{An} \cap \Lambda(\mathfrak{Eq}, \mathfrak{Eq}) = \mathcal{U} \cup \{0\}$.

Consider now the case when each individual equivalency relation consists of l classes of equivalency and social decision - equivalency relation I is of the same type as well. Let us denote the class of such equivalency relations as $\mathfrak{Eq}l$.
Then the result stated by Theorem 3.14 is not valid yet, and we obtain the following result.

Theorem 3.15 *Let* $1 < l < m$. *Then* $\Lambda^{NI^+} \cap \Lambda(\mathfrak{Eq}l, \mathfrak{Eq}l) = \Lambda^d$, *i.e. the corresponding aggregation rule is a dictatorial one.*

Proof. Since in general the rule in question is an oligarchy rule, i.e.,

$$I = \bigcap_{i \in \omega} I_i,$$

let us consider a profile $\{I_i\}$, each I_i contains l classes of equivalency, $1 < l < m$. Choose for all $i \in \omega$, $i \neq j$, the relation I_i such that the classes of equivalency is made on A in a descending order. Let the first class contains elements $x_1, ..., x_s$, and the second class contains elements $x_{s+1}, ..., x_r$. For $I_j, j \in \omega$, choose the first class being x_1, and the second class as $x_2, ..., x_r$, all other $l-2$ classes for all agents being the same. Then the social relation I contains $l+1$ classes of eqiuvalency first three being $\{x_1\}, \{x_2, ..., x_s\}, \{x_{s+1}, ..., x_r\}$. ■

Let us note that the case $l = 1$ corresponds to $I_i = A \times A$ for all i, and the case $l = m$ corresponds to $I_i = \Delta$ for all i.

3.10 Non-monotonic strongly local SDFs

In this Section we consider the case when the domain of definition of the rule F as well as the range is the class of linear orders, i.e., we study the rules from the class $\Lambda(\mathcal{LO}, \mathcal{LO})$. Let us first study how on the Venn's diagram shown at Figure 3-1 the class $\Lambda(\mathcal{LO}, \mathcal{LO})$ is disposed, i.e., study the intersection of the class $\Lambda(\mathcal{LO}, \mathcal{LO})$ with the classes $\Lambda^{NI^+}, ..., \Lambda^{U^-}$.

Theorem 3.16 *The intersection of the class* $\Lambda(\mathcal{LO}, \mathcal{LO})$ *with the classes* $\Lambda^{NI^+}, ..., \Lambda^{U^-}$ *is as shown at Venn diagram at Figure* 3-4.

Proof. Consider 20 conjunctions of conditions NI^+,..., U^- obtained in the proof of Theorem 3.2. We will prove that some of them are empty due to the following relations.
1) $\Lambda^{NI^+} \cap \Lambda^{\overline{NI^-}} \cap \Lambda^{\overline{Ne}} \cap \Lambda(\mathcal{LO}, \mathcal{AR}) = \emptyset$. Indeed, by $\overline{NI^-}$ $\exists(z, x)$ such that $\Omega(z, x) = 2^N$; by NI^+ for any (x, y) $\Omega(x, y) \neq \emptyset$. Without loss of generality consider

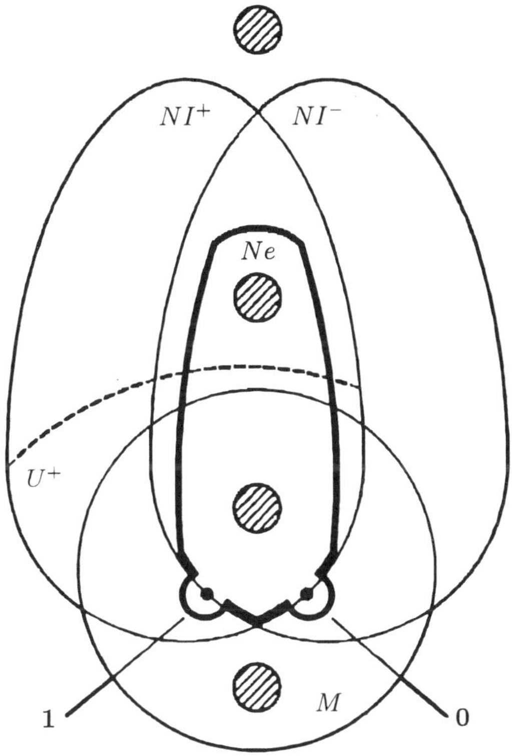

Figure 3-4

the case $m = 3$. Let $\omega_1 \in \Omega(x, y)$, $\omega_2 \in \Omega(y, z)$ and consider the following profile $\{P_i\}$.

$i \in \overline{\omega}_1 \cap \overline{\omega}_2 : \quad z \succ y \succ x;$
$i \in \omega_1 \cap \overline{\omega}_2 : \quad z \succ x \succ y;$
$i \in \overline{\omega}_1 \cap \omega_2 : \quad y \succ x \succ z;$
$i \in \omega_1 \cap \omega_2 : \quad x \succ y \succ z.$

Since $V(x, y; \overrightarrow{P}) = \omega_1$, $(x, y) \in P$; $V(y, z; \overrightarrow{P}) = \omega_2$, hence $(y, z) \in P$; from $\Omega(z, x) = 2^N$ we obtain the cycle in $P : xPyPzPx$.
2) For any rule from the class $\Lambda(\mathcal{LO}, Cn)$ the following relation holds: $\overline{NI^+} \Leftrightarrow \overline{NI^-}$. This follows from the condition cn.
3) $\Lambda^{NI^+} \cap \Lambda^{\overline{Ne}} \cap \Lambda(\mathcal{LO}, \mathcal{T}) = \emptyset$. This follows from Lemma 3.1.
4) $\Lambda^{U^+} \cap \Lambda^{\overline{M}} \cap \Lambda(\mathcal{LO}, \mathcal{T}) = \emptyset$. Follows from Lemma 3.2.
5) $\Lambda^{NI^+} \cap \Lambda^{\overline{Ne}} \cap \Lambda(\mathcal{LO}, \mathcal{LO}) = \emptyset$. It can be proved practically repeating the proof of Lemma 3.1.
Since conjunctions 6) and 10) given in the proof of Theorem 3.2 have to be excluded

as well (they define constant rules **0** and **1**), with relations 1) - 5) we obtain that only 5 conjunctions out of 20 are valid.
1) $\overline{NI^+} \cap \overline{NI^-} \cap \overline{M} \cap \overline{Ne} \cap \overline{U^+} \cap \overline{U^-}$;
2) $\overline{NI^+} \cap \overline{NI^-} \cap M \cap \overline{Ne} \cap \overline{U^+} \cap \overline{U^-}$;
15) $NI^+ \cap NI^- \cap \overline{M} \cap Ne \cap \overline{U^+} \cap \overline{U^-}$;
16) $NI^+ \cap NI^- \cap \overline{M} \cap Ne \cap \overline{U^+} \cap U^-$;
20) $NI^+ \cap NI^- \cap M \cap Ne \cap U^+ \cap U^-$.

Let us consider those non-empty intersections shown at Figure 3-4:

$$\begin{aligned} &\text{a) } \overline{NI^+} \cap \overline{NI^-} \cap \overline{M} \cap \overline{Ne} \cap \overline{U^+};\\ &\text{b) } \overline{NI^+} \cap \overline{NI^-} \cap M \cap \overline{Ne} \cap \overline{U^+};\\ &\text{c) } NI^+ \cap NI^- \cap \overline{M} \cap Ne \cap \overline{U^+};\\ &\text{d) } NI^+ \cap NI^- \cap M \cap Ne \cap U^+. \end{aligned}$$

The examples of rules for the cases a) and b) are given below.
Example 1. Let $A = \{x_1, x_2, x_3\}$, $card(N) = 3$. Consider

$$\Omega(x_i, x_i) = \emptyset;\ \Omega(x_2, x_1) = \Omega(x_3, x_1) = \emptyset;$$

$$\Omega(x_1, x_2) = \Omega(x_1, x_3) = 2^N;$$

$$\Omega(x_2, x_3) = 2^N \setminus N;\ \Omega(x_3, x_2) = \{\emptyset\}.$$

Then P is linear order, the rule violates positive and negative Non-Imposition, Neutrality, Monotonicity, and Unanimity.
Example 2. Let $A = \{x, y, z\}$, $card(N) = 3$. Consider

$$\Omega(x, y) = \Omega(y, z) = \Omega(x, z) = 2^N;$$

for all other (v, u) put $\Omega(v, u) = \emptyset$. Then P is linear order, the rule violates Non-imposition and Neutrality, but it is Monotonic.
The other non-empty intersection of the class $\Lambda(\mathcal{LO}, \mathcal{LO})$ is with the Central Class (case d)), which due to Theorem 3.5 consists of the dictatorial rules. For the cases c) and d) the complete study is provided below. ■
Let us consider the classes of rules which are isolated by the following conjunctions:

$$\begin{aligned} &\text{c) } NI^+ \cap NI^- \cap \overline{M} \cap Ne \cap \overline{U^+};\\ &\text{d) } NI^+ \cap NI^- \cap M \cap Ne \cap U^+. \end{aligned}$$

In both of them the rule under study satisfies Neutrality condition and both Non-Imposition conditions. These cases are covered by the next theorem. Before we state that theorem let us give some definition.

Definition 3.15 The rule F is called *anti-dictator rule* if there exists some $i_0 \in N$ such that $P = P_{i_0}^{-1}$.

In words, social decision is defined by anti-dictator if it is 'opposite' to the opinion of the agent i_0.

Theorem 3.17 *$F \in \Lambda^{NI^+} \cap \Lambda(\mathcal{LO}, \mathcal{LO})$ if and only if F is either dictatorial or anti-dictatorial.*

Proof. Before we prove this Theorem we state and prove several lemmas.

Lemma 3.3 *Let $F \in \Lambda^{Ne} \cap \Lambda^{\overline{U+}} \cap \Lambda(\mathcal{LO}, Cn)$. Then $\{\emptyset\} \in \Omega$.*

Proof. Since $F \in \Lambda^{\overline{U+}}$ then $N \notin \Omega$. By Theorem 3.4, statement c), we obtain $\{\emptyset\} \in \Omega$.

Lemma 3.4 *Let $F \in \Lambda^{NI^+} \cap \Lambda(\mathcal{LO}, Cn \cap \mathcal{T})$. Then there exist $i \in N$ such that $\{i\} \in \Omega$.*

Proof. First, since $F \in \Lambda^{NI} \cap \Lambda(\mathcal{LO}, \mathcal{T})$, then due to Lemma 3.1 $F \in \Lambda^{Ne}$. Now, suppose on the contrary that $\forall i \in N$, $\{i\} \notin \Omega$. Let $\{i,j\} \in \Omega$. Then by Theorem 3.4, statement c), $N \setminus \{i\} \in \Omega$. Again by Theorem 3.4, statement b), $(N \setminus \{i\}) \cap \{i,j\} = \{j\} \in \Omega$.

Lemma 3.5 *Let $F \in \Lambda^{NI^+} \cap \Lambda(\mathcal{LO}, Cn \cap \mathcal{T})$. Then either a) $\exists i_0 \in N$ such that $\{i_0\} \notin \Omega$ and $\forall j \neq i_0$ $\{j\} \in \Omega$; or b) $N \in \Omega$.*

Proof. Let $\exists j, k$ such that $\{j\}, \{k\} \notin \Omega$. Then by Theorem 3.4, statement c), we obtain $N \setminus \{j\} \in \Omega$ and $N \setminus \{k\} \in \Omega$. By Theorem 3.4, statement b), $(N \setminus \{j\}) \cup (N \setminus \{k\}) = N \in \Omega$.

Lemma 3.6 *Let $F \in \Lambda^{NI^+} \cap \Lambda^{\overline{U+}} \cap \Lambda(\mathcal{LO}, Cn)$. Then $\exists i_0 \in N$ such that $i_0 \notin \omega$ for any ω in Ω.*

Proof. By Lemma 3.5 $\exists i_0$ such that $\forall j \neq i_0$, $\{j\} \in \Omega$. By Theorem 3.4, statement b), any union of such $\{j\}$'s belong to Ω. If for some $\omega \in \Omega$, $i_0 \in \omega$ holds, then by Theorem 3.4, $N \in \Omega$ in contradiction with assumption.

Lemma 3.7 *Let $F \in \Lambda^{NI^+} \cap \Lambda^{\overline{U+}} \cap \Lambda(\mathcal{LO}, Cn)$ and there is $i_0 \in N$ such that $\{i_0\} \notin \Omega$. Then $P = P_{i_0}^{-1}$.*

Proof. Such i_0 exists due to Lemma 3.5. Now, for any $(x,y) \in P_{i_0}$ since i_0 belongs to no ω in Ω, $(x,y) \notin P$. For P to be connected, $(y,x) \in P$ holds, i.e., $P = P_{i_0}^{-1}$.
Now the statement of Theorem 3.17 follows immediately from Lemmas 3.3 - 3.7. ∎

Remark 1. As it follows from the proof of Theorem 3.17 the rule under study, i.e., $F \in \Lambda^{NI^+} \cap \Lambda(\mathcal{LO}, \mathcal{LO})$, either satisfies Positive Unanimity condition, or does not satisfy it. In the first case it is monotonic and due to Lemma 3.1 belongs to the Central Class, and due to Theorem 3.4 it is dictatorial rule. In the latter case when it does not satisfy Positive Unanimity condition, it is anti-dictator rule.

Remark 2. The statement of the Theorem 3.17 remains valid for the rules from other classes, such as $\Lambda(\mathcal{WO},\mathcal{WO})$ and $\Lambda(\mathcal{CP},\mathcal{CP})$.

Remark 3. Let us consider the following anti-olygarchic rule: there is a group ω such that the social decision is made unanimously using 'direct' opinions P_i of some members of ω and 'inverse' opinions P_j^{-1} of other members of ω, i.e.,

$$P = \bigcap_{i \in \omega} P_i^{\pm 1}.$$

Then, practically repeating the proof of Theorem 3.17 one can obtain more general result: $F \in \Lambda^{NI^+} \cap \Lambda(\mathcal{LO},\mathcal{SPO})$ if and only if F is either oligarchic or anti-oligarchic rule.

3.11 Locality

Until the end of this chapter it is assumed that the individual binary relations P_i are weak orders, i.e., acyclic, transitive and negatively transitive binary relations.
The rule F will be called a local aggregation rule if whether or not the social binary relation P contains a pair (x, y) depends entirely on the presence or absence of the pairs (x, y) and (y, x) in individual relations P_i in the agents' profile, regardless of the other pairs contained therein. To formalize the locality condition, denote as before the set of agents who includes the pair (x, y) in the given profile $\vec{P}$ as $V(x, y; \vec{P})$, i.e.,

$$V(x, y; \vec{P}) = \{i \in N \mid (x, y) \in P_i\}$$

Note that by virtue of the asymmetry of the relations P it is impossible that $(x, y) \in P_i$ and $(y, x) \in P_i$ for the same i; therefore

$$V(x, y; \vec{P}) \cap V(y, x; \vec{P}) = \emptyset.$$

Definition 3.16 Let two profiles $\{P_i\}$ and $\{P_i'\}$ be given. A rule F will be said to satisfy *locality* condition if for any pair $(x, y) \in A \times A$ for which both

$$V(x, y; \{P_i\}) = V(x, y; \{P_i'\}) \text{ and } V(y, x; \{P_i\}) = V(y, x; \{P_i'\})$$

are obeyed, the inclusion

$$(x, y) \in P \text{ holds if and only if } (x, y) \in P',$$

where $P = F(\{P_i\}), P' = F(\{P'_i\})$.

Note that in the case of strongly local rules the decision whether or not a pair (x, y) belongs to the resulting relation depends only upon the presence or absence of this pair (x, y) in the relations P_i, irrespectively of other pairs of the form (u, t), where u and t are not equal to x and y. A distinguishing feature of local rules is that in this case the individual opinions on pairs of the form (y, x) are not neglected.

Let us now show how to represent local rules in terms of logic functions and in the list form.

Remark. Let a logic variable $l_i(x, y)$, $i \in N$, be given, taking on one of three values at each pair $(x, y) \in A \times A$:

$$l_i(x,y) = \begin{cases} 1, \text{ if } (x,y) \in P_i; \\ 0, \text{ if } (x,y) \notin P_i \text{ and } (y,x) \notin P_i; \\ -1, \text{ if } (y,x) \in P_i. \end{cases}$$

It is easy to see that the locality of a rule is equivalent to the existence of the *boolean function* of the three-valued variables

$$f(x,y;\ \overrightarrow{l}(x,y)) = f(l_1(x,y),...,l_n(x,y)),$$

taking on the value 1 for $(x, y) \in P$ and 0 for $(x, y) \notin P$.

Representing the rule F in terms of the function $f(x, y;\ \overrightarrow{l}(x, y))$, one may introduce a Ω- (or, *list*) *representation* of this rule. For a certain profile $\{P_i\}$, that is, for a certain set $\overrightarrow{l}(x, y)$, let the value of the function $f(x, y;\ \overrightarrow{l}(x, y))$ be 1. Consider the set $\omega_1^{xy} = \{i \in N \mid l_i(x, y) = 1\}$ of those indices from N for which the variable $l_i(x, y)$ equals to 1, and the set $\omega_2^{xy} = \{i \in N \mid l_i(x, y) = -1\}$ of those indices for which $l_i(x, y)$ equals minus 1. It is evident that the sets ω_1^{xy} and ω_2^{xy} satisfy the condition $\omega_1^{xy} \cap \omega_2^{xy} = \emptyset$.

Let us now put each pair (x, y) into correspondence with a family $\Omega(x, y)$ of pairs $(\omega_1^{xy}, \omega_2^{xy})$ defined for all feasible profiles $\{P_i\}$ (for all sets $\overrightarrow{l}(x, y)$) by the function $f(x, y;\ \overrightarrow{l}(x, y))$. It is easy to see that for the local rule F the following is true:

$$\begin{gathered} (x,y) \in P = F(\vec{P}) \Longleftrightarrow (\omega_1^{xy}, \omega_2^{xy}) \in \Omega(x,y), \\ (V(x,y;\vec{P}), V(y,x;\vec{P})) = (\omega_1^{xy}, \omega_2^{xy}). \end{gathered} \tag{3.5}$$

The set of families $\{\Omega(x, y)\}$ for various pairs (x, y) together with the rule (3.5), forms the list representation of a local rule. It follows directly from the definition of a list representation that each local rule has its own list representation[21]. A stronger assertion may be made. Let some rule be given in its list form, i.e., let a set of families $\Omega(x, y)$

---

21 The term 'winning coalition' instead of 'list representations' is often used, though that is meaningful only for strongly local rules. In the description of local rules in the list form given in [112] the term 'decisive structure' was used.

and the rule (3.5) be specified. Since the profile contains only weak order relations P_i, the sets $\omega_1^{xy}, \omega_2^{xy}, \omega_1^{yz}, \omega_2^{yz}, \omega_1^{xz}$, and ω_2^{xz} satisfy some mutual relations of the form

$$(\omega_1^{xy} \cup \omega_1^{yz}) \cap \overline{\omega_2^{xy} \cup \omega_2^{yz}} \subseteq \omega_1^{xz} \subseteq \omega_1^{xy} \cup \omega_2^{yz},$$

$$(\omega_2^{xy} \cup \omega_2^{yz}) \cap \overline{\omega_1^{xy} \cup \omega_1^{yz}} \subseteq \omega_2^{xz} \subseteq \omega_2^{xz} \cup \omega_1^{xz}.$$

It may be shown that each rule specified in the list form which satisfies these conditions does satisfy the condition of locality.
The space (set) of all local rules will be denoted as Π_l.

3.12 Normative conditions

In formulating these conditions, we shall specify their list forms in brackets.
(NI^+) *Positive Non-Imposition.* For each pair $(x,y) \in A \times A$ a profile $\vec{P}$ exists such that $(x,y) \in P = F(\vec{P})$.
$[\forall (x,y) \in A \times A : \Omega(x,y) \neq \emptyset]$

(NI^-) *Negative Non-Imposition.* For each pair $(x,y) \in A \times A$ a profile $\vec{P}$ exists such that $(x,y) \notin P = F(\vec{P})$.
$[\forall (x,y) \in A \times A : \Omega(x,y) \neq T$, where T is the set of all pairs (ω_1, ω_2) such that $\omega_1 \subseteq N, \omega_2 \subseteq N$ and $\omega_1 \cap \omega_2 = \emptyset]$
Condition NI^+ (respectively, condition NI^-) guarantees that the aggregation rule does not exclude any pair (x,y) from the resulting decision P (include any pair in P) irrespective of the agents' opinion.

(M) *Monotonicity.* Let two profiles $\vec{P}$ and $\vec{P'}$ be given and a pair (x,y) be included in $P = F(\vec{P})$. In this case, if

$$V(x,y;\{P_i\}) \subseteq V(x,y;\{P_i'\}, \tag{3.6}$$

$$V(y,x;\{P_i'\}) \subseteq V(y,x;\{P_i\}, \tag{3.7}$$

then $(x,y) \in P' = F(\{P_i'\})$.
$[\forall (\omega_1, \omega_2) \in \Omega(x,y), \forall (x,y) \in A \times A, \forall (\widetilde{\omega}_1, \widetilde{\omega}_2)$ such that $\widetilde{\omega}_1 \cap \widetilde{\omega}_2 = \emptyset, \widetilde{\omega}_1 \supseteq \omega_1, \widetilde{\omega}_2 \subseteq \omega_2 \Rightarrow (\widetilde{\omega}_1, \widetilde{\omega}_2) \in \Omega(x,y).$]
Condition M guarantees that if the set of agents including the pair (x,y) in their relations has increased and/or the set of agents choosing (y,x) decreased, then the pair (x,y) should remain in the social decision. Note that the case of equality in (3.6) and (3.7) exactly defines the condition of locality, i.e., the monotonicity condition is what imposes that main condition.

(Ne) *Neutrality.* For any (x, y) and (z, w) such that $V(x, y; \{P_i\}) = V(z, w; \{P_i\})$ and $V(y, x; \{P_i\}) = V(w, z; \{P_i\})$ the following is true[22]: $(x, y) \in P \Leftrightarrow (z, w) \in P$.
$[\,\forall (x, y) \in A \times A : \Omega(x, y) = \Omega\,]$
According to condition Ne an aggregation rule is independent of any renaming of the alternatives, i.e., if the sets of the agents who 'vote' for and against pairs (x, y) and (z, w) coincide, so does the social decision with respect to these pairs.

(An) *Anonymity.* For any one-to-one mapping $\eta : N \leftrightarrow N$,

$$F(\{P_{\eta(i)}\}) = F(\{P_i\}).$$

[Let $\eta(\omega) = \{\eta(i) \mid i \in \omega\}$. Then

$$\forall (\omega_1, \omega_2) \in \Omega(x, y) \Rightarrow \; (\eta(\omega_1), \eta(\omega_2)) \in \Omega(x, y)]$$

If this condition is satisfied, the social binary relation is independent of re-indexing of the agents.

Next four characteristic conditions express the logic of Paretian choice discussed above.

(PC^+) *Positive Pareto condition.* If $\forall i \in N : (y, x) \notin P_i$ and $\exists i_0$ such that $(x, y) \in P_{i_0}$, then $(x, y) \in P$.
$[\forall \omega_1 \colon \emptyset \subset \omega_1 \subseteq N \Rightarrow (\omega_1, \emptyset) \in \Omega(x, y).]$
According to this condition a pair (x, y) is included in the relation P if there is at least one agent who chooses it, while nobody chooses (y, x).

(PC^-) *Negative Pareto condition.* If $\forall i \in N$: $(x, y) \notin P_i$ then $(x, y) \notin P$.
$[\,\forall \omega_2 \colon \emptyset \subseteq \omega_2 \subseteq N \Rightarrow (\emptyset, \omega_2) \notin \Omega(x, y).]$
If in the profile there is no agent including (x, y) in her P_i, then the pair is not included in the resulting relation.

(U^+) *Positive Unanimity condition.* If $\forall i \in N$: $(x, y) \in P_i$ then $(x, y) \in P$.
$[\forall (x, y) \in A \times A \Rightarrow (N, \emptyset) \in \Omega(x, y).]$
By condition U^+, a pair (x, y) is included in the P if all the agents includes (x, y) in their relations P_i.

(U^-) *Negative Unanimity condition.* If $\forall i \in N$: $(y, x) \in P_i$ then $(x, y) \notin P$.
$[\forall (x, y) \in A \times A \Rightarrow (\emptyset, N) \notin \Omega(x, y).\,]$
If all agents chooses (y, x), then the inverse pair (x, y) is not included in P.

Conditions NI^+,...,U^- may be easily formulated in terms of the boolean function $f(x, y; \overrightarrow{l}(x, y))$.
Each of the properties NI^+,...,U^- defines a certain class in the space Π_I, for which the corresponding property is characteristic. Denote these classes as Λ^{NI^+},..., Λ^{U^-}, respectively.
Let us consider mutual relationships of the classes.

Theorem 3.18 *The classes of the rules which satisfy conditions $NI^+, ..., U^-$ are related as it is shown on the Venn diagram in Figure* 3-5.

22 It is obvious that the conclusion of the condition Ne can be written as $(y, x) \in P \Leftrightarrow (w, z) \in P$.

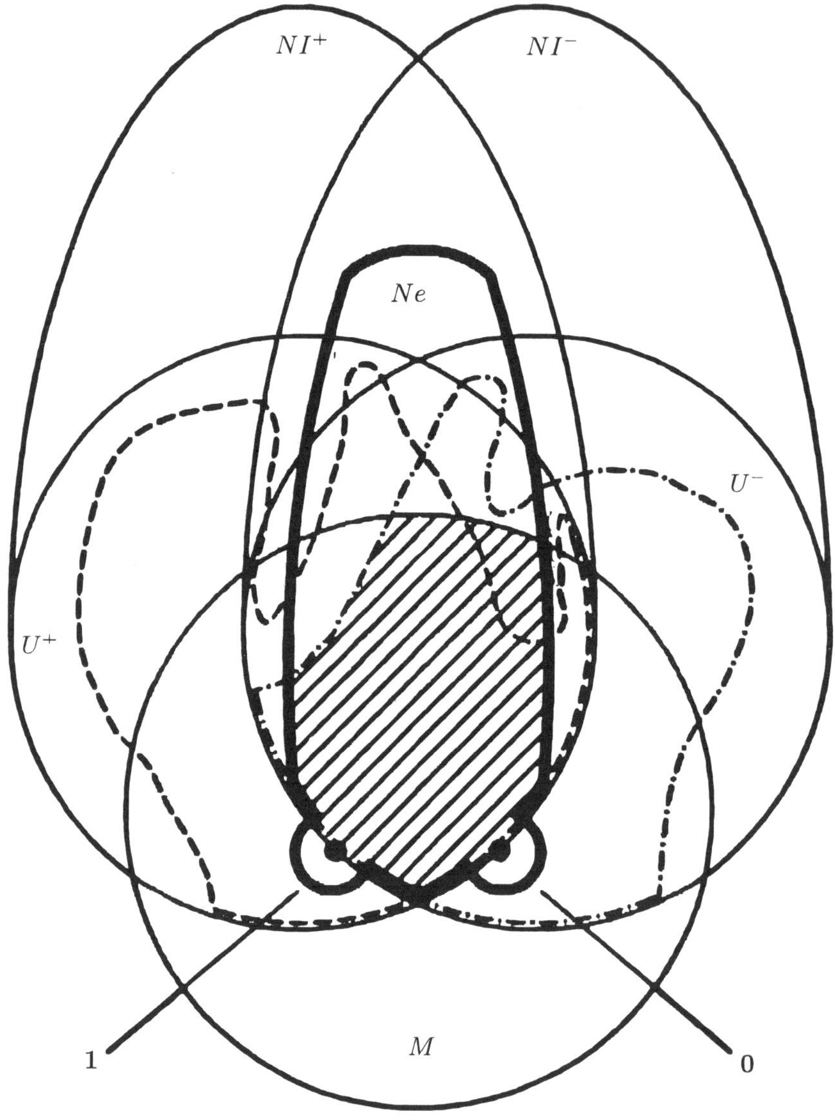

Figure 3-5

The class Λ^{An} has nonempty intersections with all the classes shown in Figure 3-5 and, for simplicity, is omitted. In this Figure the rules **0** and **1** are shown which construct the empty social relation $P = \emptyset$ and the relation $P = A \times A$, respectively, over any profile $\vec{P}$.

Proof. For conditions $NI^+, ..., U^-$ the number of the possible conjuctions and their negations is $2^9 = 512$; of these, however, 432 are empty by virtue of the following relations:

$$(1)\ PC^+ \Rightarrow U^+; (2)\ PC^- \Rightarrow U^-; (3)\ PC^+ \Rightarrow NI^+;$$

$$(4)\ PC^- \Rightarrow NI^-; (5)\ U^+ \Rightarrow NI^+; (6)\ U^- \Rightarrow NI^-;$$

$$(7)\ \overline{NI^+} \cap Ne \Rightarrow M; (8)\ \overline{NI^-} \cap Ne \Rightarrow M;$$

$$(9)\ \overline{NI^-} \cap Ne \Rightarrow PC^+; (10)\ \overline{NI^-} \cap Ne \Rightarrow U^+;$$

$$(11)\ \overline{NI^+} \cap Ne \Rightarrow PC^-; (12)\ \overline{NI^+} \cap Ne \Rightarrow U^-;$$

$$(13)\ \overline{NI^+} \cap Ne \Rightarrow U^+;$$

$$(14)\ \overline{NI^+} \cap \overline{NI^-} \cap Ne = \emptyset;$$

$$(15)\ \overline{PC^-} \cap M \cap Ne \Rightarrow PC^+; (16)\ \overline{U^-} \cap M \cap Ne \Rightarrow PC^+;$$

$$(17)\ \overline{PC^-} \cap M \cap Ne \Rightarrow U^+; (18)\ \overline{U^-} \cap M \cap Ne \Rightarrow U^+;$$

$$(19)\ \overline{NI^-} \cap Ne \Rightarrow An; (20)\ \overline{NI^+} \cap Ne \Rightarrow An;$$

$$(21)\ \overline{NI^+} \cap Ne \Rightarrow U^+; (22)\ \overline{NI^+} \cap Ne \Rightarrow \overline{PC^+};$$

$$(23)\ \overline{U^-} \cap M \cap Ne \Rightarrow An; (24)\ \overline{U} \cap M \Rightarrow \overline{NI}.$$

These relationships are satisfied by the definitions for conditions $NI^+, ..., U^-$. As an example, let us prove relation (12) above. We have $\overline{NI^+} \Rightarrow \exists(x, y) : \Omega(x, y) = \emptyset$, $Ne \Rightarrow \forall(x, y) : \Omega = \emptyset$, i.e., $\overline{NI^+} \cap Ne \Rightarrow \forall(x, y) : \Omega(x, y) = \Omega = \emptyset$; in particular $\forall(x, y) : (\emptyset, N) \notin \Omega$, which is equivalent to condition U^-.
Non-emptiness of the remaining 76 conjunctions of conditions $NI^+, ..., U^-$, which determine the relative locations of the classes $\Lambda^{NI^+}, \ldots\ldots \Lambda^{U^-}$ shown in Figure 3-5, may be cheked with appropriate examples. However, we omit both the conjunctions and the examples proving the non-emptiness of the corresponding classes.
Note that the conjunction

$$\overline{NI^+} \cap NI^- \cap M \cap Ne \cap An \cap PC^- \cap \overline{PC^+} \cap \overline{U^+} \cap U^-$$

determines the constant rule $\mathbf{0}$, while the conjuction

$$NI^+ \cap \overline{NI^-} \cap M \cap Ne \cap An \cap PC^+ \cap \overline{PC^-} \cap U^+ \cap \overline{U^-}$$

determines the constant operator $\mathbf{1}$ ■

Let us introduce some special classes in the space Π_I.

Definition 3.17 A class of rules satisfying the conditions

$$\text{(a) } NI^+ \cap NI^- \cap M \cap Ne \cap PC^-,$$

and

$$\text{(b) } NI^+ \cap NI^- \cap M \cap Ne \cap An \cap PC^-,$$

will be referred to respectively, as,
(a) the *Central*, and (b) the *Symmetrically Central Class* in Π_I.

Denote these Classes by Λ^C and Λ^{SC}, respectively.
The Central Class in Figure 3-5 is hatched.

Two constant rules, $\mathbf{0}$ and $\mathbf{1}$, were introduced above. Remind other two rules, pertaining to Central Class, which play an important role below. The Unanimity rule (denoted by $\mathcal{U}$) is defined to include the pair (x, y) in the relation P if and only if this pair belongs to the relations P_i of all agents. For this rule, obviously,

$$P = \bigcap_{i \in N} P_i.$$

The rule 'One Vote' (denoted as $\mathcal{V}$) is defined to include a pair (x, y) in P if and only if it belongs to the relation P_i of at least one agent $i \in N$, i.e.,

$$P = \bigcup_{i \in N} P_i.$$

Remark. It is worth mentioning here that in [112] two other normative conditions had been studied:
- semi-neutrality

$$\forall (x, y), (x, z) \in A^2 \; \Omega(x, y) = \Omega(x, z);$$

- decisivness

$$\begin{aligned} \forall (x, y) &\in A^2 \text{ and } \forall (\omega_1, \omega_2), (\omega_1, \omega_2') \text{ such that} \\ (\omega_1, \omega_2) &\in \Omega(x, y) \Rightarrow (\omega_1, \omega_2') \in \Omega(x, y). \end{aligned}$$

One can immediately re-write these conditions in terms of Ω–representation.

3.13 Rules from Central Class

This section studies a number of rules from the Central Class specified in the explicit form. In addition to the standard set-theoretical operations $\cup$ and $\cap$, we will use here the operation of *lexicographic composition* of relations, which for two binary relations P_1 and P_2 defines a third one as follows

$$xPy \Leftrightarrow \{xP_1y \text{ or } x\ \bar{P_1}\ y,\ y\ \bar{P_1}\ x,\ \text{but } xP_2y\}$$

In symbolic form, this operation will be denoted as $*$, i.e. $P = P_1 * P_2$.
If I_P is an indifference relation for a given P (i.e., $I_P = A^2 \setminus (P \cup P^{-1})$), the lexicographic composition may be written down as

$$P = P_1 * P_2 = P_1 \cup (I_{P_1} \cap P_2).$$

In the aggregation problem the operation $*$ reveals the inequality of agents: if P_1 is the relation presenting the opinion of the first agent, and P_2 of the second one, then the social decision P contains all pairs from P_1 as well as those pairs (x,y) from P_2 to which agent 1 does not object (the pair (y,x) being absent in P_1).
One can see that the operation $*$ is extendable to any finite number of components.
Using this operation let us introduce various rules from the Central Class Λ^C.

Definition 3.18 The local rule F is called a *hierarchical federation rule* if $P = F(\{P_i\})$ may be defined through the relations P_i as

$$P = \bigcup_{l=1}^{\gamma} \bigcap_{j=1}^{\beta_l} *_{q=1}^{\alpha_j} P_{ljq},\ P_{ljq} \in \{P_i\}_1^n.$$

The hierarchical federation rule defines a social decision as follows: the totality of individuals is divided into γ 'blocks,' which may intersect; the social decision is obtained as the union of the independent decisions of all blocks. In turn, each block decision is obtained as follows: the agents of each block are gathered in a number of subgroups (numbered as $1, ..., \beta_l$), which may intersect as well; the agents in each subgroup are ordered by their 'ranks', the decision being made hierarchically, and the decision of a block reflects the unanimous opinion of all its subgroups.
The grouping of voters into blocks and subgroups which defines a hierarchical federation rule is shown in Figure 3-6. The set N here is depicted in the form of rectangle and includes two blocks, shaded one with vertical and the other with horizontal lines. Block 1 consists of three subgroups S_1, S_2 and S_3, and block 2, of four subgroups S'_1, S'_2, S'_3, and S'_4. The subgroups S_1 and S'_1, S_2 and S'_2, etc., are intersecting. For simplicity, the block subgroups shown in the Figure 3-6 do not intersect, although in general they may.

Definition 3.19 A local rule F is called a *hierarchical representation rule* if $P =$

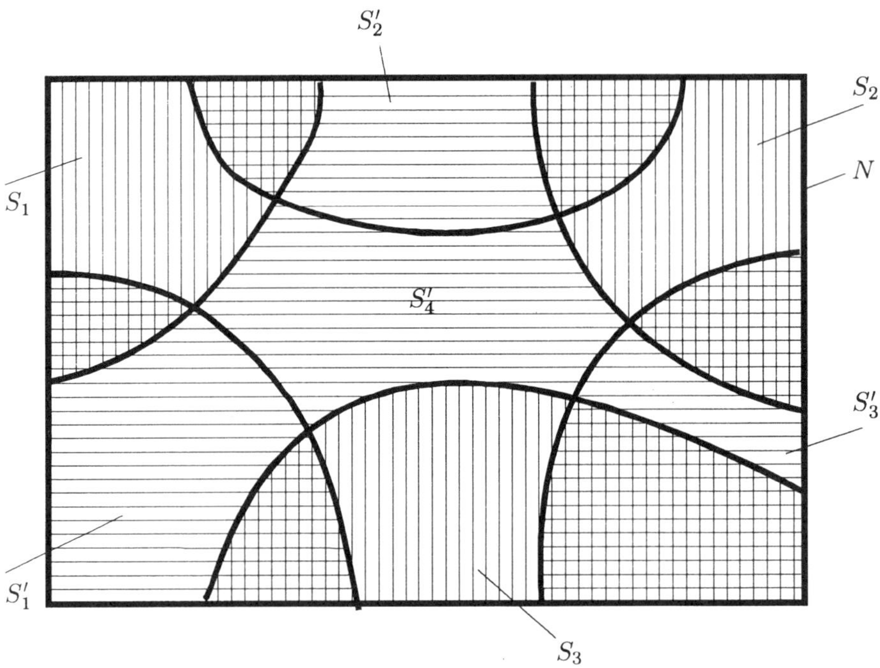

Figure 3-6

$F(\{P_i\})$ may be defined through the relations P_i as

$$P = \bigcap_{i=1}^{\rho} \bigcup_{j=1}^{\sigma_i} *_{q=1}^{\varsigma_j} P_{ijq}.$$

Denote the classes of hierarchical federation and hierarchical representation rules as $\Lambda^{\cup\cap *}$ and $\Lambda^{\cap\cup *}$, respectively.

Theorem 3.19 *The Central Class and the classes of hierarchical federation and hierarchical representation rules in Π_I coincide, i.e.,*

$$\Lambda^C = \Lambda^{\cup\cap *} = \Lambda^{\cap\cup *}.$$

Proof of the Theorem 3.19 is preceeded by the following

Lemma 3.8 *The operation $*$ is distributive from the left with respect to the operation $\cap$.*

Proof. Let $P' = P * (\bigcap_{j=1}^{s} P_j)$ and $P'' = \bigcap_{j=1}^{s}(P * P_j)$. We show that $P' = P''$. Indeed, let $(x, y) \in P'$. Then either $(x, y) \in P$ or else $(x, y) \notin P$, $(y, x) \notin P$, but

$(x,y) \in \bigcap_{j=1}^{s} P_j$. Hence it follows that $(x,y) \in \bigcap_{j=1}^{s}(P * P_j)$, i.e., $(x,y) \in P''$. The converse assertion $(x,y) \in P'' \Rightarrow (x,y) \in P'$ is proved in a similar way.

Let us now prove the theorem. Let $\Omega = \{(\omega_1^1, \omega_2^1), ..., (\omega_1^\lambda, \omega_2^\lambda)\}$ be the list of a local rule F belonging to the Central Class. Denote $\omega_3^j = N \setminus (\omega_1^j \cup \omega_2^j)$, $j = 1, ..., \lambda$, and define the following rule[23]:

$$\widehat{P} = \bigcup_{j=1}^{\lambda} \left\{ \bigcap_{r \in \omega_1^j} P_r \bigcap \left[\bigcap_{q \in \omega_3^j} \left[P_q * \left(\bigcap_{r \in \omega_1^j} P_r \right) \right] \right] \right\} \tag{3.8}$$

Let us show that $\widehat{P} = P = F(\{P_i\})$. Indeed, by the definition of list representation of F $(x,y) \in P \iff \exists j \in [1,\lambda] : V(x,y;\vec{P}) = \omega_1^j$, $V(y,x;\vec{P}) = \omega_2^j$. But the following holds: $\forall i \in N \setminus [V(x,y;\vec{P}) \cup V(y,x;\vec{P})] : (y,x) \notin P_i, (x,y) \notin P_i$. Using (3.8) we obtain $(x,y) \in \cap_{r \in \omega_1^j} P_r$, $(x,y) \in I_q$ for all $q \in \omega_3^j$, and thus $(x,y) \in \widehat{P}$.

Conversely, let $(x,y) \in \widehat{P}$. It follows that there is an index $j \in [1,\lambda]$ such that $(x,y) \in \cap_{r \in \omega_1^j} P_r$ and $(x,y) \in \cap_{r \in \omega_3^j}[P_q * (\cap_{r \in \omega_1^j} P_r)]$, i.e., $\forall q \in \omega_3^j$: $(x,y) \in P_q * (\cap_{r \in \omega_1^j} P_r)$. In this case either $(x,y) \in P_q$, or $(x,y) \notin P_q$ and $(y,x) \notin P_q$. If $(x,y) \in P_q$, then it follows that $V(x,y;\vec{P}) \supset \omega_1^j$, $V(y,x;\vec{P}) = \omega_2^j$, and, by virtue of monotonicity condition, the pair $(V(x,y;\vec{P}), V(y,x;\vec{P})) \in \Omega$, and, consequently, $(x,y) \in P$. In the second case $(x,y) \notin P_q$ and $(y,x) \notin P_q$, and then, obviously, $(x,y) \in P$.

Whether a rule of the type (3.8) belongs to the Central Class can be checked directly.

Let us now use the above Lemma to reduce the rule (3.8) to the form specified in the definition of the hierarchical federation rule. According to the Lemma, we have $\omega_1^j = \{r_s, ..., r_t\}$ and

$$P_q * (\bigcap_{r \in \omega_1^j} P_r) = (P_q * P_{r_1}) \cap ... \cap (P_q * P_{r_t}),$$

with $\omega_1^j = \{r_1, ..., r_t\}$. Then (3.8) can be rewritten as

$$\widehat{P} = \bigcup_{j=1}^{\lambda} \left\{ \bigcap_{r \in \omega_1^j} P_r \bigcap \left[\bigcap_{q \in \omega_3^j} \bigcap_{r \in \omega_1^j} (P_q * P_r) \right] \right\}$$

$$= \bigcup_{j=1}^{\lambda} \left\{ \bigcap_{r \in \omega_1^j} \bigcap_{q \in \omega_3^j} (P_q * P_r) \bigcap \left(\bigcap_{r \in \omega_1^j} P_r \right) \right\},$$

which, provided the necessary re-indexing is done, is exactly the form for the rule hierarchical federation given in the Definition 3.18.

---

23 We shall use the following special re-definition of the operation $\cap$ for the case when $\omega = \emptyset$: $\cap_{q \in \emptyset} P_q = A \times A$. We also use the obvious relationship $(\cap_{r \in \omega} P_r) \cap (A \times A) = \cap_{r \in \omega} P_r$.

We prove now the identity of the classes $\Lambda^{\cup\cap *}$ and $\Lambda^{\cap\cup *}$. Let

$$P = \bigcup_{l=1}^{\gamma} \bigcap_{j=1}^{\beta_l} *_{q=1}^{\alpha_j} P_{ljq}. \tag{3.9}$$

Denote each component of $*$ in (3.9) as P_{lj}^q. Then $P = \bigcup_{l=1}^{\gamma} \bigcap_{j=1}^{\beta_l} P_{lj}^q$, the required assertion following from permutability of the operations $\cup$ and $\cap$ ■

Below a number of particular cases of the hierarchical federation and hierarchical representation rules are considered, and their mutual relationship are found.

Definition 3.20 Let us call a hierarchical federation rule a *hierarchical veto rule*, denoted HV, if its definition contains at least one set of indices $\{1, ..., \alpha_1\}$ such that $P_{ljq} = P_{l'j'q}$, where $q \in \{\{1, ..., \alpha_1\}, l, l' = 1, ..., \gamma,\ j, j' = 1, ..., \beta_l$.

When such a set of indices is unique the rule HV may be written as follows:

$$P = \bigcup_{l=1}^{\gamma} \left[(P_{i_1} * ... * P_{i_k}) \bigcap \left(\bigcap_{j=1}^{\beta_l} *_{q=1}^{\alpha_j} P_{ljq} \right) \right]$$

i.e., each block l includes an isolated group of agents which may veto the decision of any block. The right of veto in this case is given to the agents of the given group by 'seniority'. This rule is a direct generalization of the veto rule treated above for strongly local rules.

Definition 3.21 A hierarchical federation rule is called a *hierarchical oligarchy* (denoted $\cap *$) if in the definition of the hierarchical federation $\gamma = 1$, i.e. if

$$P = \bigcap_{j=1}^{\beta} *_{q=1}^{\alpha_j} P_{jq}.$$

It is interesting to note here that first member in each hierarchical component of the rule plays a role of vetoer in veto-rules for strongly local case. Indeed, she can 'block' any decision (x, y) by choosing (y, x). On the other hand, to enforce a decision (x, y) all first members in each hierarchicl component should accept the decision, and in this sense these agents create the olygarchy.

Definition 3.22 Let us call a hierarchical representation rule a *hierarchical syndicate* (denoted $\cup *$) if $\rho = 1$.

Thus, for the hierarchical syndicate the rule is written as follows:

$$P = \bigcup_{j=1}^{\sigma} *_{q=1}^{\varsigma_j} P_{jq}.$$

Definition 3.23 A hierarchical oligarchy rule with $\beta = 1$ (or, which is the same, a hierarchical syndicate rule for which $\sigma = 1$) will be referred to as a *hierarchical dictator* rule.

In this case

$$P = *_{q=1}^{\alpha} P_q, \; \alpha \leq n.$$

The classes of rules hierarchical oligarchy, hierarchical syndicate, and hierarchical dictator will be denoted as $\Lambda^{\cap *}$, $\Lambda^{\cup *}$, and Λ^*, respectively.

Consider now other particular cases of the hierarchical federation rule, namely those satisfying the condition An of Anonymity, which is met for rules from the Symmetrically Central Class. Let us use list representation of rules for the purpose. As was shown above, the rules from the Central Class have a common list for all pairs (x, y) and satisfies Positive and Negative Non-Imposition, Monotonicity, and Negative Pareto condition. Let us introduce a definition of the Basic list Ω^B for a given list Ω satisfying the above conditions.

Definition 3.24 The pair (ω_1', ω_2') is said to dominate the pair (ω_1, ω_2) if the following inclusions are true

$$\omega_1' \supseteq \omega_1, \omega_2 \subseteq \omega_1,$$

with at least one of the inclusions being strict.

Definition 3.25 Let us call a set of pairs $\Omega^B = \{(\omega_1, \omega_2)\}$ from a given list Ω the *Basic list* for Ω if no pair (ω_1, ω_2) from Ω^B dominates any other pair from Ω^B.

One can see that the Basic list definition may be given not only for the rules from Central Class, but also for any arbitrary list $\Omega(x, y)$. However, it is only for the class of monotonic rules the Basic list may be de fined unambiguously as a set of elements of the list Ω minimal with respect to set inclusion, which are exactly those that form this Basic list. By virtue of this uniqueness we can consider Basic lists when studying list representations of the rules from Λ^C.

Let us now consider the Symmetrically Central Class. In the set of local rules, as in that of strongly local rules, the $k-$majority-type rules appear, but, unlike strongly local rules, there are several modifications of them. Let us define these rules and establish their mutual relationships as well as their location in the Symmetrically Central Class.

Definition 3.26 A rule $F \in \Lambda^C$ will be referred to as a $(k_1, k_2)-$*majority* rule (denoted as $(k_1, k_2) - maj$) if the Basic list Ω^B for it meets the following condition $\forall(\omega_1, \omega_2) \in \Omega^B$:

$$card(\omega_1) = k_1, card(\omega_2) = k_2 \Rightarrow \forall(\omega_1', \omega_2') :$$
$$card(\omega_1') = k_1, card(\omega_2') = k_2, (\omega_1', \omega_2') \in \Omega^B.$$

Definition 3.27 A $(k_1, k_2)-$majority rule will be referred to as an *absolute* $k-$*majority* (denoted as kM) if the sets ω_1 and ω_2 in its definition meets the condition $\omega_1 \cup \omega_2 = N$, or, which is the same, $k_1 + k_2 = n$, $k_1 = k$.

Definition 3.28 A $(k_1, k_2)-$majority rule will be referred to as a *relative* $k-$*majority* (denoted as RkM) if in its definition the following condition holds: $\forall(\omega_1, \omega_2) \in \Omega^B : \omega_2 = \emptyset,\ card(\omega_1) = k_1$, or, which is the same $k_1 = k,\ k_2 = 0$.

The newly introduced general (k_1, k_2)-majority rule with its subtypes of absolute k-majority and relative k-majority can be easily interpreted. Thus, using a (k_1, k_2)-majority rule, a decision is made (the pair (x, y) is included in the social binary relation P) if $n_1 \geq k_1$ agents vote for this decision and $n_2 \leq k_2$ vote against it (with the remaining $n - (n_1, n_2)$ agents abstaining from voting). Of course, when $k_1 \leq k_2$ the term "majority" is used here conditionally.
In the case of an absolute k-majority rule a decision is made if it is supported by $n_1 \geq k$ agents. The remaining $n - n_1$ agents may vote against this decision or abstain. The term 'majority' then actually can be used if $k \geq \lceil n/2 \rceil$, i.e. if more than one half of the agents support the decision.

Finally, the relative k-majority rule imply that the decision is made if it is supported by $n_1 \geq k$ agents while the remaining $n - n_1$ agents abstain (no votes against the decision are permitted). This type of rules leads to a situation described in [243] that is paradoxical in a certain sense. Consider the relative l-majority rule. A pair (x, y) in this case will be included in the social decision P if there is at least an agent who selects this pair, all others being indifferent to this decision. Then, this decision privately made by a single member of society becomes the social decision, even though it may be more appropriate to count the social decision as 'indifferent'.
Note that the hierarchical federation rule and its subtypes were introduced in Definition 3.18 to 3.23 explicitly with the use of operations $\cup$, $\cap$, and $*$, while the (k_1, k_2)-majority rule and its subtypes employed the list representation. From the proof of Theorem 3.19, one can obtain the explicit form of representation of a (k_1, k_2)-majority rule. The explicit form for a relative k-majority rule and an absolute k-majority rule is established below. The use of list forms, however, gives a better idea of these rules than the use of their explicit notation.
Denote by $\Lambda^{(k_1, k_2)}$, Λ^{kM}, and Λ^{RkM}, the classes of (k_1, k_2)-majority, absolute k-majority, and relative k-majority rules, respectively.

Let us finally introduce the rules which is a direct generalization of the (k_1, k_2)-majority rules.

Definition 3.29 A rule F from the Central Class Λ^C is referred to as a τ *system of* (k_1, k_2)*-majorities rule* (denoted as $\tau - (k_1, k_2)$) if its Basic list Ω^B satisfies the following condition:

$$\forall(\omega_1, \omega_2) \in \Omega^B : card(\omega_1) = k_1^t, card(\omega_2) = k_2^t, \ (t = 1, ..., \tau) \Rightarrow$$

$$\forall(\omega_1', \omega_2') : card(\omega_1') = k_1^t, card(\omega_2') = k_2^t, \ (\omega_1', \omega_2') \in \Omega^B$$

It should be kept in mind that from the definition of the Basic list Ω^B it follows that if $k_1^i \geq k_1^j$ then $k_2^i > k_2^j$, and if $k_2^i \leq k_2^j$ then $k_1^i < k_1^j$, i.e., the τ system of (k_1, k_2)-majorities rule consist of (k_1, k_2)-majority rules of a specific type. For instance, if $\tau = 3$, one such rule is the $(3, 2)$, $(4, 3)$, $(7, 6)$ -majorities rule, i.e., the decision is adopted if at least 3 agents select it and not more than 2 vote against it, or at least 4 agents vote for and not more than 3 agents vote against it, etc.
The class of all $\{\tau - (k_1, k_2)\}$ rules will be denoted as $\Lambda^{\{\tau-(k_1,k_2)\}}$.
Theorem 3.20 given below will establish the relationship between the introduced class $\Lambda^{\{\tau-(k_1,k_2)\}}$ and the Symmetrically Central Class.

Theorem 3.20 *The Symmetrically Central Class in the space* Π_I *of local rules coincides with the class of* τ *system of* (k_1, k_2)*-majorities rules, i.e.,* $\Lambda^{SC} = \Lambda^{\{\tau-(k_1,k_2)\}}$.

Proof. Let $\Omega^B = \{(\omega_1^1, \omega_2^1), ..., (\omega_1^\lambda, \omega_2^\lambda)\}$ be the basic list of some rule from the Symmetrically Central Class. Consider an arbitrary element of this list $\{\omega_1^j, \omega_2^j\}$ and a one-to-one mapping η of the set N onto N. Then, by virtue of condition An, there exist sets

$$\widetilde{\omega}_1^j = \{i \mid l = \omega_1^j, \ i \in \eta(l)\} \text{ and } \widetilde{\omega}_2^j = \{i \mid l \in \omega_2^j, \ i = \eta(l)\}$$

for which $card(\widetilde{\omega}_1^j) = card(\omega_1^j)$, $card(\widetilde{\omega}_2^j) = card(\widetilde{\omega}_2^j)$, and $(\widetilde{\omega}_1^j, \widetilde{\omega}_1^j) \in \Omega^B$. Since the condition An is defined for arbitrary mappings of the set N onto itself, it is evident that this list is exactly the list of the $\{(k_1, k_2)\}$-majority rule. Considering the pairs (ω_1, ω_2) from Ω^B with different cardinalities ω_1 and ω_2, one can establish that the list Ω^B consists of pairs which define different kinds of (k_1, k_2)-majority rules, i.e., a $\{(k_1, k_2)^\tau\}$-majority rule. The proof of the fact that a $\{(k_1, k_2)^\tau\}$-majority rule belongs to the Symmetrically Central Class is obvious. ■

Let us now consider the absolute k-majority rule. It follows directly from the proof of Theorem 3.19, in which the elements of list Ω were used to reconstruct the hierarchical federation rule, that the relation P for an absolute k-majority rule may be obtained in the following manner:

$$P = \bigcup_{j=1}^{l} \bigcap_{i \in \omega_1^j} P_i$$

where $\forall j = 1, ..., l$, $card(\omega_1^j) = k$, and $l = \binom{n}{k}$ is the number of combinations of n elements taken k at a tame. This representation is identical to that given above for the k-majority strongly local rule.
This is not the only case where the type of the local rule may be used to obtain an explicit representation of strongly local rules considered in Section 3.4. Other particular cases may be obtained from hierarchical federation and hierarchical representation rules provided each subgroup defining blocks contains exactly one agent, i.e., provided $\alpha_j = 1$ in the definition of the rule $\cup \cap *$, and provided $\sigma_j = 1$ in the definition of $\cap \cup *$.
Let us establish mutual relationships between the rules introduced in this Section. These relationships are stated in the following theorem.

Theorem 3.21 *The relation between the hierarchical federation and hierarchical representation classes of rules, their various subclasses, and the Central and Symmetrically Central Classes are as shown at Figures*[24] *3-7 and 3-8.*

Proof. Theorem 3.21 as depicted at Figures 3-7 and 3-8 states more than 20 assertions. The majority of them are direct corollaries of Definitions 3.18–3.23 and 3.26–3.29 for the rules considered. We need actually prove only the following assertions (which do not follow directly from these definitions):
(i) $\Lambda^{SC} \cap \Lambda^{\cap *} = \Lambda^{RkM}$, (ii) $\Lambda^{SC} \cap \Lambda^{\cup *} = \{\mathcal{V}\}$.
Let us prove them consequently.
(i): Let

$$P = (P_{11} * ... * P_{1k}) \cap ... \cap (P_{r1} * ... * P_{rk}) \tag{3.10}$$

Introduce the relation of dominance G_i for the indices within one component of the formula (3.10). Namely, let us say that index j dominates over index s (denoted as jG_is) if index j in the ith parenthesis precedes index s. The totality $D(i, s)$ of indices dominating over index s in the ith parenthesis will be called the dominating set of index s, i.e.

$$D(i, s) = \{j \mid jG_is\}.$$

The set $D^{-1}(i, s)$ will be defined as

$$D^{-1}(i, s) = \{j \mid sG_ij\}.$$

Denote by $\Psi(i)$ the totality of indices in the ith parenthesis of the rule (3.10). It may be easily seen that the element (ω_1, ω_2) of the list Ω^B in (3.10) is defined as follows:

$$\omega_1 = \{s_1, ..., s_r\},$$

where $s_i \in \Psi(i)$, $i = 1, ..., r$, i.e., the set ω_1 consists of indices taken one from each parenthesis. The set ω_2 is defined as follows:

[24] At these Figures the subclasses of the Central Class for strongly local rules are also shown.

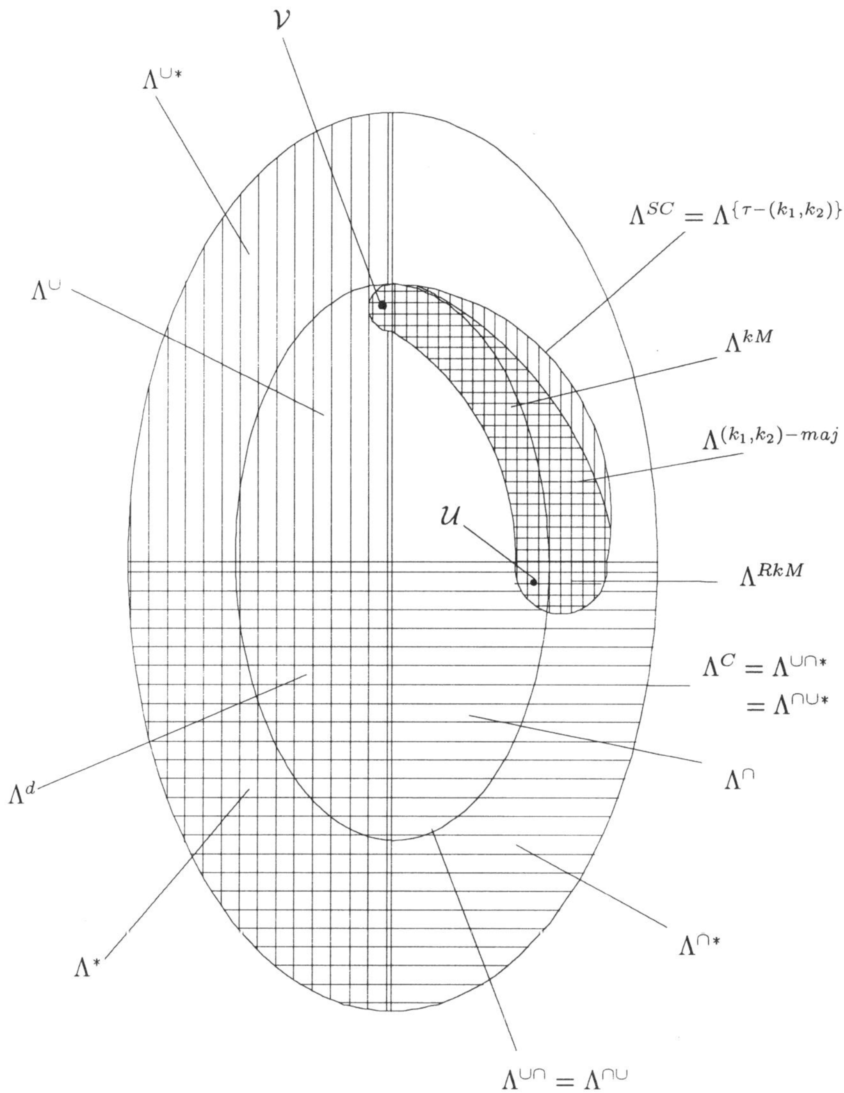

Figure 3-7

$$\omega_2 = \bigcup_i D^{-1}(i, s_i) \setminus \bigcup_i D(i, s_i).$$

Now let ω_2 for some pair $(\omega_1, \omega_2) \in \Omega^B$ be non-empty, i.e., let there be some $l \in \omega_1$

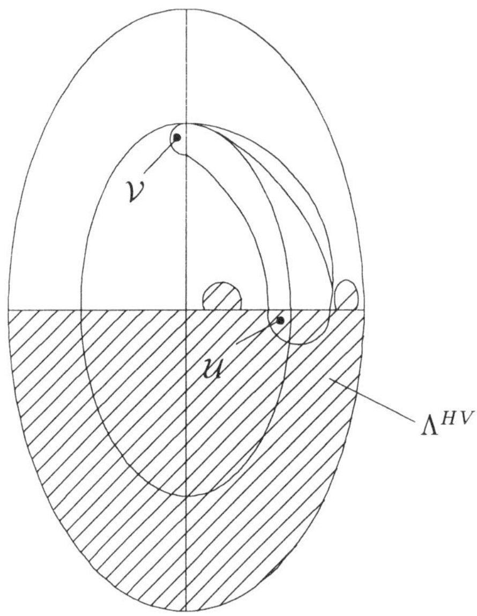

Figure 3-8

and $j \in \omega_2$. Then, by virtue of condition An, the pair $(\widetilde{\omega}_1, \widetilde{\omega}_2)$, where $\widetilde{\omega}_1 = (\omega_1 \setminus \{l\}) \cup \{j\}$ and $\widetilde{\omega}_2 = (\omega_2 \setminus \{j\}) \cup \{l\}$ belongs to Ω^B. But in this case there must exist a parenthesis $\Psi(i)$ such that $j \in \Psi(i)$ and $l\overline{G}_i j$. Consider two cases:
(a) $l \in \Psi(i)$. But then $jG_i l$ and $j \notin \omega_2$;
(b) $l \notin \Psi(i)$. Then an index $t \in \Psi(i)$ does exist such that $tG_i j$ and $t \in \omega_1$.
Since we consider a one-to-one mapping η of the form $\forall s \neq i,\ s \neq j : \eta(s) = s$, $\eta(i) = j$, $\eta(j) = i$, we have $j \notin \omega_2$, which proves the first part of assertion (i). Any rule $F \in \Lambda^{\cap *} \cap \Lambda^{An}$ was shown to be representable in the form of a relative k-majority rule. We show now that any rule $F \in \Lambda^{RkM}$ may be represented as an hierarchical olygarchy rule. Let a certain k, $1 \leq k \leq n$, be fixed. Consider an arbitrary set $R(k)$ consisting of k indices i_1,..., i_k, and the set $Q(k) = N \setminus R(k)$ containing all the other $n-k$ indices from N. Using the set $Q(k)$, let us now define $n-k$ ordered sets $S_1(k)$, ..., $S_{n-k}(k)$, each containing all indices of the $Q(k)$ but having different indices from $Q(k)$ as the first index in each set $S_l(k)$ (the order of all other indices playing no role at all). Construct the relation $P^{(k)}$ as follows:

$$P^{(k)} = \bigcap_{R(k)} \bigcap_{j \in R(k)} \bigcap_{l=1}^{n-k} \left(*_{i \in S_l(k)} P_i * P_j \right).$$

Show that the relation $P^{(k)}$ may be realized by a relative k-majority rule. Let, indeed, $(x, y) \in P = F^{(k)}(\{P_i\})$, where $F^{(k)}$ denotes an $RkM-$rule. It follows then that there are at least k indices $i_1,..., i_k$ such that $\forall j = 1,...,k$: $(x,y) \in P_{ij}$ and $\forall t \in N$: $(y,x) \notin P_t$. Consider $R(k) = \{i_1,...,i_k\}$. Then, by virtue of the condition $\forall j \in R(k) : (x,y) \in P_j$ we have $\forall i \in S_l(k) : (y,x) \notin P_i$ and

$$(x,y) \in \bigcap_{j \in R(k)} \bigcap_{l=1}^{n-k} \left(*_{i \in S_l(k)} P_i * P_j \right).$$

By construction, for all other $R(k')$ we have $j \in S_l(k')$, and consequently $(x,y) \in P^{(k)}$.
Let $(x,y) \notin P = F^{(k)}(\{P_i\})$. Two cases are possible:
(1) There is some $i \in V(y,x;\vec{P}) \neq \emptyset$. But then $i \in S_l(k')$ for some set $R(k)$, and therefore $(x,y) \notin *_{i \in S_l(k)} P_i * P_j$ and $(x,y) \notin P^{(k)}$;
(2) $V(y,x;\vec{P}) = \emptyset$, but $V(x,y;\vec{P}) = \{i_1,...,i_r\}, r < k$. Consider $R(k) \supset \{i_1,...,i_r\}$. Then

$$(x,y) \notin \bigcap_{j \in R(k)} \bigcap_{l=1}^{n-k} \left(*_{i \in S_l(k)} P_i * P_j \right),$$

and consequently, $(x,y) \notin P^{(k)}$. The first assertion of Theorem 3.21 is proved.
(ii): Let us show that the basic list of any hierarchical syndicate rule belonging to the Symmetrically Central Class consist of pairs (ω_1, ω_2) of the form $\omega_1 = \{l\}$ and $\omega_2 = N \setminus \{l\}$. Indeed, consider a rule

$$P = (P_{11} * ... * P_{1q}) \cup ... \cup (P_{r1} * ... * P_{rq}).$$

Its basic list is for obvious reasons constructed as

$$\omega_1 = \{l\}, l \in \Psi(j) \text{ for some } j;$$

$$\omega_2 = D^{-1}(j,l) \cup \left(\bigcup_{i \neq j} \Psi(i) \right).$$

Let now $\omega_2 \subset N \setminus \{l\}$, i.e., some $q \notin \omega_2$, $q \in N$ exists. Consider the one-to one mapping η of N onto itself of the following form: $\eta(q) = l$, $\eta(l) = q$; $\forall s \neq l$, $s \neq q$: $\eta(s) = s$. According to condition An, Ω^B should contain the pair $(\widetilde{\omega}_1, \widetilde{\omega}_2)$ where $\widetilde{\omega}_1 = \{q\}$. Since $q \notin \omega_2$, then $q \notin \bigcup_{i \neq j} \Psi(i)$ and $q \notin D^{-1}(j,l)$. Hence it follows that[25] $q \in \Psi(j)$ and qP_jl. But then with any ω_2' we shall have $l \in \omega_2$ in the pair $(\{q\}, \omega_2')$, which proves the assertion.
Next, it is evident that for any $l \in N$ a pair of the Basic list with $\omega_1 = \{l\}$ exists, i.e., that Ω^B has the form $\{(\{1\}, N \setminus \{1\}), ..., (\{n\}, N \setminus \{n\})\}$, which exactly coincides with the definition of the rule $\mathcal{V}$ ('One vote for'). ■

[25] The case $q \notin \Psi(j)$ is omitted, since in this case the voter q has no influence on the decision. The set N in this case can be replaced by the set $N' = N \setminus \{q\}$.

The vertical shading on Figure 3-7 shows class of hierarchical syndicate rules while the horizontal shading shows the hierarchical olygarchies rules. The inclined shading shows the $\{\tau - (k_1, k_2)\}$- -majority rules, and the crossed shading shows (k_1, k_2)-majority rules.

Some interesting results can be obtained from Theorem 3.21 pertaining to the voting systems which satisfy Anonymity condition. Thus, (k_1, k_2)-majority rules can be 'divided' into two subclasses: the proper (k_1, k_2)-majority rules, and the absolute k-majority rules. The relative k-majority rules form a proper subclass of hierarchical oligarchy rules with the intersection of classes Λ^{RkM} and $\Lambda^{\cap *}$ consisting of just a single element, the Unanimity rule $\mathcal{U}$.
The hierarchical syndicate rules show a different picture: the only rule of this type which also satisfies Anonymity condition An is that of $\mathcal{V}$ ('One Vote').

3.13.1 Representation of neutral rules

Let us at the end of this Section extend our analysis and give a representation of neutral rules, i.e., rules which satisfy only Neutrality condition Ne.

Theorem 3.22 *An arbitrary rule $F \in \Lambda^{Ne}$ with the list Ω generates the resulting relation $P = F(\{P_i\})$ in the form*

$$P = \bigcup_{i=1}^{t} \bigcap_{j=1}^{\beta_i} *_{l=1}^{\alpha_j} P_{ijl}^{\delta_{ijl}} * \Psi, \tag{3.11}$$

where δ_{ijl} is equal to ± 1, and Ψ is equal to $A \times A$ if $(\emptyset, \emptyset) \in \Omega$ or to the empty set if $(\emptyset, \emptyset) \notin \Omega$.
Conversely, each operator F generating the relation P in the form (3.11) belongs to the class Λ^{Ne}.

Proof. Let us consider without loss of generality the operator F with $\Omega = \{(\omega_1, \omega_2)\}$. Denote $\widetilde{P} = (\cap_{i \in \omega_1} P_i) \cap (\cap_{j \in \omega_2} P_j)$ and $\omega_3 = N \backslash (\omega_1 \cup \omega_2)$, and construct the relation

$$P' = \left[\bigcap_{l \in \omega_3} (P_l * \widetilde{P})\right] \cap \left[\bigcap_{l \in \omega_3} (P_l^{-1} * \widetilde{P})\right] \tag{3.12}$$

Let us show that $(x, y) \in P$ iff $(x, y) \in P'$.
(a) $(x, y) \in P$ iff $V(x, y; \{P_i\}) = \omega_1$, $V(y, x; \{P_i\}) = \omega_2$. Then $(x, y) \in P'$ by construction.
(b) $(x, y) \notin P \Rightarrow (x, y) \notin P'$. Consider the case where there exist $i \in \omega_3$ such that $V(x, y; \{P_i\}) = \omega_1 \cup \{i\}$, $V(y, x; \{P_i\}) = \omega_2$. In this case (x, y) belongs to the first component of the formula (3.12) but not to the second one, for $(x, y) \in P^{-1}$, and hence $(x, y) \notin P'$.
Other cases in which $(x, y) \notin P$ can be treated analogously.

The proof of the first statement of the Theorem 3.22 for an arbitrary list $\Omega = \{(\omega_1^i, \omega_2^i)\}_1^p$ easily follows from the construction of the relation $P'' = \cup_{i=1}^p P_i'$, where each component P_i' is constructed according to (3.12) for each compenent (ω_1^i, ω_2^i) independently, and where if, for the pair (ω_1^i, ω_2^i)in Ω, all pairs dominated by it (see Definition 3.24) are also in Ω, then the component P_i' for that pair is designed by the scheme given in the proof of Theorem 3.19. Then, making use of the left-hand distributivity of the operation $*$ with respect to the operation $\cap$ the first statement of the Theorem 3.22 can be obtained.
The second statement of the theorem can be proved directly ■

Let us note here that if the operator F satisfies Neutrality and does not satify condition NI^+ then we can obtain the constant rule **0**; when the condition NI^- is violated, then the constant rule **1** arises.

3.14 Rationality constraints

The two classes Q_d and Q_r in $\mathcal{B}$ will be called closed with respect to a local rule F if for any profile $\{P_i\}$ such that $\forall i\ P_i \in Q_d$ the following holds $F(\{P_i\}) \in Q_r$. The two classes Q_d and Q_r in $\mathcal{B}$ will be called closed with respect to a class $\mathcal{F}$ of local rules if for any rule $F \in \mathcal{F}$ and for any profile $\{P_i\}$ such that $\forall i\ P_i \in Q_d$ the following holds $F(\{P_i\}) \in Q_r$.
The maximal in set-theoretic sense class of rules relative to which the classes Q_d and Q_r are closed will be called the *complete class of closedness* for a pair (Q_d, Q_r) and will be denoted as $\Lambda(Q_d, Q_r)$.
Since as Q_d we consider only Q_d =WO, the complete class of closedness for the pair $\Lambda(\mathrm{WO}, Q_r)$ will be denoted as $\Lambda(Q_r)$.
In this part of Chapter 3 individual opinions are presented by binary relations which meet the conditions of acyclicity, transitivity, and negative transitivity, i.e., the set of weak orders, WO, will be taken as the domain Q_d, while the sets of all acyclic relations, AR, all transitive relations, $\mathcal{T}$, all strict partial orders, SPO, together with $\mathcal{WO}$, will be taken as the range Q_r. Since only the class $\mathcal{WO}$ is used for Q_d below, the complete class $\Lambda(Q_d, Q_r)$ will be denoted, for brevity, as $\Lambda(Q_r)$, specifying the corresponding class Q_r. In choosing classes Q_d and Q_r in the above manner we always consider the case $Q_d \subseteq Q_r$, which reflects the natural idea that the relation corresponding to an individual may represent the opinion of the society as well.

3.14.1 Class $\Lambda(\mathcal{AR})$

We introduce this list representation characterizing rules from the class $\Lambda(\mathcal{AR})$:

(C1) For any q, $1 < q \leq m$, for any different $x_1, ..., x_q \in A$ and any (ω_1^1, ω_2^1),...,(ω_1^q, ω_2^q) such that $(\omega_1^1, \omega_2^1) \in \Omega(x_1, x_2)$, ..., $(\omega_1^{q-1}, \omega_2^{q-1}) \in \Omega(x_{q-1}, x_q)$, $(\omega_1^q, \omega_2^q) \in \Omega(x_q, x_1)$, at least one of the following two expressions hold

$$\omega_1^i \not\subseteq \bigcup_{j \neq i} \omega_2^j \text{ for some } i \in \{1, ..., q\}, \tag{3.13}$$

or

$$\omega_2^i \not\subseteq \bigcup_{j \neq i} \omega_1^j \text{ for some } i \in \{1, ..., q\}. \tag{3.14}$$

Theorem 3.23 [112] *A local rule F belongs to the complete class of closedness $\Lambda(\mathcal{AR})$ with $Q_d = \mathcal{WO}$ if and only if its Ω–representation satisfies condition (C1).*

Proof. We will repeat the original proof given in [112] modified in the notation of this book.
Two lemmas will be proved before the proof of the theorem.

Lemma 3.9 *Suppose (3.13) and (3.14) are false. Then for all $l \in \{1, ..., p\}$, $i \in \omega_2^l \Rightarrow \exists j \neq l$ with $i \in \omega_1^j$, and $i \in \omega_1^l \Rightarrow \exists j \neq l$ with $i \in \omega_2^l$.*

Proof. If $i \in \omega_2^l$ and $i \notin \omega_1^j$ for all $j \neq l$, then (3.13) holds. If $i \in \omega_1^l$ and $i \notin \omega_2^j$ for all $j \neq l$, then (3.14) holds. Lemma is proved.

Lemma 3.10 *Suppose $x_1, ..., x_p$ are distinct alternatives in A and that, with $x_{p+1} = x_1$, P' is an asymmetric binary relation that is included in $\cup_{j=1}^p \{(x_j, x_{j+1}), (x_{j+1}, x_j)\}$ and satisfies the following: for all $l \in \{1, ..., p\}$:*

$$(i)\ x_{l+1} P' x_l \Rightarrow \exists j \neq l \text{ with } x_j P' x_{j+1};$$

$$(ii)\ x_l P' x_{l+1} \Rightarrow \exists j \neq l \text{ with } x_{j+1} P' x_j.$$

Then there is an asymmetric weak order P on $\{x_1, ..., x_p\}$ such that

$$P' = P \bigcap \left(\bigcup_{j=1}^{p} \{(x_j, x_{j+1}), (x_{j+1}, x_j)\} \right) \tag{3.15}$$

Proof. Given the lemma's hypothesis let

$$L_1 = \{l \in \{1, ..., p\} : x_l P' x_{l+1}\},$$
$$L_2 = \{l \in \{1, ..., p\} : x_{l+1} P' x_l\},$$
$$L_3 = \{1, ..., p\} \setminus (L_1 \cup L_2).$$

Then $L_1 \cap L_2 = \emptyset$ by asymmetry, and (i) and (ii) imply that $L_1 = \emptyset \Leftrightarrow L_2 = \emptyset$. Note that $P = \emptyset$ satisfies (3.15) if $L_1 = L_2 = \emptyset$. Let us denote as I' the symmetric component of P' on $\{1, ..., p\}$. Construct now a partition of $\{1, ..., p\}$ into subsets $Y_1, Y_2, ..., Y_M$ such that x_l and x_{l+1} are in the same Y_j if and only if $x_l I' x_{l+1}$, and such that $x_1 \in Y_1$ with $x_{l+1} \in Y_{j+1}$ if $\{x_l \in Y_j$, not $(x_{l+1} I' x_l)$, $j < M$ and $l < p\}$.

Note that $M = 1 \Leftrightarrow L_1 = \emptyset$. Y_1 might contain $x_p, x_{p-1}, \ldots$, as well as $x_2, x_3, \ldots$. If $p = 3$, $x_1 I' x_2, x_2 I' x_3$ and not $(x_3 I' x_1)$ then (i) or (ii) will be violated. Next, let us define Q' on $\{Y_1, \ldots, Y_M\}$ by

$$Y_j Q' Y_k \Leftrightarrow x_\alpha P' x_\beta \text{ for some } x_\alpha \in Y_j, x_\beta \in Y_k.$$

Then Q' is asymmetric and, with $Y_{M+1} = Y_1$, we have $Y_j Q' Y_{j+1}$ for some $j \in \{1, \ldots, M\}$ if and only if $Y_{k+1} Q' Y_k$ for some $k \in \{1, \ldots, M\}$. Moreover, for each $j \in \{1, \ldots, M\}$, either $Y_j Q' Y_{j+1}$ or $Y_{j+1} Q' Y_j$, and if $|k - j| > 1$ and $\{j, k\} \neq \{1, M\}$ then neither $Y_j Q' Y_k$ nor $Y_k Q' Y_j$. Next, let R' be the transitive closure of Q'. Then R' is transitive by definition and, because of the properties for Q' that were noted above, R' is asymmetric. Hence R' is an asymmetric partial order. It then follows from Szpilrajn's extension theorem (see Chapter 2) that there is a linear order R on $\{Y_1, \ldots, Y_M\}$ that includes R'. Given such an R, define P on $\{x_1, \ldots, x_m\}$ by

$$x_\alpha P x_\beta \Leftrightarrow Y_j R Y_k \text{ when } x_\alpha \in Y_j, x_\beta \in Y_k.$$

Then P is an asymmetric weak order on $\{x_1, \ldots, x_m\}$. Moreover, if $x_k P' x_{k+1}$ and $x_k \in Y_j$, then $x_{k+1} \in Y_{j+1}$ (recall that $Y_{M+1} = Y_1$), hence $Y_j Q' Y_{j+1}$, hence $Y_j R' Y_{j+1}$, hence $Y_j R Y_{j+1}$, hence $x_k P x_{k+1}$; similarly, if $x_{k+1} P' x_k$ then $x_{k+1} P x_k$; and, if $x_k I' x_{k+1}$, then x_k and x_{k+1} are in the same Y_j and therefore $x_k I x_{k+1}$. Therefore P satisfies (3.15). Lemma is proved.

Now we can prove the theorem. Suppose first that there exists a profile $\overrightarrow{P}$ and distinct $x_1, \ldots, x_p$ ($p > 2$ since $P = F(\overrightarrow{P})$ is asymmetric) such that $x_1 P x_2 P \ldots P x_p P x_1$. Then, with $(\omega_1^k, \omega_2^k) \in \Omega(x_k, x_{k+1})$ for $k < p$, and $(\omega_1^p, \omega_2^p) \in \Omega(x_p, x_1)$, the condition (C1), if true, requires that either $(\exists i \in N)(\exists k \in \{1, \ldots, p\})$ with $i \in \omega_1^k$ and $i \notin \cup_{j \neq k} \omega_2^j$ - in which case $x_1 R_i x_2 R_i \ldots R_i x_p R_i x_1$ and $x_k P_i x_{k+1}$, which contradicts the assumption that P_i is an asymmetric weak order - or else $(\exists i \in N)(\exists k \in \{1, \ldots, p\})$ with $i \in \omega_2^k$ and $i \notin \cup_{j \neq k} \omega_1^j$ which similarly contradicts weak order for P_i. Hence condition (C1) is violated.

Suppose now that condition (C1) does not hold, i.e., both conditions (3.13) and (3.14) are violated. Then let $\overrightarrow{P} = (P_1', \ldots, P_n')$ be a profile such that

$$P_i' \subseteq \bigcup_{j=1}^{p} \{(x_j, x_{j+1}), (x_{j+1}, x_j)\} \text{ for each } i \in N$$

and $(\omega_1^k, \omega_2^k) \in V(x_k, x_{k+1}; \overrightarrow{P})$ for $k = 1, \ldots, p$, with $x_{p+1} = x_1$. Then by Lemma 3.9, for all $i \in N$ and for all $k \in \{1, \ldots, p\}$, $x_{k+1} P_i' x_k \Rightarrow \exists j \neq k$ with $x_j P_i' x_{j+1}$; and $x_k P' x_{k+1} \Rightarrow \exists j \neq k$ with $x_{j+1} P_i' x_j$. Hence, by Lemma 3.10, for each $i \in N$ there is an asymmetric weak order P_i on $\{x_1, \ldots, x_p\}$ that satisfies

$$P_i' = P_i \bigcap \left[\bigcup_{j=1}^{p} \{(x_j, x_{j+1}), (x_{j+1}, x_j)\} \right].$$

Extend P_i to all A by making all alternatives in $A \setminus \{x_1, ..., x_p\}$ indifferent to one another and less preferred than everything in $\{x_1, ..., x_p\}$. Each P_i thus extended is therefore an asymmetric weak order on A so that $P_i \in \mathcal{WO}$ for any[26] $i \in N$. In addition, property (3.15) for each i implies that

$$V(x_k, x_{k+1}; \overrightarrow{P}) = (\omega_1^k, \omega_2^k) \text{ for } k = 1, ..., p.$$

Hence using Ω-representation of F we get

$$x_1 P x_2 P ... P x_p P x_1,$$

which contradicts acyclicity assumption ■

Using the condition (C1), one may locate the above class $\Lambda(\mathcal{AR})$ on the Venn diagram plotted to show the mutual relations among the classes Λ^{NI^+},..., Λ^{U^-}.

Theorem 3.24 *The intersection of the class $\Lambda(\mathcal{AR})$ with the classes Λ^{NI^+}, ..., Λ^{U^-} is as in Figure 3-9.*

Proof. The following relations hold:

$$(1)\ \Lambda^{NI^+} \cap \Lambda^{\overline{NI^-}} \cap \Lambda(\mathcal{AR}) = \emptyset;$$
$$(2)\ \Lambda^{U^+} \cap \Lambda^{\overline{U^-}} \cap \Lambda(\mathcal{AR}) = \emptyset;$$
$$(3)\ \Lambda^{PC^+} \cap \Lambda^{\overline{PC^-}} \cap \Lambda(\mathcal{AR}) = \emptyset.$$

Let us prove them.

(1) Let $\Omega(x,y) = T$; then $\forall \{P_i\} : (x,y) \in P$. It follows from condition NI^+ that $\forall (x,y)\ \Omega(x,y) \neq \emptyset$, i.e. $\exists \{P_i\} : (y,x) \in P = F(\{P_i\})$, which means that $P \notin \mathcal{AR}$.

(2) $F \in \Lambda^{U^-}$ implies that $\exists (x,y) : (\emptyset, N) \in \Omega(x,y)$, and $F \in \Lambda^{U^+}$ implies that $\forall (x,y) : (N, \emptyset) \in \Omega(x,y)$, Consider a profile $\{P_i\}$ such that $\forall i \in N : (x,y) \in P_i$. Then $(x,y) \in P$ and $(y,x) \in P$.

(3) Similar to (2).

These conditions exclude 27 conjunctions from the total of 76 possible ones (see the proof of Theorem 3.18). The remaining 49 conjunctions determine non-empty classes of rules, as may be proved by examples. By examples it can also be shown that the class $\Lambda(\mathcal{AR})$ does not cover any of the classes specified by these nonempty conjuctions. ■

3.14.2 Classes $\Lambda(\mathcal{T})$ and $\Lambda(\mathcal{SPO})$

Let us now analyze relations among the classes Λ^{NI^+},.......,Λ^{U^-}, and $\Lambda(\mathcal{T})$ and $\Lambda(\mathcal{SPO})$. A number of the statements must first be proved for this purpose. In these statements the results

$$\Lambda(\mathcal{LO}, \mathcal{T}) \cap \Lambda^{NI^+} \subset \Lambda^{Ne},$$

[26] Note that initial P' need not be a weak order.

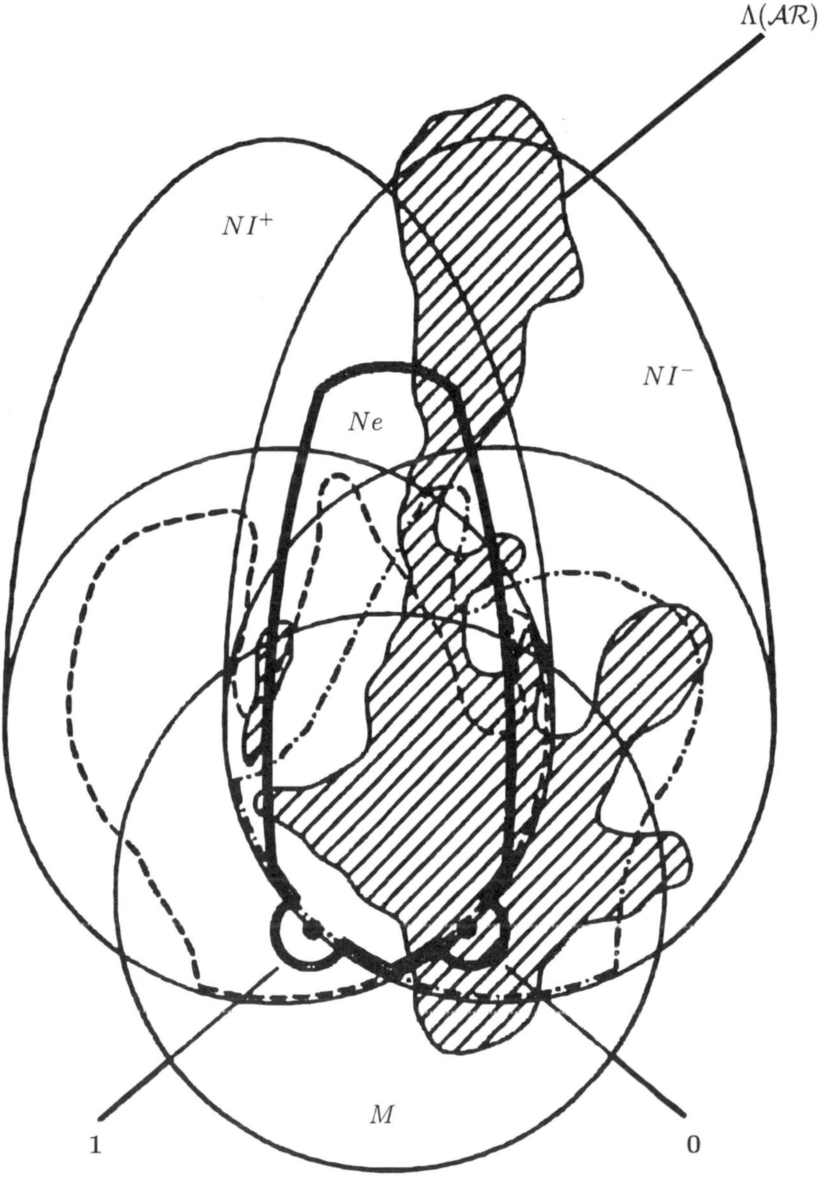

Figure 3-9

and

$$\Lambda(\mathcal{LO}, \mathcal{T}) \cap \Lambda^{U^+} \subset \Lambda^M,$$

obtained in Lemmas 3.1 and 3.2 for strongly local rules are generalized for local case. Considerations of different profiles consisting of weak orders permits to show the validity of the following theorem.

Theorem 3.25 *To obtain a profile $\{P_i\}$ consisting of weak orders, it is necessary and sufficent that the following conditions be satisfied for any three different alternatives x, y, and z and the transitive triplet (x,y) (y,z) and (x,z) :*

$$[V_1(x,y;\{P_i\}) \cup V_1(y,z)] \cap \overline{V_2(x,y) \cup V_2(y,z)} \subseteq V_1(x,z) \subseteq V_1(x,y) \cup V_1(y,z)$$
$$[V_2(x,y;\{P_i\}) \cup V_2(y,z)] \cap \overline{V_1(x,y) \cup V_1(y,z)} \subseteq V_1(x,z) \subseteq V_2(x,y) \cup V_2(y,z)$$

A direct corolary from Theorem 3.25 is the following result.

Theorem 3.26 *A local operator F transforms the profiles comprising weak orders into transitive relations, i.e., $F \in \Lambda(\mathcal{T})$ iff its $\mathbf{\Omega}$-representation meets the following condition: $\forall x, y, z, \in A$, for any (ω_1, ω_2) and (ω'_1, ω'_2) such that $(\omega_1, \omega_2) \in \Omega(x,y)$, $(\omega'_1, \omega'_2) \in \Omega(y,z)$, and for any (ω''_1, ω''_2) such that*

$$(\omega_1 \cup \omega'_1) \cup \overline{(\omega_2 \cup \omega'_2)} \subseteq \omega_1 \cup \omega'_1$$
$$(\omega_2 \cup \omega'_2) \cap \overline{(\omega_1 \cup \omega'_1)} \subseteq \omega''_2 \subseteq \omega_2 \cup \omega'_2,$$

the following is true:

$$(\omega'_1, \omega'_2) \in \Omega(x,z)$$

Thus, the theorem gives a general form of rules which transforms profiles comprising of weak orders into transitive (not necessaraly strict partial orders) binary relations. Let us study now in the serie of propositions the specific properties of the rules when some normative conditions are requested to meet.

Lemma 3.11 $F \in \Lambda(\mathcal{T}) \cap \Lambda^{NI^+} \Rightarrow \forall(\omega_1, \omega_2) \in \Omega(x,y), \forall(w,z) : \exists(\omega'_1, \omega'_2) \in \Omega(w,z)$:

$$\omega' \supseteq \omega_1, \omega'_2 \supseteq \omega_2,$$

Proof. Consider a transitive triplet (x,y), (y,w), and (x,w). $F \in \Lambda^{NI^+}$ implies that $\Omega(x,y) \neq \emptyset$. Let us choose$(\omega_1, \omega_2) \in \Omega(x,y)$, $(\omega'_1, \omega'_2) \in \Omega(y,w)$, and consider the pair (ω''_1, ω''_2) :

$$\omega''_1 = \omega_1 \cup ((\omega_1 \cup \omega'_1) \cap \overline{(\omega_2 \cup \omega'_2)}),$$
$$\omega''_2 = \omega_2 \cup ((\omega_2 \cup \omega'_2) \cap \overline{(\omega_1 \cup \omega'_1)}). \tag{3.16}$$

The check that the conditions of Theorem 3.26 are satisfied for (ω''_1, ω''_2) is straightforward; therefore (by virtue of the condition $F \in \Lambda(\mathcal{T})$) $(\omega''_1, \omega''_2) \in \Omega(x,w)$, and in particular $\omega''_1 \supseteq \omega_1$, and $\omega''_2 \supseteq \omega_2$. Giving further consideration to the triplets

(w,x), (x,y), and (w,y); (w,x),and (y,x), (w,y), (y,x) and (w,x); and (y,x), (x,w) and (y,w), we obtain that the statement of Lemma 3.11 is true for sets pairs $\Omega(x,w)$, $\Omega(w,x)$, $\Omega(y,w)$, $\Omega(y,x)$. Hence the consideration of the triplet of pairs (w,x), (x,z), and (w,z) yields the assertion. ■

Lemma 3.11 leads to several corolaries.
Let us denote by $N_+(x,y)$ $[N_-(x,y)]$ the union of all left-hand [right-hand] elements of the pairs included in the set $\Omega(x,y)$, i.e.,

$$N_+(x,y) = \bigcup_{(\omega_1,\omega_2)\in\Omega(x,y)} \omega_1,$$
$$N_-(x,y) = \bigcup_{(\omega_1,\omega_2)\in\Omega(x,y)} \omega_2.$$

Corollary 3.4 $\forall(x,y) \in A \times A$

$$N_+(x,y) = N_+$$
$$N_-(x,y) = N_-$$

The proof directly follows from Lemma 3.11.

Corollary 3.5 $\forall(\omega_1,\omega_2) \in \Omega(x,y)$ *such that* $\omega_1 \cup \omega_2 = N$, *we have*

$$\forall(x,y) \in A \times A : (\omega_1,\omega_2) \in \Omega(x,y)$$

The proof is straightforward fom Lemma 3.11.

Corollary 3.6 *Let* $\forall(x,y) \in A \times A : (\emptyset,\emptyset) \in \Omega(x,y)$. *Then* $\forall(w,z) \in A \times A$ *from* $(\omega_1,\omega_2) \in \Omega(x,y)$ *follows that* $(\omega_1,\omega_2) \in \Omega(w,z)$.

Proof. Since $(\emptyset,\emptyset) \in \Omega(x,y)$,for all $(x,y) \in A \times A$ the appropriate selection of $\omega_1' = \emptyset$ and $\omega_2' = \emptyset$ in the expression of the type (3.16) yields $\omega_1'' = \omega_1$ and $\omega_2'' = \omega_2$ (therefore all subseqeuent steps of the proof of Lemma 3.11 employ strict equalities of set-theoretic inclusions).

Corollary 3.7 $F \in \Lambda^{PC^+} \cap \Lambda(\mathcal{T}) \Rightarrow$

$$\forall(\omega_1,\omega_2) \in \Omega(x,y) : \omega_1 \cup \omega_2 \neq \emptyset,$$
$$\forall(z,w) \in A \times A : (\omega_1,\omega_2) \in \Omega(z,w)$$

Proof. Assume in (3.16) that $\omega_1' = \omega_1 \cup \omega_2$, $\omega_2' = \emptyset$. By the statement of the Corollary $F \in \Lambda^{PC^+}$; therefore $\forall(x,y)$ $\forall\omega$ such that $\emptyset \subset \omega \subseteq N$ $(\omega,\emptyset) \in \Omega(x,y)$.Taking $\omega_1' = \omega_1 \cup \omega_2$ and $\omega_2' = \emptyset$ in (3.16), we obtain $\omega_1'' = \omega_1$ and $\omega_2'' = \omega_2$.

Corollary 3.8 $\Lambda^{PC^+} \cap \Lambda(\mathcal{T}) \subseteq \Lambda^M$

Proof. Assume on the contrary $F \in \Lambda^{PC^+} \cap \Lambda(\mathcal{T})$ but $\exists(x,y) \in A \times A$, and for $(\omega_1,\omega_2) \in \Omega(x,y)$ there exist (ω_1',ω_2') such that $\omega_1' \supseteq \omega_1$, and $\omega_2' \subseteq \omega_2$,and

$(\omega_1,\omega_2) \notin \Omega(x,y)$. When the relationships $\omega_1' \supseteq \omega_1$, and $\omega_2' \subseteq \omega_2$ hold, with at least one of the inclusions strict, the following takes place: $\omega_1' \cup (\omega_2 \cap \omega_2') \neq \emptyset$, since with $\omega_1' \supset \omega_1$, $\omega_1' \neq \emptyset$, while with $\omega_2' \subset \omega_2$, $\exists i \in \omega_2'$. Therefore $(\omega_2 \cap \overline{\omega}_2') \neq \emptyset$. If $(\omega_1,\omega_2) = (\emptyset,\emptyset)$, then it follows from $F \in \Lambda^{PC^+}$ that $\forall \omega : \emptyset \subset \omega \subset N \Rightarrow (\omega,\emptyset) \in \Omega(x,y)$ for any (x,y), which contradicts our assumption. In the case $\omega_1 \cup \omega_2 \neq \emptyset$, Corollary 3.7 yields that $(\omega_1,\omega_2) \in \Omega(x,z)$ while $F \in \Lambda^{PC^+} \Rightarrow (\omega_1' \cup (\omega_2 \cap \overline{\omega}_2'),\emptyset) \in \Omega(z,y)$. It may be directly checked that the conditions of Theorem 3.26 are satisfied for (ω_1',ω_2'). Therefore, by virtue of the conditions $F \in \Lambda(\mathcal{T})$ we have $(\omega_1',\omega_2') \in \Omega(x,y)$, which contradicts our assumption. Corollary is proved.

Corollary 3.9 *Let $F \in \Lambda(\mathcal{T})$. If the condition*

$$\forall (x,y) \in A \times A, \forall \omega \neq \emptyset : (\emptyset,\omega) \in \Omega(x,y)$$

holds for Ω–representation of the operator F, then $\forall(\omega_1,\omega_2) \in \Omega(x,y)$ such that $\omega_1 \cup \omega_2 \neq \emptyset$ the following holds

$$\forall (z,w) \in A \times A \ (\omega_1,\omega_2) \in \Omega(z,w).$$

Proof. The proof is similar to that of for Corollary 3.7, in this case (ω_1',ω_2') in (3.16) is chosen as $(\emptyset,\omega_1 \cup \omega_2)$.

Definition 3.30 Let us call a local rule F *anti-monotonic* if its Ω–representation implies

$$\forall (x,y) \in A \times A, (\omega_1,\omega_2) \in \Omega(x,y), \forall(\omega_1',\omega_2') : \\ \omega_1' \subseteq \omega_1, \text{and } \omega_2' \subseteq \omega_2 \Rightarrow (\omega_1',\omega_2') \in \Omega(x,y).$$

Corollary 3.10 *Under the condition of Corollary 3.9 the operator F is anti-monotonic.*

Proof. The proof is similar to that of Corollary 3.8. The conditions considered are $\omega_1 \supseteq \omega_1'$, and $\omega_2 \subseteq \omega_2'$, $(\omega_1,\omega_2) \in \Omega(x,y)$, but $(\omega_1',\omega_2') \notin \Omega(x,y)$. Note that under these conditions $\omega_2' \cup (\omega_1 \cap \overline{\omega}_1') \neq \emptyset$; therefore $\forall (x,y) \in A \times A : (\emptyset, \omega_2' \cup (\omega_1 \cap \overline{\omega}_1')) \in \Omega(x,y)$. It is obvious that (ω_1',ω_2') satisfies the condition of Theorem 3.26; therefore, by virtue of the condition $F \in \Lambda(\mathcal{T})$, we have $(\omega_1',\omega_2') \in \Omega(x,y)$. Corollary is proved.

Lemma 3.12 *Let $F \in \Lambda^{NI^+} \cap \Lambda(\mathcal{T})$. Then its Ω-representation implies that the following conditions hold: if $(\omega_1,\omega_2) \in \Omega(x,y), (\omega_1',\omega_2') \in \Omega(x,y), \exists(\omega_1'',\omega_2''), (\omega_1''',\omega_2''')$ $(\omega_1'',\omega_2'') \in \Omega(x,y), (\omega_1''',\omega_2''') \in \Omega(x,y)$, and in particular*

$$\omega_1'' \supseteq \omega_1 \cup \omega_1', \\ \omega_2''' \supseteq \omega_2 \cup \omega_2'.$$

Proof. Let $(\omega_1,\omega_2) \in \Omega(x,y)$, $(\omega_1',\omega_2') \in \Omega(x,y)$. By virtue of Lemma 3.11, $\exists(\widetilde{\omega}_1,\widetilde{\omega}_2) \in \Omega(y,z) : \widetilde{\omega}_1 \supseteq \omega_1, \widetilde{\omega}_2 \supseteq \omega_2$. Consider $(\widetilde{\omega}_1',\widetilde{\omega}_2')$ such that

$$\widetilde{\omega}_1' = \omega_1 \cup \widetilde{\omega}_1, \\ \widetilde{\omega}_2 = (\omega_2 \cup \widetilde{\omega}_2) \cap \overline{\omega_1 \cup \widetilde{\omega}_1}$$

It may be easily seen that $(\widetilde{\omega}'_1, \widetilde{\omega}'_2)$ satisfies the condition of Theorem 3.26, and since $F \in \Lambda(T)$. then $(\widetilde{\omega}'_1, \widetilde{\omega}'_2) \in \Omega(x,z)$. According to Lemma 3.11, $\exists(\widetilde{\omega}''_1, \widetilde{\omega}''_2) \in \Omega(x,y)$ such that $\omega''_1 \supseteq \widetilde{\omega}'_1 \supseteq \omega_1 \cup \widetilde{\omega}_1 \supseteq \omega_1 \cup \omega'_1$.
In a similar way the existence of $(\omega'''_1, \omega'''_2) \in \Omega(x,y)$ such that $\omega'''_2 \supseteq \omega_2 \cup \omega'_2$ may be proved. In this case we consider $(\overline{\omega_2 \cup \widetilde{\omega}_2} \cap (\omega_1 \cup \widetilde{\omega}_1), \omega_2 \cup \widetilde{\omega}_2)$ as the pair $(\widetilde{\omega}'_1, \widetilde{\omega}'_2)$. Lemma is proved.

Corollary 3.11 $F \in \Lambda^{NI^+} \cap \Lambda(T) \Rightarrow \forall(x,y) \in A \times A\ \exists(\omega_1, \omega_2) \in \Omega(x,y)$, $(\omega'_1, \omega'_2) \in \Omega(x,y) : \omega_1 = N_+, \omega_2 = N_-$.

Proof. The proof follows from Lemma 3.12 and Corollary 3.4.

Corollary 3.12 $\forall(x,y) \in A \times A, \forall(\omega_1, \omega_2):$

$$N_+ \cap \overline{N_-} \subseteq \omega_1 \subseteq N_+,\ N_- \cap \overline{N_+} \subseteq \omega_2 \subseteq N_- \Rightarrow (\omega_1, \omega_2) \in \Omega(x,y).$$

Proof. Let us fix $z \neq x$ and $z \neq y$. By virtue of corollary 3.11, $\exists(N_+, \omega_2^{xz}) \in \Omega(x,z)$, $(\omega_1^{zy}, N_-) \in \Omega(z,y)$. It is easy to see that (ω_1, ω_2) satisfies the condition of Theorem 3.26:

$$\begin{array}{l} N_+ \cap \overline{N_-} \subseteq \omega_1 \subseteq N_+ \cup \omega_1^{zy} = N_+ \\ N_- \cap \overline{N_+} \subseteq \omega_2 \subseteq N_- \cup \omega_2^{xz} = N_- \end{array}$$

Since $F \in \Lambda(T)$ by the condition of Lemma 3.12, the use of Theorem 3.26 yields $(\omega_1, \omega_2) \in \Omega(x,y)$. Corollary is proved.

We study now the 'dual' properties of local rules which turn out to be similar to those ones defined and studied for strongly local rules.

Definition 3.31 A local rule $\overline{F}$ is said to be a *complement rule* to the rule F if for any profile $\{P_i\}$ the following is true:

$$\overline{F}(\{P_i\}) = A \times A \backslash F(\{P_i\}).$$

Let us call $\overline{\Omega}$ a complement to Ω if $\forall(x,y) \in A \times A : \overline{\Omega}(x,y) = T \backslash \Omega(x,y)$, where

$$T = \{(\omega_1, \omega_2) | \omega_1 \subseteq N,\ \omega_2 \subseteq N,\ \omega_1 \cap \omega_2 = \emptyset\}$$

One may show the validity of the following theorem.

Theorem 3.27 .

$$F = \overline{F} \Leftrightarrow \forall(x,y) \in A \times A : \Omega(x,y) = \overline{\Omega}(x,y).$$

Directly following from Theorem 3.27 are:

Corollary 3.13

$$F \in \Lambda^{Ne} \Longleftrightarrow \overline{F} \in \Lambda^{Ne},$$
$$F \in \Lambda^{An} \Longleftrightarrow \overline{F} \in \Lambda^{An}$$
$$F \in \Lambda^{NI^+} \Longleftrightarrow \overline{F} \in \Lambda^{NI^-}$$
$$F \in \Lambda^{M} \Longleftrightarrow \overline{F} \text{ is anti-monotonic}$$

Theorem 3.28 *Let $F \in \Lambda^{NI^+} \cap \Lambda^{An} \cap \Lambda(\mathcal{T})$. Then the following cases are possible:*
(a) $F \equiv \mathbf{1}$;
(b) $\Omega_F(x,y) = \Omega_F = \{(\emptyset,\emptyset)\}$;
(c) $\Omega_F(x,y)$ contains only the pairs of the form $(\omega_1^{xy},\emptyset)$;
(d) $\Omega_F(x,y)$ contains only the pairs of the form $(\emptyset,\omega_2^{xy})$;

Proof. Let $F \in \Lambda^{NI^+} \cap \Lambda^{An} \cap \Lambda(\mathcal{T})$.Then $F \in \Lambda^{NI^+}$ implies $\forall (x,y) \in A \times A$: $\Omega(x,y) \neq \emptyset$. Let $\exists (x,y) \in A \times A$, $(\omega_1,\omega_2) \in \Omega(x,y) : \omega_1 \neq \emptyset$. Then, obviously, $N_+ = N$. Similarly, let $\exists (z,w) \in A \times A, (\omega_1',\omega_2') \in \Omega(z,w) : \omega_2 \neq \emptyset$. Then obviously $N_- = N$. Therefore $\forall (x,y) \in A \times A$, for any pair $(\omega_1,\omega_2) \in \Omega(x,y)$, either $\omega_2 \neq \emptyset$ [case (c)], or $\omega_1 \neq \emptyset$ [case (d)]. Otherwise , we would have $N_+ = N_- = N$. By virtue of Corollary 3.12, $\forall (x,y) \in A \times A$, $\forall (\omega_1,\omega_2) : \omega_1 \cap \omega_2 = \emptyset$, $\emptyset \subseteq \omega_2 \subseteq N \Rightarrow (\omega_1,\omega_2) \in \Omega(x,y)$, which leads to $F \equiv \mathbf{1}$ [case (a)]. If $\forall (x,y) \in A \times A, \forall (\omega_1,\omega_2) \in \Omega(x,y)$ we have $\omega_1 = \emptyset$ and $\omega_2 = \emptyset$, then $\Omega_F(x,y) = \Omega_F = \{(\emptyset,\emptyset)\}$ [case (b)] ■

Using all the results above we can study now how the class $\Lambda(\mathcal{SPO})$ is placed on the Venn diagramm constructed for the classes of Normative conditions.

Theorem 3.29 *The intersection of the class $\Lambda(\mathcal{SPO})$ with the classes $\Lambda^{NI^+}, ..., \Lambda^{U^-}$ is as in Figure 3-10.*

Proof. Let us establish the emptiness of the intersection of some classes of operators:
(1) $\Lambda(\mathcal{SPO}) \cap \Lambda^{NI^+} \cap \Lambda^{An} \cap \Lambda^{\overline{U^+}} \cap \Lambda^{U^-} = \emptyset$;
(2) $\Lambda(\mathcal{SPO}) \cap \Lambda^{NI^+} \cap \Lambda^{M} \cap \Lambda^{Ne} \cap \Lambda^{An} \cap \Lambda^{U^+} = \emptyset$;
(3) $\Lambda(\mathcal{SPO}) \cap \Lambda^{\overline{Ne}} \cap \Lambda^{PC^+} \cap \Lambda^{PC^-} = \emptyset$;
(4) $\Lambda(\mathcal{SPO}) \cap \Lambda^{\overline{M}} \cap \Lambda^{PC^+} = \emptyset$.
Let us prove these relationships one by one.
(1): Assume on the contrary that $\exists F \in \Lambda(\mathcal{SPO}) \cap \Lambda^{NI^+} \cap \Lambda^{An} \cap \Lambda^{\overline{U^+}} \cap \Lambda^{U^-}$. By virtue of the conditions $\Lambda(\mathcal{SPO}) \subset \Lambda(\mathcal{T})$ and $\Lambda(\mathcal{SPO}) \cap \Lambda^{NI^+} \cap \Lambda^{An}$, we may use Theorem 3.28. Cases (a) and (b) of the theorem are excluded by the condition $F \in \Lambda(\mathcal{SPO})$. In cases (c) we have $\exists (\omega_1,\omega_2) \in \Omega(x,y)$ and $\omega_1 \neq \emptyset$; following the proof of Theorem 3.28 $N_+(x,y) = N_+ = N$. Then by virtue of Corollary 3.11, $\forall (x,y) \in A \times A : (N,\emptyset) \in \Omega(x,y)$, which contradicts the condition $F \in \Lambda^{\overline{U^+}}$. In case (d), $\exists (\omega_1',\omega_2') \in \Omega(x,y) : \omega_2' \neq \emptyset$ and following the proof of Theorem 3.28, $N_-(x,y)$=$N_- = N$. Then by virtue of Corollary 3.11, $\forall (x,y) \in A \times A : (\emptyset,N) \in \Omega(x,y)$, which contradicts $F \in \Lambda^{\overline{U^-}}$

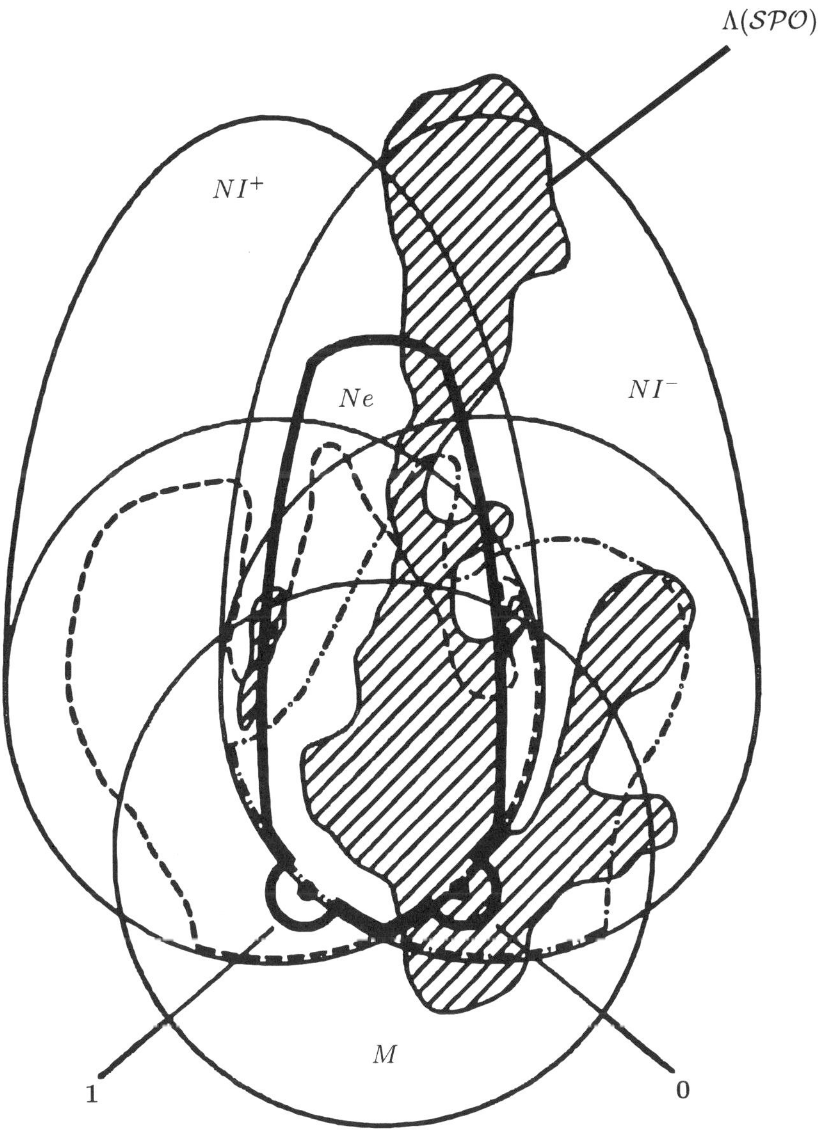

Figure 3-10

(2): Assume on the contrary that there exists

$$F \in \Lambda(\mathcal{SPO}) \cap \Lambda^{NI^+} \cap \Lambda^{\overline{M}} \cap \Lambda^{Ne} \cap \Lambda^{An} \cap \Lambda^{U^+}.$$

By virtue of the conditions $\Lambda(\mathcal{SPO}) \subseteq \Lambda(\mathcal{T})$ and $F \in \Lambda(\mathcal{SPO}) \cap \Lambda^{NI^+} \cap \Lambda^{An}$ we may use Theorem 3.28. Cases (a) and (b) of the theorem are excluded by the condition $F \in \Lambda(\mathcal{SPO})$; case (d) is excluded by$F \in \Lambda^{U^+}$. Let us prove that in case (c) $F \in \Lambda^{Ne}$ implies $F \in \Lambda^{M}$. Assume on the contrary that for $(\omega_1, \emptyset) \in \Omega$, $(N, \emptyset) \in \Omega$ there is $(\omega_1', \emptyset) \notin \Omega$ such that $\omega_1 \subset \omega_1' \subseteq N$. To check that the pair $(\omega_1', \emptyset)$ satisfies the conditions of Theorem 3.26 is straightforward; therefore, by virtue of $F \in \Lambda(\mathcal{SPO})$, $\Lambda(\mathcal{SPO}) \subseteq \Lambda(\mathcal{T})$ we have $(\omega_1', \emptyset) \in \Omega\ \forall \omega_1'$ such that $\omega_1 \subset \omega_1' \subseteq N$ which contradicts $F \in \Lambda^{\overline{M}}$.
(3) This relationship directly follows from Lemma 3.11, Corollary 3.7, and the conditions $F \in \Lambda^{PC^+}$ and $F \in \Lambda^{PC^-}$.
(4) This relationship directly follows from $F \in \Lambda^{PC^+}$, Lemma 3.11, and Corollary 3.8.
The above conditions exclude 12 more conjunctions out of the remaining after the proof of the Theorem 3.24 49 conjunctions. The other 37 conjunctions define the classes of operators non-emptiness of which may be verified by examples ■

3.14.3 Class $\Lambda(\mathcal{WO})$

For this class we will show below how it is placed relative to classes $\Lambda^{NI^+}, ..., \Lambda^{U^-}$. The study of the rules from the class $\Lambda(\mathcal{WO}) \cap \Lambda^C$ will be done in the next Section.

Theorem 3.30 *The intersection of the class $\Lambda(\mathcal{WO})$ with the classes $\Lambda^{NI^+}, ..., \Lambda^{U^-}$ is as in Figure 3-11.*

Proof. The following relations hold:
(1) $\Lambda(\mathcal{WO}) \cap \Lambda^{\overline{NI+}} \cap \Lambda^{NI^-} = \mathbf{0}$;
(2) $\Lambda(\mathcal{WO}) \cap \Lambda^{\overline{NI+}} \cap \Lambda^{NI^-} \cap \Lambda^{\overline{Ne}} = \emptyset$;
(3) $\Lambda(\mathcal{WO}) \cap \Lambda^{NI^+} \cap \Lambda^{An} = \emptyset$;
(4) $\Lambda(\mathcal{WO}) \cap \Lambda^{NI^+} \cap \Lambda^{\overline{U+}} \cap \Lambda^{U^-} = \emptyset$;
(5) $\Lambda(\mathcal{WO}) \cap \Lambda^{PC^-} \cap \Lambda^{\overline{Ne}} = \emptyset$;
(6) $\Lambda(\mathcal{WO}) \cap \Lambda^{PC^-} \cap \Lambda^{\overline{M}} = \emptyset$.
Let us prove them.
(1) The proof follows from Theorem 3.27, Lemma 3.11, Corollary 3.12, and the conditions $F \in \Lambda^{\overline{NI+}}$ and $F \in \Lambda^{NI^-}$.
(2)The proof follows from (1).
(3)Assume on the contrary that $F \in \Lambda(\mathcal{WO}) \cap \Lambda^{NI^+} \cap \Lambda^{An}$. It may be easily shown that $F \in \Lambda^{NI^-}$. Consider a dual rule $\overline{F}$. The following are true:
(a) $\overline{F} \in \Lambda(\mathcal{T})$, since $F \in \Lambda(\mathcal{WO})$;
(b) by virtue of Corollary 3.13, $\overline{F} \in \Lambda^{NI^+}$, since $F \in \Lambda^{NI^-}$.
(c) by virtue of Corollary 3.13, $\overline{F} \in \Lambda^{An}$, since $F \in \Lambda^{An}$.
From (a), (b), (c) and Theorem 3.28 it follows that either $\overline{F} \equiv \mathbf{1}$, which is impossible, for in that case $F \equiv 0$, which contradicts $F \in \Lambda^{NI^+}$; or $\Omega_{\overline{F}}(x, y) = \{(\emptyset, \emptyset)\}$ which

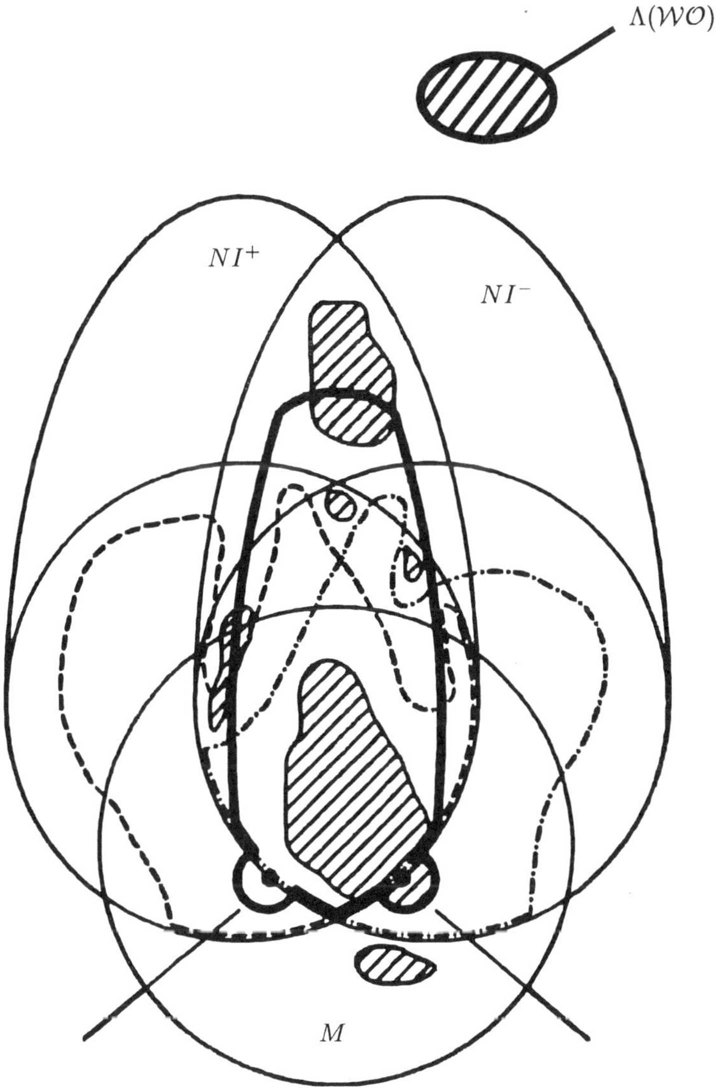

Figure 3-11

contradicts the condition $F \in \Lambda(\mathcal{WO})$ (Theorem 3.27 is used); or $\Omega_{\overline{F}}(x,y)$ contains only pairs $(\omega_1^{xy}, \emptyset)$; or $\Omega_{\overline{F}}(x,y)$ contains only pairs $(\emptyset, \omega_2^{xy})$.
Since $\Lambda(\mathcal{WO}) \subset \Lambda(\mathcal{T})$ and $F \in \Lambda^{NI^+} \cap \Lambda^{An}$, we can use Theorem 3.28. In a similar manner, the following cases are possible for F : either $F \equiv \mathbf{1}$, which is im-

possible by virtue of $F \in \Lambda(\mathcal{WO})$; or $\Omega_F = \{(\emptyset,\emptyset)\}$, which is impossible by virtue of $F \in \Lambda(\mathcal{WO})$; or $\Omega_F(x,y)$ contains only pairs of the form $(\omega_1^{xy},\emptyset)$; or $\Omega_F(x,y)$ contains only pairs $(\emptyset,\omega_2^{xy})$. For the (ω_1,ω_2) such that $\omega_1 \neq \emptyset$, $\omega_2 \neq \emptyset$ we have $(\omega_1,\omega_2) \notin \Omega_F(x,y)$, $(\omega_1,\omega_2) \notin \Omega_{\overline{F}}(x,y)$, which contradicts the relation following from Theorem 3.27:

$$\forall (x,y) \in A \times A : \Omega_F(x,y) \cup \Omega_{\overline{F}}(x,y) = T$$

Hence, $\Lambda(\mathcal{WO}) \cap \Lambda^{NI^+} \cap \Lambda^{An} = \emptyset$.
(4): Let on the contrary a certain $F \in \Lambda(\mathcal{WO}) \cap \Lambda^{NI^+} \cap \Lambda^{\overline{U^+}} \cap \Lambda^{U^-}$ exists. Consider the operator $\overline{F}$. For this operator the following relations hold:
(a) $\exists (x,y) \in A \times A : (N,\emptyset) \in \Omega_{\overline{F}}(x,y)$;
(b) $\forall (x,y) \in A \times A \ (\emptyset, N) \in \Omega(x,y)$ by virtue of $F \in \Lambda^{\overline{U^+}}$ and $F \in \Lambda^{U^-}$, and Theorem 3.27;
(c)$F \in \Lambda(\mathcal{T})$ since $F \in \Lambda(\mathcal{WO})$; and
(d)$\overline{F} \in \Lambda^{NI^+}$ by virtue of (b).
Therefore one may use Theorem 3.28 in this case. It follows from (a) and (b) and the proof of Theorem 3.28 that $N_+ = N_- = N$. Therefore, by virtue of Corollary 3.12 and Theorem 3.28, $\forall (x,y) \in A \times A, \forall (\omega_1,\omega_2) : \emptyset \subseteq \omega_1 \subseteq N, \emptyset \subseteq \omega_2 \subseteq N$, $\omega_1 \cap \omega_2 = \emptyset \Rightarrow (\omega_1,\omega_2) \in \Omega_{\overline{F}}(x,y)$, which makes $\overline{F} \equiv \mathbf{1}$ while by virtue of Theorem 3.27, $F \equiv \mathbf{0}$. which contradicts the condition $F \in \Lambda^{\overline{NI^+}}$.
(5), (6): Assume the contrary, i.e., let $F \in \Lambda(\mathcal{WO}) \cap \Lambda^{PC^-} \cap \Lambda^{\overline{Ne}}$ and $F' \in \Lambda(\mathcal{WO}) \cap \Lambda^{PC^-} \cap \Lambda^{\overline{M}}$ exist. Consider $\overline{F}$ and $\overline{F}'$. The following relations hold:
(a) $\overline{F} \in \Lambda(\mathcal{T})$, $\overline{F'} \in \Lambda(\mathcal{T})$, since $F \in \Lambda(\mathcal{WO})$, $F' \in \Lambda(\mathcal{WO})$.
(b) $\forall (x,y) \in A \times A, \forall \omega : \emptyset \subseteq \omega_1 \subseteq N \Rightarrow (\emptyset,\omega) \in \Omega_{\overline{F}}(x,y)$, $(\emptyset,\omega) \in \Omega_{\overline{F'}}(x,y)$, by virtue of the conditions $F \in \Lambda^{PC^-}$ and $F' \in \Lambda^{PC^-}$ and Theorem 3.27. It follows from (a) and (b) that one may employ Lemma 3.11 and its corollaries for the operators $\overline{F}$ and $\overline{F'}$. According to Corollary 3.6, $\overline{F} \in \Lambda^{Ne}$, and consequently, the use of Corollary 3.13 yields that $F \in \Lambda^{Ne}$, which contradicts the assumption $F \in \Lambda^{\overline{Ne}}$. By virtue of Corollaries 3.9 and 3.10, the operator $\overline{F'}$ is antimonotonic. Therefore using Corollary 3.8, we obtain $F' \in \Lambda^M$, which contradicts the assumption[27] $F \in \Lambda^{\overline{M}}$.
The relationhips obtained exclude 24 more conjunctions out of remaining after the proof of Theorem 3.29 37 conjunctions. The remaining 13 conjunctions define the classes of rules non-emptiness of which may be verified by examples ■

3.15 Comparing classes in Λ^C

In this section we will study the correlation between the above three types of classes, namely, the class isolated by the normative conditions; the complete classes of closedness for the classes $\mathcal{AR}$, $\mathcal{SPO}$, and $\mathcal{WO}$; and the hierarchical-federation rule classes

27 It follows from relations (5), (6), and (1) that $\Lambda^{PC^-} \cap \Lambda(\mathcal{WO}) \subset \Lambda^{NI^+} \cap \Lambda^{NI^-} \cap \Lambda^M \cap \Lambda^{Ne}$, i.e., the rule in the complete class $\Lambda(\mathcal{WO})$ satisfying condition PC^- belongs to the Central Class.

with its subclasses. The Central Class and the Symmetrically Central Class will be considered below as classes of the first type. For the classes under study ($Q_r = \mathcal{AR}$, $\mathcal{SPO}$, and $\mathcal{WO}$) the relative location between classes $\Lambda(Q_r)$ and the Central Class as well as the hierarchical-federation class and its subclasses are formulated in next theorem.

Theorem 3.31 *The class of hierarchical-collegium rules is strictly embedded in the intersection of the complete generating class $\Lambda(\mathcal{AR})$ with the Central Class, i.e.,*

$$\Lambda(\mathcal{AR}) \cap \Lambda^C \supset \Lambda^{HC};$$

The intersection of the complete generating class $\Lambda(\mathcal{SPO})$ with the Central Class coincides with the class of hierarchical oligarchy rules, i.e.,

$$\Lambda(\mathcal{SPO}) \cap \Lambda^C = \Lambda^{\cap *};$$

The intersection of the complete generating class $\Lambda(\mathcal{WO})$ with the Central class coincides with the class of hierarchical dictator rules, i.e.,

$$\Lambda(\mathcal{WO}) \cap \Lambda^C = \Lambda^{*}.$$

Proof. Let us write the definition for the hierarchical federation rule in the following manner: $(x,y) \in P \Leftrightarrow \exists l \in [1,p] : \ (x,y) \in \bigcap_{j=1}^{\beta_l} *_{q=1}^{\alpha_j} P_{ljq}$. It follows that $\forall j = 1,...,\beta_l : (x,y) \in (P_{lj1} * ... * P_{ljd_j})$. Therefore if the hierarchical federation rule is the hierarchical collegium rule and P contains a cycle, then the cycle must belong to at least one set of indices

$$(P_{lj1} * ... * P_{ljd_j}) \ \forall j,l \text{ such that } j \in [1,\beta_l],\ l \in [1,p],$$

which is impossible by virtue of the definition of the operation $*$ and the fact that $\forall i \in N \ P_i \in \mathcal{WO}$.

In the proof of the second statement of the theorem we will follow the original proof given in [89] and modified in notation used in this monograph.

A coalition ω_1 is said to dominate[28] a coalition ω_2 if

$$V(x,y;\ \overrightarrow{P}) = \omega_1,\ V(y,x;\ \overrightarrow{P}) = \omega_2 \text{ and } (x,y) \in F(\overrightarrow{P}).$$

A coalition ω is said to be decisive if ω dominates $\overline{\omega} = N \setminus \omega$.

Lemma 3.13 *If ω' and ω'' are decisive coalitions, then $\omega' \cap \omega''$ is a decisive coalition.*

Proof of Lemma. Consider three alternatives x, y, z and a profile $\overrightarrow{P}$ such that

$$V(x,y;\ \overrightarrow{P}) = \omega',\ V(y,x;\ \overrightarrow{P}) = \overline{\omega'},$$

$$V(y,z;\ \overrightarrow{P}) = \omega'',\ V(z,y;\ \overrightarrow{P}) = \overline{\omega''}.$$

28 Do not confuse it with the domination concepts used Sections 3.3 and 3.13.

Since ω' is a decisive coalition, then xPy, $P = F(\overrightarrow{P})$. Analogously, yPz. By transitivity P, we have xPz which implies that $\omega' \cap \omega''$ is a decisive coalition.
Lemma is proved.

Lemma implies that there exists the minimal decisive coalition ω_0 defined as the intersection of all decisive coalitions. By monotonicity of F coalition ω is decisive iff $\omega_0 \subseteq \omega$. Moreover, ω_0 is not empty.
Now for the rule $F \in \Lambda^C$, $F : \mathcal{WO}^n \to \mathcal{T}$, and for $i \in N$ let us define

$$F^{(i)} : \mathcal{WO}^n \to \mathcal{T}$$

- a rule which is obtained from F in case when agent i is always indifferent. It is obvious that $F^{(i)} \in \Lambda^C$.
By induction assumption suppose that the statement of the theorem is true for the rule $F^{(i)}$, i.e.,

$$F^{(i)} = \bigcap F_h^{(i)},$$

where h goes through some set of hierarchies $H_i \subset \mathbf{H}(N \setminus \{i\})$, $\mathbf{H}(N)$ be the set of all possible hierarchies on N.
Now for each $j \in \omega_0$ let us construct hierarchies

$$F_{(j,h)} = P_j * F_h^{(i)}.$$

We shall prove that

$$F = \bigcap_{j \in \omega_0} \left(\bigcap_{h \in H_j} F_{(j,h)} \right).$$

Consider a profile $\overrightarrow{P}$ and alternatives x and y. Assume that $(x, y) \in F(\overrightarrow{P})$. Then $V(y, x, \overrightarrow{P}) \cap \omega_0 = \emptyset$. Hence for $j \in \omega_0$ either xP_jy or xI_jy, where I_j is indifference relation for agent j. In the first case $(x, y) \in F_{(j,h)}(\overrightarrow{P})$. In the second case let us denote as $\overrightarrow{P'}$ a contruction of $\overrightarrow{P}$ to the set $N \setminus \{j\}$. Then $F(\overrightarrow{P}) = F(\overrightarrow{P'})$. Hence

$$(x, y) \in F^{(j)}(\overrightarrow{P'}) = \bigcap_{h \in H_j} F_h^{(j)}(\overrightarrow{P'}) = \bigcap_{h \in H_j} F_{(j,h)}(\overrightarrow{P}),$$

and

$$(x, y) \in \bigcap_j \left(\bigcap F_{(j,h)}(\overrightarrow{P}) \right).$$

Assume now that $(x, y) \in \bigcap_j \left(\bigcap F_{(j,h)}(\overrightarrow{P}) \right)$, i.e., for any $j \in \omega_0$ and $h \in H_j$

$$(x, y) \in F_{(j,h)}(\overrightarrow{P})$$

holds. If some j is indifferent between x and y, then again we obtain

$$F_{(j,h)}(\overrightarrow{P}) = F_h^{(j)}(\overrightarrow{P'}),$$

and

$$(x,y) \in \bigcap_{h \in H_j} F_h^{(j)}(\overrightarrow{P'}) = F^{(j)}(\overrightarrow{P'}) = F(\overrightarrow{P}).$$

If any $j \in \omega_0$ is not indifferent between x and y, then $\forall j \in \omega_0 \; xP_jy$ holds. Since ω_0 is decisive coalition, $(x,y) \in F(\overrightarrow{P})$.
The second statement of the theorem is proved.

To prove the third statement let us note that according to the second statement of the theorem the rule under question is defined by some set of hierarchies H. We should show that this set contains only one hierarchy. Let us first show that all those hierarchies begin with the same index. Indeed, let some hierarchy h in H has first index i, and other hierarchy h' has first index i', and $i \neq i'$. Consider two linear orders P and P' such that their intersection is not a week order, for instance, with $A = \{a,b,c\}$,

$$P = \{(a,b),(b,c),(a,c)\},$$

$$P' = \{(c,a),(a,b),(c,b)\}.$$

Let us construct a profile $\overrightarrow{P}$ such that $P_i = P$, and $\forall j \neq i \; P_j = P'$. It is obvious that

$$F(\overrightarrow{P}) = P \cap P',$$

i.e., $F(\overrightarrow{P}) \notin \mathcal{WO}$. Using the induction by $\mid N \mid$ will complete the proof ■

Note that, according to Theorem 3.31, the use of the hierarchical collegium rule for designing a collective decision over a profile $\{P_i\}$ guarantees acyclicity of the relation P. However, it is possible to construct an acyclic relation using hierarchical federation rules of a more general type than hierarchical collegium rule. Let us illustrate this with an example.

Example. Let $N = \{1,2,3,4\}$ and

$$P = [(P_1 * P_2 * P_3) \cap (P_4 * P_2 * P_3)] \cup [(P_1 * P_3 * P_2) \cap (P_1 * P_4 * P_2)]$$

One may check to see that the Basic list for this rule equals

$$\Omega^B = \{(1,234),(2,3),(34,2),(3,\emptyset)\}.$$

Condition (C1) is obviously satisfied, hence the relation P is acyclic.

Using condition (C1) one could find the (necessary and sufficient) conditions on the list which characterize the special sort of hierarchical federation rules generating an acyclic resulting relation P. However, these conditions, which are not quite obvious, are lengthy and thus will be omitted.

Let us analyze the rules in the intersection $\Lambda(\mathcal{AR}) \cap \Lambda^{SC}$. Since the Symmetrically Central Class coincides with the class $\Lambda^{\{\tau-(k_1,k_2)\}}$, the rules from the above intersection must belong to the class $\Lambda^{\{\tau-(k_1,k_2)\}}$. But first we shall study the cases in which the more simple (k_1, k_2)-majority rules generate the resulting relation P belonging to the class $\Lambda(\mathcal{AR})$. It turns out that the form of such rules depends of the relation between the parameters of the rule, i.e. the numbers k_1 and k_2, and the number m of alternatives in A. The corresponding result is established below.

Theorem 3.32 *The intersection of the complete class of closedness $\Lambda(\mathcal{AR})$ for the set $\mathcal{AR}$ of all acyclic relation with the class of (k_1, k_2)-majority rules is empty if $k_1 \leq k_2$.*
If $k_1 > k_2$, the intersection of $\Lambda(\mathcal{AR})$ with $\Lambda^{(k_1,k_2)-M}$ coincides with the subclass $\Lambda_m^{(k_1,k_2)-M}$ of the class of (k_1, k_2)-majority rules specified by the condition $\lceil k_1/k_2 \rceil \geq m$, i.e., $\Lambda(\mathcal{AR}) \cap \Lambda^{(k_1,k_2)-M} = \Lambda_m^{(k_1,k_2)-M}$.
With $m \geq n$ (n being the number of voters), the intersection of the complete class $\Lambda(\mathcal{AR})$ with the class $\Lambda^{(k_1,k_2)-M}$ coincides with the class of relative k-majority rules, i.e. $\Lambda(\mathcal{AR}) \cap \Lambda^{(k_1,k_2)-M} = \Lambda^{RkM}$.

Proof of Theorem 3.32 is preceded by five lemmas.

Lemma 3.14 *The acyclicity condition (C1) for a rule $F \in \Lambda^C$ is violated iff the basic list Ω^B of F includes p pairs $\{\omega_1^j, \omega_2^j\}$, $j = 1, ..., p$, such that*

$$\bigcup_{j=1}^{p} \omega_1^j = \bigcup_{j=1}^{p} \omega_2^j. \tag{3.17}$$

Proof. Let condition (C1) be violated, i.e., there exist p pairs $\{\omega_1^j, \omega_2^j\}$ such that $\forall i$ $\omega_1^i \subseteq \cup_{j\neq i}\omega_2^j$ and $\omega_2^i \subseteq \cup_{j\neq i}\omega_1^j$, i.e., $\omega_1^1 \subseteq \cup_{i=2}^{p}\omega_2^i$, ..., $\omega_1^p \subseteq \cup_{i=1}^{p-1}\omega_2^i$. Hence it follows that $\cup_{i=1}^{p}\omega_1^i \subseteq \cup_{i=1}^{p}\omega_2^i$. On the other hand, from the fact that $\omega_2^1 \subseteq \cup_{i=2}^{p}\omega_1^i$,..., $\omega_2^p \subseteq \cup_{i=1}^{p-1}\omega_1^i$ it follows that $\cup_{i=1}^{p}\omega_2^i \subseteq \cup_{i=1}^{p}\omega_1^i$. Therefore, we have $\cup_{i=1}^{p}\omega_1^i = \cup_{i=1}^{p}\omega_2^i$.

Let condition (3.17) holds. Since $\forall i = 1, ..., p$ we have $\omega_1^i \cap \omega_2^i = \emptyset$, then obviously the following inclusions occur $\forall i$ $\omega_1^i \subseteq \cup_{i\neq j}\omega_2^j$ and $\omega_2^i \subseteq \cup_{i\neq j}\omega_2^j$. Lemma 3.14 is proved.

Lemma 3.15 *Under the conditions of Lemma 3.14,*

$$\text{(a) } \cap_i \omega_1^i = \emptyset,$$
$$\text{(b) } \cap_i \omega_2^i = \emptyset.$$

Proof. (a): Let $j \in \cap_i \omega_1^i$; then the violation of condition (C1) yields that $\forall i_0$

$$j \in \omega_1^{i_0} \subseteq \bigcap_{i \neq i_0} \omega_2^i.$$

But since $\forall i : j \in \omega_1^i$ and $\forall i : \omega_1^i \cap \omega_2^i = \emptyset$, then j cannot belong to $\cup_{j \neq i_0} \omega_2^j$. (b) is proved similarly to (a). Thus, Lemma 3.15 is proved.

Definition 3.32 Let a rule $F \in \Lambda^C$ with its list Ω be given. The totality of pairs $\{(\omega_1^i, \omega_2^i)\}_1^\rho \subseteq \Omega$, $\rho > 1$, satisfying the condition $\cup_i \omega_1^i = \cup_i \omega_2^i$ will be referred to as a *cyclic set*. A cyclic set $\{(\omega_1^i, \omega_2^i)\}_1^{\rho_0}$ such that Ω does not contain any other cyclic set with $\rho < \rho_0$ will be called minimal.

Lemma 3.16 *For an arbitrary profile $\vec{P}$ such that $\forall i \in N$ $P_i \in \mathcal{WO}$, the minimal length of the cycle in the relation $P = F(\vec{P})$, where $F \in \Lambda^C$ equals the cardinality ρ_0 of the minimal cyclic set in the list Ω of the rule F.*

The proof of Lemma 3.16 follows from Theorem 3.23 and Lemmas 3.14 and 3.15. Let us now estimate the cardinality ρ_0 of the minimal cyclic set for an arbitrary (k_1, k_2)-majority rule with fixed $n = card(N)$.

Lemma 3.17 *Let $k_1 \leq k_2$. Then $\rho_0 = 2$.*

Proof. First, let us consider an arbitrary pair (ω_1, ω_2) in Ω^B. Let $\omega_1 = \{i_1, ..., i_{k_1}\}$, $\omega_2 = \{j_1, ..., j_{k_2}\}$, and consider a pair (ω_1, ω_2') such that $\omega_2' = \{j_1, ..., j_{k_2}\}$. By virtue of the monotonicity condition the pair $(\omega_2', \omega_1) \in \Omega$ also belongs to Ω. It is obvious then that neither of the pairs (ω_1', ω_2) and (ω_2', ω_1) meets condition (C1). Lemma 3.17 is proved.

Lemma 3.18 *Let $k_1 > k_2$. Then $\rho_0 = \lceil k_1/k_2 \rceil$.*

Proof. Let $(\omega_1, \omega_2) \in \Omega^B$, $\omega_1 = \{i_1, ..., i_{k_1}\}$, $\omega_2 = \{j_1, ..., j_{k_2}\}$. Consider the substitution of indices in ω_1 and ω_2 in accordance with the following procedure: $\omega_2' = \{i_1, ..., i_{k_1}\}$, $\omega_1' = \{j_1, ..., j_{k_2}, i_{k_2+1}, ..., i_{k_1}\}$, i.e., k_2 indices from ω_1 are replaced with indices from ω_2 at each step of the procedure. It is easy to see that one needs exactly $\lceil k_1/k_2 \rceil$ substitutions of indices in order to satisfy the condition $\bigcup_i \omega_1^i = \bigcup_i \omega_2^i$. The minimality of ρ_0 follows from the fact that such a substitution always requires $k_1 + k_2$ indices, while in substituting the indices from $\omega \subseteq N \setminus \omega_1$ for those in ω_1 one would require $k_1 + k_2 + card(\omega \setminus \omega_2)$. Lemma 3.18 is proved.

Let us now prove Theorem 3.32. Since by virtue of Lemma 3.16 the minimal length cycle for an arbitrary profile $\{P_i\}$ is determined by the number ρ_0, we have $m < \rho_0$. According to Lemma 3.17, $\rho_0 = 2$ for $k_1 \leq k_2$, and consequently, m should equal to 1. The proof of the second assertion follows directly from the condition $m < \rho_0$ and Lemma 3.18. Finally, to prove the third assertion of the theorem we note that when n is fixed, ρ_0 has its maximum with $k_1 = n - 1$ and $k_2 = 1$; hence it follows that with $m \geq n$ we have $m \geq \rho_0$ irrespective of the values of k_1 and k_2 ■

The second and third assertions of Theorem 3.32 may be illustrated with the case of $m = 5$. Then any (k_1, k_2)-majority rule will generate an acyclic relation P for any weak order profile with $\lceil k_1/k_2 \rceil \geq m$. Such rules may, for instance, be $(5,1)$-, $(9,2)$-, or $(15,3)$-majority rules. The number of voters n is important only if $m \geq n$, for instance, if $n = 3$. In this case an acyclic relation P may be obtained only with the use of the relative k-majority rules, because the only (k_1, k_2)-majority rule with $k_1 > k_2 \neq 0$ here is the $(2,1)$-majority rule, for which a profile $\{P_i\}_1^3$ exists such that the resulting relation does not belong to region $\Lambda(\mathcal{AR})$. A simple corollary of Theorem 3.32 deals with an intersection of $\Lambda(\mathcal{AR})$ with the class of absolute k-majority rules.

Corollary 3.14 *The intersection of the complete class $\Lambda(\mathcal{AR})$ with the class of absolute k-majority rules consists of rules satisfying the condition $\lceil k/(n-k) \rceil \geq m$. With $m \geq n$, this intersection contains only Unanimity rule $\mathcal{U}$.*

Remark. For the general case, i.e., for the rules from the intersection of the classes $\Lambda(\mathcal{AR})$ and $\Lambda^{\{\tau-(k_1,k_2)\}}$, the proof of Theorem 3.32 taking into account the equality $\Lambda^{SC} = \Lambda^{\{\tau-(k_1,k_2)\}}$ is easily seen to imply that
(a) if there exist some $t = 1, ..., \tau$, such that $k_1^t \leq k_2^t$, then $\Lambda(\mathcal{AR}) \cap \Lambda^{SC} = \emptyset$;
(b) if $\forall t \in 1$, $k_1^t > k_2^t$, then $\Lambda(\mathcal{AR}) \cap \Lambda^{SC} = \Lambda_m^{\{\tau-(k_1,k_2)\}}$ with $m \leq \min_t \lceil k_1^t, k_2^t \rceil$;
(c) if $m \geq n$, then $\Lambda(\mathcal{AR}) \cap \Lambda^{SC} = \Lambda^{RkM}$.

Let us now turn to consideration of intersections of the classes $\Lambda(\mathcal{SPO})$ and $\Lambda(\mathcal{WO})$ for strict partial orders and weak orders with Symmetrically Central Class. As a direct consequence of Theorems 3.19 and 3.21 and previous Remark, we have

Theorem 3.33 *The intersection of the class $\Lambda(\mathcal{SPO})$ with the Symmetrically Central Class coincides with the class of relative k-majority rules, i.e.,*

$$\Lambda(\mathcal{SPO}) \cap \Lambda^{SC} = \Lambda^{RkM}.$$

The intersection of the class $\Lambda(\mathcal{WO})$ with the Symmetrically Central Class is empty, i.e.,

$$\Lambda(\mathcal{WO}) \cap \Lambda^{SC} = \emptyset.$$

Note that by virtue of the assertions made in Theorem 3.32 and 3.33, the intersection of the classes $\Lambda(\mathcal{SPO})$ when $m \geq n$ and $\Lambda(\mathcal{WO})$ with the Symmetrically Central Class coincide with each other. Then it follows that with $m \geq n$ and with any profile $\vec{P}$, rules from the intersection of the class $\Lambda(\mathcal{AR})$ with the Symmetrically Central Class will generate partial orders rather than just acyclic relations.

Figure 3-12 illustrates the assertions made in Theorems 3.31 to 3.33. This picture shows the intersection $\Lambda(\mathcal{AR}) \cap \Lambda^C$ containing class Λ^{HC}, the class $\Lambda(\mathcal{AR}) \cap \Lambda^{SC}$ being shaded, and the class of relative k-majority rules double-shaded.

The case with the number of alternatives m exceeding 2 was considered above. The special case $m = 2$ will be interesting to analyze as well. The availability of only two alternatives x and y in A may be interpreted as some unique decision such that if P_i

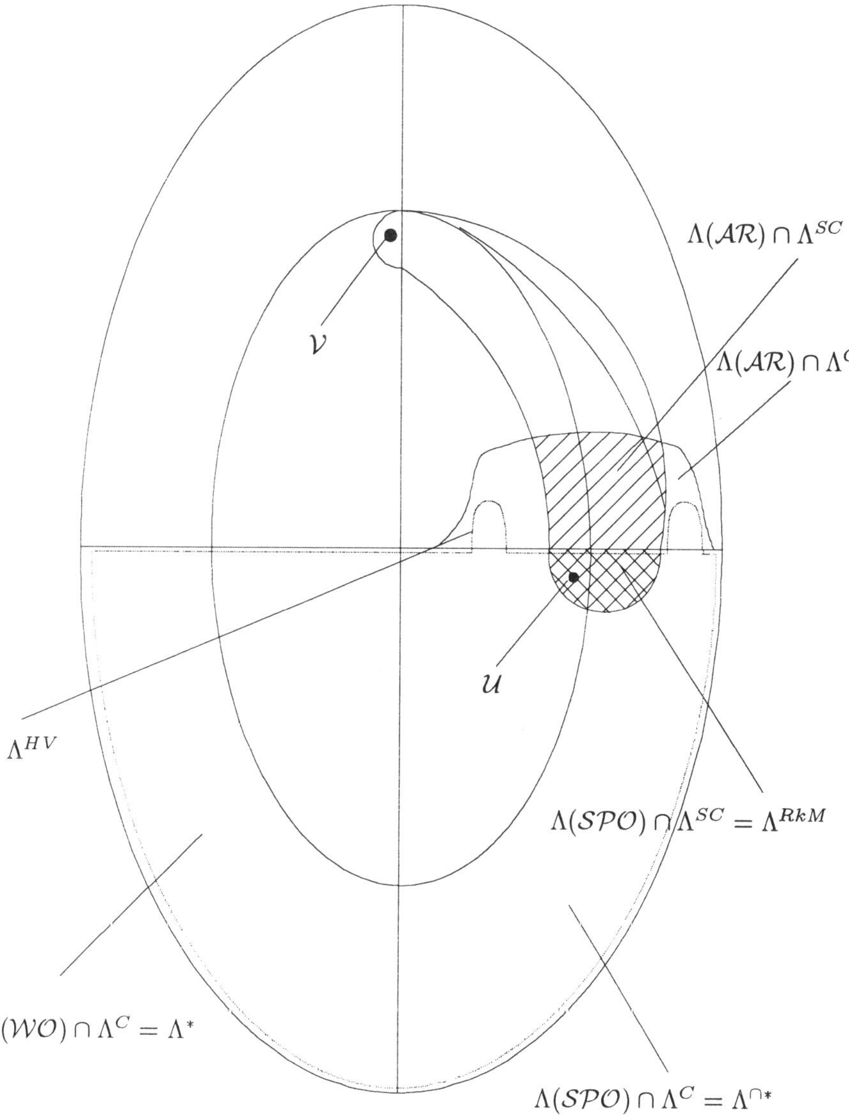

Figure 3-12

consists of the pair (x, y), voter i prefers to make this decision, while if P_i consists of the inverse pair (y, x), voter i prefers to reject it.
From Theorem 3.31 immediately follows

Corollary 3.15 *If $m = 2$, any (k_1, k_2)-majority rule with $k_1 > k_2$ generates an acyclic relation P for an arbitrary profile $\vec{P}$.*

Since any acyclic relation is a weak order when $m = 2$, then any (k_1, k_2)-majority rule with $k_1 > k_2$ determines a social weak order P. This assertion is true, in particular, of the absolute k-majority rules with $k \geq \lceil n/2 \rceil$, to which special consideration was given in [29] .

The assertion stated in the above Corollary explains two principles widely used in grouping voters into small groups for making a collective decision: such groups normally consist of an odd number of voters, or the chairman is given an additional vote.

Four remarks will complete this Section.

Remark 1. Let us summarize the results obtained above for local rules in the Central Class. In Table 3-1 the columns correspond to different rationality constraints, and rows correspond to Central and Symmetrically Central Classes. At the intersection of rows and columns one can find the subclasses of the class of hierarchical federation rules which correspond to the case under question.

Table 3-1

	$\Lambda(\mathcal{AR})$	$\Lambda(\mathcal{SPO})$	$\Lambda(\mathcal{WO})$
Λ^C	rules which satisfy (C1)	$\Lambda^{\cap *}$	Λ^*
Λ^{SC}	Λ^{RkM}, if $m \geq n$; $\Lambda_m^{\{\tau-(k_1,k_2)\}}$, $m \leq \min_t \left\lceil \frac{k_1^t}{k_2^t} \right\rceil$	Λ^{RkM}	$\emptyset$

Thus, we have an analogue of Arrow's Theorem - hierarchical dictator when we consider the intersection of Central Class with $\Lambda(\mathcal{WO})$, and the analogue of the theorem about olygarchy - hierarchical olygarchy when we study the intersection of Central Class with $\Lambda(\mathcal{SPO})$.

Remark 2. The statements of Theorems 3.31-3.33 did not relate the class of hierarchical syndicate rules to the complete generating class for some region Q_r. The reason is that these rules, as well as the general type of hierarchical federation rules (and, by virtue of Theorem 3.19, the hierarchical representation rules), determine a social binary relation for a given profile $\{P_i\}$ which generally contains cycles, and this has been always interpreted in social choice theory as an unacceptable result (see Chapter 2).

Remark 3. The statements of Theorems 3.31-3.33 directly yield the results described above for strongly local rules: the intersection of the class $\Lambda(\mathcal{AR})$ with the Central Class defined for strongly local rules includes the collegium rules; the intersection of

$\Lambda(\mathcal{SPO})$ with this Central Class coincides with the oligarchic class of rules; etc. Note that in the case of strongly local rules, the intersection $\Lambda(\mathcal{SPO}) \cap \Lambda^{SC}$ consists of a single rule $\mathcal{U}$. Generally, local rules provide wider possibilities in that this intersection coincides with the class of rules Λ^{RkM}. Thus an 'insignificant' extension of the strong locality condition has made it possible to theoretically describe the procedures pertaining to the Symmetrically Central Class which generate acyclic and transitive relations, i.e., the relations corresponding to the logic of rational choice as it is understood in social choice theory.

Remark 4. Using this representation of rules from the class Λ^{Ne} (see Theorem 3.22), the explict form of the oprators from the intersections $\Lambda^{Ne} \cap \Lambda(\mathcal{AR})$, $\Lambda^{Ne} \cap \Lambda(\mathcal{SPO})$, and $\Lambda^{Ne} \cap \Lambda(\mathcal{WO})$ can be obtained. The results about such rules are direct generalizations of those about anti-oligarchy and anti-dictatorship considered in Section 3.10.

3.16 Concluding remarks and guide to the literature

Remark 1. The assumption that the domain of Social Decision Rules consists of all $n-$tuples of of binary relations of a special type, say, all $n-$tuples of linear orders, or all $n-$tuples of weak oredrs, etc., plays a crucial role in a theory developed. In the applications to economic environment this assumption should be weakened. The first result applying Arrow's model to economic environment was obtained in [151]. Further results on this way were got in [66,70,78,79,101]. In [81,82] the impossibility results were obtained in topological spaces even without Independence of Irrelevant Alternatives condition. A complete analysis of publications in this direction was done in [74,79].
The case with infinite number of voters was studied by P.Fishburn [117] and A.Kirman and D.Sondermann [160] (see also [25,266,267]).

Remark 2. Another constraint on the domain of a local rule - single-peakedness - was introduced by D.Black [48,49]. It was proved that simple majority rule preserves all axioms need with that restriction on the domain Q_d.
In general, the problem of preserving transitivity (or other necessary rationality constraints) when majority rule (or, in general, local rule) is used was studied in many publications. Since with Unrestricted Domain condition preserving of this property is impossible, so the restrictions on the agents' binary relations were elaborated. The corresponding results (see, e.g., [43,44,53,69,97,116,128,149,150,208,228,230,233, 251,275] show how these restrictions should be constructed.

Remark 3. Very interesting model in which the locality condition has been re-formulated for the case of hyper-relations was considered in [201]. It is considered the aggregation of binary relations defined on A to social binary relation defined on $\mathcal{A}^k$ where $\mathcal{A}^k$ is a family of subsets of A of cardinality k. It is worth discussing here their counterpart of IIA. Let X_1 and X_2 be two subsets of A of the cardinality k, a and b be some alternatives from the set $X_1 \cup X_2 \backslash (X_1 \cap X_2)$. Let for two profiles of linear orders $\overrightarrow{R}$

and $\overrightarrow{R'}$ the following holds: $\forall i$

$$aR_ib \Leftrightarrow aR'_ib.$$

Then in the corresponding social orders $\mathcal{R}$ and $\mathcal{R}'$ it takes place

$$X_1\mathcal{R}X_2 \Leftrightarrow X_1\mathcal{R}'X_2.$$

The conditions analogous to the normative conditions considered above are introduced, and it is shown that there are rules which satisfy the axioms introduced.
The model extends that one studied in [153] .

The studies of local rules in Π_I had been initiated by the classic monograph [27] by K.Arrow. He first proved the theorem which in our notation is expressed as follows: with $|A| > 2$, $|N| > 2$

$$\Lambda^C \cap \Lambda(\mathcal{WO}) = \Lambda^d.$$

In the framework of strongly local rules A.Gibbard, A.S.Guha, A.Mas-Colell and H.Sonnenshein [130, 136, 179] obtained the result

$$\Lambda^C \cap \Lambda(\mathcal{SPO}) = \Lambda^{\cap},$$

which shows that the Arrow's Paradox can be weakened when the range of the rule is the class of strict partial orders. For the discussion of this result see [120, 122, 154, 155] .
The Veto Rule and Collegium rule were introduced and the theorem

$$\Lambda^C \cap \Lambda(\mathcal{AR}) = \Lambda^{VR}$$

was first proved by D.Brown [76] (see also [55, 60, 62, 197]).
Federation and representation rules and the theorem

$$\Lambda^C = \Lambda^{\cup\cap} = \Lambda^{\cap\cup}$$

were first obtained by B.Mirkin [186, 187] . He had studied the problem of the aggregation of equivalences as well [186] .

R.Wilson showed [277] that if in the formulation of the Arrow's General Impossibility Theorem the monotonicity condition (Pareto principle) is omitted then the anti-dictator rule arises, i.e.,

$$\Lambda^{NI} \cap \Lambda^{Ne} \cap \Lambda(\mathcal{WO}) = \Lambda^d \cup \Lambda^{d-}.$$

For further discussions and extensions of this result the reader is referred to [66, 127, 207] .
Very detailed studies of aggregation rules in Π_I had been made by B.Monjardet [188–190] , which elaborate the problem of tournament aggregation, and give the characterization of the class $\Lambda^{\cup\cap}$ in the algebraic form.

The study of acyclicity of rules made in Section 3.6 is based on [202] (see, also, [193, 194]).
New constraints on the range of the strongly local rules , namely, $l-$acyclic and single-source relations had been studied in [3] .

The local rules seem are first studied by P.Fishburn [122, 125] and T.Schwartz (see [241] and the references there). T.Schwartz obtained that the class $\Lambda^C \cap \Lambda(\mathcal{WO})$ consists of weak dictators, which was later understood to be the first by seniority agent in the Hierarchy rule. P.Fishburn proved the theorem

$$\Lambda^C \cap \Lambda(\mathcal{WO}) = \Lambda^*.$$

V.Danilov [89, 90] was the first who proved that

$$\Lambda^C \cap \Lambda(\mathcal{WO}) = \Lambda^{\cap *}.$$

He also studied the problem of aggregation of the equivalency relations and relations of tolerancy (reflexive and symmetric relations) using local rules [87, 88] .
In the exposition of the results concerning local rules in Π_I I have followed mainly [12, 22, 89] . In 1995 these results partly were re-discovered in [38, 75]

V.Levchenkov [162, 163] obtained another representation of local rules using algebraic polynomials. He made an extensive study of local neutral rules, and, in particular, he showed that Monotonicity condition M can be changed with the Positive Pareto condition PC^+ when the range Q_r of the rule in Π_I is $Q_r = \mathcal{AR}$. Another algebraic approach to local rules has been used in [86, 184, 193] .

The use of three-valued logic functions to study the problem of social choice is due to Y.Murakami [200] . In the monograph by I.Makarov et al. [170] these approach was used very widely to describe different choice problems.

A.Vladimirov [271, 272] showed that the locality of the rule in Π_I is equivalent to the existence of a boolean function $\varphi(x, y)$ of $2n$ variables, which is constructed as follows: let Z be a vector of $2n$ variables such that $Z = Z(x, y, \overrightarrow{P})$, and components of Z are defined as $\forall i \in N$

$$\begin{aligned} z_{2i-1}(Z) &= 1 \Leftrightarrow (x, y) \in P_i, \\ z_{2i}(Z) &= 0 \Leftrightarrow (y, x) \notin P_i. \end{aligned}$$

The function φ is defined as follows

$$\varphi(x, y)(Z) = 1 \Leftrightarrow (x, y) \in F(\overrightarrow{P}).$$

The set of boolean vectors $\{Z\}$ turns out to make the boolean algebra according to co-ordinate-wise defined operations of disjunction, conjunctions and negation; it is partially ordered by the relation $\leq$ $(Z_1 \leq Z_2 \Leftrightarrow Z_1 \cdot \overline{Z}_2 = \{0, ..., 0\})$, It is closed with respect to unary operation

$$Z^- : \forall i\; z_{2i-1}(Z^-) = z_{2i}(Z), z_{2i}(Z^-) = z_{2i-1}(Z).$$

This approach allowed to cosiderably extent the analysis of local rules with respect to given above. In particular, weaker assumption about individual relations had been used, namely,

$$Q_d \subseteq Q_r$$

instead of the assumption $Q_d = \mathcal{WO}$ used above.

L.Sholomov in [253–256] studied the aggregation problem using the representation of local rules via boolean functions of three-valued variables. In particular, he seems was the first to obtain the following theorems

$$\begin{aligned} \Lambda^C \cap \Lambda(\mathcal{SO}) &= \Lambda^*, \text{ and} \\ \Lambda^C \cap \Lambda(\mathcal{IO}) &= \Lambda^*, \end{aligned}$$

for the classes of semi-orders $\mathcal{SO}$, and interval orders $\mathcal{IO}$. He also obtained the class of weighted majority rules for monotonic and non-monotonic cases of local rules.

4

FUNCTIONAL AGGREGATION RULES

4.1 Introduction

In this Chapter the rules from the space Π_{II} are studied, i.e., the rules which transform individual choice functions into a social choice function. We called these rules in Chapter 1 functional aggregation rules, or, briefly, FARs. It is worth mentioning here that in general neither individual functions nor a social one are assumed to be rationalizable by some binary relation.
In Section 4.2 we give the definition of local functional aggregation rule and provide the representation of such rules via winning coalitions and in terms of boolean functions. The locality condition is formulated in such a way that the decision about inclusion an alternative x in the choice from the set X is made depending on the inclusion of x into the choice from X by agents, and the information about other alternatives and/or sets is not taken into account. Section 4.3 describes normative conditions to which the rules under study may satisfy and defines the Central Class in the set of all local FARs. This Class contains the rules which satisfy non-imposedness, monotonicity and neutrality conditions. In Section 4.4 an explicit form of the rules from the Central Class is given. It turns out that the same types of rules as in Π_I^s are obtained in the case under study - federation, olygarchy, syndicate, dictator, etc. Sections 4.5 and 4.6 study main rationality constraints imposed on FARs. In Section 4.5 we study the constraints of non-emptyness and resoluteness, and in Section 4.6 - the rules which transform individual choice functions from the domains **H**, **C**, **O** and their intersections to social choice functions from the same domains. In Section 4.7 the classes of rules which satisfy those rationality constraints are compared with the subclasses of the Central Class. One can observe here deep analogy with the strongly local rules in Π_I^s. In particular, the direct counterpart of Arrow's General Impossibility Theorem is established. In Sections 4.8 - 4.10 more detailed study of FARs is given. In Section 4.8 we consider monotonic non-neutral rules, and in Sections 4.9 and 4.10 - non-monotonic neutral rules. Section 4.11 contains concluding remarks and gives a guide to the literature.

4.2 Locality

Before we formulate and discuss the locality condition let us briefly remind the framework of the problem. Consideration is given to a group consisting of a finite number $N \geq 2$ of individuals choosing from the same (any) presentation $X \in \mathcal{A}$. Let $N = \{1, 2, \ldots, n\}$ be the set of individuals. We are interested in external (I/O) description of their actions, i.e., their choice functions $C_i(\cdot)$. The functions $C_i(\cdot)$ are assumed to be independent, i.e., each agent makes her choice independently. In what follows, the ordered set of functions $C_i(\cdot)$ ($i \in N$) is referred to as profile and is denoted as $\vec{C}$ or $\{C_i(\cdot)\}$.
The problem of aggregation consists in determining, via the profile $\{C_i(\cdot)\}$, the choice function $C(\cdot)$ which defines social choice $Y = C(X)$ for each $X \in \mathcal{A}$.

Definition 4.1 A mapping F of profile $\{C_i(\cdot)\}$ into a social choice function $C(\cdot)$ will be called a *functional aggregation rule.* A rule F is defined over the n–tuples of functions from $\mathcal{C}$, and its values are the functions from $\mathcal{C}$, i.e., F is the mapping

$$F : \mathcal{C}^n = \mathcal{C} \times \ldots \times \mathcal{C} \to \mathcal{C}.$$

The functional aggregation rule F may determine, generally, the value of $C(X)$ for some X depending on all the values $C_i(Z),\ Z \in \mathcal{A},\ i \in N$. Below we consider a narrower class of rules F, the rules determining inclusion of an alternative $x \in X$ into the social choice $C(X)$ depending only on whether this alternative x is included into the choice from X by the individual choice functions $C_i(X),\ i \in N$. The rules of this kind are defined as follows.

Definition 4.2 The functional aggregation rule F is said to satisfy *locality condition* if

$$x \in C(X) \Longleftrightarrow x \in C'(X)$$

holds for any $X \in \mathcal{A}$ and $x \in X$ and any two profiles $\{C_i(\cdot)\}$ and $\{C_i'(\cdot)\}$ such that

$$\forall i \in N\ x \in C_i(X) \Longleftrightarrow x \in C_i'(X)).$$

The set (space) of all local rules is denoted by Π_{II}.

Remark. The notion of Locality is similar to that of Strong Locality defined in the previous Chapter for the social decision rules. Indeed, in that case the decision about the inclusion of a pair (x, y) in the social binary relation P depends on the inclusion of this very pair in agents' preferences, and does not depend on other pairs (x, z) or (z, w). Locality in Π_{II} is based on the same idea but instead of a pair (x, y) we consider a pair (x, X).

As usual, four special FARs play a special role in the next sections.

Constant rule $\mathbf{1}$ generating the choice function $C(X) = X$ for all $X \in \mathcal{A}$ independently of the profile $\{C_i(\cdot)\}$;

Constant rule $\mathbf{0}$ generating the choice function $C(X) = \emptyset$ for all $X \in \mathcal{A}$ independently of the profile $\{C_i(\cdot)\}$;

Rule $\mathcal{U}$, *Unanimity*, generating $C(\cdot)$ as follows: $\forall X \in \mathcal{A}$

$$C(X) = \bigcap_{i \in N} C_i(X);$$

Rule $\mathcal{V}$, *One vote*, generating $\forall X \in \mathcal{A}$

$$C(X) = \bigcup_{i \in N} C_i(X).$$

The notations $\mathbf{1}, \mathbf{0}, \mathcal{U}$ and $\mathcal{V}$ are used in the text below and in the figures.

Let us define now the representation of local FARs using winning coalitions approach. Let $\omega^{(x,X)}$ be a subset of N, and $\Omega(x, X)$ be an arbitrary family of such subsets ω. The set $\{\Omega(x, X)\}_{(x,X)}$ of families $\Omega(x, X)$ being given, let us define the aggregation rule ψ in the following way

$$x \in \psi(\vec{C}, X) \text{ if and only if } V(x, X; \vec{C}) \in \Omega(x, X), \tag{4.1}$$

where $V(x, X; \vec{C}) = \{i \in N \mid x \in C_i(X)\}$. In other words, x is included in the social choice from X if and only if the set of agents including x into their choice from X constitutes a group from the list $\Omega(x, X)$ for the pair (x, X). The set of lists $\{\Omega(x, X) \mid x \in X \in \mathcal{A}\}$ forms Ω- *(or, list) representation* of the rule ψ.

Denote the class of all such rules ψ arising with different $\{\Omega(x, X)\}_{(x,X)}$ as Ψ.

Theorem 4.1 *The sets Π_{II} and Ψ coincide.*

Proof. Let a local rule F be given. Construct $\Omega(x, X)$ for each x and X $(x \in X)$ as follows: for any profile $\vec{C}$ if $x \in F(\vec{C}, X)$, then include $V(x, X; \vec{C})$ to $\Omega(x, X)$. Via the lists $\{\Omega(x, X)\}_{(x,X)}$ and (4.1) we obtain the aggregation rule ψ. Show that $F = \psi$. Let $x \in F(\vec{C}, X)$. Then by construction of $\Omega(x, X)$, $x \in \psi(\vec{C}, X)$. Let $x \notin F(\vec{C}, X)$ and suppose $x \in \psi(\vec{C}, X)$. Then there exists a profile $\vec{C'}$ such that $V(x, X; \vec{C}) = V(x, X; \vec{C'})$ and $V(x, X; \vec{C'}) \in \Omega(x, X)$. But then, by locality of F, $x \in F(\vec{C}, X)$. It is evident that any rule ψ defined via $\{\Omega(x, X)\}_{(x,X)}$ and (4.1) is local. ■

Using Theorem 4.1 one can obtain the representation of any given local rule F via the set of families $\Omega(x, X)$. Since $\Omega(x, X)$ contains (for any x and X) a set of winning coalitions $\omega^{(x,X)}$, each coalition $\omega^{(x,X)}$ can enforce x to be socially chosen out of X, when the members of $\omega^{(x,X)}$ choose x even all other agents reject it.

Remark. Consider logic variable $l_i(x, X)$ defined as follows:

$$l_i(x, X) = \begin{cases} 1, \text{ if } x \in C_i(X); \\ 0, \text{ otherwise.} \end{cases}$$

and function $f_{(x,X)}(l_1, \ldots, l_n)$ such that

$$f_{(x,X)}(l_1, \ldots, l_n) = \begin{cases} 1, \text{ if } x \in C(X), \\ 0, \text{ otherwise.} \end{cases}$$

One can see that satisfaction of the aggregation rule locality condition is equivalent to the existence of a corresponding *boolean function* $f_{(x,X)}(l_1, \ldots, l_n)$.
The main theorem of boolean logic states (see, e.g., [183]) that the function f can be written explicitly is disjunctive normal form as[29]

$$f(x, X; \vec{l}\,(x, X)) = \bigvee_{\omega \in \Omega(x,X)} \bigwedge_{i \in \omega} l_i^{\omega}(x, X),$$

where $\Omega(x, X) = \{\omega_1^{(x,X)}, ..., \omega_{q(x,X)}^{(x,X)}\}$ is a collection of $q(x, X)$ sets of individuals varying with x and X, and

$$l_i^{\omega}(x, X) = \begin{cases} l_i(x, X) \text{ if } i \in \omega, \\ |\; l_i(x, X) - 1 \;| \text{ else} \end{cases}$$

Alternatively, according to the theorem, f can be written explicitly in conjunctive normal form as

$$f(x, X; \vec{l}\,(x, X)) = \bigwedge_{\varepsilon \in E(x,X)} \bigvee_{i \in \varepsilon} l_i^{\varepsilon}(x, X),$$

where $E(x, X) = \{\varepsilon_1^{(x,X)}, ..., \varepsilon_{p(x,X)}^{(x,X)}\}$ and l_i^{ε} is defined in the same fashion as $l_i^{\omega}(x, X)$.
If $f(x, X)$ is represented in disjunctive normal form (DNF), the list $\Omega(x, X)$ will consist for $X \in \mathcal{A},\ x \in X$, of the groups $\omega(x, X)$ corresponding to the terms of DNF (i.e., conjunctions of variables l_i or their negations $\bar{l}_i,\ i = 1, \ldots, n$, in it). In doing so, each group $\omega(x, X)$ is composed of the indices of variables that are involved positively (i.e., as l_i and not as $\bar{l}_i$) into the given term.

Similarly, consideration can be given to representation of $f(x, X)$ in the conjunctive normal form (CNF), and another list $E(x, X)$ can be constructed. This list consists of groups $\varepsilon(x, X)$ corresponding to the terms of a given CNF, each group as before consisting of indices j belonging to the positively involved (into the corresponding

[29] $\bigvee$ and $\bigwedge$ are boolean addition and multiplication, respectively, defined by $l_i \bigvee l_j = 1$ if $l_i + l_j \geq 1$ and $l_i \bigvee l_j = 0$ otherwise, and $l_i \bigwedge l_j = 1$ if $l_i + l_j = 2$ and $l_i \bigwedge l_j = 0$ otherwise.

term) variables l_j. Using this dual list $E(x, X)$, one can define dual list representation for the original rule F:

$$x \notin C(X) \Leftrightarrow (\exists \varepsilon(x, X) \in E(x, X) \ : \ V(x, X; \vec{C}) = N \backslash \varepsilon(x, X)).$$

4.3 Normative conditions

We now introduce a number of normative conditions on FARs. Each condition separates the class of all local rules in Π_{II}. The conditions introduced below are counterparts of those conditions which were introduced in Chapter 3 for social decision rules. As before, in parenthesis the list representation of the normative conditions will be given.

(NI). *Non–Imposition*. This condition breaks down into two conditions, NI^+ and NI^-.
(NI^+). *Positive Non–Imposition*: for any $X \in \mathcal{A}$ and any x from X there exists a profile $\{C_i(\cdot)\}$ such that $x \in C(X)$, where $C(\cdot) = F(\{C_i(\cdot)\}_{i \in N})$.
$[\forall X, \forall x \in X, \Omega(x, X) \neq \emptyset]$
(NI^-). *Negative Non–Imposition*: for any $X \in \mathcal{A}$ and any x from X there exists a profile $\{C_i(\cdot)\}$ such that $x \notin C(X)$;
$[\forall X, \forall x \in X, \Omega(x, X) \neq 2^N]$
If both conditions NI^+ and NI^- are satisfied, the non–imposedness condition NI will be said to be satisfied.

(M). *Monotonicity*,. Let two profiles $\{C_i(\cdot)\}$ and $\{\widetilde{C}_i(\cdot)\}$ be given and $x \in C(X)$ be satisfied for some $X \in \mathcal{A}$ and $x \in X$. Let $V(x, X; \{C_i(\cdot)\}) \subseteq V(x, X; \{\widetilde{C}_i(\cdot)\})$ holds. Then, $x \in \widetilde{C}(X)$.
[Let $\omega(x, X) \in \Omega(x, X)$. Then, $\widetilde{\omega} \in \Omega(x, X)$ holds for any $\widetilde{\omega}$ such that $\omega(x, X) \subseteq \widetilde{\omega} \subseteq N$];
Monotonicity condition ensures that if all agents including the alternative x in the choice from X keep to their opinion and some of the agents who previously, in $\{C_i(\cdot)\}$ did not choose x from X change their opinion and include it in the choice from X, the social choice of x is valid. In doing so, opinions of the agents on the alternatives y from $X \backslash \{x\}$ can vary arbitrarily.
As follows directly from the definition, Monotonicity condition is stronger than that of locality: if a rule F locality of which is not pre-assumed obeys Monotonicity condition, it obviously meets the locality condition.

(Ne). *Neutrality*. Let two profiles $\{C_i'(\cdot)\}$ and $\{C_i''(\cdot)\}$ be given and let the following assertion holds for any X', X'', x', x'' such that $x' \in X'$ and $x'' \in X''$: $x' \in C_i'(X')$ for each $i \in N$ if and only if $x'' \in C_i''(X'')$. Then, $x' \in C'(X')$ if and only if $x'' \in C''(X'')$, where $C'(\cdot) = F(\{C_i'(\cdot)\})$ and $C''(\cdot) = F(\{C_i''(\cdot)\})$.

$[\forall x', X' : x' \in X', \forall x'', X'' : x'' \in X''\ \Omega(x, X) = \Omega(x', X')]$;

Condition Ne consists of two following conditions:
(Ne_X). *Context (presentation X) independence*. Let two profiles $\{C_i'(\cdot)\}$ and $\{C_i''(\cdot)\}$ be given and let for some X', X'' and x such that $x \in X'$ and $x \in X''$ the following be true: for each $i \in N$ $x \in C_i'(X')$ if and only if $x \in C_i''(X'')$. Then, $x \in C'(X')$ if and only if $x \in C''(X'')$.
$[\forall x, X, X' : x \in X, x \in X'\ \Omega(x, X) = \Omega(x, X')]$;
It is obvious that if this condition holds, then the lists $\Omega(x, X)$ are independent of the set X ($\Omega(x, X)) \equiv \Omega(x)$ for any $X : x \in X$, i.e., the rule is defined by $m =| A |$ lists of the form of $\Omega(x_1), \Omega(x_2), \ldots, \Omega(x_m)$).

(Ne_x). *Alternatives* (x) *independence*. Let two profiles $\{C_i'(\cdot)\}$ and $\{C_i''(\cdot)\}$ be given and let for some X, x', x'' such that $x' \in X$ and $x'' \in X$ the following hold: $\forall i \in N$ $x' \in C_i'(X)$ if and only if $x'' \in C_i''(X)$. Then $x' \in C'(X)$ if and only if $x'' \in C''(X)$.
$[\forall x, x' : x, x' \in X\ \Omega(x, X) = \Omega(x', X)]$;
The class of rules satisfying the condition of alternatives independence consists of rules defined by $2^m - 1$ lists $\Omega(X_1), \ldots, \Omega(X_{2^m-1})$ for all the non–empty subsets X from A. Thus, the rules satisfying the condition of Neutrality are defined for all X and $x \in X$ by a single list $\Omega(\omega_1, \ldots, \omega_q)$. In particular, for $\Omega = 2^N$ this list defines the trivial rule **1** (generating for all the profiles $\vec{C}$ the same function $C(X) = X$ for all X), and for $\Omega = \emptyset$ the trivial rule **0**.
Each of the conditions Ne_X and Ne_x are stronger than the locality condition[30] per se.

(An). *Anonymity*. Let η be some one–to–one mapping of N to N. Then, $F(\{C_i(\cdot)\} = F(\{C_{\eta(i)}(\cdot)\})$.
[Let $\Omega(x, X) = \{\omega_1, \ldots, \omega_q\}$ and η be arbitrary one–to–one mapping of N on N. Denote

$$\eta(\omega_i) = \{\eta(j) \mid j \in \omega_i\}$$

and

$$\eta(\Omega(x, X)) = \{\eta(\omega_1), \ldots, \eta(\omega_q)\}$$

Then, $\eta(\Omega(x, X)) = \Omega(x, X)$];
This condition guarantees that rules satisfying it operate identically with the opinions of all the agents.

Remark. The list representation of the rules satisfying Anonymity condition may be characterized also by the following condition:

$$\forall X, x :\ x \in X\ (\omega \in \Omega(x, X),\ | \omega' |=| \omega |) \Rightarrow \omega' \in \Omega(x, X).$$

30 It suffices to assume in Ne_X and Ne_x that, respectively, $X' = X''$ and $x' = x''$.

(U). *Unanimity condition (Pareto principle).* If $x \in C_i(X)$ for all $i \in N$, then $x \in C(X)$ (*positive Unanimity*, U^+);
$[\forall X, \forall x \in X \; N \in \Omega(x, X)]$;
if for all $i \in N \; x \notin C_i(X)$, then $x \notin C(X)$ (*negative Unanimity*, U^-);
$[\forall X, \forall x \in X \; \emptyset \notin \Omega(x, X)]$.

In contrast to the conditions M and Ne which are stronger than the locality condition, the rest of them, i.e., NI, An and U, are not related to a locality condition and are equally applicable to both local and non-local rules.
The classes in the space Π_{II} satisfying the condition $NI^+, ..., U^-$ will be denoted as $\Lambda^{NI^+}, \Lambda^{NI^-}, \ldots, \Lambda^{U^-}$. Obviously, $\Lambda^{r \cap t} = \Lambda^r \cap \Lambda^t$ holds for any two classes of rules defined by the conditions r and t $(r, t \in \{NI^+, \ldots, U^-\})$.

Definition 4.3 The class in Π_{II}, where conditions NI and M are satisfied simultaneously (i.e., the intersection of domains $\Lambda^{NI} \bigcap \Lambda^M$) will be referred to as the *Basic Class*, and that satisfying simultaneously three conditions NI, M and Ne as the *Central Class*; finally, the class satisfying the four conditions NI through An as the *Symmetrically Central Class*. These classes will be denoted as Λ^{Bas}, Λ^C and Λ^{SC}, respectively.

Let us now look on mutual positions in Π_{II} of the classes identified by the conditions NI through U, not limiting, for the time being, the domains and ranges of rules, i.e., assuming that the profile $\{C_i(\cdot)\}$ may consist of any choice functions, and $C(\cdot)$ may be also any choice function, i.e., the domain of a rule is $(Q_d)^n$ with $Q_d = \mathcal{C}$, and the range is $Q_r = \mathcal{C}$; $\mathcal{C}$ as usual stands for the set (space) of all choice functions on A.

Theorem 4.2 *a) The mutual relations of the classes* $\Lambda^{NI^+}, ..., \Lambda^{U^-}$ *are as shown at the Venn's diagrams on the Fig.*4-1*;*
b) The class Λ^{An} *has non empty intersections with all those classes;*
c) The intersection of $\Lambda^M \cap \Lambda^{Ne}$ *with* $\Lambda^{\overline{NI^-}}$ *contains only one constant rule* **1***, and the intersection of* $\Lambda^M \cap \Lambda^{Ne}$ *with* $\Lambda^{\overline{NI^+}}$ *contains only one constant rule* **0**.

Proof. In total 128 conjunctions of the conditions NI^+ through U^- and their negations are possible[31]. The following relations hold which follow directly from list representation of FARs: $U^+ \Rightarrow NI^+$; $U^- \Rightarrow NI^-$; $\overline{NI^+} \cap Ne \Rightarrow M$; $\overline{NI^-} \cap Ne \Rightarrow M$; $\overline{NI^-} \cap Ne \Rightarrow U^+$; $\overline{NI^+} \cap Ne \Rightarrow U^-$; $NI^+ \cap M \Rightarrow U^+$; $NI^- \cap M \Rightarrow U^-$.
Let us prove some other relations:
a) $\overline{NI^+} \cap \overline{NI^-} \cap Ne = \emptyset$. Indeed, $\overline{NI^+} \cap Ne$ implies $\Omega(x, X) = \emptyset$ for all $X \in \mathcal{A}$; from $\overline{NI^-} \cap Ne$ follows $\Omega(x, X) = 2^N$ for all $X \in \mathcal{A}$ and $x \in X$.
b) $\overline{NI^+} \cap Ne \Rightarrow An$; $\overline{NI^-} \cap Ne \Rightarrow An$. Indeed, the conjunction $\overline{NI^+} \cap Ne$ defines a rule for which $\forall X \in \mathcal{A}, \forall x \in X \; \Omega(x, X) = \emptyset$ and $\overline{NI^-} \cap Ne$ a rule with $\forall X \in \mathcal{A}, \forall x \in X \; \Omega(x, X) = 2^N$. Obviously, An is satisfied.

31 Conditions Ne_X and Ne_x separately are not studied in this Theorem.

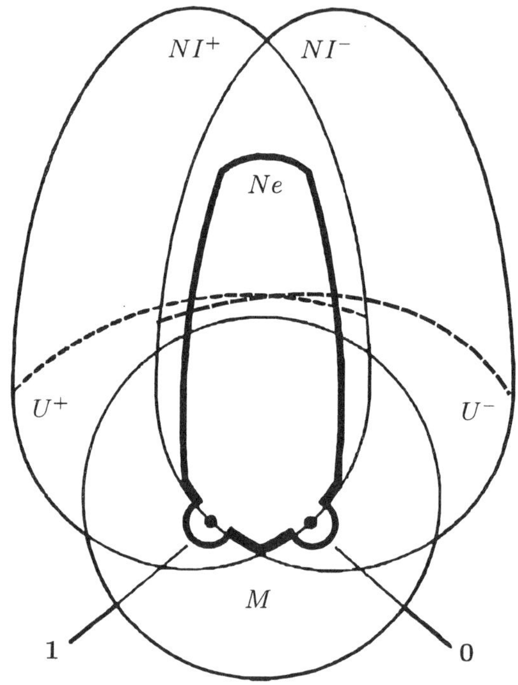

Figure 4-1

The listed properties leave only 38 of 128 conjunctions of the conditions NI^+ through U^- and their negations. The rest of 90 conjunctions separate empty domains having no rule. Non–emptiness of the classes separated by the above 38 conjunctions in Π_{II} is shown below by examples of particular rules. Since these 38 conjunctions will be used in what follows, we enumerate and present them:

1. $\overline{NI^+} \cap \overline{NI^-} \cap \overline{M} \cap \overline{Ne} \cap \overline{An} \cap \overline{U^+} \cap \overline{U^-}$,
2. $NI^+ \cap \overline{NI^-} \cap \overline{M} \cap \overline{Ne} \cap \overline{An} \cap \overline{U^+} \cap \overline{U^-}$,
3. $\overline{NI^+} \cap NI^- \cap \overline{M} \cap \overline{Ne} \cap \overline{An} \cap \overline{U^+} \cap \overline{U^-}$,
4. $NI^+ \cap NI^- \cap \overline{M} \cap \overline{Ne} \cap \overline{An} \cap \overline{U^+} \cap \overline{U^-}$,
5. $\overline{NI^+} \cap \overline{NI^-} \cap M \cap \overline{Ne} \cap \overline{An} \cap \overline{U^+} \cap \overline{U^-}$,
6. $NI^+ \cap NI^- \cap \overline{M} \cap Ne \cap \overline{An} \cap \overline{U^+} \cap \overline{U^-}$,
7. $\overline{NI^+} \cap \overline{NI^-} \cap \overline{M} \cap \overline{Ne} \cap An \cap \overline{U^+} \cap \overline{U^-}$,
8. $NI^+ \cap \overline{NI^-} \cap \overline{M} \cap \overline{Ne} \cap An \cap \overline{U^+} \cap \overline{U^-}$,
9. $\overline{NI^+} \cap NI^- \cap \overline{M} \cap \overline{Ne} \cap An \cap \overline{U^+} \cap \overline{U^-}$,
10. $NI^+ \cap NI^- \cap \overline{M} \cap \overline{Ne} \cap An \cap \overline{U^+} \cap \overline{U^+}$,
11. $\overline{NI^+} \cap \overline{NI^-} \cap M \cap \overline{Ne} \cap An \cap \overline{U^+} \cap \overline{U^-}$,

12. $NI^+ \cap NI^- \cap \overline{M} \cap Ne \cap An \cap \overline{U^+} \cap \overline{U^-}$,
13. $NI^+ \cap \overline{NI^-} \cap \overline{M} \cap \overline{Ne} \cap \overline{An} \cap U^+ \cap \overline{U^-}$,
14. $NI^+ \cap NI^- \cap \overline{M} \cap \overline{Ne} \cap \overline{An} \cap U^+ \cap \overline{U^-}$,
15. $NI^+ \cap \overline{NI^-} \cap M \cap \overline{Ne} \cap \overline{An} \cap U^+ \cap \overline{U^-}$,
16. $NI^+ \cap NI^- \cap \overline{M} \cap Ne \cap \overline{An} \cap U^+ \cap \overline{U^-}$,
17. $NI^+ \cap \overline{NI^-} \cap \overline{M} \cap \overline{Ne} \cap An \cap U^+ \cap \overline{U^-}$,
18. $NI^+ \cap \overline{NI^-} \cap \overline{M} \cap \overline{Ne} \cap An \cap U^+ \cap \overline{U^-}$,
19. $NI^+ \cap \overline{NI^-} \cap M \cap \overline{Ne} \cap An \cap U^+ \cap \overline{U^-}$,
20. $NI^+ \cap NI^- \cap \overline{M} \cap Ne \cap An \cap U^+ \cap \overline{U^-}$,
21. $NI^+ \cap \overline{NI^-} \cap M \cap Ne \cap An \cap U^+ \cap \overline{U^-}$,
22. $\overline{NI^+} \cap NI^- \cap \overline{M} \cap \overline{Ne} \cap \overline{An} \cap \overline{U^+} \cap U^-$,
23. $NI^+ \cap NI^- \cap \overline{M} \cap \overline{Ne} \cap \overline{An} \cap \overline{U^+} \cap U^-$,
24. $\overline{NI^+} \cap NI^- \cap M \cap \overline{Ne} \cap \overline{An} \cap \overline{U^+} \cap U^-$,
25. $NI^+ \cap NI^- \cap \overline{M} \cap Ne \cap \overline{An} \cap \overline{U^+} \cap U^-$,
26. $\overline{NI^+} \cap NI^- \cap \overline{M} \cap \overline{Ne} \cap An \cap \overline{U^+} \cap U^-$,
27. $NI^+ \cap NI^- \cap \overline{M} \cap \overline{Ne} \cap An \cap \overline{U^+} \cap U^-$,
28. $\overline{NI^+} \cap NI^- \cap M \cap \overline{Ne} \cap An \cap \overline{U^+} \cap U^-$,
29. $NI^+ \cap NI^- \cap \overline{M} \cap Ne \cap An \cap \overline{U^+} \cap U^-$,
30. $\overline{NI^+} \cap NI^- \cap M \cap Ne \cap An \cap \overline{U^+} \cap U^-$,
31. $NI^+ \cap NI^- \cap \overline{M} \cap \overline{Ne} \cap \overline{An} \cap U^+ \cap U^-$,
32. $NI^+ \cap NI^- \cap M \cap \overline{Ne} \cap \overline{An} \cap U^+ \cap U^-$,
33. $NI^+ \cap NI^- \cap \overline{M} \cap Ne \cap \overline{An} \cap U^+ \cap U^-$,
34. $NI^+ \cap NI^- \cap M \cap Ne \cap \overline{An} \cap U^+ \cap U^-$,
35. $NI^+ \cap NI^- \cap \overline{M} \cap \overline{Ne} \cap An \cap U^+ \cap U^-$,
36. $NI^+ \cap NI^- \cap M \cap \overline{Ne} \cap An \cap U^+ \cap U^-$,
37. $NI^+ \cap NI^- \cap \overline{M} \cap Ne \cap An \cap U^+ \cap U^-$,
38. $NI^+ \cap NI^- \cap M \cap Ne \cap An \cap U^+ \cap U^-$.

Table 4-1 gives examples of 26 choice functions from these intersections which proves their non–emptiness. In all the examples $A = \{x, y, z\}$, $N = \{1, 2, 3\}$. To each of the 26 conjunctions we show lists $\Omega(x, X)$ for the following pairs

$$(x, A),\ (x, \{x, y\}),\ (x, \{x, z\}),\ (x, \{x\}).$$

For the remaining pairs of the form of (t, X), $t \neq x$, $X \in \mathcal{A}$, the lists are the same as for the corresponding pairs (x, X), i.e., one can assume that $\Omega(z, A) = \Omega(y, A) = \Omega(x, A)$, $\Omega(y, \{y, z\}) = \Omega(z, \{y, z\}) = \Omega(x, \{x, y\})$, etc. One can readily check that with these lists the conditions are met for corresponding conjunctions from Theorem 4.2 and, thus, the domain it defines is non–empty.
The examples of rules for conjunctions 6, 12, 16, 20, 21, 25, 29, 30, 33, 34, 37 and 38 (omitted in Table 4-1) are constructed regarding the examples 4, 10, 14, 18, 19, 23, 27, 28, 31, 32, 35 and 36, respectively, if one takes into account that the condition Ne is obeyed and the list $\Omega(x, A)$ is used as Ω.
Conjunction 30 defines the rule with $\forall X, x : x \in X \in \mathcal{A}$, $\Omega(x, X) = \emptyset$, generating

Table 4-1

Conjunction	$\Omega(x, A)$	$\Omega(x, \{x,y\})$	$\Omega(x, \{x,z\})$	$\Omega(x, \{x\})$
1	$\{\emptyset\}$	2^N	$\{1\}$	$\emptyset$
2	$\{1\}$	2^N	$\{1\}$	$\{1\}$
3	$\emptyset$	$\emptyset$	$\{1\}$	$\{\emptyset\}$
4	$\{\emptyset\},\{1\}$	$\{\emptyset\}$	$\{1\}$	$\{\emptyset\}$
5	$\{1\}, \quad \{1,2\}$ $\{1,3\} \quad N$	$\emptyset$	2^N	$\emptyset$
7	$\{1\},\{2\},\{3\}$	$\emptyset$	2^N	$\emptyset$
8	$\{1\},\{2\},\{3\}$	2^N	2^N	2^N
9	$\{1\},\{2\},\{3\}$	$\emptyset$	$\emptyset$	$\{\emptyset\}$
10	$\{\emptyset\},\{1\},\{2\},\{3\}$	$\{\emptyset\}$	$\{\emptyset\}$	$\{\emptyset\}$
11	N	$\emptyset$	2^N	2^N
13	$\{1\},N$	2^N	2^N	2^N
14	$\{\emptyset\},\{1\},N$	N	N	N
15	2^N	$\{1,2\},N$	N	N
17	$\{1\},\{2\},N$	2^N	N	N
18	$\{\emptyset\},\{1\},\{3\},N$	N	N	N
19	2^N	N	N	N
22	$\{1\}$	$\emptyset$	$\emptyset$	$\emptyset$
23	$\{1\}$	$\{1\},\{2\}$	$\{1\}$	$\{1\}$
24	$\{1,2\},N$	$\emptyset$	$\emptyset$	$\emptyset$
26	$\{1\},\{2\},\{3\}$	$\emptyset$	$\emptyset$	$\emptyset$
27	$\{1\},\{2\},\{3\}$	N	N	N
28	$\emptyset$	N	$\emptyset$	$\emptyset$
31	$\{1\},N$	N	N	N
32	$\{1,2\},\{2\},\{3\},N$	N	N	N
35	$\{1\},\{1,3\},\{2,3\},N$	N	N	N
36	$\{1,2\},N$	N	N	N

$C(X) = \emptyset$ independently of the profile $\{C_i(\cdot)\}$, i.e., the rule $\mathbf{0}$. Conjunction 21 defines the rule with $\forall X, x : x \in X \in \mathcal{A}$, $\Omega(x, X) = 2^N$, generating $C(X) = X$ independently of the profile $\{C_i(\cdot)\}$, i.e., the rule $\mathbf{1}$.

The examples presented here were constructed for $|N| = 3$ and $|A| = 3$. The same examples can be easily generalized to the cases of $|N| > 3$ and $|A| > 3$. In the first case, for all the conjunctions where An is met one must add the corresponding rows of the index set of the same type as in the sets given in the rows of Table 4-1.

In the second case, N may be inserted in all the rows for lists of the form of (x, X) apart those presented in Table 4-1.

Theorem 4.2 follows from the established fact that the above 38 conjunctions are non–empty and the remaining 90 are empty ■

Let us introduce next the notion of the Basic list of a local rule F.

Definition 4.4 The subset of a given list $\Omega(x, X)$ will be called the *Basic list* of the list $\Omega(x, X)$ and denoted as $\Omega^B(x, X)$ if
a) for any $\omega(x, X) \in \Omega^B(x, X)$ any superset belongs to $\Omega(x, X)$, i.e.,

$$\forall \omega(x, X) \in \Omega^B(x, X) \text{ and } \forall \widetilde{\omega} \supset \omega(x, X) \Rightarrow \widetilde{\omega} \in \Omega(x, X);$$

and
b) no subset of any $\omega(x, X)$ from $\Omega^B(x, X)$ belongs to $\Omega(x, X)$, i.e.,

$$\forall \omega(x, X) \in \Omega^B(x, X) \text{ and } \forall \widetilde{\omega} \subset \omega(x, X) \Rightarrow \widetilde{\omega} \notin \Omega(x, X).$$

For the rules F which satisfy Monotonicity condition the Basic list $\Omega^B(x, X)$ is a set of minimal (by inclusion) groups $\omega(x, X)$ from $\Omega(x, X)$. Thus, for monotone rules the Basic list is defined by condition b), since condition a) follows from monotonicity, and via $\Omega^B(x, X)$ the list $\Omega(x, X)$ for a given monotone rule F is defined uniquely.

4.4 Rules from Central Class

Below, consideration is given to the rules defined explicitly by indicating a procedure that determines whether alternative x is included into social choice $Y = C(X)$ by the fact that x is present in the choice made by individuals from X.

The classes of aggregation rules described below are distinguished by the fact that they represent different degrees of individuals' inequality in social choice. The importance of the classes thus introduced will be established after the study of interrelations between classes defined in three different ways: by normative conditions, by rationality constraints and via definition of explicit form of rules.

Definition 4.5 Let us call the rule a *federation rule* if there exists a family $\Omega = (\omega_1, \dots, \omega_q)$ (where $q \geq 1$) of non–empty coalitions such that for all $j = 1, \dots, q$, $\omega_j \subseteq N$, and for any x and X $(x \in X \in \mathcal{A})$ $x \in C(X)$ if and only if there is at least one set of indices ω_j from Ω such that for all $i \in \omega_j$, $x \in C_i(X)$.

Denote the class of federation rules as $\Lambda^{\cup\cap}$.

By virtue of this definition, a federation rule describes the case where privileged groups are separated within the set of all agents N, and social decision about inclusion of x into $C(X)$ is made only if all the individuals of at least one such group make this decision (i.e., include x into the choice from X).

A federation rule may be formally described as follows:

$$C(X) = \bigcup_{j=1}^{q} \bigcap_{i \in \omega_j} C_i(X). \tag{4.2}$$

Since the non–emptiness of the intersection $\cap_{i\in\omega_j} C_i(X)$ corresponds to unanimous decision of the group ω_j, the union of group decisions comprises the alternatives unanimously chosen by the agents of at least one group.

Definition 4.6 Let us call a local rule a *representation rule* if there exists a family $E = \{\varepsilon_1, \dots, \varepsilon_t\}$ $(t \geq 1)$ of non–empty coalitions such that for all $j = 1, \dots, t$, $\varepsilon_j \subseteq N$, and for all x and X $(x \in X \in \mathcal{A})$, $x \in C(X)$ if and only if in any index set $\varepsilon_1, \dots, \varepsilon_t$ there is at least one index i such that $x \in C_i(X)$.

Denote the class of all the representation rules by $\Lambda^{\cap\cup}$. The fact that the representation rule constructs $C(\cdot)$ directly in the following manner

$$C(X) = \bigcap_{j=1}^{t} \bigcup_{i\in\varepsilon_j} C_i(X), \tag{4.3}$$

follows directly from Definition 4.6, i.e., the alternative x is included into the collective choice if at least one agent (representative) of each privileged group includes this alternative into her choice.

As follows from comparison of (4.2) and (4.3) and from distributiveness of the operations $\bigcup$ and $\bigcap$, the classes of federation and representation rules coincide, i.e., $\Lambda^{\cup\cap} = \Lambda^{\cap\cup}$.

Theorem 4.3 *The Central Class Λ^C in Π_{II} coincides with the class of federation (representation) rules, i.e., $\Lambda^C = \Lambda^{\cup\cap} = \Lambda^{\cap\cup}$.*

Proof. Let some rule from Λ^C be given with basic list $\Omega^B = (\omega_1, ..., \omega_r)$, $r \geq 1$. Due to the conditions NI and M $\forall i = 1, ..., r$, $\omega_i \neq \emptyset$. Construct the federation rule φ as follows:

$$\varphi(\vec{C}, X) = \bigcup_{i=1}^{r} \bigcap_{j\in\omega_i} C_j(X).$$

Show that $F \equiv \varphi$. Let $x \in F(\vec{C}, X)$. Then $\exists \omega_i \in \Omega^B$ such that $V(x, X; \vec{C}) \supseteq \omega_i$. This implies that $\forall j \in \omega_i$, $x \in C_j(X)$. Hence $x \in \varphi(\vec{C}, X)$. Let $x \notin F(\vec{C}, X)$. Then $V(x, X; \vec{C}) \notin \Omega$, i.e., $x \notin \cap_{j\in\omega_i} C_j(X)$ for any ω_i. Hence, $x \notin \varphi(\vec{C}, X)$. The fact that any federation rule belongs to Λ^C is obvious. ■

Consider now special cases of federation (representation) rules.

Definition 4.7 The federation rule representable as

$$C(X) = \bigcap_{i\in\omega} C_i(X),$$

will be called the *oligarchy rule.*

Here ω is one group from N.

Definition 4.8 The representation procedure representable as

$$C(X) = \bigcup_{i \in \varepsilon} C_i(X),$$

will be called the *syndicate* rule.

Definition 4.9 The oligarchy (correspondingly, syndicate) rule representable as

$$C(X) = C_i(X),$$

will be referred to as the dictatorial rule, or, simply, *dictator.*

Denote the classes of above introduced rules by $\Lambda^{\cap}$, $\Lambda^{\cup}$ and Λ^{d}, respectively. The class Λ^{d}, obviously, consists of $n = | N |$ dictatorial rules.

Let us define now *k-majority* rule in Λ^{C}. This rule includes alternative x into $C(X)$ if at least k agents include it in their choices from X. Obviously, this rule is a special case of the federation rule, where the family Ω in its definition comprises all the k-element coalitions and no coalitions with less than k members are in Ω.

Denote the class of k-majority rules by Λ^{kM}.

All the rules introduced above are defined by some set Ω (or E) of agents groups. For all rules, with the exception of the k-majority rule, the groups Ω may be such that the agents are included into them in different manner. Moreover, some agents may be out of all groups. In contrast, in the k-majority rule agents are equally included in corresponding groups.

The following theorem holds.

Theorem 4.4 *The Symmetrically Central Class Λ^{SC} coincides with the class of k-majority rules, i.e.,*

$$\Lambda^{SC} = \Lambda^{kM}.$$

The intersection of the class Λ^{kM} with the classes a) dictator, b) oligarchy and c) syndicate is a) empty, b) consists of the only unanimity rule $\mathcal{U}$, or c) consists of the only one vote rule $\mathcal{V}$, i.e.,

$$\Lambda^{kM} \cap \Lambda^{d} = \emptyset,$$

$$\Lambda^{kM} \cap \Lambda^{\cap} = \{\mathcal{U}\},$$

$$\Lambda^{kM} \cap \Lambda^{\cup} = \{\mathcal{V}\}.$$

Moreover, the class $\Lambda^{C} \backslash (\Lambda^{\cap} \cup \Lambda^{\cup} \cup \Lambda^{d})$ is not empty, whereas $(\Lambda^{\cap} \cap \Lambda^{\cup}) \backslash \Lambda^{d}$ is empty.

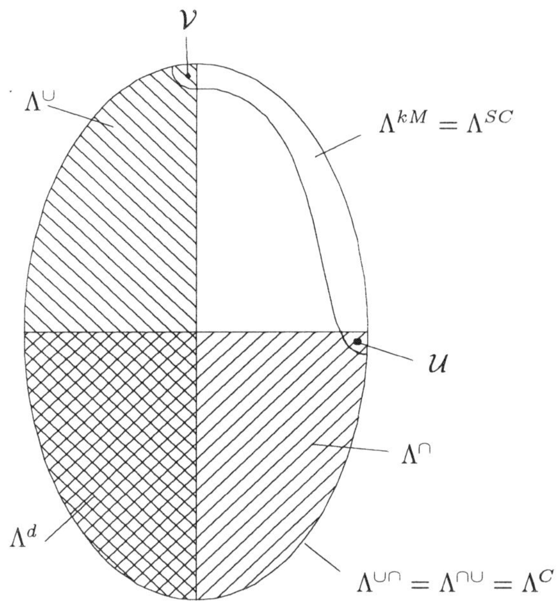

Figure 4-2

Proof. The assertion of Theorem 4.4 that the classes Λ^{SC} and Λ^{kM} coincide follows from their definitions in terms of list representation.
The cases a), b) and c) will be proved separately.
Case a). For the $k-$majority rule and $k = 1$, the list Ω^B must comprise all the $k-$element subsets N, for the dictatorial rule the list Ω^B consists of only one index i^*. Hence, $\Lambda^{kM} \bigcap \Lambda^d = \emptyset$.
Case b). The oligarchy rule is defined by the list $\Omega^B = \{\omega\}$. If it is also the k-majority rule, then $\omega = N$, i.e., $\Omega^B = \Omega = (N)$, which is the list representation of the rule $\mathcal{U}$.
Case c). The syndicate rule is defined by the list $\Omega^B = \{\omega_1, \ldots, \omega_t\}$ for $\mid \omega_i \mid = 1, \forall\ i = 1, \ldots, t, 1 \leq t \leq N$. If it is also the k-majority rule, obviously, $\Omega^B = (\{1\}, \ldots, \{N\})$, which is the list representation of rule $\mathcal{V}$. ■

Figure 4-2 illustrates the mutual relations between rule classes following from Definitions 4.5-4.9 and Theorems 4.3 and 4.4.

4.5 Rationality constraints: non-emptiness

Until now we did not restrict the domain and range of functional aggregation rules, i.e., the rule F was defined over the n–tuples of functions from C, and its values were

the functions from $\mathcal{C}$, i.e., F was considered as the mapping $F : \mathcal{C}^n \to \mathcal{C}$.
Let the domain of definition Q_d and range Q_r coincide: $Q_d = Q_r = Q$, and $Q \subset \mathcal{C}$.

Definition 4.10 The domain of choice functions $Q \subset \mathcal{C}$ will be called closed with respect to a rule F if for any profile $\{C_i(\cdot)\}$ such that for all $i \in N$ $C_i(\cdot) \in Q$,

$$F(\{C_i(\cdot)\}) = C(\cdot) \in Q$$

holds.
The domain $Q \subset \mathcal{C}$ will be called closed with respect to the class of rules $\mathcal{F}$ if Q is closed with respect to each rule $F \in \mathcal{F}$.
If $\mathcal{F}$ consists of all the rules with respect to which Q is closed, $\mathcal{F}$ will be called the *complete class of closedness* for the domain Q and denoted by $\Lambda(Q)$.

Obviously, $\Lambda(Q)$ is the largest (in the sense of set theoretical inclusion) class with respect to which Q is closed.

In this Section we consider two important rationality constraints on a functional aggregation rule. First one is a non-emptiness of social choice functions, i.e., the case when $C(X) \neq \emptyset$ for any X and any profile $\vec{C}$, such that $\forall i$ $C_i(X) \neq \emptyset$. The second rationality constraint is that of resoluteness, i.e., $C(X) \subset X$ for any X and any profile $\vec{C}$ such that $\forall i$ $C_i(X) \subset X$. First the case will be considered when social choice function is not empty only on A, and the case when $C(A) \subset A$. Then, these results will be extended for the case of an arbitrary X. For simplicity we will consider only the rules from Λ^C and then give a remark about the extension of obtained results on general case.

Definition 4.11 A rule F is called a *non-empty choice rule*, or briefly, non-empty rule if for any profile $\vec{C}$ and for any X such that $\forall i$ $C_i(X) \neq \emptyset$, $C(X) \neq \emptyset$. A rule F is called *weakly non-empty rule* if for any profile $\vec{C}$ such that $\forall i$ $C_i(A) \neq \emptyset$, $C(A) \neq \emptyset$ holds.
A rule F is called a *resolute rule* if for any X and any $\vec{C}$ such that $\forall i$ $C_i(X) \subset X$, $C(X) \subset X$. A rule F is called a *weakly resolute rule* if $C(A) \subset A$ for any $\vec{C}$ such that $\forall i$ $C_i(A) \subset A$.

The classes of these rules will be denoted as $\Lambda(NE)$, $\Lambda(wNE)$, $\Lambda(Re)$, and $\Lambda(wRe)$, respectively.

In Section 4.3 the dual list $E(x, X)$ for a local rule was defined. Let us study now the notion of duality of functional aggregation rule in detail.

We will say that the choice function $C^-(\cdot)$ is *dual* to the function $C(\cdot)$ if $C^-(X) = X \setminus C(X)$ for any X . It is obvious that $(C^-(\cdot))^- = C(\cdot)$, where $(C^-(\cdot))^-$ is the function dual to the choice function $C^-(\cdot)$.

Definition 4.12 Let F be a functional aggregation rule. The *dual rule* for F is the functional aggregation rule $\overline{F}$ such that

$$\overline{F}(\{C_i(\cdot)\} = \overline{F(\{C_i^-(\cdot)\})}$$

for all profiles $\{C_i(\cdot)\}$.

It is obvious that $\overline{\overline{F}}= F$, where $\overline{\overline{F}}$ is the dual of $\overline{F}$. Let us first note that $C(\cdot)$ is non-empty (weakly non-empty) if and only if $C^-(\cdot)$ is resolute (weakly resolute) choice function. Analogously, F is a non-empty (weakly non-empty) rule if and only if $\overline{F}$ resolute (weakly resolute rule).

Definition 4.13 The family of sets $\overline{\Omega}$ is called the *dual list* to the list Ω if

$$\overline{\Omega} = \{\omega \subseteq N \mid \overline{\omega} \notin \Omega\}.$$

The following obvious statement holds.

Lemma 4.1 *The functional aggregation rule F is local if and only if the dual rule $\overline{F}$ is also local, and $\forall X \in \mathcal{A}$ and $\forall x \in X$*

$$\Omega_{\overline{F}}(x, X) = \overline{\Omega}_F(x, X).$$

Let us study the properties of the rules dual to the rules from Central and Symmetrically Central Classes.

Lemma 4.2 *$F \in \Lambda^C$ if and only if $\overline{F} \in \Lambda^C$; $F \in \Lambda^{SC}$ if and only if $\overline{F} \in \Lambda^{SC}$.*

Proof. Since $F \in \Lambda^C$, $\Omega \equiv \Omega_F$ monotonic. Let us prove that $\Omega_{\overline{F}} \equiv \overline{\Omega}$ is monotonic. Let $\omega \in \overline{\Omega}$. This means that $\overline{\omega} \notin \Omega$. Monotonicity of Ω implies that any subset of $\overline{\omega}$ does not belong to Ω. So $\overline{\omega}' \subset \omega$, $\overline{\omega}' \notin \Omega$ and then $\omega' =\overline{\overline{\omega}}' \supseteq \omega$, $\omega' \in \overline{\Omega}$. $\overline{\Omega}$ is neutral by definition. Since $\emptyset \notin \Omega$, $N \in \Omega$, then $N \in \overline{\Omega}$, $\emptyset \notin \overline{\Omega}$. The proof about Symmetrically Central Class is analogous. ■

As in the previous Chapter 3 let us define the notion of the rank of the list Ω.

Definition 4.14 The *rank* (or *Nakamura number*) of the list Ω is a natural number $\nu(\Omega)$ such that Ω contains $\nu(\Omega)$ sets intersection of which is empty, while the intersection of fewer sets from Ω is not empty. If $\bigcap_{\omega\in\Omega} \omega \neq \emptyset$, then by definition $\nu(\Omega) = \infty$.

Let us study now under which conditions the functional aggregation rule F is the weakly non-empty rule.

Theorem 4.5 *$F \in \Lambda(wNE) \cap \Lambda^C$ if and only if $m < \nu(\overline{\Omega})$, i.e. F is the weakly non-empty rule if and only if the rank of the dual list $\overline{\Omega}$ is greater than the number of elements in the set A.*

Proof. Let $F \in \Lambda(wNE) \cap \Lambda^C$. Suppose $m \geq \nu(\overline{\Omega})$. Consider $\omega_1,...,\omega_m$ from $\overline{\Omega}$ such that $\bigcap_{i=1}^m \omega_i = \emptyset$. Construct the profile $\vec{C}$ such that if $i \notin \omega_j$ then $C_i(A) = \{x_i\}$. Then $V(x_i, A; \vec{C}) = \{i\} \subseteq N \backslash \omega_j$. Then $V(x_i, A; \vec{C}) \notin \Omega$, since otherwise due to the Lemma 4.1 $N \backslash V(x_i, A; \vec{C}) \notin \overline{\Omega}$. This case is impossible since $N \backslash V(x_i, A; \vec{C}) \supseteq \omega_j$ and $\omega_j \in \overline{\Omega}$. Then due to the monotonicity of $\overline{\Omega}$, $N \setminus V(x_i, A; \vec{C})$ should belong to $\overline{\Omega}$. Hence $V(x_i, A; \vec{C}) \notin \Omega$ for any x_i and $C(A) = \emptyset$.
Suppose now that $F \in \Lambda^C$ and $m < \nu(\overline{\Omega})$ and show that $F \in \Lambda(wNE)$, i.e. $\forall \vec{C}$, $F(\vec{C}, A) \neq \emptyset$. Then for any $i \in N$ $\exists l \in \{1, ..., m\}$ such that $x_l \in C_i(A)$. Then $i \in V(x_l, A; \vec{C})$ and $i \notin N \setminus V(x_l, A; \vec{C})$. Hence $\bigcap_{j=1}^m (N \setminus V(x_j, A; \vec{C})) = \emptyset$. Since $m < \nu(\overline{\Omega})$ it follows that $N \setminus V(x_j, A; \vec{C}) \notin \overline{\Omega}$. This implies that $V(x_j, A; \vec{C}) \in \Omega$; hence $x_j \in C(A)$. ■

Thus, this result is the direct counterpart of Nakamura's theorem proved in previous Chapter for strongly local Social Decision Functions.

Now we make two remarks about an extensions of this theorem.
Remark 1. Since weak non-emptiness and weak resoluteness are dual constraints on choice functions, Theorem 4.5 can be immediately reformulated for the case of weak resolute functional aggregation rules. Thus we have

$$F \in \Lambda(wRe) \cap \Lambda^C \text{ if and only if } m < \nu(\Omega).$$

Remark 2. From the prove of Theorem 4.5 immediately follows how one can extend that result for the non-neutral case: A rule F is a non-empty functional aggregation rule if and only if for any X, $card(X) = t$, and any $\omega_i \in \overline{\Omega}(x_i, X)$, $i = 1, ..., t$,

$$\bigcap_{i=1}^{t} \omega_i \neq \emptyset.$$

An analogous result holds for the case $F \in \Lambda(Re)$.

One can immediately extend the result stated by Theorem 4.5 taking into account Remark 2 for an arbitrary X, i.e., extend this result for non-empty and resolute cases. So we have

Theorem 4.6 *a)* $F \in \Lambda(NE) \cap \Lambda^C$ *if and only if* $m < \nu(\overline{\Omega})$;
b) $F \in \Lambda(Re) \cap \Lambda^C$ *if and only if* $m < \nu(\Omega)$.

Proof. Indeed, since a social choice function is defined on any X, then for X such that $card(X) = 2$ it should be that for any two sets ω_1 and ω_2 in $\overline{\Omega}$ their intersection is non-empty, for X such that $card(X) = 3$ any three sets in $\overline{\Omega}$ have non-empty intersection, etc. All these cases are covered by $m < \nu(\overline{\Omega})$ for A is the set with maximal cardinality. ■

Let us study now the structure of a list Ω for the case when $\nu(\overline{\Omega}) = \infty$, i.e. the case when all ω in $\overline{\Omega}$ have a non-empty intersection.

Definition 4.15 An agent $i \in N$ is called *weak dictator* if $C_i(X) \subseteq C(X)$ for any X and any profile $\vec{C}$.

Otherwise speaking, weak dictatorship pre-defines that the alternatives chosen by the weak dictator are always included in the social choice independently of opinions of other agents. In terms of list representation the existence of weak dictator means that $\{i\} \in \Omega^B$. If such set $\{i\}$ is unique, we have a usual dictator, introduced above.

Theorem 4.7 *Let $F \in \Lambda^C$. If $\nu(\overline{\Omega}) = \infty$, then F is a weak dictatorial rule.*

Proof. Let $\omega_0 = \bigcap_{\omega \in \overline{\Omega}} \omega$. We show that if $i \in \omega_0$, then $\{i\} \in \Omega$. Let $x \in C_i(X)$ for some X. Then $i \in V(x, X; \vec{C})$. This implies that $N \setminus V(x, X; \vec{C}) \notin \overline{\Omega}$. Indeed, if $\omega' = N \setminus V(x, X; \vec{C}) \in \overline{\Omega}$, then $\omega' \cap \omega_0 = \omega'' \subset \omega_0$, which contradicts the minimality of ω_0. Then $V(x, X; \vec{C}) \in \Omega$ and $x \in C(X)$. ■

Consider now the rules from the Symmetrically Central Class. Since this Class coincides with the class of k-majority rules, we can answer the question about the non-emptiness of those rules in terms of relations between k, $n = card(N)$ and $m = card(A)$.

Theorem 4.8 *Let F be a k-majority rule. Then F is a non-empty rule if and only if*

$$m < \left\lceil \frac{n}{k-1} \right\rceil.$$

Proof. First we formulate and prove two lemmas.

Lemma 4.3 *Let $\overline{\Omega}$ consists of the sets ω with cardinality greater than or equal to q. Then*

$$\nu(\overline{\Omega}) = \left\lceil \frac{n}{n-q} \right\rceil.$$

Proof of Lemma 4.3. If Ω contains r coalitions $\omega_1, ..., \omega_r$ of the cardinality q such that $\bigcap_{i=1}^{r} \omega_i = \emptyset$, then $\bigcup_{i=1}^{r} \overline{\omega}_i = N$, where $card(\overline{\omega}_i) = n - q$ for all i. But it is possible iff $r(n-q) \geq n$, i.e. $r \geq \left\lceil \frac{n}{n-q} \right\rceil$. Hence, $\nu(\overline{\Omega}) = \left\lceil \frac{n}{n-q} \right\rceil$.

Lemma 4.4 *Let F be a k-majority rule. Then $\overline{\Omega}$ for F consists of all sets ω with cardinality greater or equal $n-k+1$.*

Proof of Lemma 4.4. Let us consider several cases
a) $k < \lceil \frac{n}{2} \rceil$,
Indeed, due to the monotonicity condition all sets of cardinality greater than or equal to $n-k$ are in Ω. Hence, the sets ω, $card(\omega) = n-k$, do not belong to $\overline{\Omega}$. Since the sets ω with $card(\omega) \leq k-1$ do not belong to Ω, then all sets ω with $card(\omega) \geq n-k+1$ belong to $\overline{\Omega}$.
b) $k > \lceil \frac{n}{2} \rceil$. Proof is analogous to a).
c) n is even and $k = \frac{n}{2}$. Then $\overline{\Omega}$ consists of all sets of cardinality greater than or equal k, i.e. of cardinality $q \geq n-k+1$. Proof is analogous to a).
d) n is odd and $k = \lceil \frac{n}{2} \rceil$. Then $\overline{\Omega}$ consists of all sets ω of cardinality greater than or equal to k, hence of cardinality $q \geq n-k+1$. Proof is analogous to a).
Now the statement of the Theorem directly follows from Lemmas 4.3 and 4.4. ■

Remark. 1) From Theorem 4.8 one can obtain the following obvious result: The rule $\mathcal{V}$ (one vote for) is non-empty rule for any m;
2) The other simple corollary from Theorem 4.8 is also obvious: simple majority rule is non-empty if and only if $m < 3$.

From the duality of the properties of non-emptiness and resoluteness we have

Theorem 4.9 *Let F be a k-majority rule. Then F is a resolute functional aggregation rule from Λ^C, i.e., $F \in \Lambda(Re) \cap \Lambda^C$ if and only if*

$$m < \left\lceil \frac{n}{n-k} \right\rceil .$$

Let us conclude this section with the following remark.
Remark. Let $F \in \Lambda^C$ be such that that intersection of all ω from Ω is not empty, i.e., $\emptyset \neq \omega_0 = \cap_{\omega_i \in \Omega} \omega_i$. Consider two cases: a) $\omega_0 \in \Omega$; and b) $\omega_0 \notin \Omega$. In the case a) we have an oligarchy rule. The case b) is more interesting - individuals from ω_0 have a veto power, i.e. any agent $i \in \omega_0$ can 'block' any alternative x just not choosing it. However, if every member from ω_0 chooses x, it is not enough for x to be socially chosen. In this case it is necessary that agents from some group $\omega_i \setminus \omega_0$ also choose it. Thus it is the counterpart of *Veto rule* studied in previous Chapter.

Let us consider Anonymity condition in a restricted form: let η be a one- to -one mapping from N to N with $\eta(\omega_0) = \omega_0$. Then we obtain the rule which is a direct counterpart of *Collegium rule*, studied in Chapter 3 as well. This rule is defined by a parameter l, $l > card(\omega_0)$, and an alternative x is socially chosen if all agents from ω_0 choose it as well as $l - card(\omega_0)$ agents from $N \setminus \omega_0$. Let us consider in which case a collegium rule is a non-empty one. It is easy to prove that $\nu(\overline{\Omega}) = 2$ and from Theorem 4.6 we obtain the following result: a collegium rule is a rule of non-empty choice if and only if $m = 1$.

4.6 Rationality constraints: domains H, C, and O

Denote by $\Lambda(\mathbf{H}), \Lambda(\mathbf{C}), \ \Lambda(\mathbf{O}), \ \Lambda(\mathbf{H} \cap \mathbf{C})$, etc., the complete classes of closedness for the fundamental domains defined, respectively, by the conditions $\mathbf{H}, \mathbf{C}, \mathbf{O}, \mathbf{H} \cap \mathbf{C}$, etc.

4.6.1 Domain H

Let us introduce the condition (h), which restricts a list representation of a functional aggregation rule from Π_{II}.

(h). For any $X, X', x, \omega, \widetilde{\omega}$ such that $X, X' \in \mathcal{A}, \ x \in X' \subset X, \ \ \omega \in \Omega(x, X)$ and $\omega \subseteq \widetilde{\omega} \subseteq N, \ \widetilde{\omega} \in \Omega(x, X')$ holds.

Theorem 4.10 *Condition (h) is necessary and sufficient for the closedness of the domain* $\mathbf{H}$ *with respect to the rules from* Π_{II}.

Proof. Let condition (h) be satisfied. Show that $C(\cdot) \in \mathbf{H}$ if $\forall \ i \in N \ C_i(\cdot) \in \mathbf{H}$. Assume the contrary, i.e., let there be X, X', x and profile $\{C_i(\cdot)\}$ such that $x \in X' \subset X \subseteq A, \ x \in C(X)$ and $x \notin C(X')$. Since $x \in C(X)$, then $V(x, X; \{C_i(\cdot)\}) \in \Omega(x, X)$. Since $\forall \ i \in N \ C_i(\cdot) \in \mathbf{H}$ and $\forall \ i \in V(x, X; \{C_i(\cdot)\})$ and $X' \subset X$ takes place $x \in C_i(X')$, i.e. $V(x, X; \{C_i(\cdot)\}) \subseteq V(x, X'; \{C_i(\cdot)\})$. By virtue of the assumption $x \notin C(X')$, $V(x, X'; \{C_i(\cdot)\}) \notin \Omega(x, X')$ holds, which violates the condition (h).
Let now the domain $\mathbf{H}$ be closed with respect to the rule F from Π_{II}. Demonstrate that condition (h) is obeyed. Assume the contrary, i.e., let there exist $X, X', x, \omega, \widetilde{\omega}$ such that $x \in X' \subset X \subseteq A, \omega \in \Omega(x, X), \widetilde{\omega} \supseteq \omega$ and $\widetilde{\omega} \notin \Omega(x, X')$. Consider a profile $\{C_i(\cdot)\}$ consisting of functions such that the following three conditions holds for each of them:
1) $\forall \ i \in N \setminus \widetilde{\omega}$, then $x \notin C_i(X)$ and $x \notin C_i(X')$ hold;
2) $\forall \ i \in \widetilde{\omega} \setminus \omega$, then $x \notin C_i(X)$ and $x \in C_i(X')$ hold;
3) $\forall \ i \in \omega$, then $x \in C_i(X) \bigcap C_i(X')$ hold.
The above listed requirements for $C_i(\cdot)$ do not contradict the condition $\mathbf{H}$. The described profile $\{C_i(\cdot)\}$, thus, can be constructed of functions belonging to the domain $\mathbf{H}$. Then $V(x, X; \{C_i(\cdot)\}) = \omega, \ V(x, X'; \{C_i(\cdot)\}) = \widetilde{\omega}$, whence by assumption $x \in C(X), x \notin C(X')$ which contradicts the condition $C(\cdot) \in \mathbf{H}$. ■

Remark. As is evident from the proof of Theorem 4.10, its assertion is valid already for $\mid A \mid = 2$, i.e., condition (h) is necessary and sufficient for the closedness of the domain $\mathbf{H}$ even in that case.

4.6.2 Domain C

We introduce the next condition (c) on FARs F.

(c). For any $X', X'', x, \omega', \omega'', \widetilde{\omega}$ such that $X' \nsubseteq X'', X'' \nsubseteq X', \ x \in X' \in \mathcal{A}, \ x \in X'' \in \mathcal{A}, \ \omega' \in \Omega(x, X'), \omega'' \in \Omega(x, X'')$ and $\omega' \cap \omega'' \subseteq \widetilde{\omega} \subseteq N, \ \widetilde{\omega} \in \Omega(x, X' \cup X'')$

holds.

Theorem 4.11 *Condition (c) is necessary and sufficient for the closedness of the domain* **C** *with respect to the rules from* Π_{II}.

Proof. Let condition (c) be satisfied. Demonstrate that $C(\cdot) \in \mathbf{C}$ if $\forall\, i \in N\ C_i(\cdot) \in \mathbf{C}$. Assume the contrary, i.e., let there exists a profile $\{C_i(\cdot)\}$ and X', X'' and x such that $x \in C(X')\bigcap C(X'')$ and $x \notin C(X'\bigcup X'')$. It should be also noted that in this case $X' \not\subseteq X''$ and $X'' \not\subseteq X'$. Considering that $x \in C(X')$, then $V(x, X'; \{C_i(\cdot)\}) \in \Omega(x, X')$.
Similarly, $V(x, X''; \{C_i(\cdot)\}) \in \Omega(x, X'')$. Let

$$i \in V(x, X'; \{C_i(\cdot)\})\bigcap V(x, X''; \{C_i(\cdot)\}).$$

By virtue of $C_i(\cdot) \in \mathbf{C}$, obtain $x \in C_i(X'\bigcup X'')$, i.e.,

$$V(x, X'; \{C_i(\cdot)\})\bigcap V(x, X''; \{C_i\cdot)\}) \subseteq V(x, X'\bigcup X''; \{C_i(\cdot)\}).$$

Since $x \notin C(X'\bigcup X'')$ then $V(x, X'\bigcup X'', \{C_i(\cdot)\}) \notin \Omega(x, X'\bigcup X'')$ whence it follows that condition (c) is violated.
Let now the domain **C** be closed with respect to some $F \in \Pi_{II}$. Show that Condition (c) holds for it. Assume the contrary, i.e., that there exists $X', X'', x, \omega', \omega''$ and $\widetilde{\omega}$ such that $X' \not\subseteq X'', X'' \not\subseteq X'$, $x \in X'\bigcap X''$, $\omega' \in \Omega(x, X')$, $\omega'' \in \Omega(x, X'')$, $\omega'\bigcap\omega'' \subseteq \widetilde{\omega} \subseteq N$ and $\widetilde{\omega} \notin \Omega(x, X'\bigcup X'')$. Construct a profile $\{C_i(\cdot)\}$ satisfying the conditions of Table 4-2 for $X' = \{x, y\}$, $X'' = \{x, z\}$ assuming that $C_i(X) = X$ if $|X| = 1$.

Table 4-2

$i \in$	$C_i(X')$	$C_i(X'')$	$C_i(X' \cup X'')$
$\omega' \cap \omega'' \cap \widetilde{\omega}$	$\{x\}$	$\{x\}$	$\{x\}$
$(N \setminus \omega') \cap \omega'' \cap \widetilde{\omega}$	$\{y\}$	$\{x\}$	$\{x, z\}$
$\omega' \cap (N \setminus \omega'') \cap \widetilde{\omega}$	$\{x\}$	$\{z\}$	$\{x, y\}$
$\omega' \cap (N \setminus \omega'') \cap (N \setminus \widetilde{\omega})$	$\{x\}$	$\{z\}$	$\{z\}$
$(N \setminus \omega') \cap \omega'' \cap (N \setminus \widetilde{\omega})$	$\{y\}$	$\{x\}$	$\{y\}$
$(N \setminus \omega') \cap (N \setminus \omega'') \cap \widetilde{\omega}$	$\{y\}$	$\{z\}$	$\{x, y, z\}$
$(N \setminus \omega') \cap (N \setminus \omega'') \cap (N \setminus \widetilde{\omega})$	$\emptyset$	$\emptyset$	$\emptyset$

None of the conditions violates the condition **C**. Therefore, the profile $\{C(\cdot)\}$, $C_i(\cdot) \in$ **C**, can be constructed for which the following is satisfied:

$$V(x, X'; \{C_i(\cdot)\}) \;\; = \;\; \omega',$$

$$V(x, X''; \{C_i(\cdot)\}) = \omega''$$

and

$$V(x, X' \bigcup X''; \{C_i(\cdot)\}) = \widetilde{\omega}.$$

According to the assumption, obtain $x \in C(X')$, $x \in C(X'')$ and $x \notin C(X' \bigcup X'')$ which violates the requirement that $C(\cdot) \in \mathbf{C}$. ■

Remark. The statement of Theorem 4.11 requires implicitly that $|A| \geq 3$.

4.6.3 Domain O

The next condition (o) consists of two parts.

(o). For any $X', x, y, \omega, \omega', \widetilde{\omega}$ such that $x, y \in X \in \mathcal{A}$, $x \neq y$, $\omega \in \Omega(x, X)$, $\omega' \notin \Omega(y, X)$ and $\omega \backslash \omega' \subseteq \widetilde{\omega} \subseteq \omega \cup \omega'$, $\widetilde{\omega} \in \Omega(x, X \backslash \{y\})$ holds.
If $z \in X$, $z \neq y$, then $\widetilde{\omega}'' \notin \Omega(z, X \backslash \{y\})$ is obeyed for any $\widetilde{\omega}'', \omega''$, such that $\omega'' \notin \Omega(z, X)$, $\omega'' \backslash \omega' \subseteq \widetilde{\omega}'' \subset \omega'' \cup \omega'$.

Theorem 4.12 *Condition (o) is necessary and sufficient for the closedness of the domain* **O** *with respect to the rules from Π_{II}.*

Proof. Two lemmas precede the proof of the theorem.

Lemma 4.5 *Let $x, y \in X$, $x \neq y$, $\omega \in \Omega(x, X)$, $\omega' \notin \Omega(y, X)$, $\omega \setminus \omega' \subseteq \widetilde{\omega} \subseteq \omega \bigcup \omega'$. Then there exists a profile $\{C_i(\cdot)\}$ such that $\forall\ i \in N$ $C_i(\cdot) \in$* **O** *and $V(x, X; \{C_i(\cdot)\}) = \omega$, $V(y, X; \{C_i(\cdot)\}) = \omega'$, $V(x, X \setminus \{y\}; \{C_i(\cdot)\}) = \widetilde{\omega}$.*

Proof. Eight intersections of the sets $\omega, \omega', \widetilde{\omega}$ and their complements are possible of which two are empty by virtue of $\widetilde{\omega} \subseteq \omega \bigcup \omega'$.
Consider the profile $\{C(\cdot)\}$ given in Table 4-3 for $X = \{x, y, z\}$ and $X' \subset X, x \in X'$, where $C_i(\cdot) \in$ **O** for all $i \in N$ and all the desired relations are satisfied.

Table 4-3

$i \in$	$C_i(\{x,y,z\})$	$C_i(\{x,z\})$	$C_i(\{x,y\})$	$C_i(\{x\})$
$\overline{\omega} \cap \overline{\omega'} \cap (N \setminus \widetilde{\omega})$	$\emptyset$	$\emptyset$	$\emptyset$	$\emptyset$
$\overline{\omega} \cap \omega' \cap (N \setminus \widetilde{\omega})$	$\{y\}$	$\emptyset$	$\{y\}$	$\emptyset$
$\overline{\omega} \cap \omega' \cap \widetilde{\omega}$	$\{y\}$	$\{x\}$	$\{y\}$	$\{x\}$
$\omega \cap \omega' \cap (N \setminus \widetilde{\omega})$	$\{x,y\}$	$\{z\}$	$\{x,y\}$	$\{x\}$
$\omega \cap \overline{\omega'} \cap \widetilde{\omega}$	$\{x\}$	$\{x\}$	$\{x\}$	$\{x\}$
$\omega \cap \omega' \cap \widetilde{\omega}$	$\{x,y\}$	$\{x\}$	$\{x,y\}$	$\{x\}$

Lemma 4.6 *Let* $y, z \in X, y \neq z, \omega' \notin \Omega(y, X), \omega'' \notin \Omega(z, X), \omega'' \setminus \omega' \subseteq \widetilde{\omega''} \subseteq \omega'' \bigcup \omega'$. *There exists then a profile* $\{C_i(\cdot)\}, \forall C_i(\cdot) \in \mathbf{O}$ *and* $V(y, X; \{C_i(\cdot)\}) = \omega'$, $V(z, X; \{C_i(\cdot)\}) = \omega''$, $V(z, X \setminus \{y\}; \{C_i(\cdot)\}) = \widetilde{\omega}''$.

Proof. Consider $X = \{y, z\}$ without loss of generality. Eight intersections of the sets $\omega', \omega'', \widetilde{\omega''}$ and their complements are possible of which two are empty by virtue of $\omega'' \setminus \omega' \subseteq \widetilde{\omega''} \subseteq \omega'' \bigcup \omega'$. Consider the profile $\{C_i(\cdot)\}$ shown in Table 4-4, where $C_i(\cdot) \in \mathbf{O}$ and all the desired requirements are satisfied.

Table 4-4

$i \in$	$C_i(\{y, z\})$	$C_i(\{z\})$
$(N \setminus \omega') \cap (N \setminus \omega'') \cap (N \setminus \widetilde{\omega''})$	$\emptyset$	$\emptyset$
$\omega' \cap (N \setminus \omega'') \cap (N \setminus \widetilde{\omega''})$	$\{y\}$	$\emptyset$
$(N \setminus \omega') \cap \omega'' \cap \widetilde{\omega''}$	$\{z\}$	$\{z\}$
$\omega' \cap (N \setminus \omega'') \cap \widetilde{\omega''}$	$\{y\}$	$\{z\}$
$\omega' \cap \omega'' \cap (N \setminus \widetilde{\omega''})$	$\{y, z\}$	$\emptyset$
$\omega' \cap \omega'' \cap \widetilde{\omega''}$	$\{y, z\}$	$\{z\}$

Let us prove now the theorem. Let condition (o) be satisfied. Show that $C(\cdot) \in \mathbf{O}$ if $\forall\, i \in N\ C_i(\cdot) \in \mathbf{O}$. Assume the contrary, i.e., let for some X either
A) $x \in C(X), y \notin C(X), x \notin C(X \setminus \{y\})$, or
B) $z \notin C(X), y \notin C(X), z \in C(X \setminus \{y\})$.

Case A). Since $x \in C(X)$, $y \notin C(X)$, then $\omega = V(x, X; \{C_i(\cdot)\}) \in \Omega(x, X)$, $\omega' = V(y, X; \{C_i(\cdot)\}) \notin \Omega(y, X), \widetilde{\omega} = V(x, X \setminus \{y\}; \{C_i(\cdot)\}) \notin \Omega(x, X \setminus \{y\})$. Demonstrate that $\omega \setminus \omega' \subseteq \widetilde{\omega} \subseteq \omega \bigcup \omega'$ is obeyed. Indeed, as follows from $i \in \omega \setminus \omega'$, $x \in C_i(X), y \notin C_i(X)$. Considering that $C_i(\cdot) \in \mathbf{O}$, obtain $x \in C_i(X \setminus \{y\})$ and, therefore, $i \in \widetilde{\omega}$. Further, $i \in \omega \bigcup \omega'$ follows from $i \in \widetilde{\omega}$.
Indeed, let it be, on the contrary, that $i \notin \omega \bigcup \omega'$. Then $x \notin C_i(X), y \notin C_i(X)$, but $x \in C_i(X \setminus \{y\})$, which violated the condition $\mathbf{O}$. $\omega \setminus \omega' \subseteq \widetilde{\omega} \subseteq \omega \bigcup \omega'$ is shown to be satisfied. Since $\omega \in \Omega(x, X), \omega' \notin \Omega(y, X), \widetilde{\omega} \notin \Omega(x, X \setminus \{y\})$, the first part of condition (o) is violated.

Case B). Since $y, z \notin C(X)$, $z \in C(X \setminus \{y\})$ obtain that $V(y, X; \{C_i(\cdot)\}) = \omega' \notin \Omega(y, X), V(z, X; \{C_i(\cdot)\}) = \omega'' \notin \Omega(z, X), V(z, X \setminus \{y\}; \{C_i(\cdot)\}) = \widetilde{\omega''} \in \Omega(z, X \setminus \{y\})$. As above, one can demonstrate that $\omega'' \setminus \omega' \subseteq \widetilde{\omega}'' \subseteq \omega'' \bigcup \omega'$ holds and that the second part of condition (o) is violated.
Let the domain $\mathbf{O}$ be closed with respect to some $F \in \Pi_{II}$. Show that condition (o) is met for it. Assume the contrary. By virtue of Lemmas 4.5 and 4.6, violation of $C(\cdot) \in \mathbf{O}$ immediately follows from violation of condition (o). ■

Remark 1. As is evident from the proof of Theorem 4.12, its assertion is valid already for $|A| = 2$, i.e., even for $|A| = 2$ the condition (o) is necessary and sufficient for the closedness of the domain $\mathbf{O}$.

Remark 2. The assertion of Theorems 4.10-4.12 about closedness of the choice function domains Q may be treated as investigation of the case $Q_d = Q_r = Q \subset \mathcal{C}$ for $Q = \mathbf{H}, \mathbf{C}$ or $\mathbf{O}$. These theorems admit generalization to the cases where consideration is given to $Q_d \subset Q_r \subset \mathcal{C}$. Namely, one can check that for $C(\cdot)$ to belong to the class 1) $Q_r = \mathbf{H}$ for $Q_d = \mathbf{H} \cap \mathbf{C} \cap \mathbf{O}$, or $\mathbf{H} \cap \mathbf{O}$, or $\mathbf{H} \cap \mathbf{C}$, 2) $Q_r = \mathbf{C}$ for $Q_d = \mathbf{C} \cap \mathbf{O}$, or 3) $Q_r = \mathbf{O}$ for $Q_d = \mathbf{H} \cap \mathbf{C} \cap \mathbf{O}$, or $\mathbf{H} \cap \mathbf{O}, \mathbf{C} \cap \mathbf{O}$, it is necessary and sufficient that the list representation of a rule meet the conditions 1) (h), 2) (c) and 3)(o).

For $Q_r = \mathbf{C}$ to hold, it is necessary and sufficient that the following weakened version of condition (c) be satisfied for $Q_r = \mathbf{C}$, $Q_d = \mathbf{H} \cap \mathbf{C} \cap \mathbf{O}$ or $\mathbf{H} \cap \mathbf{C}$: $\forall X', X''$, $x, \omega', \omega'', \widetilde{\omega} : X' \not\subseteq X'', X'' \not\subseteq X', x \in X' \in \mathcal{A}, x \in X'' \in \mathcal{A}, \omega' \in \Omega(x, X')$, $\omega'' \in \Omega(x, X''), \widetilde{\omega} = \omega' \cap \omega'' \Longrightarrow \widetilde{\omega} \in \Omega(x, X' \cup X'')$.
For monotone rules, this condition coincides with the original condition (c).

Let us conclude this subsection with the following lemma.

Lemma 4.7 *If a rule F belongs to the intersection $\Lambda(\mathbf{O}) \bigcap \Lambda^{NI}$, then it belongs to the Central Class, i.e., $\Lambda(\mathbf{O}) \bigcap \Lambda^{NI} \subseteq \Lambda^C$.*

Proof. Lemma is proved in several steps.
a) First, show that the rule from the intersection $\Lambda(\mathbf{O}) \bigcap \Lambda^{NI}$ satisfies the Neutrality condition Ne.
a_1) Demonstrate that for any $\omega \in \Omega(x, X)$ and any $X' \subset X$ such that $x \in X'$, $\omega \in \Omega(x, X')$ holds. Indeed, it follows from the fact that the condition NI^- is satisfied that $\forall y \in X$ exists ω' such that $\omega' \notin \Omega(y, X)$. Let $y \neq x$. Then, $\widetilde{\omega} \in \Omega(x, X \setminus \{y\})$ follows from condition (o) for any $\widetilde{\omega}$ such that $\omega \setminus \omega' \subseteq \widetilde{\omega} \subseteq \omega \cup \omega'$.
In particular, ω itself satisfies this condition, whence $\omega \in \Omega(x, X \setminus \{y\})$. Considering now the set $X \setminus \{y\}$ as new X and an arbitrary alternative $y^1 \neq x$ from $X \setminus \{y\}$ as y, we see that a_1) holds for any $X' \subset X$ such that $x \in X'$.

a_2) Show that $\omega \in \Omega(x, X')$ holds for any $\omega \in \Omega(x, X)$ and any $X' \supset X$. Let, on the contrary, $\omega \notin \Omega(x, X')$. Consider profile $\{C_i(\cdot)\}$ such that $\forall i \in N$ $C_i(\cdot) \in \mathbf{O}, \forall i \in \omega$ $C_i(X') = \{x\}, \forall i \notin \omega$, $C_i(X') = \emptyset$. Obviously, $x \notin C(X')$, and $x \notin C(X)$ since $C(\cdot) \in \mathbf{O}$. However, $C_i(\cdot)$ also belong to $\mathbf{O}$. Therefore, $C_i(X) = \{x\}$ for any $i \in \omega$ and $C_i(X) = \emptyset$ for any $i \notin \omega$. This and $\omega \in \Omega(x, X)$ lead to $x \in C(X)$ which contradicts the above relation $x \notin C(X)$.
Hence, for all $\omega \in \Omega(x, X)$ and $X' \in \mathcal{A}$ for $x \in X'$, $\omega \in \Omega(x, X')$ takes place (this is easily proved by considering the set $X'' = X \cup X'$ and the fact that $X'' \supset X$ and $X'' \supset X'$).
The latter assertion shows that the condition Ne_X is met, i.e., the lists $\Omega(x, X)$ for $x \in X$ are representable as $\Omega(x)$. Show now that the condition Ne_x is satisfied.

a$_3$) Let $\omega' \in \Omega(x)$. Let us show that $\widetilde{\omega} \in \Omega(x)$ is satisfied for any $\widetilde{\omega}$ such that $\omega' \subseteq \widetilde{\omega}$, i.e., that condition (M) is obeyed. Let $\widetilde{\omega} \notin \Omega(x)$. Consider the set $\omega'' \notin \Omega(y)$ for an arbitrary $y \neq x$. Since the condition NI holds, such a set does exist. Then it follows from condition (o) that $\widetilde{\omega}'' \notin \Omega(x)$ is satisfied for any $\widetilde{\omega}''$ such that $\widetilde{\omega} \setminus \omega'' \subseteq \widetilde{\omega}'' \subseteq \widetilde{\omega} \cup \omega''$. Similarly, $\widetilde{\omega}'' \notin \Omega(y)$ follows for any $\widetilde{\omega}''$ such that $\omega'' \setminus (\widetilde{\omega} \cup \omega'') = \emptyset \subseteq \widetilde{\omega}'' \subseteq \widetilde{\omega} \cup \omega''$. In this case, $\widetilde{\widetilde{\omega}} \notin \Omega(x)$ follows for any $\widetilde{\widetilde{\omega}}$ such that $\widetilde{\omega} \setminus (\omega'' \cup \widetilde{\omega}) = \emptyset \subseteq \widetilde{\widetilde{\omega}} \subseteq \widetilde{\omega} \cup \omega''$. Considering that $\widetilde{\widetilde{\omega}} \supset \omega'$, $\omega' \notin \Omega(x)$ follows which contradicts the assumption.

a$_4$) Demonstrate that $\omega \in \Omega(y)$ takes place for any $\omega \in \Omega(x)$ and any $y \in A$. Let, on the contrary, $\omega \notin \Omega(y)$. Then, obtain from condition (o) that any $\widetilde{\omega}$ such that $\omega \setminus \omega \subseteq \widetilde{\omega} \subseteq \omega$, satisfies the condition $\widetilde{\omega} \in \Omega(x)$. Considering $\widetilde{\omega} = \emptyset$ of a$_3$), obtain $\Omega(x) = 2^N$ which leads to contradiction if NI is satisfied. Hence, Ne is satisfied, i.e., $\forall x \in A\ \Omega(x) = \Omega$.

b) It follows from a_3) for all $F \in \Lambda^{NI} \bigcap \Lambda^{Ne} \bigcap \Lambda(\mathbf{O})$ that $F \in \Lambda^M$. This fact and a) shows that $\Lambda(\mathbf{O}) \bigcap \Lambda^{NI} \subset \Lambda^C$. ■

It is worth noting that this Lemma is a counterpart of Lemmas 3.1 and 3.2 for strongly local rules in Π_I, and it is a counerpart of Lemma 3.11 and Corollary 3.8 for local rules in Π_I. It is interesting that Condition **O** plays in Π_{II} a role similar to that of transitivity in the space Π_I.

4.6.4 Intersections of domains H, C, and O

Now, we study the closedness conditions for intersections of the classes **H**, **C** and **O** of choice functions with respect to the rules from Π_{II}.
The following lemma is important for investigation of complete closedness classes for the domains in question.

Lemma 4.8 *Let Q' and Q'' be some fundamental domains in $\mathcal{C}$ (i.e., domains* **H**, **C** *or* **O**). *The complete class of closedness for the intersection of domains Q' and Q'' coincides with the intersection of complete classes of closedness for Q' and Q'', i.e.,*

$$\Lambda(Q' \cap Q'') = \Lambda(Q') \cap \Lambda(Q'').$$

Proof. Let $F \in \Lambda(Q') \cap \Lambda(Q'')$. Then consider a profile $\{C_i(\cdot)\}$ such that $\forall i\ C_i(\cdot) \in Q' \cap Q''$. Since $\forall i\ C_i(\cdot) \in Q'$ and $F \in \Lambda(Q')$, $C(\cdot) \in Q'$. Analogously, $C(\cdot) \in Q''$, i.e., $C(\cdot) \in Q' \cap Q''$. Hence $F \in \Lambda(Q' \cap Q'')$.
The proof that $F \in \Lambda(Q' \cap Q'') \Rightarrow F \in \Lambda(Q') \cap \Lambda(Q'')$ follows from the Remark 2 from the subsection 4.6.3 ■

By virtue of the Lemma 4.8 joint satisfaction of Conditions (h) and (c), or (h) and (o), or (c) and (o), as well as (h), (c), and (o) defines the form of list representation of rules with respect to which the intersections $\mathbf{H} \cap \mathbf{C}$, $\mathbf{H} \cap \mathbf{O}$, $\mathbf{C} \cap \mathbf{O}$, and $\mathbf{H} \cap \mathbf{C} \cap \mathbf{O}$ are closed.

4.6.5 Rationality constraints in Central Class

We have obtained the list representation of the rules form Π_{II}, which guarantee the closedness of the fundamental domains in the space C with respect to these rules. Let us study now those restrictions for the case when functional aggregation rules belong to the Central Class, i.e., when the normative conditions NI, M, and Ne hold. To this end let us re-write the conditions (h), (c), and (o) for that case: $\forall \omega$, ω', ω'', $\widetilde{\omega}$ and $\widetilde{\omega}''$.
(h^C): $\omega \in \Omega$ and $\omega \subseteq \widetilde{\omega} \subseteq N \Rightarrow \widetilde{\omega} \in \Omega$;
(c^C): $\omega' \in \Omega, \omega'' \in \Omega$ and $\omega' \cap \omega'' \subseteq \widetilde{\omega} \subseteq N \Rightarrow \widetilde{\omega} \in \Omega$;
(o^C): $\omega \in \Omega$, $\omega' \notin \Omega$ and $\omega \backslash \omega' \subseteq \widetilde{\omega} \subseteq N \Rightarrow \widetilde{\omega} \in \Omega$; $\widetilde{\omega}'' \notin \Omega$ is obeyed for any $\widetilde{\omega}'', \omega''$, such that $\omega', \omega'' \notin \Omega$, $\omega'' \backslash \omega' \subseteq \widetilde{\omega}'' \subset \omega'' \cup \omega'$.

One can easily see that the condition (h^C) coincides in the Central Class with Monotonicity condition, i.e., a rule $F \in \Lambda^C$, which transforms individual choice functions from the domain $\mathbf{H}$ to the social choice function from the same domain, is always monotonic. This leads to the following obvious statement.

Lemma 4.9 $\Lambda^C \subset \Lambda(\mathbf{H})$, *i.e. any rule in the Central Class from the profile, comprising of the functions, which satisfy* $\mathbf{H}$, *constructs a social choice function, which satisfies* $\mathbf{H}$.

4.6.6 Mutual relations of the classes $\Lambda(\mathbf{H})$, $\Lambda(\mathbf{C})$, and $\Lambda(\mathbf{O})$ with Λ^{NI^+}, ..., Λ^{U^-}

As in the case of the rules from Π_I, let us construct in Π_{II} mutual relations of complete classes $\Lambda(\mathbf{H})$, $\Lambda(\mathbf{C})$, and $\Lambda(\mathbf{O})$ with the classes of rules isolated by normative conditions. These relations are shown on Figs.4-3 - 4-5. We will not prove these relations. The reader can find the proofs in [14] . Let us note here that there are no interections of corresponding classes $\Lambda(\mathbf{H})$, $\Lambda(\mathbf{C})$, and $\Lambda(\mathbf{O})$ with the class $\Lambda^{NI} \cap \Lambda^{\overline{M}} \cap \Lambda^{Ne}$, or, in other words, the rules from these complete classes which satisfy Non-Imposition and Neutrality are always monotonic.

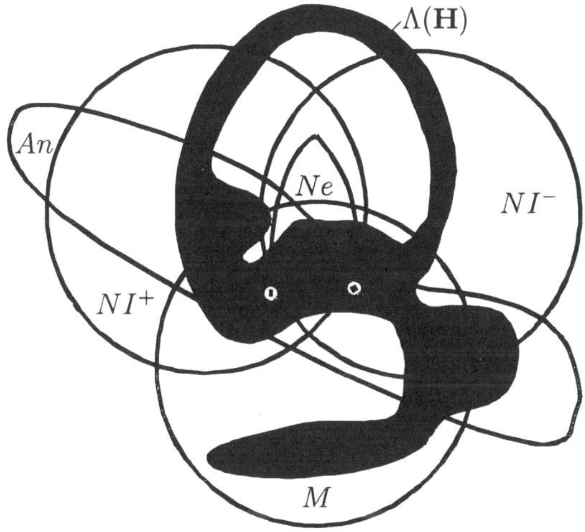

Figure 4-3

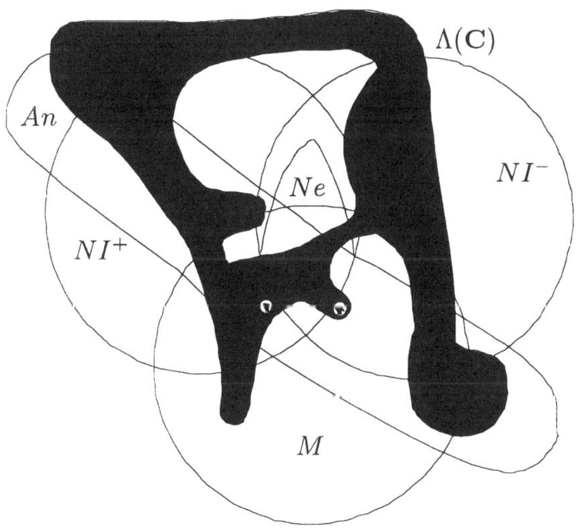

Figure 4-4

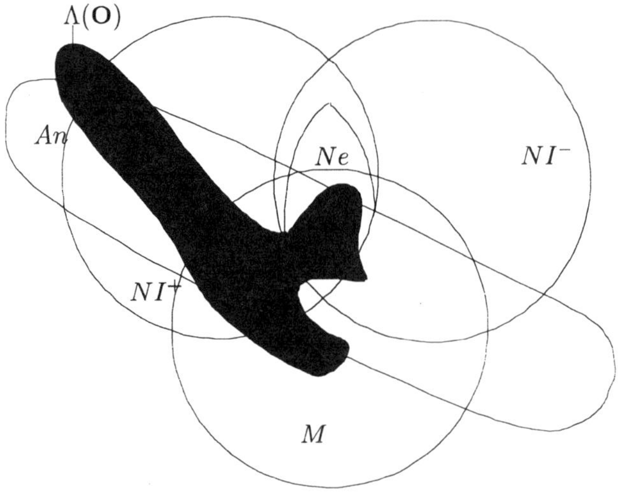

Figure 4-5

4.7 Comparing classes in Λ^C

Now we come to the problem of mutual relation of the classes of rules closedness for the domains $Q = \mathbf{H}, \mathbf{C}$ and $\mathbf{O}$, and the class of federation rules and its subclasses. We will solve this problem below for the rules from the Central Class; further generalization will be done at the next Section.

Theorem 4.13 *In Table* 4-5, *cells list the classes of rules satisfying corresponding normative conditions and rationality constraints.*

Table 4-5

	$\Lambda(\mathbf{H})$	$\Lambda(\mathbf{C})$	$\Lambda(\mathbf{O})$	$\Lambda(\mathbf{H}\cap\mathbf{C})$	$\Lambda(\mathbf{H}\cap\mathbf{O})$	$\Lambda(\mathbf{C}\cap\mathbf{O})$	$\Lambda(\mathbf{H}\cap\mathbf{C}\cap\mathbf{O})$	$\Lambda(\mathbf{ACA})$
Λ^C	$\Lambda^{\cup\cap}$	$\Lambda^{\cap}$	$\Lambda^{\cup}$	$\Lambda^{\cap}$	$\Lambda^{\cup}$	Λ^d	Λ^d	Λ^d
Λ^{SC}	Λ^{kM}	$\mathcal{U}$	$\mathcal{V}$	$\mathcal{U}$	$\mathcal{V}$	$\emptyset$	$\emptyset$	$\emptyset$

Proof. Theorem 4.13 consists of 14 statements. Let us prove them consequently.
1. $\Lambda^C \cap \Lambda(\mathbf{H}) = \Lambda^{\cup\cap}$. This fact follows directly from the Theorem 4.3 and Lemma 4.9, according to which $\Lambda^C \subset \Lambda(\mathbf{H})$.

2. $\Lambda^C \cap \Lambda(\mathbf{C}) = \Lambda^{\cap}$. Indeed, according to the condition (c^C), if $\omega', \omega'' \in \Omega$, then for any $\widetilde{\omega}$ such that $\omega' \cap \omega'' \subseteq \widetilde{\omega} \subseteq N$, it follows that $\widetilde{\omega} \in \Omega$. This means that $\omega_0 = \bigcap_{\omega \in \Omega} \omega \in \Omega$. Due to the condition NI $\omega_0 \neq \emptyset$. Then $\Omega^B = \{\omega_0\}$,which coincides with the definition of the oligarchy rule.
3. $\Lambda^C \cap \Lambda(\mathbf{O}) = \Lambda^{\cup}$. Without loss of generality suppose $\{i, j\} \in \Omega$, but neither $\{i\}$, nor $\{j\}$ belongs to Ω. But according to the first part of condition (o^C) $\{i, j\} \setminus \{i\} = \{j\} \in \Omega$, and this holds for $\{i\}$ as well. Due to Monotonicity condition M the basic list for Ω in this case is as follows: $\Omega^B = (\{i_1\}, ..., \{i_r\})$ which coincides with the definition of syndicate rule.
4. $\Lambda^C \cap \Lambda(\mathbf{H} \cap \mathbf{C}) = \Lambda^{\cap}$. Due to 1), 2), Lemma 4.8 and Theorems 4.3 and 4.8, $\Lambda^C \cap \Lambda(\mathbf{H} \cap \mathbf{C}) = \Lambda^C \cap \Lambda(\mathbf{H}) \cap \Lambda(\mathbf{C}) = \Lambda^{\cup\cap} \cap \Lambda^{\cap} = \Lambda^{\cap}$.
5. $\Lambda^C \cap \Lambda(\mathbf{H} \cap \mathbf{O}) = \Lambda^{\cup}$. Due to 1), 3), Lemma 4.8 and Theorem 4.8,$\Lambda^C \cap \Lambda(\mathbf{H} \cap \mathbf{O})$ $= \Lambda^C \cap \Lambda(\mathbf{H}) \cap \Lambda(\mathbf{O}) = \Lambda^{\cup\cap} \cap \Lambda^{\cup} = \Lambda^{\cup}$.
6. $\Lambda^C \cap \Lambda(\mathbf{C} \cap \mathbf{O}) = \Lambda^d$. Due to 2), 3), Lemma 4.8 and Theorem 4.8, $\Lambda^C \cap \Lambda(\mathbf{C} \cap \mathbf{O})$ $= \Lambda^C \cap \Lambda(\mathbf{C}) \cap \Lambda(\mathbf{O}) = \Lambda^{\cap} \cap \Lambda^{\cup} = \Lambda^d$.
7. $\Lambda^C \cap \Lambda(\mathbf{H} \cap \mathbf{C} \cap \mathbf{O}) = \Lambda^d$. Due to 1), 2), 3), Lemma 4.8 and Theorem 4.8, $\Lambda^C \cap \Lambda(\mathbf{H} \cap \mathbf{C} \cap \mathbf{O}) = \Lambda^C \cap \Lambda(\mathbf{H}) \cap \Lambda(\mathbf{C}) \cap \Lambda(\mathbf{O}) = = \Lambda^{\cup\cap} \cap \Lambda^{\cap} \cap \Lambda^{\cup} = \Lambda^d$.
All statements about the intersection of Λ^{SC} with the classes in question are direct implications from the above statements 1)-7), and Theorem 4.4 ■

Three remarks are in order.
Remark 1. As follows from Theorem 4.13, the domain of classically rational choice functions[32] $\mathbf{H} \cap \mathbf{C}$ is closed within the Central Class only with respect to oligarchy rules. The domain of classically rational choice functions[33] $\mathbf{H} \cap \mathbf{C} \cap \mathbf{O}$ is closed only with respect to dictatorial rules. Similarly, the Plott's functions domain[34] $\mathbf{H} \cap \mathbf{O}$ is closed with respect to the syndicate rules.

Remark 2. Also of interest is the problem of domain $\mathbf{ACA}$ closedness. It may be shown that the domain $\mathbf{ACA}$ is closed with respect to the rules from the Central Class if and only if this is dictatorial rule.
This result, which is a direct counterpart to the Arrow's General Impossibility Theo rem, reflects the extreme degree of violating Anonymity condition An.

Remark 3. The theorems of this Section define the spirit of violations of An. It has turned out that it consists in isolation of privileged groups of individuals (in particular, this may be a single group or even a single agent) that actually make decisions.

---

[32] Choice functions from that domain are rationalizable via an arbitrary binary relation (see Section 2.5).
[33] Choice functions from that domain are rationalizable via a strict partial order, and they are rationalizable via vector of criteria $\overrightarrow{u}$ using Pareto rule (see Section 2.5).
[34] Choice functions from $\mathbf{H} \cap \mathbf{O}$ are rationalizable via vector of criteria and joint-extremal rule (see Section 2.5).

4.8 Rules from Basic Class

Section 4.4 discussed explicit representation of the rules from Central Class. Now we generalize these results to the case when the condition Ne of Neutrality is obeyed partially, if at all.

We begin the study of explicit representation of rules with the case when the condition Ne of Neutrality is not satisfied while those of Non–Imposition NI and Monotonicity M are satisfied, i.e., we are going to consider the rules from the Basic Class Λ^{Bas}.

It will be recalled that while we considered the rules from the Central Class, the sets ω_j and ε_j in the definitions of federation, representation, oligarchy, etc., rules were independent of the alternative x and context X. This fact implies that inclusion into social choice of any alternative x for any presentation X may be decided by the same set of coalitions (or even by the same oligarchy and syndicate, or by the same dictator).

In this Section analysis of a more general case runs across a different situation: for each pair x, X there exists its own set of coalitions, i.e., the set Ω (or E) is dependent on x and $X (\Omega = \Omega(x, X))$, and the notions of federation, representation, etc., rules are generalized to the case where such a dependence takes place.
Bearing this in mind, we extend the definitions of rules introduced in the Section 4.4 to the case of dependence on x and X and write: $\Omega(x, X)$, $\Lambda^{\cup\cap(x,X)}$, etc.
Obviously, anonymity is violated for all but the $k(x, X)$ -majority rules, whereas the $k(x, X)$-majority rules are anonymous as before in the sense that each agent is equally included into the corresponding groups.

The rules are formally described in terms of the logic function language.
The normative conditions NI^+ through U^- of Section 4.3 are naturally formulated in terms of logic functions $f_{(x,X)}$. Namely, $\forall x, X$ such that $x \in X \in \mathcal{A}$:

(NI^+): $f_{(x,X)}(l) \not\equiv 0$;

(NI^-): $f_{(x,X)}(l) \not\equiv 1$;

(M): function $f_{(x,X)}(l)$ is monotone, i.e., if $(l_1, \ldots, l_N) \leq (l'_1, \ldots, l'_N)$, then $f_{(x,X)}(l) \leq f_{(x,X)}(l')$;

(Ne): $\forall x', X' : x' \in X' \in \mathcal{A}$, $f_{(x,X)}(l) = f_{(x',X')}(l)$, i.e., $f_{(x,X)}(l) \equiv f(l)$;

(Ne_X): $\forall X' \in \mathcal{A} : x \in X'$, $f_{(x,X)}(l) = f_{(x,X')}(l)$, $f_{(x,X)}(l) \equiv f_{(x)}(l)$;

(Ne_x): $f_{(x,X)}(l) \equiv f_{(X)}(l)$;

(An): function $f_{(x,X)}(l)$ is symmetrical with respect to its arguments, i.e., for any index permutation (one–to–one transformation $\eta : N \to N$)

$$f_{(x,X)}(l_1, \ldots, l_N) = f_{(x,X)}(l_{\eta(1)}, \ldots, l_{\eta(N)})$$

holds;

(U^+): $f_{(x,X)}(1, \ldots, 1) = 1$;

(U^-): $f_{(x,X)}(0, \ldots, 0) = 0$.

Any boolean (binary) function of boolean variables is representable by means of disjunction, conjunction and negation ([183]) in the disjunctive normal form

$$f_{(x,X)}(l_1,\ldots,l_n) = \bigvee_{j=1}^{q} \bigwedge_{j\in\omega_j(x,X)} \widetilde{l_i},$$

where $\widetilde{l_i}$ depends on x and X, and is either l_i or its negation l_i, it being assumed as usual that $\vee_{i\in\emptyset} l_i = 0,\ \wedge_{i\in\emptyset} l_i = 1$.

In the case where the function $f_{(x,X)}(l)$ is monotone (condition M), it is representable as

$$f_{(x,X)}(l_1,\ldots,l_n) = \bigvee_{j=1}^{q} \bigwedge_{j\in\omega_j(x,X)} l_i \tag{4.4}$$

or

$$f_{(x,X)}(l_1,\ldots,l_n) = \bigwedge_{j=1}^{t} \bigvee_{i\in\varepsilon_j(x,X)} l_i \tag{4.5}$$

i.e., in the form where the terms have no elements with negation.

It might be well to note that if all the sets $\omega_j(x,X)$ and $\varepsilon_j(x,X)$ are non–empty, (4.4) and (4.5) are formal definitions of federation and representation rules.

Correspondingly, the rules 'oligarchy,' 'syndicate,' and 'dictator' in the case under study may be defined as follows:

$$f_{(x,X)}(l_1,\ldots,l_N) = \bigwedge_{i\in\omega_1(x,X)} l_i;$$

$$f_{(x,X)}(l_1,\ldots,l_N) = \bigvee_{i\in\varepsilon_1(x,X)} l_i;$$

$$f_{(x,X)}(l_1,\ldots,l_N) = l_{i^*},$$

and the $k(x,X)-$ votes rule as

$$f_{(x,X)}(l_1,\ldots,l_N) = \bigvee_{j=1}^{q(x,X)} \bigwedge_{i\in\omega_j(x,X)} l_i,\ |\,\omega_j(x,X)\,| = k(x,X),$$

for all $j = 1,\ldots,q(x,X)$, where $q(x,X) = \binom{N}{k(x,X)}$ is the number of combinations of $k(x,X)$ out of N.

Attention is drawn to the fact that if the indices (x,X) in groups $\omega(x,X)$ and $\varepsilon(x,X)$ and in the function $f_{(x,X)}$ are omitted, the same logic formulas describe the rules from the Central Class. Whereas by virtue of the Neutrality condition one could use in the Central Class the set-theoretic operations, in this case the language of logic functions is adequate for rule description.

A theorem similar to Theorems 4.3 and 4.4 (Figure 4-6) holds.

Theorem 4.14 *The Basic Class Λ^{Bas} coincides with the class of federation rules $\Lambda^{\cup\cap(x,X)}$ (and with the class of representation rules $\Lambda^{\cap\cup(x,X)}$), i.e.,*

$$\Lambda^{Bas} = \Lambda^{\cup\cap(x,X)} = \Lambda^{\cap\cup(x,X)}.$$

The intersection of the Basic Class with the class An coincides with the class of '$k(x,X)$-majority' rules, i.e.,

$$\Lambda^{Bas} \bigcap \Lambda^{An} = \Lambda^{kM(x,X)}$$

The intersection of the class of $k(x,X)-$ majority rules with the classes of 1) dictatorial rules $\Lambda^{d(x,X)}$; 2) oligarchy rules $\Lambda^{\cap(x,X)}$, and 3) syndicate rules $\Lambda^{\cup(x,X)}$ is 1) empty, or consists of the only rule 2) $\mathcal{U}$, or 3)$\mathcal{V}$, respectively.
Moreover, the following relations hold

$$\Lambda^{Bas} \backslash (\Lambda^{\cap(x,X)} \bigcup \Lambda^{\cup(x,X)} \bigcup \Lambda^{d(x,X)}) \neq \emptyset,$$

$$(\Lambda^{\cap(x,X)} \bigcap \Lambda^{\cup(x,X)}) \backslash \Lambda^{d(x,X)} = \emptyset,$$

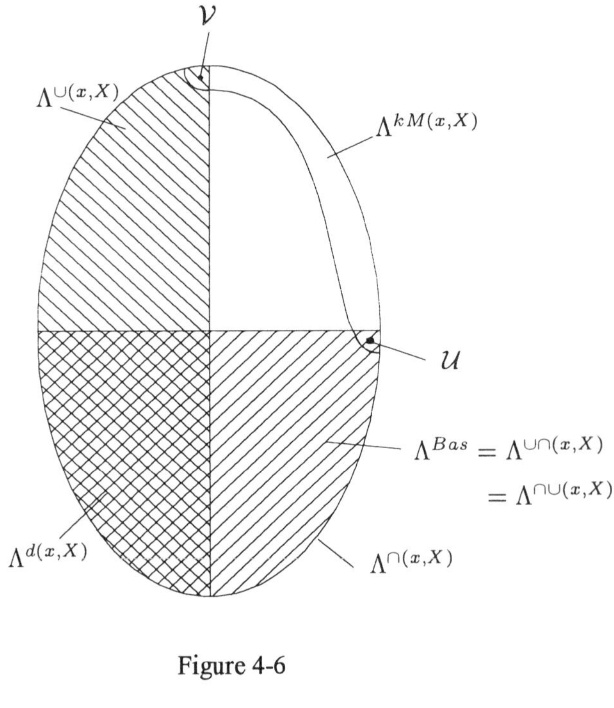

Figure 4-6

Proof. The statements of Theorem 4.14 becomes obvious if we rewrite the rules introduced above in Λ^{Bas} in list forms. Since Monotonicity condition M is obeyed we will write the list form of rules using basic lists.
- *Federation:* $\forall X, x \in X$,

$$\Omega^B(x,X) = \{\omega_1(x,X), \ldots, \omega_q(x,X)\}$$

is an arbitrary non–empty set of non–empty coalitions corresponding to the definition of Basic list.
- *Oligarchy*: $\forall X, x \in X, \Omega^B(x,X) = \{\omega(x,X)\}$;
- *Syndicate*: $\forall X, x \in X$

$$\Omega^B(x,X) = \{\omega_1(x,X), \ldots, \omega_q(x,X)\},$$

$\forall i = \overline{1,q}, 1 \leq q \leq N, \mid \omega_i(x,X) \mid = 1$;
- '$k(x,X)$-majority': $\forall X, x \in X$

$$\Omega^B(x,X) = \{\omega_1(x,X), \ldots, \omega_q(x,X)\},$$

$\mid \omega_i(x,X) \mid = k(x,X)$, for all $i = \overline{1,q}$, where $q = \binom{N}{k(x,X)}$ is the $k(x,X)$–fold combination of N elements.
Now the proof of Theorem 4.14 repeats the proof of Theorems 4.3 and 4.4 ■

When introducing in Section 4.3 the Neutrality condition Ne we drew attention to the possibility of considering it as consisting of two conditions: context independence Ne_X, and alternative independence Ne_x.
If now condition Ne_X is assumed to be satisfied and not Ne, the structure of intersection of Λ^{Bas} with Λ^{Ne_X} may be described in a precisely similar manner if one takes into account that all the sets $\omega_j(x,X)$ and $\varepsilon_j(x,X)$ defining the federation and representation rules will be dependent on x rather than on X. In doing so, denote the corresponding rule classes by $\Lambda^{\cup\cap(x)}$, $\Lambda^{\cup(x,X)}$, $\Lambda^{\cap(x)}$, etc. The structure of intersection $\Lambda^{Bas} \bigcap \Lambda^{Ne_x}$ can be described correspondingly. For us, however, of special interest is the intersection $\Lambda^{Bas} \bigcap \Lambda^{Ne_X}$, which is wider than the Central Class, but narrower than Λ^{Bas}, i.e., the class satisfying the following enclosures:

$$\Lambda^C \subset \Lambda^{Bas} \bigcap \Lambda^{Ne_X} \subset \Lambda^{Bas}.$$

The following theorem establishes relations between complete rule closedness classes, the Basic Class Λ^{Bas} and the class $\Lambda^{Bas} \bigcap \Lambda^{Ne_X}$.

Theorem 4.15 *In Table 4-6, the cells list the classes of rules satisfying corresponding normative conditions and rationality constraints.*

Table 4-6

	$\Lambda(\mathbf{H})$	$\Lambda(\mathbf{C})$	$\Lambda(\mathbf{O})$	$\Lambda(\mathbf{H}\cap\mathbf{C})$
Λ^{Bas}	–	–	$\Lambda^{\cup}$	–
$\Lambda^{Bas}\cap\Lambda^{Nex}$	$\Lambda^{\cup\cap(x)}$	$\Lambda^{\cap(x)}$	$\Lambda^{\cup}$	$\Lambda^{\cap(x)}$
$\Lambda^{Bas}\cap\Lambda^{Nex}\cap\Lambda^{An}$	$\Lambda^{kM(x)}$	$\mathcal{U}$	$\mathcal{V}$	$\mathcal{U}$

	$\Lambda(\mathbf{H}\cap\mathbf{O})$	$\Lambda(\mathbf{C}\cap\mathbf{O})$	$\Lambda(\mathbf{H}\cap\mathbf{C}\cap\mathbf{O})$
Λ^{Bas}	$\Lambda^{\cup}$	Λ^{d}	Λ^{d}
$\Lambda^{Bas}\cap\Lambda^{Nex}$	$\Lambda^{\cup}$	Λ^{d}	Λ^{d}
$\Lambda^{Bas}\cap\Lambda^{Nex}\cap\Lambda^{An}$	$\mathcal{V}$	$\emptyset$	$\emptyset$

Proof. This theorem contains 21 statements.
1) $\Lambda^{Bas}\cap\Lambda(\mathbf{H})$. From Theorems 4.10 and 4.14 follows that it is some subclass of $\Lambda^{\cup\cap(x,X)}$ for which condition (h) holds.
2) $\Lambda^{Bas}\cap\Lambda(\mathbf{C})$. Again from Theorems 4.10 and 4.14 follows that it is some subclass of $\Lambda^{\cap(x,X)}$ for which condition (c) holds.
3) $\Lambda^{Bas}\cap\Lambda(\mathbf{O})$. From Lemma 4.7 follows that $\Lambda^{NI}\cap\Lambda(\mathbf{O})\subset\Lambda^{C}$. Then by Theorem 4.13 we have the corresponding statement.
4) $\Lambda^{Bas}\cap\Lambda(\mathbf{H}\cap\mathbf{C})$. From Theorems 4.10 and 4.14 and Lemma 4.8 follows that it is some subclass of $\Lambda^{\cap(x,X)}$ for which conditions (h) and (c) holds.
5) $\Lambda^{Bas}\cap\Lambda(\mathbf{H}\cap\mathbf{O})$. Follows from 3) and Theorem 4.13.
6) $\Lambda^{Bas}\cap\Lambda(\mathbf{C}\cap\mathbf{O})$. Analogously to 5).
7) $\Lambda^{Bas}\cap\Lambda(\mathbf{H}\cap\mathbf{C}\cap\mathbf{O})$. Analogously to 5).
Next 14 statements can be obtained from first 7 taking into account that whereas the condition of context independence Ne_X holds, the conditions (h) and (c) just coincide with the definitions of federation and oligarchy rules, respectively. ■

The lines drawn in the cells for $\Lambda^{Bas}\cap\Lambda(\mathbf{H})$, $\Lambda^{Bas}\cap\Lambda(\mathbf{C})$ and $\Lambda^{Bas}\cap\Lambda(\mathbf{H}\cap\mathbf{C})$ are due to the fact that they should have contained some special, rather than general form rules from the class $\Lambda^{\cup\cap(x,X)}$. Description of their specific form is given in the proof of Theorem 4.15.

The reader's attention is drawn to the fact that, as Table 4-6 demonstrates, if one abandons the Neutrality condition or that of alternative independence, one meets with the same difficulties as in Section 4.7 at discussion of Central Class rules: the closedness requirement to the classical domains $\mathbf{H}\cap\mathbf{C}$ and $\mathbf{H}\cap\mathbf{C}\cap\mathbf{O}$ can be satisfied only with a privileged group of agents or even a single privileged agent (dictator).

Consider another special cases, namely the classes $\Lambda^{M}\cap\Lambda^{Ne}$ and $\Lambda^{M}\cap\Lambda^{Ne}\cap\Lambda^{An}$. To this end, return to the definition of federation rule dependent on the pair (x, X).

This rule can be defined to the cases where the number q of index sets in the family Ω is zero, i.e., where $\Omega = \emptyset$, or where there is at least one empty index set $\omega_j = \emptyset$ in the non–empty family $\Omega = \{\omega_j\}$, i.e., $\emptyset \in \Omega$. In compliance with the conventions $\vee_{i \in \emptyset} l_i = 0$ and $\wedge_{i \in \emptyset} l_i = 1$, assume that

$$f_{(x,X)}(l_1, \ldots, l_N) \equiv 0 \text{ and } f_{(x,X)}(l_1, \ldots, l_N) \equiv 1$$

in the first and the second cases, respectively.
For similar cases $E = \emptyset$ and $E \ni \emptyset$, the representation rule is defined, respectively, as $f_{(x,X)} \equiv 1$ or $f_{(x,X)} \equiv 0$. It is evident that $E(x,X) \ni \emptyset$ and $E(x,X) = \emptyset$ in the representation rule correspond, respectively, to $\Omega(x,X) = \emptyset$ and $\emptyset \in \Omega(x,X)$ in the federation rule. It is only natural to call these federation and representation rules constant. If Ne is obeyed, such a definition leads to the rules $\mathbf{1}$ and $\mathbf{0}$. In particular, for the neutral federation rule (i.e., for $\Omega(x,X) \equiv \Omega$) the rules $\mathbf{0}$ and $\mathbf{1}$ correspond to the cases $\Omega = \emptyset$ and $\emptyset \in \Omega$, respectively. Obviously, the classes of federation and representation rules completed with corresponding constant rules coincide as well.

Below, the rule classes introduced above will be used both with and without the constant rules. Therefore, to separate classes with constant rules we use the term *replenished class* of rules that is denoted by $*$. For example, the completed class of federation rules with Ne satisfied is the result of adding the rules $\mathbf{1}$ and $\mathbf{0}$ to the neutral federation class, i.e., $\Lambda_*^{\cup\cap} = \Lambda^{\cup\cap} \cup \{\mathbf{1}\} \cup \{\mathbf{0}\}$, etc.
Replenished classes 'federation' and 'representation' and their various subclasses leads to more general formulations of Theorems 4.14 and 4.15. For example, the first assertion of Theorem 4.14 can be restated as follows: the class of monotone rules Λ^M coincides with the replenished class $\Lambda_*^{\cup\cap(x,X)}$ of federation rules (and, thus, with the replenished class of representation rules), i.e.,

$$\Lambda^M = \Lambda_*^{\cup\cap(x,X)} = \Lambda_*^{\cap\cup(x,X)}.$$

The formulations of Theorems 4.14 and 4.15 can be generalized owing to the fact that elimination of the Non–Imposition condition NI in their list of conditions leads precisely to admission of constant rules and, thus, to the possibility of establishing in the theorems correspondences between rule classes defined by one or another property and completed by classes of explicitly defined rules.
Without NI, Table 4-2 becomes for the class $\Lambda^M \cap \Lambda^{Ne}$ Table 4-7.

Table 4-7

	$\Lambda(\mathbf{H})$	$\Lambda(\mathbf{C})$	$\Lambda(\mathbf{O})$	$\Lambda(\mathbf{H} \cap \mathbf{C})$
$\Lambda^M \cap \Lambda^{Ne}$	$\Lambda_*^{\cup\cap}$	$\Lambda_*^{\cap}$	$\Lambda_*^{\cup}$	$\Lambda_*^{\cap}$
$\Lambda^M \cap \Lambda^{Ne} \cap \Lambda^{An}$	Λ_*^{kM}	$\mathcal{U}, \mathbf{1}, \mathbf{0}$	$\mathcal{V}, \mathbf{1}, \mathbf{0}$	$\mathcal{U}, \mathbf{1}, \mathbf{0}$

	$\Lambda(\mathbf{H} \cap \mathbf{O})$	$\Lambda(\mathbf{C} \cap \mathbf{O})$	$\Lambda(\mathbf{H} \cap \mathbf{C} \cap \mathbf{O})$
$\Lambda^M \cap \Lambda^{Ne}$	$\Lambda_*^{\cup}$	Λ_*^{d}	Λ_*^{d}
$\Lambda^M \cap \Lambda^{Ne} \cap \Lambda^{An}$	$\mathcal{V}, \mathbf{1}, \mathbf{0}$	$\mathbf{1}, \mathbf{0}$	$\mathbf{1}, \mathbf{0}$

As can be seen from Table 4-7, in these special cases the closedness requirement to the classical domains of choice functions leads to the same asymmetry forms for the agents.

4.9 Non-monotonic rules

In the previous Section we gave an exhaustive analysis of the class Λ^M of local monotonic rules in Π_{II}. However, we left untouched those local rules which fail Monotonicity. Here we present the results for the classes $\Lambda^{NI} \cap \Lambda^{Ne}$ and $\Lambda^{NI} \cap \Lambda^{Ne} \cap \Lambda^{An}$.

An example of a non-monotonic rule is that defined by $C(X) = C_i(X) \cap C_j^-(X)$, where $C^-(X) = X \setminus C(X)$, for all admissible X. It does not follow, however, that a rule is non-monotonic merely from the fact that it can be written as a union of intersections of choice functions with some negative terms: the rule defined by

$$C(X) = [C_1(X) \cap C_2^-(X)] \cup [C_1^-(X) \cap C_2(X)] \cup [C_1(X) \cap C_2(X)]$$

is actually monotonic since it can be rewritten as $C(X) = C_1(X) \cup C_2(X)$. Larger classes of rules which contain non-monotonic rules are introduced next:

Definition 4.16 A rule $F \in \Lambda$ is
- a *generalized federation rule* if there exists a collection $\Omega = \{\omega_1, ..., \omega_q\}$ with $0 < q < 2^n$ such that

$$C(X) = \bigcup_{\omega \in \Omega} \bigcap_{i \in N} C_i^{\omega}(X),$$

where

$$C_i^{\omega}(X) = \begin{cases} C_i(X) \text{ if } i \in \omega; \\ C_i^-(X) \text{ else;} \end{cases}$$

- a *generalized representation rule* if there exists a collection $E = (\varepsilon_1, ..., \varepsilon_p\}$ with $0 < p < 2^n$ such that

$$C(X) = \bigcap_{\varepsilon \in E} \bigcup_{i \in N} C_i^{\varepsilon}(X),$$

where

$$C_i^{\varepsilon}(X) = \begin{cases} C_i(X) \text{ if } i \in \varepsilon; \\ C_i^-(X) \text{ else;} \end{cases}$$

- an *anti-oligarchy* rule if there exists $\emptyset \subset \omega^* \subseteq N$ such that

$$C(X) = \bigcap_{i \in \omega^*} C_i^-(X);$$

- an *anti-syndicate rule* if there exists $\emptyset \subset \varepsilon^* \subseteq N$ such that

$$C(X) = \bigcup_{i \in \varepsilon^*} C_i^-(X);$$

- an *anti-dictator rule* if there exists $d \in N$ such that

$$C(X) = C_d^-(X);$$

- a *T-majority rule* if T is a non-empty set of integers between zero and n with $T \neq \{0, ..., n\}$, $M = \{\mu \subseteq N \mid card(\mu) \in T\}$, and

$$C(X) = \bigcup_{\mu \in M} \bigcap_{i \in N} C_i^\mu(X),$$

where

$$C_i^\mu(X) = \begin{cases} C_i(X) \text{ if } i \in \mu; \\ C_i^-(X) \text{ else;} \end{cases}$$

These classes are denoted $\Lambda^{\cup\cap\pm}$, $\Lambda^{\cap\cup\pm}$, $\Lambda^{\cap-}$, $\Lambda^{\cup-}$, Λ^{d-}, and $\Lambda^{T\pm}$, respectively.

It follows that T–majority is the special case of generalized federation with $\Omega = \{\omega \subseteq N \mid card(\omega) \in T\}$; an anti-oligarchy is the special case of generalized federation with $\Omega = \{\omega \subseteq N \mid \omega^* \cap \omega = \emptyset\}$; an anti-syndicate is the special case of generalized representation with $E = \{\varepsilon \subseteq N \mid \varepsilon^* \cap \varepsilon = \emptyset\}$; and anti-dictatorship is the special case of both anti-oligarchy and anti-syndicate with $card(\omega^*) = card(\varepsilon^*) = 1$.

As an example of a generalized T-majority rule, let n=5 and $T = \{3, 5\}$. Then an alternative x is socially chosen from an admissible X whenever exactly 3 or exactly 5 individuals choose x - but if first, second, or fourth agent chooses x then it is socially rejected.

We also define the non-monotonic counterparts of Unanimity and One vote rules by

$$\mathcal{U}^- : C(X) = \bigcap_{i \in N} C_i^-(X);$$

$$\mathcal{V}^- : C(X) = \bigcup_{i \in N} C_i^-(X),$$

for all admissible X. $\mathcal{U}^-$ is the special case of generalized federation and anti-oligarchy when $\Omega = \{\emptyset\}$ and it is the special case of T-majority when $T = \{0\}$. The rule $\mathcal{V}^-$ is the special case of generalized representation and anti-syndicate when $E = \{\emptyset\}$ and it is the special case of T-majority when $T = \{0, 1, ..., n-1\}$.

Let us consider the representation of neutral rules in general. To this end let us generalize the definition of the replenished classes of rules given in the previous Section for monotonic non-neutral rules. So, we can define

- *replenished class of generalized federation rules*

$$\Lambda_*^{\cup\cap\pm} = \Lambda^{\cup\cap\pm} \cup \{0, 1\};$$

- *replenished class of generalized representation rules*

$$\Lambda_*^{\cap\cup\pm} = \Lambda^{\cap\cup\pm} \cup \{0, 1\};$$

- *replenished class of T–majority rules*

$$\Lambda_*^{T\pm} = \Lambda^{T\pm} \cup \{0, 1\}.$$

That is, we replenish $\Lambda^{\cup\cap\pm}$ by allowing $q = 0$ and $q = 2^n$ in Definition 4.15, so that $F \in \Lambda_*^{\cup\cap\pm}$ if there exists a collection $\Omega = \{\omega_1, ..., \omega_q\}$ with $0 \leq q \leq 2^n$ such that $C(X) = \cup_{\omega\in\Omega} \cap_{i\in\omega} C_i^\omega(X)$. Similarly, we replenish $\Lambda^{\cap\cup\pm}$ by allowing $p = 0$ and $p = 2^n$, and we replenish $\Lambda^{T\pm}$ by allowing $T = \emptyset$ and $T = N \cup \{0\}$.
We then have the following general results:

Theorem 4.16 $\Lambda^{Ne} = \Lambda_*^{\cup\cap\pm} = \Lambda_*^{\cap\cup\pm}$.

Proof. Consider a rule $F \in \Lambda^{Ne}$. We will show that $F \in \Lambda_*^{\cup\cap\pm}$. We know from the reformulation of neutrality in terms of boolean functions that F can be represented by a function $f(x, X; \vec{l}\ (x, X)) = \bigvee_{\omega\in\Omega(x,X)} \bigwedge_{i\in\omega} l_i^\omega(x, X)$, and we will show that $F(\vec{C}, X) = C(X) = = \bigcup_{\omega\in\Omega} \bigcap_{i\in N} C_i^\omega(X)$, for every profile $\vec{C}$ and admissible X. Assume that $x \in C(X)$ for some profile $\vec{C}$ and admissible X. Then there is an $\omega \in \Omega$ such that $V(x, X; \vec{C}) = \omega$. Then $x \in C_i(X)$ for all $i \in \omega$ and $x \in C_j^-(X)$ for all $j \notin \omega$, so $x \in \bigcap_{i\in N} C_i^\omega(X) \subseteq \bigcup_{\omega\in\Omega} \bigcap_{i\in N} C_i^\omega(X)$. Now assume that $x \in \bigcup_{\omega\in\Omega} \bigcap_{i\in N} C_i^\omega(X)$ for some profile $\vec{C}$ and admissible X . Then there is $\omega \in \Omega$ such that $x \in \bigcap_{i\in N} C_i^\omega(X)$, so $x \in C_i(X)$ for all $i \in \omega$ and $x \in C_j^-(X)$ for all $j \notin \omega$. That is, $V(x, X; \vec{C}) = \omega \in \Omega$, so $x \in C(X)$. Therefore, the desired equality holds and $F \in \Lambda_*^{\cup\cap\pm}$.
The proof that $F \in \Lambda_*^{\cap\cup\pm}$ is similar, using the conjunctive list for F. It is obvious that rules in replenished classes of generalized federation and generalized representation rules satisfy Neutrality, giving us the desired equalities ■

Theorem 4.17 $\Lambda^{Ne} \cap \Lambda^{An} = \Lambda_*^{T\pm}$.

Proof. From Theorem 4.16, we know that $F \in \Lambda^{Ne} \cap \Lambda^{An}$ satisfies

$$C(X) = \bigcup_{\omega\in\Omega} \bigcap_{i\in N} C_i^\omega(X)$$

for some collection Ω. By An, we know that if $\omega \in \Omega$ and $card(\omega) = card(\omega')$ then $\omega' \in \Omega$. Now set $T = \{card(\omega) \mid \omega \in \Omega\}$ and note that $F \in \Lambda_*^{T\pm}$. It is obvious that rules in the replenished class of $T-$majority rules satisfy Neutrality and Anonimity, giving us the desired equality ■

We now extend Theorems 4.3 and 4.4 to the non-monotonic case. Together with next Theorem 4.19, this provides the explicit form of all non-monotonic local rules isolated by Non-Imposition and Neutrality

Theorem 4.18 *1).* $\Lambda^{NI} \cap \Lambda^{Ne} = \Lambda^{\cup\cap\pm} = \Lambda^{\cap\cup\pm}$;
2). $\Lambda^{NI} \cap \Lambda^{Ne} \cap \Lambda^{An} = \Lambda^{T\pm}$.

Proof. 1) Consider a rule $F \in \Lambda^{NI} \cap \Lambda^{Ne}$. From Theorem 4.16, we know that $F \in \Lambda_*^{\cup\cap\pm}$, and by Non-Imposition it cannot be the case that $\Omega = \emptyset$ or $\Omega = 2^N$. Then $\Omega = \{\omega_1, ..., \omega_q\}$ with $0 < q < 2^n$, and $F \in \Lambda^{\cup\cap\pm}$. It is obvious that generalized federation rule satisfy non-imposedness and neutrality. The proof that $\Lambda^{NI} \cap \Lambda^{Ne} = \Lambda^{\cap\cup\pm}$ is similar.
2) Consider a rule $F \in \Lambda^{NI} \cap \Lambda^{Ne} \cap \Lambda^{An}$. From Theorem 4.17, we know that $F \in \Lambda_*^{T\pm}$, and by non-imposedness it cannot be the case that $T = \emptyset$ or $T = \{0, ...n\}$. But then $F \in \Lambda^{T\pm}$. It is obvious that T-majority rule satisfy Non-Imposition, Neutrality and Anonimity ■

The next theorem extends Theorem 4.2 to the case of non-monotonic rules, revealing the structure of the class of generalized federation rules:

Theorem 4.19 *1.* $\Lambda^{\cup\cap} \cup \Lambda^{\cup-} \cup \Lambda^{\cap-} \cup \Lambda^{T\pm} \subset \Lambda^{\cup\cap\pm} = \Lambda^{\cap\cup\pm}$;
2. $\Lambda^{\cup-} \cap \Lambda^{\cap-} = \Lambda^{d-}$;
3. $\Lambda^{\cap-} \cap \Lambda^{\cup\cap} = \Lambda^{\cup-} \cap \Lambda^{\cup\cap} = \Lambda^{T\pm} \cap \Lambda^{d-} = \emptyset$;
4. $\Lambda^{t} \subset \Lambda^{T\pm}$;
5. $\Lambda^{T\pm} \cap \Lambda^{\cup-} = \{\mathcal{V}^-\}$;
6. $\Lambda^{T\pm} \cap \Lambda^{\cap-} = \{\mathcal{U}^-\}$;
7. $\Lambda^{T\pm} \cap \Lambda^{\cup\cap} - \Lambda^{t}$.

These relationships are represented by a Venn diagram in Figure 4-7.

Proof. (1) It is shown in Theorem 4.16 that $\Lambda^{\cup\cap\pm} = \Lambda^{\cap\cup\pm}$. We know that T-majority, anti-oligarchy, and anti-syndicate are special cases of generalized federation and generalized representation, so we must show that $\Lambda^{\cup\cap} \subseteq \Lambda^{\cup\cap\pm}$. Consider $F \in \Lambda^{\cup\cap}$ with disjunctive list Ω and construct Ω' from Ω by $\Omega' = \{\omega' \subseteq N \mid \omega \subseteq \omega'$ for some $\omega \in \Omega\}$. Then for every profile $\vec{C}$ we have $C(X) = \bigcup_{\omega\in\Omega} \bigcap_{i\in N} C_i^{\omega}(X)$ for all admissible X and $0 < card(\Omega) < 2^n$, so that $F \in \Lambda^{\cup\cap\pm}$. To see that the inclusion is strict, consider the rule defined by $\forall X\ C(X) = C_1(X) \cap C_2^-(X)$.

(2) Consider an rule $F \in \Lambda^{\cap-} \cap \Lambda^{\cup-}$. Since F is an anti-syndicate rule, there is an individual i who can secure the social choice of every alternative x from every admissible X by rejecting it. And since F is an anti-oligarchy rule, there is an $\omega \subseteq N$ such that any member of ω can ensure that alternative x is socially rejected from an

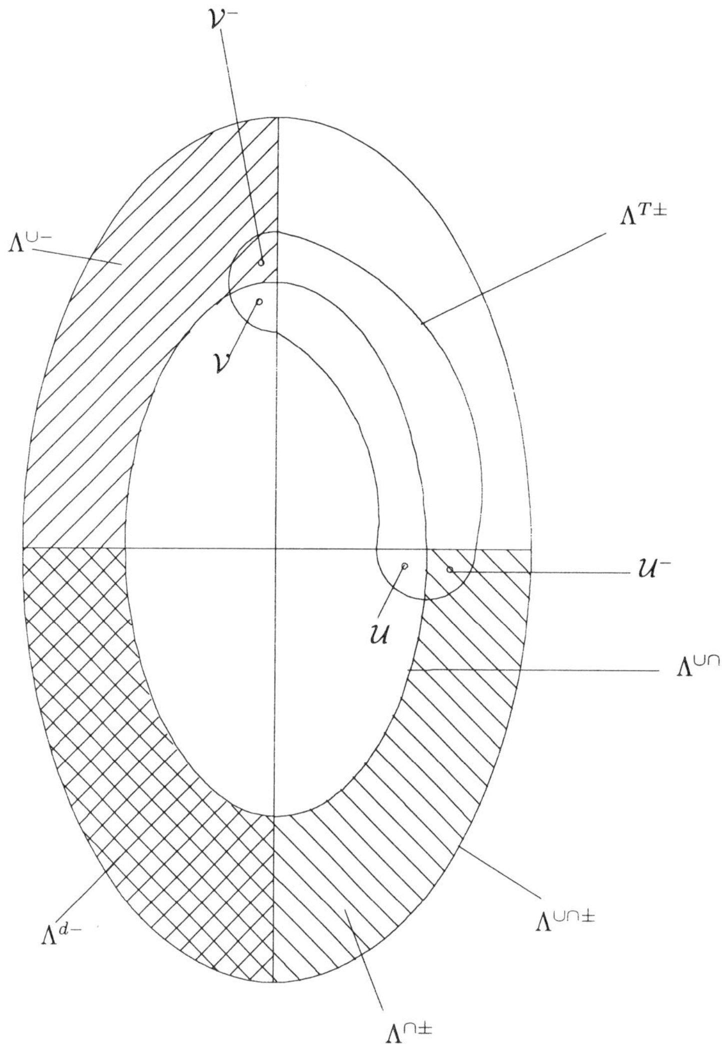

Figure 4-7

admissible X by choosing it. It must be that $\{i\} = \omega$. But then i is an anti-dictator and $F \in \Lambda^{d-}$. The opposite inclusion is obvious, giving us the desired equality.

(3) It is clear that $\Lambda^{\cap-} \cap \Lambda^{\cup\cap} = \emptyset$, since anti-syndicate rules are non-monotonic and federation rules are monotonic. Similarly, we have $\Lambda^{\cup-} \cap \Lambda^{\cup\cap} = \emptyset$. To see that $\Lambda^{T\pm} \cap \Lambda^{d-} = \emptyset$, suppose a T-majority rule is an anti-dictator rule. Then it must be that $T = \{1\}$, but then every agent would be an anti-dictator. This is, of course,

impossible.
(4) For $F \in \Lambda^t$, set $T = \{t, ..., n\}$ and $M = \{\mu \subseteq N \mid card(\mu) \in T\}$, and note that for every profile $\vec{C}$ we have $C(X) = \bigcup_{\mu \in M} \bigcap_{i \in N} C_i^{\mu}(X)$ for all admissible X, so that $F \in \Lambda^{T\pm}$. To see that the inclusion is strict, consider the example of T-majority in Section 4.9.
(5) Consider $F \in \Lambda^{T\pm} \cap \Lambda^{\cup -}$. Since F is an anti-syndicate rule, there is an ε such that every member of it can secure the social choice of x out of each admissible X by rejecting it. Then it must be that $T = \{0, ..., n-1\}$, but then every agent can ensure the social choice of x from X by rejecting it. Therefore, $F = \mathcal{V}^-$. The opposite inclusion is obvious, giving us the desired equality.
(6) Consider $F \in \Lambda^{T\pm} \cap \Lambda^{\cap -}$. Since F is an anti-oligarchy rule, there is an $\omega \subseteq N$ such that x is choosen out of each admissible X if and only if $\omega \subseteq N \setminus V(x, X; \vec{C})$. Then it must be that $T = \{0, ..., n - card(\omega)\}$. Now if $card(\omega) < n$ then we can find $i \in \omega$ and $j \notin \omega$, and construct ω' by replacing i with j, so that $card(\omega) = card(\omega')$. Since $F \in \Lambda^{T\pm}$ it follows that x is choosen out of X if $\omega' = N \setminus V(x, X; \vec{C})$, but this is impossible because $i \in \omega \cap V(x, X; \vec{C})$. Therefore, $card(\omega) = n$ and $T = \{0\}$. That is, $F \in \Lambda^{\cup -}$. The opposite inclusion is obvious, giving us the desired equality.
(7) Note that any rule $F \in \Lambda^{T\pm} \cap \Lambda^{\cup\cap}$ must be monotonic, so T must be the set of all integers between some t and n. Therefore, $F \in \Lambda^t$. The opposite inclusion is obvious, giving us the desired equality ■

Let us consider now the classes of local rules isolated by various rationality constraints combined with non-imposedness and neutrality, with and without anonymity. The first result is immediate, and extends Theorem 4.13 by adding two more rows to Table 4-5.

Theorem 4.20 *In Table 4-8, cells list the classes of rules satisfying the corresponding normative and rationality conditions.*

Table 4-8

	$\Lambda(\mathbf{H})$	$\Lambda(\mathbf{C})$	$\Lambda(\mathbf{O})$	$\Lambda(\mathbf{H} \cap \mathbf{C})$
$\Lambda^{NI} \cap \Lambda^{Ne}$	$\Lambda^{\cup\cap}$	$\Lambda^{\cap}$	$\Lambda^{\cup}$	$\Lambda^{\cap}$
$\Lambda^{NI} \cap \Lambda^{Ne} \cap \Lambda^{An}$	Λ^t	$\mathcal{U}$	$\mathcal{V}$	$\mathcal{U}$

	$\Lambda(\mathbf{H} \cap \mathbf{O})$	$\Lambda(\mathbf{C} \cap \mathbf{O})$	$\Lambda(\mathbf{H} \cap \mathbf{C} \cap \mathbf{O})$	$\Lambda(\mathbf{ACA})$
$\Lambda^{NI} \cap \Lambda^{Ne}$	$\Lambda^{\cup}$	Λ^d	Λ^d	Λ^d
$\Lambda^{NI} \cap \Lambda^{Ne} \cap \Lambda^{An}$	$\mathcal{V}$	$\emptyset$	$\emptyset$	$\emptyset$

Proof. Let us first rewrite conditions (h), (c), and (o) for the case, when condition of Neutrality (Ne) holds:
(h) $[\omega \in \Omega$ and $\omega \subseteq \omega'] \Rightarrow [\omega' \in \Omega]$;

(c) $[\omega_1 \in \Omega, \omega_2 \in \Omega,$ and $\omega_1 \cap \omega_2 \subseteq \omega] \Rightarrow [\omega \in \Omega]$;
(o) $[\omega_1 \in \Omega, \omega_2 \notin \Omega,$ and $\omega_1 \setminus \omega_2 \subseteq \omega \subseteq \omega_1 \cup \omega_2] \Rightarrow [\omega \in \Omega]$,
and $[\omega_2 \notin \Omega, \omega_3 \notin \Omega,$ and $\omega_3 \setminus \omega_2 \subseteq \omega \subseteq \omega_3 \cup \omega_2] \Rightarrow [\omega \notin \Omega]$.
Next, we will re-define the notion of closedness of domains $Q \subseteq C$ admitting now the posibility $Q_d \subset Q_r$.

Definition 4.17 The domain Q from $\mathcal{C}$ will be said to be closed with respect to the local rule F for $Q_d = Q' \subseteq \mathcal{C}$ if $F(\{C_i(\cdot)\}) \in Q$ for any profile $\{C_i(\cdot)\}$ such that $\forall i\ C_i(\cdot) \in Q'$.
The domain Q will be said to be closed with respect to the class of rules $\mathcal{F}$ for $Q_d = Q'$ if Q is closed with respect to any rule $F \in \mathcal{F}$ for $Q_d = Q'$.
The largest (in the sense of set theoretical inclusion) class of rules $\mathcal{F}$ with respect to which Q is closed for $Q_d = Q'$ will be referred to as the complete closedness class for mapping $(Q')^n \to Q$ and denoted by $\Lambda(Q', Q)$.

Let us study the properties of classes $\Lambda(Q', Q)$.

Lemma 4.10 *Let Q', Q_1 and Q_2 be some domains in the choice function space $\mathcal{C}$, and $\Lambda(Q', Q_1)$ and $\Lambda(Q', Q_2)$ be complete closedness classes for the mappings $(Q')^n \to Q_1$ and $(Q')^n \to Q_2$, respectively. Then, the complete closedness class for the mapping $(Q')^n \to Q_1 \bigcap Q_2$ is equal to the intersection of complete closedness classes for $(Q')^n \to Q_1$ and $(Q')^n \to Q_2$, i.e.,*

$$\Lambda(Q', Q_1 \bigcap Q_2) = \Lambda(Q', Q_1) \bigcap \Lambda(Q', Q_2)$$

Proof. Consider the domains Q', Q_1 and Q_2 in $\mathcal{C}$, and let $\Lambda(Q', Q_1)$ and $\Lambda(Q', Q_2)$ be complete closedness classes for $(Q')^n \to Q_1$ and $(Q')^n \to Q_2$, respectively. Consider rules F belonging to $\Lambda(Q', Q_1 \bigcap Q_2)$. As follows from definition 4.17, the rule F belongs to the intersection of complete classes $\Lambda(Q', Q_1) \bigcap \Lambda(Q', Q_2)$. And conversely, let $F \in \Lambda(Q', Q_1) \bigcap \Lambda(Q', Q_2)$ and F does not belong to $\Lambda(Q', Q_1 \bigcap Q_2)$. Consider an arbitrary profile $\{C_i(\cdot)\}$ consisting of functions belonging to the domain Q'. Since $F \in \Lambda(Q', Q_1)$, $F(\{C_i(\cdot)\}) \in Q_1$ holds. Similarly, $F(\{C_i(\cdot)\}) \in Q_2$, i.e., $F(\{C_i(\cdot)\}) \in Q_1 \bigcap Q_2$; therefore, F belongs to the complete closedness class $\Lambda(Q', Q_1 \bigcap Q_2)$.
Lemma 4.10 is proved.

Lemma 4.11 *If $Q_1 \subseteq Q_2 \subseteq Q \subseteq \mathcal{C}$, then $\Lambda(Q_2, Q) \subseteq \Lambda(Q_1, Q)$. Furthermore, $\Lambda(Q, Q_1) \subseteq \Lambda(Q, Q_2)$.*

Proof. Consider $F \in \Lambda(Q_2, Q)$ and a profile $\vec{C} \in \times_{i \in N} Q_1$. Then since $\vec{C} \in \times_{i \in N} Q_2$ it immediately follows that $F(\vec{C}) \in Q$ and $F \in \Lambda(Q_1, Q)$. Now consider $F \in \Lambda(Q, Q_1)$ and a profile $\vec{C} \in \times_{i \in N} Q$. Then $F(\vec{C}) \in Q_1 \subseteq Q_2$, and it follows that $F \in \Lambda(Q, Q_2)$.
Lemma 4.11 is proved.

Let us prove now the theorem. The proof follows for columns $\Lambda(\mathbf{H})$, $\Lambda(\mathbf{C})$, $\Lambda(\mathbf{O})$, $\Lambda(\mathbf{H} \cap \mathbf{O})$, and $\Lambda(\mathbf{C} \cap \mathbf{O})$ by noting that conditions $\mathbf{H}$ and $\mathbf{C}$ obviously imply the reformulation M of monotonicity, so all of these classes are contained in Λ^M. That $\mathbf{O}$ also implies monotonicity can be seen by considering a rule $F \in \Lambda(\mathbf{O})$ with $\omega' \notin \Omega$. Setting $\omega_2 = \omega_3 = \omega'$ in $(\mathbf{O})$, it follows that $[\emptyset \subseteq \omega \subseteq \omega'] \Rightarrow [\omega \notin \Omega]$, which is equivalent to (M).
Columns $\Lambda(\mathbf{H} \cap \mathbf{C})$, $\Lambda(\mathbf{H} \cap \mathbf{C} \cap \mathbf{O})$, and $\Lambda(\mathbf{ACA})$ require a little more work. Since $\mathbf{ACA} \subseteq \mathbf{H} \cap \mathbf{C} \cap \mathbf{O} \subseteq \mathbf{H} \cap \mathbf{C}$, the desired result will follow from Lemma 4.11 if we can show that $\Lambda(\mathbf{ACA}, \mathbf{H}) \subseteq \Lambda^M$. To this end, consider a rule $F \in \Lambda(\mathbf{ACA}, \mathbf{H} \cap \mathbf{C})$, assume that $\omega \in \Omega$, and $\omega \subseteq \omega'$, and suppose that $\omega' \notin \Omega$. Now construct the following profile for admissible $X_1 \subseteq X_2$ and $x \in X_1$:

$$i \in N \setminus \omega' \Rightarrow x \notin C_i(X_1) \cup C_i(X_2);$$

$$i \in \omega' \setminus \omega \Rightarrow x \in C_i(X_1), C_i(X_2) \subseteq X_2 \setminus X_1;$$

$$i \in \omega \Rightarrow x \in C_i(X_1) \cap C_i(X_2),$$

and note that $C_i(\cdot)$ is consistent with $\mathbf{ACA}$ for every individual, so we can assume $\vec{C} \in \times_{i \in N} \mathbf{ACA}$. Furthermore, $V(x, X_1; \vec{C}) = \omega' \notin \Omega$ and $V(x, X_2; \vec{C}) = \omega \in \Omega$. Then $x \in C(X_2)$ and $x \notin C(X_1)$, violating $\mathbf{H}$. Therefore, $\omega' \in \Omega$ and F is monotonic ■

Note that this is just the table of Theorem 4.13 with the rows appropriately relabeled! In other words, there are no non-monotonic rules which close these important domains. This is in stark contrast to the classic framework, in which the only non-dictatorial social welfare function satisfying appropriate formulations of locality, Non-Imposition, and Neutrality are inversely dictatorial ([277] , see also Chapter 3). This difference is partly accounted for by an attribute of rules in the classic framework which is not shared by rules in the non-binary framework: the inverse of a weak order is a weak order, but the function dual to a choice function satisfying $\mathbf{ACA}$ does not necessarily satisfy $\mathbf{ACA}$.

4.10 Non-monotonic rules: dual domains

Are there any interesting domains which are closed by non-monotonic rules? We next introduce several additional rationality constraints for rules in an attempt to answer this question. For a class $Q \subseteq \mathcal{C}$, let $Q^- = \{C(\cdot) \mid C^-(\cdot) \in Q\}$. That is, Q^- is the set of choice functions which are dual to choice functions in Q. We then have the following result:

Theorem 4.21 *The explicit forms of the conditions* $\mathbf{H}^-$, $\mathbf{C}^-$, $\mathbf{O}^-$, *and* $\mathbf{ACA}^-$ *are*
$(\mathbf{H}^-)$ $[X_1 \subseteq X_2] \Rightarrow [C(X_1 \subseteq C(X_2)]$;

$(\mathbf{C}^-)$ $[Y \subseteq X_1 \cap X_2$ *and* $C(X_1) \cap Y = C(X_2) \cap Y = \emptyset] \Rightarrow [C(X_1 \cup X_2) \cap Y = \emptyset]$;
$(\mathbf{O}^-)$ $[X_1 \subseteq C(X_2)] \Rightarrow [C(X_2 \setminus X_1) = C(X_2) \setminus X_1]$;
$(\mathbf{ACA}^-)$ $[X_1 \subseteq X_2]$ *and* $[X_1 \setminus C(X_2) \neq \emptyset$ *or* $C(X_2) = X_2] \Rightarrow [C(X_1) = C(X_2) \cap X_1]$,
for all admissible X_1, X_2 *and* Y.

Proof. $(\mathbf{H}^-)$. Consider admissible $X_1 \subseteq X_2$, $C(\cdot) \in \mathbf{H}^-$, and $x \in C(X_1)$. Then $x \notin C^-(X_1)$ and since $C^-(\cdot) \in \mathbf{H}$, it follows that $x \notin C^-(X_2)$. Therefore, $x \in C(X_2)$.
Now consider admissible $X_1 \subseteq X_2$ and $C(\cdot)$ satisfying the above condition. We know that $C(X_1) \subseteq C(X_2)$, so $C^-(X_2) = X_2 \setminus C(X_2) \subseteq X_2 \setminus C(X_1)$. Then $C^-(X_2) \cap X_1 \subseteq (X_2 \setminus C(X_1)) \cap X_1 = X_1 \setminus C(X_1) = C^-(X_1)$. Therefore, $C^-(\cdot) \in \mathbf{H}$ and $C(\cdot) \in \mathbf{H}^-$.

$(\mathbf{C}^-)$. Consider $C(\cdot) \in \mathbf{C}^-$, $Y \subseteq X_1 \cap X_2$ admissible, and $C(X_1) \cap Y = C(X_2) \cap Y = \emptyset$. Since $Y \subseteq X_1$ and $C(X_1) \cap Y = \emptyset$, we know $Y \subseteq C^-(X_1)$. Similarly, $Y \subseteq C^-(X_2)$. Since $C^-(\cdot) \in \mathbf{C}$, it follows that $Y \subseteq C^-(X_1) \cap C^-(X_2) \subseteq C^-(X_1 \cup X_2)$. Therefore, $C(X_1 \cup X_2) \cap Y = \emptyset$.
Now consider $C(\cdot)$ satisfying the above condition. Let $x \in C^-(X_1) \cap C^-(X_2)$. Then $\{x\} \subseteq X_1 \cap X_2$ and $C(X_1) \cap \{x\} = C(X_2) \cap \{x\}$, so $C(X_1 \cup X_2) \cap \{x\} = \emptyset$. We then have $\{x\} \subseteq C^-(X_1 \cup X_2)$. Therefore, $C^-(\cdot) \in \mathbf{C}$ and $C(\cdot) \in \mathbf{C}^-$.

$(\mathbf{O}^-)$ Consider $C(\cdot) \in \mathbf{O}^-$ and admissible $X_1 \subseteq C(X_2)$. Then $X_1 \subseteq X_2 \setminus C^-(X_2)$ and $C^-(X_2 \setminus X_1) = C^-(X_2)$, since $C^-(\cdot) \in \mathbf{O}$. This implies $(X_1 \setminus X_2) \setminus C^-(X_2 \setminus X_1) == (X_2 \setminus X_1) \setminus C^-(X_2)$, which implies $C(X_2 \setminus X_1) = (X_2 \setminus C^-(X_2)) \setminus X_1 = C(X_2) \setminus X_1$.
Now consider $C(\cdot)$ satisfying the above condition and admissible $X_1 \subseteq X_2 \setminus C^-(X_2)$. Then $X_1 \subseteq C(X_2)$, so we have $C(X_2 \setminus X_1) = C(X_2) \setminus X_1$, which implies $(X_2 \setminus X_1) \setminus C(X_2 \setminus X_1) = (X_2 \setminus X_1) \setminus (C(X_2) \setminus X_1)$. This in turn implies $C^-(X_2 \setminus X_1) = [(X_2 \setminus X_1) \setminus C(X_2)] \cup [\, C(X_2) \cap X_1 \cap (X_2 \setminus X_1)] = [(X_2 \setminus C(X_2) \setminus X_1] = [C^-(X_2) \setminus X_1] = C^-(X_2)$. Therefore, $C^-(\cdot) \in \mathbf{O}$ and $C(\cdot) \in \mathbf{O}^-$.

$(\mathbf{ACA}^-)$ Consider $C(\cdot) \in \mathbf{ACA}^-$ and admissible $X_1 \subseteq X_2$ with $C(X_2) = X_2$ or $X_1 \setminus C(X_2) \neq \emptyset$. First assume $C(X_2) = X_2$. Then $C^-(X_2) = \emptyset$, where $C^-(\cdot) \in \mathbf{ACA}$. It follows that $C^-(X_1) = C^-(X_2) \cap X_1 = \emptyset$, so $C(X_1) = X_1 = C(X_2) \cap X_1$.
Next assume $X_1 \setminus C(X_2) \neq \emptyset$, and suppose that $X_1 \cap C^-(X_2) = X_1 \cap (X_2 \setminus C(X_2)) = \emptyset$. But then $X_1 \setminus C(X_2) \neq \emptyset$, a contradiction. So $X_1 \setminus C^-(X_2) \neq \emptyset$, and since $C^-(\cdot) \in \mathbf{ACA}$ we have $C^-(X_1) = C^-(X_2) \cap X_1$, which implies $X_1 \setminus C^-(X_1) = X_1 \setminus (C^-(X_2) \cap X_1)$. This in turn implies $C(X_1) = X_1 \setminus C^-(X_2) = X_1 \setminus (X_2 \setminus C(X_2)) = (X_1 \setminus X_2) \cup (X_1 \cap X_2 \cap C(X_2)) = X_1 \cap C(X_2)$.
Now consider $C(\cdot)$ satisfying the above condition and $C^-(X_2) = \emptyset$ or $X_1 \cap C^-(X_2) \neq \emptyset$ for admissible $X_1 \subseteq X_2$. First assume $C^-(X_2) = \emptyset$. Then $C(X_2) = X_2$, so $C(X_1) = C(X_2) \cap X_1 = X_1$, which implies $C^-(X_1) = \emptyset = X_1 \cap C^-(X_2)$.
Next assume $X_1 \cap C^-(X_2) \neq \emptyset$. But then $X_1 \cap (X_2 \setminus C(X_2) = X_1 \setminus C(X_2)) = X_1 \setminus (X_2 \setminus C^-(X_2)) = (X_1 \setminus X_1) \cup (X_1 \cap X_2 \cap C^-(X_2)) == X_1 \cap C^-(X_2) \neq \emptyset$, so $X_1 \setminus C(X_2) \neq \emptyset$. Then $C(X_1) = C(X_2) \cap X_1$, which implies $X_1 \setminus C(X_1) =$

$X_1 \setminus (C(X_2) \cap X_1)$. This in turn implies $C^-(X_1) = (X_1 \setminus C(X_2)) \cup (X_1 \setminus X_1) = X_1 \setminus (X_2 \setminus C^-(X_2)) =. (X_1 \setminus X_2) \cup \cup(X_1 \cap X_2 \cap C^-(X_2)) = X_1 \cap C^-(X_2)$. Therefore, $C^-(\cdot) \in \mathbf{ACA}$ and $C(\cdot) \in \mathbf{ACA}^-$ ■

Note that this condition $\mathbf{H}^-$ was called in Chapter 2 as Choice Monotonicity condition. For a choice function satisfying $\mathbf{C}^-$, if an element is rejected from two sets of alternatives then it is rejected from their union. For a choice function satisfying $\mathbf{O}^-$, a subset of chosen alternatives may be deleted without disturbing the choice set in any other way. Lastly, a choice function satisfying $\mathbf{ACA}^-$ behaves much like one satisfying $\mathbf{ACA}$, but it exhibits the peculiar property that the alternatives chosen from an admissible set are not necessarily chosen from the smaller admissible set consisting of just the originally chosen alternatives.
The classes of rules which close these new domains are investigated next:

Theorem 4.22 *In Table 4-9, cells list the classes of rules satisfying the corresponding normative and rationality constraints.*

Table 4-9

	$\Lambda(\mathbf{H}^-)$	$\Lambda(\mathbf{C}^-)$	$\Lambda(\mathbf{O}^-)$	$\Lambda(\mathbf{H}^- \cap \mathbf{C}^-)$
$\Lambda^{NI} \cap \Lambda^{Ne}$	$\Lambda^{\cup\cap}$	$\Lambda^{\cup}$	$\Lambda^{\cap}$	$\Lambda^{\cup}$
$\Lambda^{NI} \cap \Lambda^{Ne} \cap \Lambda^{An}$	Λ^t	$\mathcal{V}$	$\mathcal{U}$	$\mathcal{V}$

	$\Lambda(\mathbf{H}^- \cap \mathbf{O}^-)$	$\Lambda(\mathbf{C}^- \cap \mathbf{O}^-)$
$\Lambda^{NI} \cap \Lambda^{Ne}$	$\Lambda^{\cap}$	Λ^d
$\Lambda^{NI} \cap \Lambda^{Ne} \cap \Lambda^{An}$	$\mathcal{U}$	$\emptyset$

	$\Lambda(\mathbf{H}^- \cap \mathbf{C}^- \cap \mathbf{O}^-)$	$\Lambda(\mathbf{ACA}^-)$
$\Lambda^{NI} \cap \Lambda^{Ne}$	Λ^d	Λ^d
$\Lambda^{NI} \cap \Lambda^{Ne} \cap \Lambda^{An}$	$\emptyset$	$\emptyset$

Proof. Let us first state and prove two lemmas, in which C^0 denotes the choice function $C(X) = \emptyset$ for all admissible X and C^1 denotes the choice function $C(X) = X$ for all admissible X:

Lemma 4.12 *For all $Q \subseteq \mathcal{C}$, $\Lambda^{\cap} \subseteq \Lambda(Q)$ if and only if $\Lambda^{\cup} \subseteq \Lambda(Q^-)$.*

Proof of Lemma 4.12. We prove only the 'only if' direction, as the 'if' direction follows by a similar argument. Assume that $\Lambda^{\cap} \subseteq \Lambda(Q)$ and consider the rule $F \in \Lambda^{\cup}$, so there is $\omega \subseteq N$ such that for all profiles $\vec{C}$ we have $C(X) = \cup_{i\in\omega} C_i(X)$, for all admissible X. Pick a profile $\vec{C}$, relabel indexes so that $\omega = \{1, ..., card(\omega)\}$, and for each $k \in \omega$ define the choice function $C(\cdot, k)$ by $C(X, k) = \bigcup_{i=1}^{k} C_i(X)$ for all admissible X. $C(\cdot, 1) = C_1(\cdot) \in Q^-$ follows immediately, so assume that $C(\cdot, k) \in Q^-$. Note that $C(\cdot, k+1)$ is defined by $C(X, k+1) = C(X, k) \cup C_{k+1}(X)$ for all

admissible X. We know the rule defined by $C^-(X, k+1) = C^-(X,k) \cap C^-_{k+1}(x)$ belongs to Q since $C^-(\cdot, k)$, $C_{k+1}(\cdot) \in Q$ and $\Lambda^\cap \subseteq \Lambda(Q)$. But then $C(\cdot, k+1) \in Q^-$, and by induction we have $C(\cdot) = C(\cdot, card(\omega)) \in Q^-$.
Lemma 4.12 is proved.

Lemma 4.13 *For all $Q \subseteq C$ such that $C^1, C^0 \in Q$,*
1. $[\Lambda^d \subset \Lambda(Q) \cap \Lambda^{\cup\cap}] \Rightarrow [\Lambda^\cap \subseteq \Lambda(Q)$ *or* $\Lambda^\cup \subseteq \Lambda(Q)]$;
2. $[\Lambda^\cap \subset \Lambda(Q) \cap \Lambda^{\cup\cap}] \Rightarrow [\Lambda^{\cup\cap} \subseteq \Lambda(Q)]$;
3. $[\Lambda^\cup \subset \Lambda(Q) \cap \Lambda^{\cup\cap}] \Rightarrow [\Lambda^{\cup\cap} \subseteq \Lambda(Q)]$.

Proof of Lemma 4.13. (1) In words, we must show that if the dictatorship rules are strictly contained in the class of federation rules which close Q, then Q is either closed with respect to intersection or union. Consider $F \in (\Lambda(Q) \cap \Lambda^{\cup\cap}) \setminus \Lambda^d$. We know that there is a basic list Ω^B such that for every profile $\vec{C}$ we have $C(X) = \bigcup_{\omega \in \Omega^B} \bigcap_{i \in \omega} C_i(X)$ for all admissible X. Since F is not a dictatorship, we know that either $| \Omega^B | > 1$ or $\Omega^B = \{\omega\}$ with $| \omega | > 1$.
Assume the first case holds and define $\Omega_i = \{\omega \in \Omega^B \mid i \in \omega\}$ for every individual. We need two individuals i and j such that Ω_i is not a proper subset of Ω_j and *vice versa.* If such a pair does not exist then for all pairs $\{i,j\} \subseteq N$ either $\Omega_i \subseteq \Omega_j$ or $\Omega_j \subseteq \Omega_i$, so we can order N according to set inclusion of the Ω_i's. Denote the set of maximal individuals by N^*, and note that $N^* \in \Omega^B$ and $N^* \subseteq \omega$ for all $\omega \in \Omega^B$. That is, $\Omega^B = \{N^*\}$ and $C(X) = \bigcap_{i \in N^*} C_i(X)$. Since F is not a dictatorial rule we know that $| N^* | > 1$, so $C(X)$ is the intersection of several choice functions from Q, and it follows that $\Lambda^\cap \subseteq \Lambda(Q)$. To see this, suppose there are $C'(\cdot)$, $C''(\cdot)$ such that $C_\cap(\cdot) = C'(\cdot) \cap C''(\cdot) \notin Q$. Pick $i \in N^*$ and consider the profile $\vec{C} = \times_{i \in N} Q$ in which $C_i(\cdot) = C'(\cdot)$ and $C_j(\cdot) = C''(\cdot)$ for $j \neq i$. Then $C(\cdot) = C_\cap(\cdot) \notin Q$, contradicting the assumption that $F \in \Lambda(Q)$.
So assume such a pair $\{i^*, j^*\}$ does exist and consider $\omega_{i^*} \in \Omega^B$ such that $i^* \in \omega_{i^*}$ and $j^* \notin \omega_{i^*}$ along with $\omega_{j^*} \in \Omega^B$ such that $j^* \in \omega_{j^*}$ and $i^* \notin \omega_{j^*}$. We will show that without loss of generality we can assume there is no $\omega \in \Omega^B$ such that $\omega \subseteq (\omega_{i^*} \cup \omega_{j^*}) \setminus \{i^*, j^*\}$. To see this, suppose there is such an ω. Since Ω^B is a basic list, we know that $\omega \cap \omega_{i^*} \neq \emptyset$ and $\omega \cap \omega_{j^*} \neq \emptyset$. Pick an individual $j \in \omega \cap \omega_{j^*}$ and relabel j as j^* and ω as ω_{j^*}, and note that for the new pair $\{i^*, j^*\}$ Ω_{i^*} is not a subset of Ω_{j^*} and vice versa. This process will eventually terminate at a pair with the desired property.
Then consider the profile $\vec{C} \in \times_{i \in N} Q$ in which $C_{i^*}(\cdot)$ and $C_{j^*}(\cdot)$ are arbitrary elements of Q, $C_i(\cdot) = C^1$ for all other $i \in \omega_{i^*} \cup \omega_{j^*}$, and $C_i(\cdot) = C^0$ for all $i \notin \omega_{i^*} \cup \omega_{j^*}$. Then $C(X) = C_{i^*}(X) \cup C_{j^*}(X)$ for all admissible X, since $\bigcap_{i \in \omega_{i^*}} C_i(X) = C_{i^*}(X)$, $\bigcap_{i \in \omega_{j^*}} C_i(X) = C_{j^*}(X)$, and

$$\bigcap_{i \in \omega} C_i(X) = \begin{cases} \emptyset & \text{if } \omega \setminus (\omega_{i^*} \cup \omega_{j^*}) \neq \emptyset; \\ C_{i^*}(X) & \text{if } i^* \in \omega \subseteq (\omega_{i^*} \cup \omega_{j^*}) \setminus \{j^*\}; \\ C_{j^*}(X) & \text{if } j^* \in \omega \subseteq (\omega_{i^*} \cup \omega_{j^*}) \setminus \{i^*\}; \\ C_{i^*}(X) \cup C_{j^*}(X) & \text{if } \{i^*, j^*\} \subseteq \omega \subseteq \omega_{i^*} \cup \omega_{j^*}, \end{cases}$$

where we have dismissed without loss of generality the case $\omega \subseteq (\omega_{i^*} \cup \omega_{j^*}) \setminus \{i^*, j^*\}$. Since $F \in \Lambda(Q)$ we know $C(\cdot) \in Q$, and it follows by an induction argument that $\Lambda^{\cup} \subseteq \Lambda(Q)$.
If the first case does not hold then $\Omega^B = \{\omega\}$, where $|\ \omega\ | > 1$. Then F is just an oligarchy and it follows that $\Lambda^{\cap} \subseteq \Lambda(Q)$.
(2) Consider $F \in (\Lambda(Q) \cap \Lambda^{\cup\cap}) \setminus \Lambda^{\cap}$. We know that there is a basic list Ω^B such that for every profile $\vec{C}$ we have $C(X) = \bigcup_{\omega \in \Omega^B} \bigcap_{i \in \omega} C_i(X)$ for all admissible X. Since F is not an oligarchy, we know that $card(\Omega^B) > 1$, which is just the first case in the proof of (1). Again, we need two individuals i and j such that Ω_i is not a subset of Ω_j and vice versa. If such a pair does not exist then we know from the above argument that F is an oligarchy with $\Omega^B = \{N^*\}$, a contradiction. It follows that we can find such a pair, and by the above argument we have $\Lambda^{\cup} \subseteq \Lambda(Q)$. Since Q is closed with respect to union and intersection, it follows that $\Lambda^{\cup\cap} \subseteq \Lambda(Q)$.
(3) Consider $F \in (\Lambda(Q) \cap \Lambda^{\cup\cap}) \setminus \Lambda^{\cup}$. We know that there is a basic list Ω^B such that for all profiles $C(X) = \bigcup_{\omega \in \Omega^B} \bigcap_{i \in \omega} C_i(X)$ for all admissible X. Since F is not a syndicate, we know that there is $\omega' \in \Omega^B$ with $card(\omega') > 1$, and since Ω^B is a basic list we know that there does not exist an $\omega \in \Omega^B$ with $\omega \subset \omega'$.
Now consider the profile $\vec{C} \in \times_{i \in N} Q$ in which $C_i(\cdot) \in Q$ is arbitrary for every $i \in \omega'$ and $C_j(\cdot) = C^0$ for every $j \notin \omega'$. Then $C(X) = \bigcap_{i \in \omega'} C_i(X)$ for all admissible X, and since $F \in \Lambda(Q)$ we have $C(\cdot) \in Q$. It follows by an induction argument that $\Lambda^{\cap} \subseteq \Lambda(Q)$. Since Q is closed with respect to union and intersection, it follows that $\Lambda^{\cup\cap} \subseteq \Lambda(Q)$.
Lemma 4.13 is proved.

Let us prove now the theorem. The $\Lambda^{NI} \cap \Lambda^{Ne}$ row follows from the application of Theorem 4.20, Lemma 4.12, and Lemma 4.13, while the $\Lambda^{NI} \cap \Lambda^{Ne} \cap \Lambda^{An}$ row then follows by application of the definition of anonimity. As an example, consider the cell $\Lambda^{NI} \cap \Lambda^{Ne} \cap \Lambda(\mathbf{C}^-)$. By Theorem 4.20, $\Lambda^{\cap} \subseteq \Lambda(\mathbf{C})$, so it follows from Lemma 4.12 that $\Lambda^{\cup} \subseteq \Lambda(\mathbf{C}^-) \cap \Lambda^{\cup\cap}$. Now suppose this inclusion is strict, so that $\Lambda^{\cup} \subset \Lambda(\mathbf{C}^-) \cap \Lambda^{\cup\cap}$. Then by Lemma 4.13 we have $\Lambda^{\cup\cap} \subset \Lambda(\mathbf{C}^-)$, and in particular, $\Lambda^{\cap} \subseteq \Lambda(\mathbf{C}^-)$. But then Lemma 4.12 implies that $\Lambda^{\cup} \subseteq \Lambda(\mathbf{C})$, contradicting Theorem 4.20. Therefore, $\Lambda^{\cup} = \Lambda(\mathbf{C}^-) \cap \Lambda^{\cup\cap} = \Lambda(\mathbf{C}^-) \cap \Lambda^{NI} \cap \Lambda^{Ne}$. The results for the other cells follow by similar arguments ■

Once again none of the eight domains is closed with respect to a non-monotonic rule. One domain which is closed relative the entire class of generalized federation rules is defined next. Let us remind the condition $\mathbf{ACA}^*$ defined in Section 2.4: a choice function $C(\cdot)$ satisfies condition $\mathbf{ACA}^*$ if there exists $A^* \subseteq A$ such that $C(X) = A^* \cap X$ for all admissible X.
Choice over all admissible sets according to $\mathbf{ACA}^*$ is entirely given by the choice A^* from the set of all alternatives A. If X is the set of alternatives presented for choice then the alternatives chosen from X are just the elements of A^*, and it follows that when $X \cap A^* = \emptyset$ the choice out of X is empty.
Now we obtain the following theorem:

Theorem 4.23 $\Lambda(\mathbf{ACA}^*) \cap \Lambda^{NI} \cap \Lambda^{Ne} = \Lambda^{\cup\cap\pm}$.

Proof. It suffices to show that $\mathbf{ACA}^*$ is closed with respect to union, intersection, and complementation. Consider $C_1(\cdot), C_2(\cdot) \in \mathbf{ACA}^*$ given by A_1^* and A_2^*, respectively, and consider the choice function $C(\cdot)$ defined by $C_1(\cdot) \cap C_2(\cdot)$ for all admissible X. Since $x \in C(X)$ if and only if $x \in A^* = A_1^* \cap A_2^*$, it follows immediately that $C(\cdot) \in \mathbf{ACA}^*$. Similarly, the choice function $C(\cdot)$ defined by $C_1(\cdot) \cup C_2(\cdot)$ for all admissible X satisfies $x \in C(X)$ if and only if $x \in A^* = A_1^* \cup A_2^*$, so $C(\cdot) \in \mathbf{ACA}^*$. Lastly, $C(\cdot) = C_1^-(\cdot) \in \mathbf{ACA}^*$, since $x \in C(X)$ if and only if $x \in A \setminus A_1^*$ ■

Although none of the sixteen domains considered in Theorems 4.20 and 4.22 is closed with respect to a non-monotonic rule, there are many other combinations which might be. Of particular interest are $\mathbf{H} \cap \mathbf{H}^-$, $\mathbf{O} \cap \mathbf{O}^-$ and $\mathbf{C} \cap \mathbf{C}^-$. The first two of these domains and their relationship to $\mathbf{ACA}^*$ is the subject of the next theorem and corollary:

Theorem 4.24 $\mathbf{H} \cap \mathbf{H}^- = \mathbf{O} \cap \mathbf{O}^- = \mathbf{ACA}^*$.

Proof. The statement $\mathbf{H} \cap \mathbf{H}^- \equiv \mathbf{H} \cap \mathbf{CM} = \mathbf{ACA}^*$ was proved in Chapter 2. Consider $C(\cdot) \in \mathbf{O} \cap \mathbf{O}^-$ and set $A^* = C(A)$. For an admissible X, partition $A \setminus X$ into $X_1 = (A \setminus X) \cap A^*$ and $X_2 = (A \setminus X) \setminus A^*$. Note that $X_1 \subseteq A^*$ and $X_2 \subseteq (A \setminus X_1) \setminus (A^* \setminus X_1)$. To see this last inclusion, note that $X_2 = (A \setminus X) \setminus A^* \subseteq A \setminus A^* = (A \setminus X_1) \setminus A^* = (A \setminus X_1) \setminus (A^* \setminus X_1)$. Then $C(A \setminus X_1) = (A^* \setminus X_1)$ and $C((A \setminus X_1) \setminus X_2) = (A^* \setminus X_1) \setminus X_2 = A^* \cap X$. But $X = (A \setminus X_1) \setminus X_2$, so we have $C(X) = A^* \cap X$. That is, $\mathbf{O} \cap \mathbf{O}^- \subseteq \mathbf{ACA}^*$. It is obvious that $\mathbf{ACA}^* \subseteq \mathbf{O} \cap \mathbf{O}^-$, so equality follows ■

Corollary 4.1 $\Lambda(\mathbf{H} \cap \mathbf{H}^-) \cap \Lambda^{NI} \cap \Lambda^{Ne} = \Lambda(\mathbf{O} \cap \mathbf{O}^-) \cap \Lambda^{NI} \cap \Lambda^{Ne} = \Lambda^{\cup\cap\pm}$.

We have then shown that there are no non-monotonic rules which satisfy Non-Imposition and Neutrality and close the usual domains, and that there is one extremely rational domain closed by every non-imposed and neutral rule - non-monotonic as well as monotonic. The domain $\mathbf{C} \cap \mathbf{C}^-$ is more interesting , as it does not demand the extreme rationality of $\mathbf{ACA}^*$; for example, consider a choice function $C(\cdot)$ such that $C(\{x,y,z\}) = \{x,y,z\}$, $C(\{x,y\}) = \{x\}$, $C(\{y,z\}) = \{y\}$, and $C(\{x,z\}) = \{z\}$. This choice function satisfies $\mathbf{C}$ and $\mathbf{C}^-$, but obviously violates $\mathbf{H}$. Nevertheless, this domain is closed by exactly one kind of monotonic rules and exactly one kind of non-monotonic rules.

Theorem 4.25 $\Lambda(\mathbf{C} \cap \mathbf{C}^-) \cap \Lambda^{NI} \cap \Lambda^{Ne} = \Lambda^d \cup \Lambda^{d-}$.

Proof. Theorem 4.25 is proved in a scrics of stcps, in which we derive the explicits forms of rules in the classes $\Lambda(\mathbf{C} \cap \mathbf{C}^-, \mathbf{C})$ and $\Lambda(\mathbf{C} \cap \mathbf{C}^-, \mathbf{C}^-)$ and offer two corollaries of independent interest. In what follows, an interval is a collection of subsets of N such as $[\omega', \omega''] = \{\omega \subseteq N \mid \omega' \subseteq \omega \subseteq \omega''\}$.

Lemma 4.14 $F \in \Lambda(\mathbf{C} \cap \mathbf{C}^-, \mathbf{C}) \cap \Lambda^{NI} \cap \Lambda^{Ne}$ *if and only if* $\Omega \neq 2^N$, $\Omega \neq \emptyset$, *and for all* $\omega', \omega'' \in \Omega$ $[\omega' \cap \omega'' \subseteq \omega \subseteq \omega' \cup \omega''] \Rightarrow [\omega \in \Omega]$.

Proof. We first prove the 'only if' direction. Consider $F \in \Lambda(\mathbf{C} \cap \mathbf{C}^-, \mathbf{C}) \cap \Lambda^{NINe}$, so F has a disjunctive list Ω. It follows from non-imposedness that $\Omega \neq 2^N$ and $\Omega \neq \emptyset$. Suppose there are $\omega', \omega'' \in \Omega$ and $\omega \in \Omega$ such that $\omega' \cap \omega'' \subseteq \omega \subseteq \omega' \cup \omega''$ but $\omega \notin \Omega$. For $x \in X_1 \cap X_2$ both admissible, construct the following profile $\vec{C}$:

$$i \in N \setminus (\omega' \cup \omega'') \Rightarrow x \notin C_i(X_1),\ x \notin C_i(X_2),\ x \notin C_i(X_1 \cup X_2);$$

$$i \in \omega' \setminus \omega \Rightarrow x \in C_i(X_1),\ x \notin C_i(X_2),\ x \notin C_i(X_1 \cup X_2);$$

$$i \in \omega'' \setminus \omega \Rightarrow x \notin C_i(X_1),\ x \in C_i(X_2),\ x \notin C_i(X_1 \cup X_2);$$

$$i \in \omega \setminus \omega' \Rightarrow x \notin C_i(X_1),\ x \in C_i(X_2),\ x \in C_i(X_1 \cup X_2);$$

$$i \in \omega \setminus \omega'' \Rightarrow x \in C_i(X_1),\ x \notin C_i(X_2),\ x \in C_i(X_1 \cup X_2);$$

$$i \in \omega' \cap \omega'' \Rightarrow x \in C_i(X_1),\ x \in C_i(X_2),\ x \in C_i(X_1 \cup X_2).$$

Note that this profile is consistent with $\mathbf{C}$ and $\mathbf{C}^-$, so we can assume $\vec{C} \in \times_{i \in N} \mathbf{C} \cap \mathbf{C}^-$. Now, since $V(x, X_1; \vec{C}) = \omega' \in \Omega$ we have $x \in C(X_1)$, and since $V(x, X_2; \vec{C}) = \omega'' \in \Omega$ we have $x \in C(X_2)$. But $V(x, X_1 \cup X_2; \vec{C}) = \omega \in \Omega$, so $x \notin C(X_1 \cup X_2)$ and $C(\cdot) \notin \mathbf{C}$. This, of course, contradicts the assumption that $F \in \Lambda(\mathbf{C} \cap \mathbf{C}^-, \mathbf{C}) \cap \Lambda^{NI} \cap \Lambda^{Ne}$.

We next prove the 'if' direction. Consider an rule F with disjunctive list Ω satisfying the above condition and a profile $\vec{C} \in \times_{i \in N} \mathbf{C} \cap \mathbf{C}^-$. Assume $x \in C(X_1) \cap C(X_2)$ for arbitrary admissible X_1 and X_2. Since $x \in C(X_1)$ we know $V(x, X_1; \vec{C}) \in \Omega$, and since $x \in C(X_2)$ we know $V(x, X_2; \vec{C}) \in \Omega$. The desired result will follow if it can be shown that

$$V(x, X_1; \vec{C}) \cap V(x, X_2; \vec{C}) \subseteq V(x, X_1 \cup X_2; \vec{C}) \subseteq V(x, X_1; \vec{C}) \cup V(x, X_2; \vec{C})$$

for then the above list condition implies that $V(x, X_1 \cup X_2; \vec{C}) \in \Omega$ and $x \in C(X_1 \cup X_2)$. Now, consider $i \in V(x, X_1; \vec{C}) \cap V(x, X_2; \vec{C})$, which implies $x \in C_i(X_1) \cap C(X_2)$. Since $C_i(\cdot) \in \mathbf{C}$, it follows that $x \in C_i(X_1 \cup X_2)$ and $i \in V(x, X_1 \cup X_2; \vec{C})$, giving us one inclusion. Consider $i \in V(x, X_1 \cup X_2; \vec{C})$ and suppose $i \notin V(x, X_1; \vec{C}) \cup V(x, X_2; \vec{C})$. Then $x \notin C_i(X_1)$ and $x \notin C_i(X_2)$, and it follows from Theorem 4.21 and $C_i(\cdot) \in \mathbf{C}^-$ that $x \notin C_i(X_1 \cup X_2)$. In other words, $i \notin V(x, X_1 \cup X_2; \vec{C})$, a contradiction. This gives us the second inclusion and the desired result. Lemma is proved.

Lemma 4.15 *$F \in \Lambda(\mathbf{C} \cap \mathbf{C}^-, \mathbf{C}) \cap \Lambda^{NI} \cap \Lambda^{Ne}$ if and only if there is an interval $[\omega', \omega''] \neq 2^N$, $[\omega', \omega''] \neq \emptyset$ such that for all profiles $\vec{C}$ and for all admissible X*

$$C(X) = \bigcup_{\omega \in [\omega', \omega'']} \bigcap_{i \in N} C_i^{\omega}(X)$$

Proof of Lemma 4.15. First the 'only if' direction. Since $F \in \Lambda^{NI} \cap \Lambda^{Ne} = \Lambda^{\cup\cap\pm}$, we know from Theorem 4.18 that there is a collection Ω such that for all profiles $C(X) = \bigcup_{\omega \in \Omega} \bigcap_{i \in \omega} C_i^{\omega}(X)$. And since $F \in \Lambda(\mathbf{C} \cap \mathbf{C}^-, \mathbf{C})$, it follows from Lemma 4.14 that Ω is an interval $[\omega', \omega'']$. To see this, note that Lemma 4.14 implies $\bigcup_{\omega \in \Omega} \omega \in \Omega$ and $\bigcap_{\omega \in \Omega} \omega \in \Omega$. Then another application of Lemma 4.14 implies $[\bigcap_{\Omega} \omega, \bigcup_{\Omega} \omega] \subseteq \Omega$. Equality then follows since $\Omega \subseteq [\bigcap_{\Omega} \omega, \bigcup_{\Omega} \omega]$. Since $F \in \Lambda^{NI}$, it must be that $[\omega', \omega''] \neq 2^N$ and $[\omega', \omega''] \neq \emptyset$.
The 'if' direction follows easily by noting that any rule with an interval disjunctive list is neutral and also non-imposed if the interval is not $\emptyset$ and not 2^N. Furthermore, such an rule closes $\mathbf{C} \cap \mathbf{C}^-$ since it satisfies the condition of Lemma 4.14. Lemma is proved.

In words, Lemma 4.15 establishes that there is an interval $[\omega', \omega'']$ such that an alternative x is chosen from each admissible X if and only if, for at least one group in the interval, all members choose x from X and all non-members reject x from X.

Lemma 4.16 *$F \in \Lambda(\mathbf{C} \cap \mathbf{C}^-, \mathbf{C}^-) \cap \Lambda^{NI} \cap \Lambda^{Ne}$ if and only if there is an interval $[\omega', \omega''] \neq 2^N$, $[\omega', \omega''] \neq \emptyset$ such that for all profiles $\vec{C}$ and for all admissible X*

$$C(X) = \bigcap_{\omega \in [\omega', \omega'']} \bigcup_{i \in N} C_i^{-\omega}(X),$$

where

$$C_i^{-\omega}(X) = \begin{cases} C_i^-(X) \text{ if } i \in \omega; \\ C_i(X) \text{ else,} \end{cases}$$

for all admissible X.

Proof of Lemma 4.16. We know that $F \in \Lambda(\mathbf{C} \cap \mathbf{C}^-, \mathbf{C}^-) \cap \Lambda^{NI} \cap \Lambda^{Ne}$ if and only if $F \in \Lambda^{NI} \cap \Lambda^{Ne}$ and $F(\vec{C}) = C(\cdot) \in \mathbf{C}$ for all profiles $\vec{C} \in \times_{i \in N} \mathbf{C} \cap \mathbf{C}^-$. This is true if and only if $F \in \Lambda^{NI} \cap \Lambda^{Ne}$ and for all profiles $\vec{C} \in \times_{i \in N} \mathbf{C} \cap \mathbf{C}^-$ we have $C^-(\cdot) \in \mathbf{C}$, which by Lemma 4.15 is true if and only if there exists an interval $[\omega', \omega''] \neq \emptyset$ and $[\omega', \omega''] \neq 2^N$ such that for all profiles

$$C(X) = \bigcup_{\omega \in [\omega', \omega'']} \bigcap_{i \in N} C_i^{\omega}(X)$$

for all admissible X. By DeMorgan's Law, this is true if and only if there exists an interval $[\omega', \omega''] \neq \emptyset$ and $[\omega', \omega''] \neq 2^N$ such that for all profiles

$$C(X) = \bigcap_{\omega \in [\omega', \omega'']} \bigcup_{i \in N} C_i^{-\omega}(X)$$

for all admissible X. The desired result follows by setting $[\omega_1, \omega_2] = [\omega', \omega'']$. Lemma is proved.

In words, Lemma 4.16 establishes that there is an interval $[\omega_1, \omega_2]$ such that an alternative x is rejected from an admissible X if and only if, for at least one group in the interval, all members choose x from X and all non-members reject x from X.

These results allow us to prove two interesting corollaries, and after the proof of an additional lemma we can prove Theorem 4.25 as well:

Corollary 4.2 $\Lambda^{\cap} \cup \Lambda^{\cap -} \subset \Lambda(\mathbf{C} \cap \mathbf{C}^-, \mathbf{C})$

Proof: Note that an oligarchy rule F is given by a list $\Omega = \{\omega \subseteq N \mid \omega^* \subseteq \omega\}$ with $\emptyset \subset \omega^* \subseteq N$. This is just the interval $[\omega^*, N]$, and by Lemma 4.15 it follows that $F \in \Lambda(\mathbf{C} \cap \mathbf{C}^-, \mathbf{C})$.

We know that an anti-oligarchy rule F is given by a list $\Omega = \{\omega \subseteq N \mid \omega \cap \omega^* = \emptyset\}$ with $\emptyset \subset \omega^* \subseteq N$. This is just the interval $[\emptyset, N \setminus \omega^*]$, and by Lemma 4.15 it follows that $F \in \Lambda(\mathbf{C} \cap \mathbf{C}^-, \mathbf{C})$.

Corollary 4.3 $\Lambda^{\cup} \cup \Lambda^{\cup -} \subset \Lambda(\mathbf{C} \cap \mathbf{C}^-, \mathbf{C}^-)$.

Proof: Note that a syndicate rule F is given by a list $E = \{\varepsilon \subseteq N \mid \varepsilon^* \subseteq \varepsilon\}$ with $\emptyset \subset \varepsilon^* \subseteq N$. Then the interval $[\emptyset, N \setminus \varepsilon^*]$ satisfies the condition of Lemma 4.16 and it follows that $F \in \Lambda(\mathbf{C} \cap \mathbf{C}^-, \mathbf{C}^-)$.

We know that an anti-syndicate rule F is given by a conjunctive list $E = \{\varepsilon \subseteq N \mid \varepsilon \cap \varepsilon^* = \emptyset\}$ with $\emptyset \subset \varepsilon^* \subseteq N$. Then the interval $[\varepsilon^*, N]$ satisfies the condition of Lemma 4.16 and it follows that $F \in \Lambda(\mathbf{C} \cap \mathbf{C}^-, \mathbf{C}^-)$.

Lemma 4.17 $\Lambda(\mathbf{C} \cap \mathbf{C}^-, \mathbf{C}) \cap \Lambda(\mathbf{C} \cap \mathbf{C}^-, \mathbf{C}^-) = \Lambda(\mathbf{C} \cap \mathbf{C}^-)$.

Proof of Lemma 4.17: Consider $F \in \Lambda(\mathbf{C} \cap \mathbf{C}^-, \mathbf{C}) \cap \Lambda(\mathbf{C} \cap \mathbf{C}^-, \mathbf{C}^-)$ and a profile $\vec{C} \in \times_{i \in N} \mathbf{C} \cap \mathbf{C}^-$. Then $F(\vec{C}) \in \mathbf{C}$ and $F(\vec{C}) \in \mathbf{C}^-$, so $F \in \Lambda(\mathbf{C} \cap \mathbf{C}^-)$. Conversely, $F \in \Lambda(\mathbf{C} \cap \mathbf{C}^-)$ maps each profile in $\mathbf{C} \cap \mathbf{C}^-$ to $\mathbf{C}$ and $\mathbf{C}^-$, so $F \in \Lambda(\mathbf{C} \cap \mathbf{C}^-, \mathbf{C}) \cap \Lambda(\mathbf{C} \cap \mathbf{C}^-, \mathbf{C}^-)$. Lemma is proved.

Proof of Theorem 4.25. Obviously, $\mathbf{C} \cap \mathbf{C}^-$ is closed with respect to complementation, so we have $\Lambda^d \cup \Lambda^{d-} \subseteq \Lambda(\mathbf{C} \cap \mathbf{C}^-) \cap \Lambda^{NI} \cap \Lambda^{Ne}$.

Now consider $F \in \Lambda(\mathbf{C} \cap \mathbf{C}^-) \cap \Lambda^{NI} \cap \Lambda^{Ne}$. By Lemma 4.17, we know that $F \in \Lambda(\mathbf{C} \cap \mathbf{C}^-, \mathbf{C}) \cap \Lambda(\mathbf{C} \cap \mathbf{C}^-, \mathbf{C}^-)$. Lemma 4.15 then implies that F is given by an interval $[\omega', \omega'']$ such that for every profile $\vec{C}$ an alternative x is socially chosen from each admissible X if and only if $V(x, X; \vec{C}) \in [\omega', \omega'']$. And Lemma 4.16 implies that F is given by an interval $[\omega_1, \omega_2]$ such that x is socially rejected from each admissible

X if and only if $V(x, X; \vec{C}) \in [\omega_1, \omega_2]$. It follows immediately that $[\omega', \omega''] = 2^N \setminus [\omega_1, \omega_2]$ and $[\omega', \omega''] \cap [\omega_1, \omega_2] = \emptyset$. Also from Lemma 4.15 we have $[\omega', \omega''] \neq [\emptyset. N]$, $[\omega', \omega''] \neq \emptyset$, and similarly for $[\omega_1, \omega_2]$. Note that $F \in \Lambda^d$ if and only if there is a $d \in N$ such that $[\omega_1, \omega_2] = [\emptyset, N \setminus \{d\}]$ and $F \in \Lambda^{d-}$ if and only if there is a $d \in N$ such that $[\omega_1, \omega_2] = [\{d\}, N]$.
Suppose that $F \notin \Lambda^d$ and $F \notin \Lambda^{d-}$. We consider three cases:
1) there is a $d \in N$ such that $d \in \omega$ for all $\omega \in [\omega_1, \omega_2]$;
2) there is a $d \in N$ such that $d \notin \omega$ for all $\omega \in [\omega_1, \omega_2]$;
3) for all $i \in N$ there are $\omega_i^1, \omega_i^0 \in [\omega_1, \omega_2]$ such that $i \in \omega_i^1$ and $i \notin \omega_i^0$.
We shall see that a contradiction arises in each case, giving us the desired result.
(1) Since $[\omega_1, \omega_2] \neq [\{d\}, N]$, there exists an $\omega^d \subseteq N$ with $d \in \omega^d$ such that $\omega^d \notin [\omega_1, \omega_2]$. Note that we then have $[\emptyset, N \setminus \{d\}] \cup \omega^d \subseteq [\omega', \omega'']$. In particular, $N \setminus \omega^d \in [\omega', \omega'']$. It follows from Lemma 4.14 that $\omega^d \cap (N \setminus \omega^d) = \emptyset \in [\omega', \omega'']$ and that $\omega^d \cup (N \setminus \omega^d) = N \in [\omega', \omega'']$. But then $[\omega', \omega''] = [\emptyset, N]$, violating non-imposedness.
(2) Since $[\omega', \omega''] \neq [\emptyset, N]$, there exists an $\omega^d \subseteq N$ with $d \notin \omega^d$ such that $\omega^d \notin [\omega', \omega'']$. Note that we then have $[\{d\}, N] \cup \{\omega^d\} \subseteq [\omega', \omega'']$. It follows from Lemma 4.14 that $\omega^d \cap \{d\} = \emptyset \in [\omega', \omega'']$. But then $[\omega', \omega''] = [\emptyset, N]$, violating non-imposedness.
(3) Since $[\omega', \omega'']$ is an interval, we know $\bigcap_{i \in N} \omega_i^0 = \emptyset \in [\omega', \omega'']$ and $\bigcup_{i \in N} \omega_i^1 = N \in [\omega', \omega'']$. But then $[\omega', \omega''] = [\emptyset, N]$, violating Non-Imposition. ■

Thus, Theorem 4.25 is a direct non-binary counterpart to Wilson's theorem.
There are 63 non-empty domains isolated by combinations of the rationality constraints $\mathbf{H}, \mathbf{C}, \mathbf{O}, \mathbf{H}^-, \mathbf{C}^-$, and $\mathbf{O}^-$. Of these, 14 are covered by Theorems 4.20 and 4.22, and 28 reduce to the domain $\mathbf{ACA}^*$ and are covered by Theorem 4.23. One more is treated in Theorem 4.25, leaving 20 domains which may be closed by a non-monotonic rule. Moreover, we have not considered the classes of rules which close domains which are strictly smaller than their ranges, such as $\Lambda(\mathbf{H} \cap \mathbf{C}, \mathbf{H})$. It is possible to show, however, that of all these possibilities $\mathbf{C} \cap \mathbf{C}^-$ is the only domain other than $\mathbf{ACA}^*$ which is closed by a non-monotonic rule.

4.11 Concluding remarks and guide to the literature

Remark 1. The following facts have been established in the above sections of this chapter under the assumption of locality:
1. There is no local rule satisfying the set of characteristic conditions NI through An with respect to which the domains of classically rational choice functions ($\mathbf{H} \bigcap \mathbf{C} \bigcap \mathbf{O}$ or $\mathbf{ACA}$) are closed. It implies that, if all agents use some classically rational functions, there exists no local rule satisfying those conditions whose application would guarantee classical rationality of the social choice function.
The difficulties remain even if the domain in C checked for closedness with respect to voting rules is outside the limits of the classical intersection $\mathbf{H} \bigcap \mathbf{C}$. For example, if profiles from the non–classical domain $\mathbf{C}$ (or $\mathbf{O}$) are permitted, the conditions NI

through An and the requirement of domain closedness are satisfied by only Uunanimity (or One vote) rule which is of little interest from the application point of view.
At the same time, the domain **H** was found to be, in contrast to **C** and **O**, remarkable in a sense. Namely, if the agents are restricted in their choice of functions $C_i(\cdot)$ only by the condition **H**, no difficulty arises with construction of the desired rules: social choice function belonging to **H** is constructed for any rule satisfying the characteristic conditions NI through An and any profile from **H**. Moreover, such rules are k - majority rules.
As follows from the aforesaid, as long as consideration is confined only to local voting rules and the conditions NI through An are regarded as necessary, the indicated difficulties can be overcome only if one abandons the classical rationality requirements and accepts as reasonable all the choice functions from the domain **H** in $\mathcal{C}$. Generally speaking, this assumption tolerating violation of the conditions **C** and **O** is necessary only in reference to the choice function $C(\cdot)$ generated by the aggregation rule, whereas the individual agent choice functions $C_i(\cdot)$ can be arbitrarily limited by any subdomain of **H** (e.g., even $\mathbf{ACA} \subset \mathbf{H}$).

Remark 2. Throughout Chapter 4, it was assumed that $Q_d \subseteq Q_r$, i.e., any kind of choice functions which is used by agents is admissible as social choice function. However, the question arises what kind of rules can be obtained if this restriction is omitted, i.e., the domains Q_d and Q_r are not enclosed. The answer on that question given in [14] is that if $Q_d \not\subseteq Q_r$, then the intersection of the Basic Class and the corresponding complete class $\Lambda(Q_d, Q_r)$ is empty. Moreover, practically in all cases such mappings violate Non-Imposition condition.

Remark 3. In the classic framework Monotonicity is a binding constraint: when it is relaxed dictatorship and inverse dictatorship both satisfy the remaining conditions NI and Ne. In the non-binary framework considered in this Chapter 4, however, we find that Monotonicity in conjunction with Non Imposition, Neutrality, and the usual rationality constraints is not binding. A more thorough investigation reveals that all non-imposed and neutral rules - monotonic and non-monotonic - close the extremely rational domain $\mathbf{ACA}^*$, so that Monotonicity is binding for such rules. Moreover, Wilson's theorem (see Chapter 3) carries over to the non-binary framework in an extremely interesting way: there is one and only one domain $\mathbf{C} \cap \mathbf{C}^-$ closed by just dictatorship and anti-dictatorship rules.

In contrast to the social decision rules there are only several publications in which local functional aggregation rules have been studied.
First article on local FARs was [211], but in that work the problem of axiomatic synthesis had not even been stated. The problem of axiomatic synthesis of local aggregation rules was stated in [10] ,[2] , in the latter article practically all results concerning the Central Class of local FARs were obtained. Detailed study of those rules was done in [4] . Classes of rules under different kind of rationality constraints and their relations

with Basic and Central Classes were studied in [14] . The conditions which guarantee the non-emptyness of local FARs were obtained in [223] . Non-neutral but monotonic FARs were subject of study in [4] , [14] and [6] , and non-monotonic neutral rules - in [20] .

Recently, the article [261] was published in which the results for local functional aggregation rules are generalized for infinite case.

5

SOCIAL CHOICE CORRESPONDENCES

5.1 Introduction

In this Chapter we study the rules from the space Π_{III}, i.e., the rules which transform individual binary relations to social choice functions. These rules were called in Chapter 1 Social Choice Correspondences.
The locality condition is given in Section 2, as well as the list–form representation of local rules. It is important to note that since domain and range of the rules under study are of different nature, Ω—lists for such kind of rules consists of the ordered sets of subsets of the set A rather than the subsets of N as in both previous cases of rules in Π_I and Π_{II}.
In Section 3 some normative conditions on rules are given, and the Central Class of rules in Π_{III} is defined. As usual, this Class is defined by Non-Imposition, Monotonicity and Neutrality conditions. In Section 4 boolean representation of local social choice correspondences is given. In Sections 5 and 6 the rules from Central Class, and in Section 7 the rules from Symmetrically Central Class are studied. Again, we obtain the rules of federation type, however, in the case under study much more reach classes of rules arise. In Sections 8-10 rationality constraints on the rules are studied. In Section 8 the case of single-valued social choice functions are studied. A famous Muller-Satterthwaite Theorem is proved in this Section. In Section 9 the class of coa;itional q-federation rules introduced in Section 5, and its intersections with the complete classes of closedness for fundamental domains in C are elaborated. Section 10 provides an analysis of those rationality constraints in general. In Section 11 different classes of rules isolated by normative conditions and rationality constraints are investigated. The final Section of Chapter 5, Section 12, contains as usual concluding remarks and giude to the literature.

5.2 Locality

First, let us remind the problem under study: we consider the set A ($| A |= m \geq 2$) of alternatives, and the set N ($| N |= n \geq 2$) of individuals. Each agent $i \in N$ is independent from the other agents, and expresses her opinion on the alternatives using a binary relation P_i, which can be interpreted in terms of preference. In this case, the pair (a,b) is in P_i if 'the alternative a is preferred to the alternative b' by agent i.

For simplicity, the binary relation $P_i, i = 1, \dots, n$, is assumed to be a linear order, i.e., satisfy the following conditions:
– irreflexivity ($\forall x \in A$, $x\overline{P_i}x$);
– transitivity ($\forall x, y, z \in A$, $xP_iy, yP_iz \Rightarrow xP_iz$);
– connectedness ($\forall x, y \in A$, $x \neq y$, xPy or yPx).

Note that a linear order admits the obvious following interpretation: for any pair of alternatives, it is possible to establish that one alternative is more preferable than the other.

The totality of all linear orders is denoted by $\mathcal{LO}$.

Now we introduce the notion of the upper contour (dominant) and lower contour sets for the alternative x.

Definition 5.1 The *upper contour* (or, *dominant*) *set* $\mathcal{D}(x)$ for the alternative x in the binary relation P is defined as follows:

$$\mathcal{D}(x) = \{y \in A \mid (y, x) \in P\},$$

i.e., the dominant set for x is a set of all alternatives which are more preferable in P than x.
The lower contour set $\mathcal{L}(x)$ for the alternative x in the binary relation P is defined as follows:

$$\mathcal{L}(x) = \{z \in A \mid (x, z) \in P\},$$

i.e., the *lower contour set* for x is a set of all alternatives which are less preferable in P than x.

We consider the aggregation rules in Π_{III} which transform the profiles $\{P_i\}$ in the choice functions $C(\cdot)$, or strictly speaking, transform the domain defined by the n–tuple cartesian product $\mathcal{LO}^n = \mathcal{LO} \times \ldots \times \mathcal{LO}$ to the space $\mathcal{C}$. The space $\mathcal{C}$ as before is the set of all choice functions on A. Thus, the rule $F \in \Pi_{III}$ is defined as

$$F : \mathcal{LO}^n \to \mathcal{C}.$$

These rules are called Social Choice Correspondences.

For the moment being, we will not restrict somehow the set $\mathcal{C}$, i.e., all choice functions are admissible as a collective decision.
There are many rules which implement the mapping $\mathcal{LO}^n \to \mathcal{C}$. As before, we study the rules which satisfy a special locality condition.

Definition 5.2 A SCC $F : \mathcal{LO}^n \to \mathcal{C}$ will be called to satisfy *locality* condition if for any two profiles $\overrightarrow{P}, \overrightarrow{P'}$ and any x, X, $x \in X \in \mathcal{A}$, such that

$$\forall i \in N \ X \cap \mathcal{D}_i(x) = X \cap \mathcal{D}'_i(x)$$

follows

$$x \in C(X) \text{ if and only if } x \in C'(X),$$

where $C(\cdot) = F(\overrightarrow{P})$ and $C'(\cdot) = F(\overrightarrow{P'})$.

The set of all local Social Choice Correspondences will be hereafter denoted as Π_{III}.

Consider two profiles $\overrightarrow{P}$ and $\overrightarrow{P'}$ of linear orders on the set $A = \{a, b, c, d\}$, with $N = \{1, 2, 3\}$:

$$\begin{array}{llll} P_1: & b \succ a \succ c \succ d; & P'_1: & a \succ b \succ c \succ d; \\ P_2: & d \succ c \succ a \succ b; & P'_2: & d \succ c \succ b \succ a; \\ P_3: & a \succ c \succ b \succ d; & P'_3: & a \succ c \succ d \succ b. \end{array}$$

It can be easily seen that for the subset $X = \{a, b, c\}$ the dominant sets for alternative c coincide for all binary relations $P_i, P'_i, i = 1, 2, 3$. Thus, the locality condition is satisfied if c is included (or not included) in $C(X)$ and also if c is included (respectively, not included) in $C'(X)$. Note, that for the alternative b we obtain $\mathcal{D}_1(b) \cap X = \emptyset$, and $\mathcal{D}'_1(b) \cap X = \{a\}$. In this case nothing can be said about social decisions concerning the alternative b in X with respect to profiles $\overrightarrow{P}$ and $\overrightarrow{P'}$.

Below two examples of Social Choice Correspondences are given.

Example 1. Let us consider the weak Pareto rule introduced above in Chapter 2, and re-write it for the case when agents' opinions are represented in the form of linear orders rather than criteria:

$$C(X) = \{x \in X \mid \overline{\exists} y \in X \text{ such that } \forall i \in N \; yP_ix\}.$$

This rule will be denoted by F_{Par}. It means that x is included in the choice $C(X)$ if and only if another alternative y is not preferred to x in all relations P_i.
It can be proved that the rule F_{Par} satisfies the locality condition.

Example 2. Let us consider now another rule which will be called *Borda*[35] *rule* and denoted as F_{Borda}. Let for each alternative a in binary relation P_i $r_i(a)$ be the number of elements in the lower contour set of the alternative a in P_i. As an aggregation rule we consider the rule which includes in the social choice those alternatives which have maximum sum value $\Sigma_{i \in N} r_i(a)$. This rule can be written in the following form:

$$x \in C(X) \Leftrightarrow (x \in X \mid x = \arg\max_{a \in X} \Sigma_{i \in N} r_i(a)).$$

Let us consider now two profiles $\overrightarrow{P}$ and $\overrightarrow{P}'$ with the sets $A = \{x, y, z\}$, $N = \{1, 2, 3\}$:

35 This operator is analogus to that studied by Borda [65] ..

$$\begin{array}{llll} P_1: & x \succ y \succ z; & P_1': & x \succ y \succ z; \\ P_2: & z \succ x \succ y; & P_2': & z \succ x \succ y; \\ P_3: & y \succ z \succ x; & P_3': & z \succ y \succ x. \end{array}$$

Let us note that $\forall i \in N$ $\mathcal{D}_i(x) \cap A = \mathcal{D}_i'(x) \cap A$ and according to condition of locality x is included (or is not included) in choice $C(A)$ if and only if x belongs (or does not belong) to $C'(A)$. Let us apply now the Borda rule to profile $\overrightarrow{P}$. One can see that $\Sigma_{i \in N} r_i(x) = \Sigma_{i \in N} r_i(y) = \Sigma_{i \in N} r_i(z) = 3$ and hence $C(A) = A$.
However, in the profile $\overrightarrow{P'}$, $\Sigma_{i \in N} r_i'(x) = 3$, but $\Sigma_{i \in N} r_i'(y) = 2$ and $\Sigma_{i \in N} r_i'(z) = 4$ and thus $z \in C'(A)$ and $x \notin C'(A)$. In other words, according to this example the Borda rule is not local.

5.2.1 List representation of local rules

Now let us introduce a new language for the study of Social Choice Correspondences. The totality of sets $\{\vec{Z}\}_1^s, \vec{Z} = (Z_1, \ldots, Z_n)$ such that $\forall i \in N$ $Z_i \subseteq X \backslash \{x\}$ is called a list for the pair $(x, X), x \in X \in \mathcal{A}$. The list for pair (x, X) will be denoted $\Omega(x, X) : \Omega(x, X) = (\{\vec{Z}\}_1^s)$.
The Ω- *(or, list) representation* of a rule $F \in \Pi_{III}$ is defined by the set of lists $\Omega_F = \{\Omega(x, X)\}_{(x,X)}$ and the rule which for any profile $\overrightarrow{P}$ determines a social choice on any pair (x, X) as follows:

$$x \in C(X) \Leftrightarrow (X \cap D_1(x), \ldots X \cap D_n(x)) \in \Omega(x, X) \in \Omega_F \qquad (5.1)$$

Theorem 5.1 *Each rule in Π_{III} has a list representation. Each Social Choice Correspondence which admits the list representation is a local rule.*

Proof. Let us consider the whole set of profiles on linear orders, the arbitrary set $X \in \mathcal{A}$ and the option $x \in X$. Construct a list for local operator F according to the following algorithm: for a given profile $\overrightarrow{P}$, if $x \in C(X)$, then include the set $\vec{Z} = (Z_1, \ldots, Z_n)$, as an element in the list $\Omega(x, X)$. Each component Z_i of $\vec{Z}$ is defined as $\forall i \in N$ $Z_i = \mathcal{D}_i(x) \cap X$. All such lists $\Omega(x, X)$ define the whole list Ω_F for the rule F. This list and rule (5.1) define some operator $\tilde{F}$. Let us show that $\tilde{F} \equiv F$. The functions generated by the operators F and $\tilde{F}$ will be denoted as $C(\cdot)$ and $\tilde{C}(\cdot)$, respectively. Consider the profile $\overrightarrow{P}$ and assume that there exists X and x such that $x \in \tilde{C}(X)$ and $x \notin C(X)$. Because of the fact that $x \in \tilde{C}(X)$, according to the construction of the operator $\tilde{F}$ it means that there exists a profile $\overrightarrow{P'}$ such that $X \cap \mathcal{D}_i(x) = Z_i$ for all i. Since F is local, the condition $\forall i$ $\mathcal{D}_i(x) \cap X = \mathcal{D}_i'(x) \cap X$ and $x \in C'(X)$ imply that $x \in C(X)$. Let now a rule F has a list representation Ω_F. Let us prove its locality. Let us consider two profiles $\overrightarrow{P}$ and $\overrightarrow{P'}$ such that $\forall i \in N$ $\mathcal{D}_i(x) \cap X = \mathcal{D}_i'(x) \cap X$. If $\{\mathcal{D}_i(x) \cap X\} \in \Omega_F(x, X)$, then $x \in C(X)$ and

$x \in C'(X)$. On the other hand if $\forall i \in N$ $\{\mathcal{D}_i(x) \cap X\} \notin \Omega_F(x, X)$ then $x \notin C(X)$ and $x \notin C'(X)$ ■

Remark 1. Let us emphasize that in contrast with previous cases of the local rules in Π_I and Π_{II} for which lists in Ω–representation contain winning coalitions or pairs of coalitions, i.e., subsets of the set of agents N, in the case of local rules in Π_{III} lists in Ω–representation are subsets of the set of alternatives A.

Remark2. Strongly local rules.
Let us assume first that agents' binary relations are represented as weak orders, i.e., as irreflexive, transitive, and negatively transitive ($\forall x, y, z \in A$ $x\overline{P}y, y\overline{P}z \rightarrow x\overline{P}z$) binary relations. Strongly local rules differ from local rules - to make a decision about an inclusion (or exclusion) an alternative to the social choice from X, one should check not only upper but also lower contour sets in agents' weak orders.

Definition 5.3 The rule $F : \mathcal{WO}^n \rightarrow \mathcal{C}$ will be called a strongly local one if it satisfies the following condition: Let two profiles $\overrightarrow{P}, \overrightarrow{P'}$ are given and suppose that for some x, X, such that $x \in X \in \mathcal{A}$ the following equalities hold

$$\forall i \in N \; X \cap \mathcal{D}_i(x) = X \cap \mathcal{D}'_i(x);$$
$$\forall i \in N \; X \cap \mathcal{L}_i(x) = X \cap \mathcal{L}'_i(x),$$

which means that the upper contour sets as well as lower contour sets for the alternative x in X in the relations P_i and P'_i coincide. Then

$$x \in C(X) \text{ if and only if } x \in C'(X),$$

where $C(\cdot) = F(\overrightarrow{P})$ and $C'(\cdot) = F(\overrightarrow{P'})$.

Consider now Pareto rule (not weak Pareto rule!) introduced in Chapter 2, Section 2.3, and re-write it for the case when agents' opinions are represented in the form of weak orders rather than criteria:

$$C(X) = \{x \in X \mid \overline{\exists} y \in X \text{ such that } (\forall i \in N \text{ either } yP_ix \text{ or } yI_ix \text{ and } \exists i_0 \text{ such that } yP_{i_0}x)\},$$

where I is an indifference relation for P_i. In words, x is not chosen even if every agent but one is indifferent between x and y, and that one agent prefers x to y.
Consider an example given at Fig.5-1. Using Pareto rule for the profile $\overrightarrow{P}$, one can obtain social choice on A being equal to $C(\overrightarrow{P}, A) = \{b, c\}$. Now consider the profile $\overrightarrow{P'}$. For the alternative b $D_i(b) = D'_i(b)$ for any i, however, $C(\overrightarrow{P'}, A) = \{c\}$ since bI'_1c and bI'_2c, but cP'_3b. This means that Pareto rule is not local. Nevertheless it is strongly local which can be proved directly.
Immediately from the proof of Theorem 5.1 follows how to construct Ω–representation for strongly local rules. In this case the list $\Omega(x, X)$ contains the ordered set of pairs of subsets of A such that

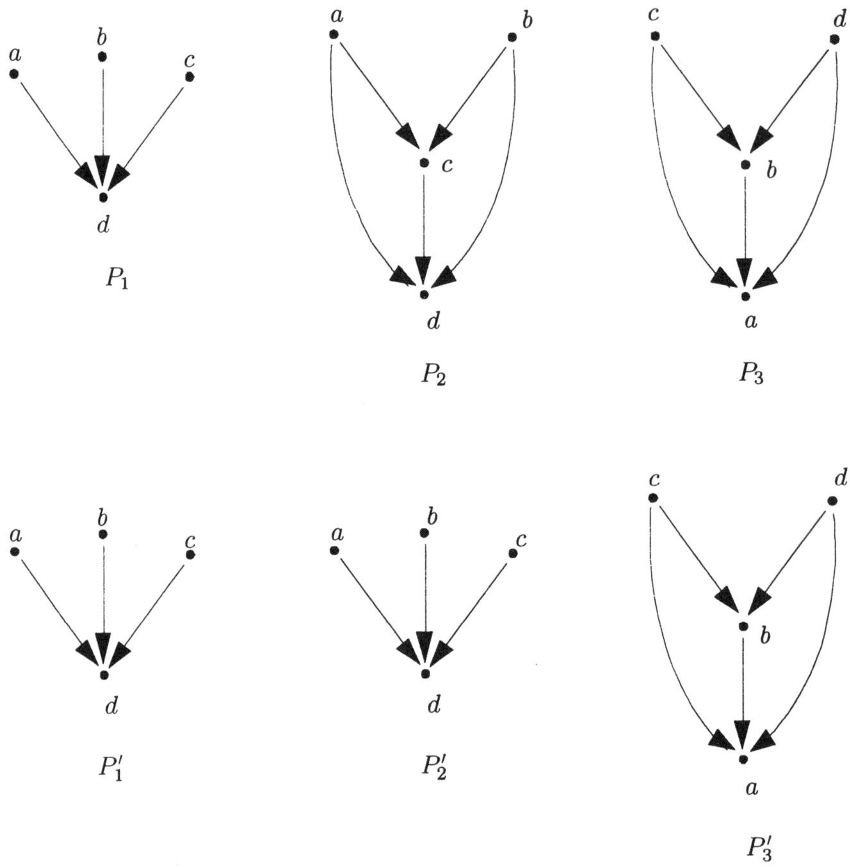

Figure 5-1

$$\Omega(x, X) = \{(Z_1^1, Z_2^1), ..., (Z_1^s, Z_2^s)\},$$

with the following property $Z_1^i \cap Z_2^i = \emptyset$ for any $i = 1, ..., s$. The rule how to define social choice on each X from a given profile $\overrightarrow{P}$ is written down as follows

$$x \in C(X) \Leftrightarrow ((X \cap \mathcal{D}_1(x), X \cap \mathcal{L}_1(x)), ..., \\ (X \cap \mathcal{D}_s(x), X \cap \mathcal{L}_s(x))) \in \Omega(x, X)$$

5.3 Normative conditions

Let us now introduce the normative conditions.

(NI). *Non–Imposition*. This condition consists of two conditions.

(NI^+). *Positive Non–Imposition*. For all x, X $(x \in X \in \mathcal{A})$ there exists a profile $\overrightarrow{P}$ such that $x \in C(X)$, where $C(\cdot) = F(\overrightarrow{P})$.

(NI^-). *Negative Non–Imposition*. For all x, X $(x \in X \in \mathcal{A})$ there exists a profile $\overrightarrow{P}$ such that $x \notin C(X)$.
In other words, while constructing the function $C(\cdot)$, the rule F takes into consideration the individual opinions: there are no x, X for which the condition that x is always in $C(X)$ or x is never in $C(X)$ is predetermined independently of profile.

(MM). *Monotonicity*. Let us consider some profile $\overrightarrow{P}$, and for some x and X $(x \in X \in \mathcal{A})$, $\mathcal{D}_i \cap X$ for all i in N. Let now in the profile $\overrightarrow{P'}$: $\forall i \in N$ $\mathcal{D}'_i(x) \cap X \subseteq D_i(x) \cap X$ holds. Then, $x \in C(X) \Rightarrow x \in C'(X)$.
Let us explain this condition. At the illustrative example for locality condition above, for the profile $\overrightarrow{P}$, $D_1(d) \cap A = \{a, b, c\}$, $D_2(d) \cap A = \emptyset$ and $D_3(d) \cap A = \{a, b, c\}$ and for the profile $\overrightarrow{P'}$ $D'_1(d) \cap A = \{a, b, c\}$, $D'_2(d) \cap A = \emptyset$ and $D'_3(d) \cap A = \{a, c\}$. In these two profiles $D_1(d) \cap A$ and $D'_1(d) \cap A$ coincide, as well as $D_2(d) \cap A$ and $D'_2(d) \cap A$. However, for P_3, the dominant set of d consists of a, b, c, and for P'_1 it consists of a, c. It can be interpreted in terms of preference relations: the set of alternatives preferred to d in P'_3 is narrower than in relation P_1. So, if d is in social choice $C(A)$ with profile $\overrightarrow{P}$, then d is to be in $C'(A)$ with the profile $\overrightarrow{P'}$.
It is obvious that the condition of monotonicity is a reinforcement of the condition of locality, i.e., the monotonic rule is local.
This condition of monotonicity was introduced using lower contour sets by E.Maskin [180], and is known as Maskin's Monotonicity. We will denote this condition as MM.

(Ne). *Neutrality*. This condition is divided into two conditions:

(Ne_x). *Independence of alternative* (of x). Let for some x and y in X $\forall i$ $X \cap \mathcal{D}_i(x) = X \cap \mathcal{D}_i(y)$. Then $y \subset C(X)$ iff $x \subset C(X)$;

(Ne_X). *Independence of context* (of the subset X). Let us consider two subsets X and X' of $\mathcal{A}$ with the condition $\forall i$ $\mathcal{D}_i(x) \cap X = \mathcal{D}_i(x) \cap X'$. Then $x \in C(X)$ iff $x \in C(X')$. Conditions (Ne_X) and (Ne_x) are stronger of locality condition: put $x = y$ in Ne_xor $X' = X$ in Ne_X.
Neutrality condition, as usual, guarantees that the alternatives are treated equally (even in different contexts X) by the aggregation rule.

(An). *Anonymity*. Let $\eta :$ $N \Rightarrow N$ be a one–to–one mapping from the set N to N. Then $C(\cdot) = C'(\cdot)$ where $C(\cdot) = F(P_1, \dots, P_n)$ and $C'(\cdot) = F(P_{\eta(1)}, \dots, P_{\eta(n)})$. Anonymity condition, as usual, guarantees that the agents are treated equally by the aggregation rule.

(ND). *Non–Dominance*. This condition is divided into two following conditions:

(ND^+). *Positive Non–Dominance*. For all x, X $(x \in X \in \mathcal{A})$, if it exists $i_o \in N$ such that $\mathcal{D}_{i_o}(x) \cap X = \emptyset$, then $x \in C(X)$.
Positive Non–Dominance means that if at least one agent put x as a top element in X with respect to her weak order, then this x will belong to social decision.
(ND^-). *Negative Non–Dominance*. For all x, X $(x \in X \in \mathcal{A})$, if $\forall i \in N$ $\mathcal{D}_i(x) \cap X \neq \emptyset$, then $x \notin C(X)$.
Negative Non–Dominance states that if x is not a best element in X for all agents, then this x will not be socially chosen.
(wPO). *Weak Pareto Optimality*. If $\bigcap_{i \in N}(\mathcal{D}_i(x) \cap X) \neq \emptyset$, then $x \notin C(X)$.
This condition means that if there exists some y which unanimously is accepted to be better than x in X, then x will not belong to social choice. It is obvious that Negative Non–Dominance is stronger than Weak Pareto Optimality. Indeed, in the condition of Negative Non–Dominance alternatives which are better than x in X for different agents may be different.
(U^+). *Positive Unanimity*. If for some x, X $(x \in X \in \mathcal{A})$, and for all $i \in N$ $\mathcal{D}_i(x) \cap X = \emptyset$, then $x \in C(X)$.
If in X there is the best alternative for all agents, then it is socially chosen.
(U^-). *Negative Unanimity*. If for some x, X $(x \in X \in \mathcal{A})$ $\exists i \in N$ $\mathcal{D}_i(x) \cap X \neq \emptyset$, then $x \notin C(X)$.
If at least for one agent x is not the best option in X, then x may not be socially chosen.
(NVP) *No Veto Power*. Let

$$card(\{i \mid X \cap \mathcal{D}_i(x) = \emptyset\}) = n - 1.$$

Then $x \in C(X)$.
The NVP condition states that if $n-1$ agents evaluate some alternative x as their best, the last agent cannot 'veto' this decision to be social one, i.e., x will be socially chosen. This condition was first introduced in [180] .

Example. Let us consider Pareto rule F_{Par} and check to what conditions it satisfies. The satisfaction of the Non–Imposition condition is obvious. Let us show that this rule satisfies to Maskin's Monotonicity condition. Consider two profiles $\overrightarrow{P}$ and $\overrightarrow{P'}$; let us put that for subset X and $x \in X$ there exists no y such that $\forall i \in N$ $y \in \mathcal{D}_i(x) \cap X$. Then $x \in C(X)$. Now let $\forall i \in N$ $\mathcal{D}'_i(x) \cap X \subseteq \mathcal{D}_i(x) \cap X$. But then, obviously, $\bigcap_i(\mathcal{D}'_i(x) \cap X) = \emptyset$ again, and according to the Pareto rule, $x \in C'(X)$. Satisfaction to conditions Ne, An, ND^+, and U^+ can be easily shown. Thus, Pareto rule belongs to the class separated by conditions $NI \cap MM \cap Ne \cap An \cap ND^+ \cap U^+$.

Let us introduce some special rules.
The *constant rule* **1** is defined as follows:

$$\forall \overrightarrow{P} \text{ and } \forall X \in A \quad C(X) = X;$$

constant rule **0** :

$$\forall \overrightarrow{P} \text{ and } \forall X \in A \quad C(X) = \emptyset\,;$$

Unanimity rule:

$$\mathcal{U} : C(X) = \{x \in X \mid \forall i \in N \; X \cap D_i(x) = \emptyset\};$$

One vote rule:

$$\mathcal{V} : C(X) = \{x \in X \mid \exists i_o \in N \;\; D_{i_o}(x) \cap X = \emptyset\}.$$

Let us note that the constant rule **0** satisfies the conditions $NI^- \cap MM \cap Ne \cap An \cap ND^-$, the constant rule **1** satisfies to the conditions $NI^+ \cap MM \cap Ne \cap An \cap ND^+ \cap U^+$. Unanimity rule $\mathcal{U}$ satisfies $NI \cap MM \cap Ne \cap An \cap ND^- \cap U^+$, and, finally, the rule One vote $\mathcal{V}$ satisfies $NI \cap MM \cap Ne \cap An \cap ND \cap U^+$.

Let us define now Central and Symmetrically Central Classes in Π_{III}.

Definition 5.4 The class in Π_{III} satisfying simultaneously three Normative conditions NI, MM and Ne will be referred to as the *Central Class*; the class satisfying the four conditions NI, MM, Ne and An will be referred to as the *Symmetrically Central Class*.

These classes will be denoted as Λ^C and Λ^{SC}, respectively.

Let us give at the end of this Section an example of Normative condition which is valid for the case when agents' preferences are weak orders, and strongly local rules are considered.

(sPO). *Strong Pareto Optimality*. If there exists y in X such that a) $y \in \cap_{i \in N}(A \setminus \mathcal{L}_i(x)) \cap X \neq \emptyset$, and b) there is i_0 such that $y \in \mathcal{D}_i(x) \cap X$, then $x \notin C(X)$.

Strong Pareto Optimality is also stronger than Weak Pareto Optimality but it is weaker than Negative Non Dominance since for x not to be socially chosen from X it is sufficient that there is y which is not less preferable than x for all agents, and for at least one agent y is strictly preferable than x.

The reformulation of the normative conditions on local rules in terms of list representation is given below.
Hereafter, when we define ordered n-tuple $\vec{Z} = (Z_1, \ldots, Z_n)$ for some x and X it is necessary to remember that $\forall i \; Z_i \subseteq X \setminus \{x\}$.

(NI). Non-Imposition. This condition consists of two conditions.

(NI^+). Positive Non-Imposition. For all x, X $(x \in X \in \mathcal{A})$ $\Omega(x, X) \neq \emptyset$.

In order to formalize the condition of negative Non-Imposition it is necessary to define $T(x, X)$ as the list which contains all possible ordered n-tuples $\vec{Z}$, i.e.,

$$T(x, X) = 2^A \times 2^A \times \ldots \times 2^A.$$

(NI^-). Negative Non-Imposition. For all x, X $(x \in X \in \mathcal{A})$ $\Omega(x, X) \neq T(x, X)$.

(MM). Maskin's Monotonicity. For any x and X, $(x \in X \in \mathcal{A})$ and any $\vec{Z} = (Z_1, \ldots, Z_n) \in \Omega(x, X)$ and $\vec{Z}'$ such that $\forall i \in N\ Z_i' \subseteq Z_i$, $\vec{Z}' \in \Omega(x, X)$.

(Ne). Neutrality. Let $\vec{Z} = (Z_1, \ldots, Z_n) \in \Omega(x, X)$. For any permutation $\sigma : A \to A$ let us denote

$$\begin{aligned} \sigma\vec{Z} &= (\sigma Z_1, \ldots, \sigma Z_n), \\ \text{and } \sigma Z_i &= \{u \mid u = \sigma(v) \text{ for } v \in Z_i\}. \end{aligned}$$

Then Neutrality condition states that

$$\sigma\vec{Z} \in \Omega(x, X) \text{ and } \sigma_{xy}\vec{Z} \in \Omega(y, X),$$

where σ_{xy} is any permutation $\sigma : A \to A$ such that $\sigma(x) = y$ and $\sigma(y) = x$.

(An). Anonymity. Let $\eta :\ N \Rightarrow N$ is a one–to–one mapping and $\vec{Z} \in \Omega(x, X)$. Then $\eta\vec{Z} \in \Omega(x, X)$, where $\eta\vec{Z} = (Z_{\eta(1)}, \ldots, Z_{\eta(n)})$.

(ND). Non–Dominance. This condition is divided into two following conditions:

(ND^+). Positive Non–Dominance. For all $\vec{Z} = (Z_1, \ldots, Z_n)$ where one of its components Z_{i_o} is such that $Z_{i_o} = \emptyset$, $\vec{Z} \in \Omega(x, X)$ holds.

(ND^-). Negative Non–Dominance. For all $\vec{Z} = (Z_1, \ldots, Z_n)$ if $\forall i \in N\ Z_i \neq \emptyset$ $\vec{Z} \notin \Omega(x, X)$.

(wPO) Weak Pareto Optimality. For all $\vec{Z} = (Z_1, \ldots, Z_n)$ such that $\bigcap_{i \in N} Z_i \neq \emptyset$ $\vec{Z} \in \Omega(x, X)$ holds.

(U^+). Positive Unanimity. The ordered n-tuple $(\emptyset, \ldots, \emptyset)$ belongs to $\Omega(x, X)$.

(U^-) Negative Unanimity. For all $\vec{Z} = (Z_1, \ldots, Z_n)$ if there is $i \in N$ such that $Z_i \neq \emptyset$ $\vec{Z} \in \Omega(x, X)$ holds.

(NVP) No Veto Power. For all $\vec{Z} = (Z_1, \ldots, Z_n)$ such that

$$card(\{i \mid Z_i \neq \emptyset\}) = n - 1$$

follows $\vec{Z} \in \Omega(x, X)$.

Let us now study using Ω–representation how the classes of rules isolated by the conditions introduced above are related.

Theorem 5.2 *The relative position of the classes* $(NI^+) - (U^+)$ *in the space* Π_{III} *is shown on Figure* 5-2

Proof. Since there 2048 conjunctions of the conditions (NI^+), ..., (NVP) and their negations, only 8 conditions will be studied in this Theorem. There are 256 conjunctions of those 8 conditions and their negations.

The following relations between these conditions $NI^+, \ldots, U^+$ hold:

$ND^+ \Rightarrow NI^+; ND^- \Rightarrow NI^-; U^+ \Rightarrow NI^+; ND^+ \Rightarrow U^+;$

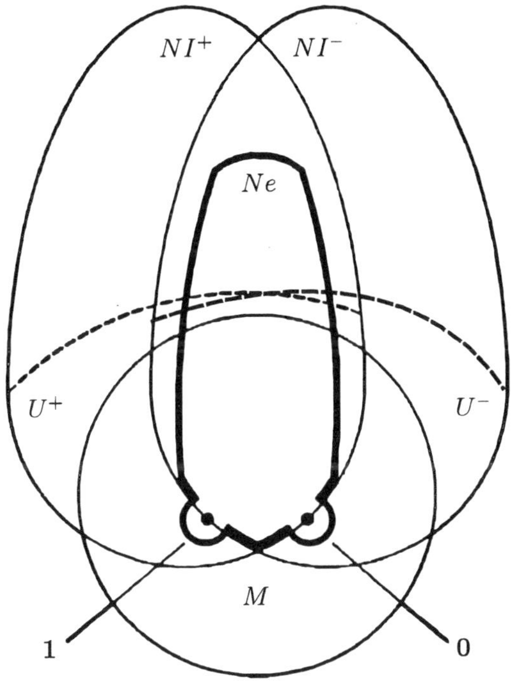

Figure 5-2

$\overline{NI^+} \cap Ne = \mathbf{0}; \overline{NI^+} \cap Ne \Rightarrow \overline{U^+}; \overline{NI^+} \cap Ne \Rightarrow \overline{ND^+}.$
$\overline{NI^+} \cap Ne \Rightarrow MM; \overline{NI^+} \cap Ne \Rightarrow An; \overline{NI^+} \cap Ne \Rightarrow ND^-;$
$\overline{NI^-} \cap Ne = \mathbf{1}; \overline{NI^-} \cap Ne \Rightarrow MM; \overline{NI^-} \cap Ne \Rightarrow An;$
$\overline{NI^-} \cap Ne \Rightarrow ND^+ : \overline{NI^-} \cap Ne \Rightarrow U^+;$
$\overline{NI^+} \cap \overline{NI^-} \cap Ne = \emptyset;$
$\overline{ND^-} \cap MM \Rightarrow ND^+; \overline{ND^-} \cap MM \Rightarrow U^+;$
These relations follow from the definitions of corresponding conditions. As an example we prove here only one relation $\overline{ND^-} \cap MM \Rightarrow U^+$. Since $\overline{ND^-}$ holds, $\Omega(x, X)$ contains $\vec{Z} = (Z_1, \ldots, Z_n)$ and $\forall j = 1, \ldots, n\ Z_j \neq \emptyset$. Then Maskin's Monotonicity implies that $\vec{Z}' = (\emptyset, \ldots, \emptyset)$ will belong to Ω ∎

The class of rules satisfying the conditions of Positive Non-Imposition, Neutrality, Anonymity, Maskin's Monotonicity, etc., will be denoted as Λ^{NI^+}, Λ^{Ne}, Λ^{An}, Λ^{MM}, respectively.

Two special classes in the space Π_{III} of all local operators are of a special interest: that one which isolated by the conditions of Non-Imposition, Maskin's Monotonicity, and Neutrality - this class will be called Central Class in Π_{III} and denoted as Λ^C; and the other one which is isolated inside Central Class by Anonymity condition—the latter one will be denoted as Λ^{SC} and called Symmetrically Central Class in Π_{III}.

We will use operations $\cup$ and $\cap$ over rules and will denote it briefly as $F_1 \cup F_2$, $F_1 \cap F_2$. However, it should be kept in mind that it is just shortened notation for

$$F_1(X, \overrightarrow{P}) \cup F_2(X, \overrightarrow{P}),$$
$$F_1(X, \overrightarrow{P}) \cap F_2(X, \overrightarrow{P}),$$

etc.

For the lists in the definitions of local rules we will use also the notation Ω_F often without emphasizing for which set X and alternative x it was constructed. Naturally, such notation will be used only in cases when it does not lead to some ambiguity.

Three lemmas are given next which are widely used below.

Lemma 5.1 *Let Ω be a list for a rule $F \in \Lambda^C$, and $\vec{Z} \in \Omega$. Then the set $\vec{Z}' = (Z_1 \cap B_1, \dots, Z_n \bigcap B_n)$ belongs to Ω, where $B_i \subseteq A, i = 1, \dots, n$, are arbitrary subsets of A.*

Proof of this Lemma immediately follows from the monotonicity of F ■

It is obvious that the statement of Lemma 5.1 can be immediately extended for the case of monotonic but not neutral rules.

Lemma 5.2 *Let F_1 and F_2 be some rules from the Central Class Λ^C. Then the rules $F = F_1 \cup F_2$ and $F = F_1 \cap F_2$ belong to Central Class as well.*

Proof is obvious ■

Lemma 5.3 *Let F_1 and F_2 be some rules from the Central Class Λ^C, and Ω_1 and Ω_2 be their lists, respectively. Then the list $\Omega_{F_1 \cup F_2}$ of rule $F = F_1 \cup F_2$ is just a union of Ω_1 and Ω_2, i.e.*

$$\Omega_{F_1 \cup F_2} = \{\vec{Z} \mid \vec{Z} \in \Omega_1 \text{ or } \vec{Z} \in \Omega_2\}$$

Proof follows from the definition of the list representation of local rules ■

Lemma 5.4 *Let F_1, F_2 be some rules from Λ^C, and Ω_1, Ω_2 be their lists, respectively. Then the list $\Omega_{F_1 \cap F_2}$ of the rule $F_1 \cap F_2$ is equal to*

$$\Omega_{F_1 \cap F_2} = \{\overrightarrow{Z} \mid \overrightarrow{Z} = \overrightarrow{Z}_i \cap \overrightarrow{Z}_j, \overrightarrow{Z}_i \in \Omega_1, \overrightarrow{Z}_j \in \Omega_2,$$
$$\overrightarrow{Z}_i \cap \overrightarrow{Z}_j = (Z_1^i \cap Z_1^j, \dots, Z_n^i \cap Z_n^j)\}$$

Proof. Let $\overrightarrow{Z}_1 \in \Omega_1$, $\overrightarrow{Z}_2 \in \Omega_2$. Then by Lemma 5.1 $\overrightarrow{Z} = \overrightarrow{Z}_1 \cap \overrightarrow{Z}_2$ belongs to both Ω_1 and Ω_2. Now, $x \in F_1(\overrightarrow{P}, X) \cap F_2(\overrightarrow{P}, X)$ iff there exist $\overrightarrow{Z}_1 \in \Omega_1$ and $\overrightarrow{Z}_2 \in \Omega_2$ such that $\forall i$

$$X \cap \mathcal{D}_i(x) = Z_i^1 \in \overrightarrow{Z}_1,$$
$$X \cap \mathcal{D}_i(x) = Z_i^2 \in \overrightarrow{Z}_2,$$

which implies $Z_i^1 = Z_i^2$ for all i, i.e., $\overrightarrow{Z}_1 = \overrightarrow{Z}_2$. This equality holds for such elements $\overrightarrow{Z}$ of Ω_1 and Ω_2 which can be represented as

$$\overrightarrow{Z} = \overrightarrow{Z}_1 \cap \overrightarrow{Z}_1$$

for all $\overrightarrow{Z}_1 \in \Omega_1$ and $\overrightarrow{Z}_2 \in \Omega_2$ ■

As before we can define the Basic list for $\Omega(x, X)$.

Definition 5.5 The set $\vec{Z}$ is called to be a *monotonic extension* of $\vec{Z}'$ if $\forall\ i \in N\ Z_i \supseteq Z_i'$.

Definition 5.6 We will call the subset $\Omega^B(x, X)$ of a list $\Omega(x, X)$ the *Basic list* if for no $\overrightarrow{Z} \in \Omega^B(x, X)$ its monotonic extension belongs to $\Omega^B(x, X)$.

It is immediately seen that for SCCs which satisfy Maskin's Monotonicity, the Basic list is defined from a general list $\Omega(x, X)$ uniquely. In this case Basic list contains ordered n-tuples $\overrightarrow{Z}$ maximal by set inclusion.

Example. Consider the list $\Omega^B(x, X)$ for alternative x for monotonic rule F such that

$$\Omega^B(x, X) = \begin{bmatrix} Z_1 = (\{y\}, \{y, z\}, \{t\}); \\ Z_2 = (\{y\}, \{y, t\}, \{z\}); \\ Z_3 = (\{z\}, \{z, t\}, \{y\}); \\ Z_4 = (\{z\}, \{y, z\}, \{t\}); \\ Z_5 = (\{t\}, \{y, t\}, \{z\}); \\ Z_6 = (\{t\}, \{z, t\}, \{y\}). \end{bmatrix}$$

By Lemma 5.1 any $\overrightarrow{Z'}$ such that $Z_i' = B_i \cap Z_i$ for any $i \in N$ and for any $B_i \subseteq A$ with $(Z_1, ..., Z_n) \in \Omega(x, X)$ also belongs to $\Omega(x, X)$. For example, the n-tuple $(\oslash, \{y, z\}, \{t\})$ which is obtained from $\overrightarrow{Z_1}$ (or from $\overrightarrow{Z_4}$) also belongs to $\Omega(x, X)$. But it can be seen that for no $\overrightarrow{Z}, \overrightarrow{Z'}$ in this $\Omega^B(x, X)$ we have $\forall i$

$$Z_i' \subseteq Z_i \text{ or } Z_i' \supseteq Z_i.$$

Below we illustrate the list representation of local social choice correspondences.

Example. Let $A = \{x, y, z\}$ and $N = \{1, 2, 3\}$. Consider the list for the rule F given in the Table 5-1. For simplicity, the lists for the pairs $(t, \{t\}), t \in A$, in this Table are not shown. In the first column of Table 5-1 the pairs (t, X) are given $(t \in X \in \mathcal{A})$, and in other columns the corresponding lists are shown.

Table 5-1

(x, A)	$(\emptyset, \{y\}, \{y\})$	$(\emptyset, \{z\}, \{z\})$	$(\emptyset, \{y, z\}, \{y, z\})$
(y, A)	$(\emptyset, \{x\}, \{x\})$	$(\emptyset, \{z\}, \{z\})$	$(\emptyset, \{x, z\}, \{x, z\})$
(z, A)	$(\emptyset, \{x\}, \{x\})$	$(\emptyset, \{y\}, \{y\})$	$(\emptyset, \{x, y\}, \{x, y\})$
$(x, \{x, y\})$	$(\emptyset, \{y\}, \{y\})$		
$(x, \{x, z\})$	$(\emptyset, \{z\}, \{z\})$		
$(y, \{x, y\})$	$(\emptyset, \{x\}, \{x\})$		
$(y, \{y, z\})$	$(\emptyset, \{z\}, \{z\})$		
$(z, \{x, z\})$	$(\emptyset, \{x\}, \{x\})$		
$(z, \{y, z\})$	$(\emptyset, \{y\}, \{y\})$		

It is easily seen that the lists $\{\Omega(t, X)\}_{t,X}$ satisfy the Neutrality condition. Moreover, if we exclude the lists $(\emptyset, \{y, z\}, \{y, z\})$, $(\emptyset, \{y, z\}, \{y, z\})$, $(\emptyset, \{y, z\}, \{y, z\})$ from the Table, then still the lists will satisfy condition Ne. If the list given in the Table is considered as the Basic list for the rule F, then there is no need to show in $\Omega(x, A)$ the lists $(\emptyset, \{y\}, \{y\})$ and $(\emptyset, \{z\}, \{z\})$ since the list $(\emptyset, \{y, z\}, \{y, z\})$ is the monotonic extension of these lists. Naturally, the analogous reasons are applied to lists $\Omega(y, A)$ and $\Omega(z, A)$.

5.4 Boolean representation of Social Choice Correspondences

In this Section we study a representation of Social Choice Correspondences in general form using boolean variables and functions.

We introduce a boolean variable

$$l_i(x, y; X, \overrightarrow{P}) = \begin{cases} 1, \text{ if } x, y \in X \text{ and } xP_iy; \\ 0, \text{ else,} \end{cases}$$

i.e., this variable is defined for a pair (x, y) and is equal to 1 if x dominates y in the preference relation P_i of i-th agent.

Next we define a function $g_i(y, Z_i, X, \overrightarrow{P})$ in the following form

$$g_i(y, Z_i, X, \overrightarrow{P}) = \bigwedge_{x \in Z_i \cap X} l_i(x, y; X, \overrightarrow{P}),$$

i.e., it is a conjunction of values of all variables $\{l_i(x, y; X, \overrightarrow{P})\}_{x \in Z_i \cap X}$. In words, $g_i(y, z, X, \overrightarrow{P})$ is equal to 1 if $D_i(y) \cap X = Z_i$. Then we can define a function $h(y, \overrightarrow{Z}; X, \overrightarrow{P})$ such that

$$h(y, \overrightarrow{Z}; X, \overrightarrow{P}) = \bigwedge_{i \in N} g_i(y, Z_i, X, \overrightarrow{P}),$$

i.e., $h(y, \overrightarrow{Z}; X, \overrightarrow{P})$ is equal to 1 if for each i upper contour set for y is equal to Z_i, i.e., $\forall i\ D_i(y) \cap X = Z$.
Now let us define a boolean function $\widetilde{F}(y, X, \overrightarrow{P})$ in the following way

$$\widetilde{F}(y, X, \overrightarrow{P}) = \bigvee_{\overrightarrow{Z} \in \Omega(y,X)} h(y, \overrightarrow{Z}; X, \overrightarrow{P}),$$

i.e., $\widetilde{F}(y, X, \overrightarrow{P})$ is equal to 1 if there exists at least one $\overrightarrow{Z}$ in $\Omega(y, X)$ such that in the profile $\overrightarrow{P}$ upper contour sets for alternative y coincide for every agent with the corresponding set Z_i.
Finally, we define *boolean function* $\widetilde{F}(X, \overrightarrow{P})$ as

$$\widetilde{F}(X, \overrightarrow{P}) = \bigvee_{y \in X} \widetilde{F}(y, X, \overrightarrow{P}). \tag{5.2}$$

If we re-write the rule $\widetilde{F}(X, \overrightarrow{P})$ using initial boolean variable $l_i(x, y; X, \overrightarrow{P})$, we obtain the following representation:

$$\widetilde{F}(X, \overrightarrow{P}) = \bigvee_{y \in X} \bigvee_{\overrightarrow{Z^y} \in \Omega(y,X)} \bigwedge_{i \in N} \bigwedge_{\substack{x \in Z_i^y \cap X, \\ Z_i^y \in Z^y}} l_i(x, y; X, \overrightarrow{P}), \tag{5.3}$$

Theorem 5.3 *Any rule $F \in \Pi_{III}$ admits a representation in the form (5.3).*

Proof. Consider $X = \{x_1, ..., x_s\}$ and without loss of generality assume that $F(X, \overrightarrow{P}) = \{x_1, ..., x_r\}$ for some $\overrightarrow{P}$. Since $x_k \in F(X, \overrightarrow{P})$ for some $k = 1, ..., r$, then $\exists \overrightarrow{Z^{x_k}} \in \Omega(x_k, X)$ such that $\forall i$

$$V(x_k, X, P_i) = Z_i^{x_k}$$

Thus, $\bigwedge_{i \in N} \bigwedge_{\substack{x \in Z_i^{x_k} \cap X, \\ Z_i^{x_k} \in \overrightarrow{Z} \in \Omega(x_k, X)}} l_i(x, y; X, \overrightarrow{P}) = 1$, and $x_k \in \widetilde{F}(X, \overrightarrow{P})$. Assume now that some $x_t \notin F(X, \overrightarrow{P})$. Then $\exists i$ such that

$$V(x_t, X, P_i) \neq Z_i.$$

Then, $\bigwedge_{\substack{x \in Z_i^{x_k} \cap X, \\ Z_i^{x_k} \in \overrightarrow{Z} \in \Omega(x_k, X)}} l_i(x, y; X, \overrightarrow{P}) = 0$, and $x_t \notin \widetilde{F}(x, \overrightarrow{P})$ ■

For the case of monotonic social choice correspondencces, i.e., for rules $F \in \Lambda^{MM}$ we re-define the function

$$g_i(y, z, X, \overrightarrow{P}) = \begin{cases} 1, \text{ if } l_i(x, y; X, \overrightarrow{P}) = 1 \text{ for any } x \in Z \subseteq Z_i; \\ 0, \text{ else.} \end{cases}$$

Then it is obvious that the statement of Theorem 5.3 holds for rules $F \in \Lambda^{MM}$ and $\widetilde{F}(x, \overrightarrow{P})$ re-defined in the above way.

Example. Consider the rule $f(P_1 * P_2, 0)$, i.e., we choose undominated alternatives on the weak order $P = P_1 * P_2$ obtained by lexicographic composition[36] of weak orders of the first and second agents. This rule turns out to be non-local. Indeed, consider the profile xI_1y , yP_2x . For this profile , obviosly, $f(P_1 * P_2, 0) = \{y\}$. For the profile $xP_1'y$, $yP_2'x$, we have $f(P_1 * P_2, 0) = \{x\}$. However, $D_1(x) = D_1'(x) = \emptyset$, $D_2(x) = D_2'(x) = \{y\}$. In other words, upper contour sets for x for both agents in both profiles coincide in contrast with the social choices from those profiles.

On the other hand, if strougly local rules are considered, then

$$\begin{gathered} D_1(x) = D_1'(x) = \emptyset, \\ D_2(x) = D_2'(x) = \{y\} \\ L_1(x) = \emptyset \neq L_1'(x) = \{y\} \\ L_2(x) = L_2'(x) = \emptyset. \end{gathered}$$

It can be proved that the rules using lexicographic composition are strougly local rather than local.

5.5 Rules from Central Class, I

Representation of the rules from Central Class Λ^C is established below. Because the variety of the rules from this class is very large, we first introduce some particular cases of these rules, and then give their generalizations.

Consider now the following rule:

$$\pi(N,0) : \forall x, X \; x \in C(X) \Leftrightarrow \mid \bigcap_{i \in N} (X \bigcap \mathcal{D}_i(x)) \mid = 0.$$

In words, x belongs to the social choice $C(X)$ if the number of alternatives which are more preferable than x in each P_i is null, or, otherwise speaking, there is no alternative y which is more preferable than x for each agent. One can see that this rule is exactly the Pareto rule F_{Par} introduced above, i.e., $F_{Par} = \pi(N, 0)$.

The following generalization of this rule can be defined not for all set N, but for some coalition $I \subset N$ and will be denoted by $\pi(I, 0)$, i.e.,

$$\pi(I,0) : \forall x, X \; x \in C(X) \Leftrightarrow \mid \bigcap_{i \in I} (X \bigcap \mathcal{D}_i(x)) \mid = 0.$$

This rule chooses Pareto-optimal alternative(s) for some coalition I and can be called as *partial Pareto rule*.

Generalizing these definitions, let us introduce the following rule:

[36] Lexicographic composition of two weak orders P_1 and P_2 is defined as $P = P_1 * P_2 = P_1 \cup (I_{P_1} \cap P_2)$, where I_P is an indifference relation for a given P, $I_P = A^2 \setminus (P \cup P^{-1})$ - see Section 3.11.

$$\pi(I,q^I) : x \in C(X) \Leftrightarrow \mid \bigcap_{i\in I}(X \bigcap \mathcal{D}_i(X)) \mid \leq q^I,$$

i.e., the alternative x is chosen even if there are at least q^I alternatives which are more preferable than x for every member of coalition I.

Example. Consider the profile $\overrightarrow{P}$

$$\begin{array}{ll} P_1: & a \succ b \succ y \succ x; \\ P_2: & a \succ b \succ x \succ y; \\ P_3: & a \succ y \succ b \succ x. \end{array}$$

Then, $\bigcap_{i\in\{2,3\}}(A \bigcap \mathcal{D}_i(y)) = \{a,b,x\} \cap \{a\} = \{a\}$. For the alternative x one can obtain

$$\bigcap_{i\in\{2,3\}}(A \bigcap \mathcal{D}_i(x)) = \{a,b\} \cap \{a,b,y\} = \{a,b\}.$$

If the rule $\pi(\{2,3\},1)$ is used, then from the set A the alternative y is chosen together with alternatives a and b, while x will not be chosen.

Let us consider the generalization of this rule constructed by the same 'scenario' as in the cases of strongly local social decision rules and functional aggregation rules. Namely, we construct the rule which will be called *coalitional q-federation rule* as follows: for a given totality of sets of coalitions we consider q-Pareto optimal elements unanimously chosen in each set of coalitions, and unify these elements over the sets from the given totality of sets. It is important to note that the parameter q^I for each coalition in each set can be different. Stated it formally, we obtain

$$F = \bigcup_{t=1}^{s} \bigcap_{I\in\mathcal{I}_t} \pi(I,q^I), \tag{5.4}$$

The class of these rules will be denoted as $\Lambda^{q\cup\cap}$.

Consider now some other rule

$$\pi_{\cup}(N,0) : x \in C(X) \Leftrightarrow \mid \bigcup_{i\in N}(X \bigcap \mathcal{D}_i(x)) \mid = 0,$$

i.e., x is chosen if there is no y which is preferred to x at least by one agent from N.

Generalization of this rule is immediate

$$\pi_{\cup}(I,p) = \{y \in X \mid card(\cup_{i\in I}(\mathcal{D}_i(y) \cap X) \leq p^I\},$$

i.e., the rule $\pi_{\cup}$ defines the social choice as those alternatives y which have no more than p alternatives better than y in all linear orders from the coalition I. Thus, y may be top element in all but one preference from I, and in that one preference relation it may have more than p better alternatives. Then, y will not be chosen.

However, the rule $\pi_{\cup}$ can be represented as coalitional $q-$federation rule. We will show it via illustrative example.
Let $N = \{1,2,3\}$. Consider the rule $\pi_{\cup}(N,2)$. Construct the rule

$$\pi(\{1\},0) \cap \pi(\{2\},0) \cap \pi(\{3\},2).$$

It is obvious that it chooses those alternatives y which are top elements in the preferences of the first and second agents, and those y's have no more than 2 preferred alternatives in the preference relation of the third agent. In other words, for these alternatives y the following holds

$$card(\bigcup_{i\in N}(\mathcal{D}_i(y) \cap X)) \leq 2.$$

Analogously, the following rule possesses the same property

$$\pi(\{1\},1) \cap \pi(\{2\},1) \cap \pi(\{3\},0).$$

This rule chooses alternatives which are first or second best in the preferences of first and second agents, and which at the same time are top elements in the linear order of the third agent.

Considering all such kind of rules and unifying the corresponding choices, it is obvious that one can represent the rule $\pi_{\cup}(N,2)$ as follows

$$\begin{aligned}
\pi_{\cup}(N,2) \quad = \quad & (\pi(\{1\},0) \cap \pi(\{2\},0) \cap \pi(\{3\},2)) \cup \\
& \cup(\pi(\{1\},2) \cap \pi(\{2\},0) \cap \pi(\{3\},0)) \cup \\
& \cup(\pi(\{1\},0) \cap \pi(\{2\},2) \cap \pi(\{3\},0)) \cup \\
& \cup(\pi(\{1\},1) \cap \pi(\{2\},1) \cap \pi(\{3\},0)) \cup \\
& \cup(\pi(\{1\},1) \cap \pi(\{2\},0) \cap \pi(\{3\},1)) \cup \\
& \cup(\pi(\{1\},0) \cap \pi(\{2\},1) \cap \pi(\{3\},1)).
\end{aligned}$$

Using this very argument one can find general representation of these rules as coalitional q-federation rules. Let us consider the set of all n-tuples of integers $(q^1, ..., q^n)$ which satisfy the following properties:

$$\begin{aligned}
1)\, \forall i \quad & \in \quad I \quad 0 \leq q^i \leq p^I; \\
2)\, \forall i \quad & \in \quad N \setminus I \quad q^i = |A|; \\
3)\, \sum_{i\in I} q^i \quad & = \quad p^I.
\end{aligned}$$

Let us denote this set as $\mathcal{K}$. Then, the following statement is obviously holds

Lemma 5.5

$$\pi_{\cup}(I,p^I) = \bigcup_{\mathcal{K}} \bigcap_{i\in I} \pi(\{i\},q^i).$$

Let us mention finally that if in the definition of rule $\pi(I,q^I)$ the coalition I contains only one element i, then this rule will be denoted as $\pi(\{i\},q^i)$, and according to this rule the alternative x is chosen if there are no more than q alternatives which are better than x in P_i.

Consider now the rules introduced above with extremal values of parameter q. The following equalities obviously take place: $\forall i$ and $\forall I$
- if $q \geq m-1$ then

$$\pi(\{i\},q) = \pi(I,q) = \mathbf{1};$$

- if $q < 0$ then

$$\pi(\{i\},q) = \pi(I,q) = \mathbf{0}.$$

All the rules introduced above are local and satisfy additionally the conditions of Non-Imposition (if $0 < q < m-1$), Maskin's Monotonicity and Neutrality which can be checked directly. So, these rules belong to the Central Class Λ^C. Varying coalition I and number q in the definition of these rules, one can obtain the class of rules, depending on I and q; i.e., I, q are parameters in the definition of these classes.

The importance of the rules introduced above is explicated in the following Theorem.

Theorem 5.4 *The rule F belongs to Central Class Λ^C iff there exists an integer $s \geq 0$, a set of coalitions $\mathcal{I}_t, t=1,...,s$, the integers $\{q^I\}$,such that for any X $\forall I$ $0 < q^I < |X|-1$ and for any $\overrightarrow{P}$*

$$F = \bigcup_{t=1}^{s} \bigcap_{I\in\mathcal{I}_t} \pi(I,q^I), \tag{5.5}$$

i.e., any rule from Λ^C can be represented as coalitional q-federation rule, and any coalitional q-federation rule is the rule from Central Class.

Proof. Let $F \in \Lambda^C$, and let Ω_F be its list. For any $\overrightarrow{Z} \in \Omega_F(x,X)$, $\overrightarrow{Z} = (Z_1,...,Z_n)$, let us construct the following rules

$$\varphi(\{i\},q^i) \equiv \pi(\{i\},|Z_i|\}, \tag{5.6}$$

$$\varphi(I,q^I) \equiv \pi(I, card(\bigcap_{i\in I} Z_i)\}, \tag{5.7}$$

$$\psi(I, q^I) \equiv \pi_\cup(I, card(\bigcup_{i \in I} Z_i)\}. \tag{5.8}$$

In other words, for a given ordered n-tuple $\overrightarrow{Z}$ we construct $2^n - 1$ rules for any combinations of sets $Z_1, ..., Z_n$. Next we prove several lemmas about these rules.

Lemma 5.6 *Let $\Omega_{\varphi(\{i\},q^i)}(x, X)$ be the list of a rule $\varphi(\{i\}, q^i)$ constructed according to (5.6) by $Z_i \in \overrightarrow{Z} \in \Omega_F(x, X)$. Then*
1) for any $\overrightarrow{Z''} \in \Omega_{\varphi(\{i\},q^i)}(x, X)$ and for any i $Z''_i \supseteq Z_i$ holds;
2) there exists $\overrightarrow{Z'} \in \Omega_{\varphi(\{i\},q^i)}(x, X)$ such that $Z'_i = Z_i$, and $\forall j \neq i$ $Z'_j = X \setminus \{x\}$.

Proof. For the rule $\varphi(\{i\}, q^i)$ it is obvious that its Basic list (for a given X and x) contains the following $\overrightarrow{Z''}$:

$$\overrightarrow{Z''} = (X \setminus \{x\}, ..., Z''_i, X \setminus \{x\}, ..., X \setminus \{x\}),$$

where Z''_i has the same cardinality as Z_i.
Since the rule $\varphi(\{i\}, q^i)$ is neutral, there exists $\overrightarrow{Z'}$ in $\Omega_{\varphi(\{i\},q^i)}(x, X)$ such that $Z'_i = Z_i$. Lemma is proved.

Lemma 5.7 *Let $\Omega_{\varphi(I,q^I)}(x, X)$ be the list of a rule $\varphi(I, q^I)$ constructed according to (5.7) by $\{Z_i\}_{i \in I}$, $Z_i \in \overrightarrow{Z} \in \Omega_F(x, X)$. Then*
1) for any $\overrightarrow{Z''} \in \Omega_{\varphi(I,q^I)}(x, X)$ and for any i $Z''_i \supseteq Z_i$ holds;
2) there exists $\overrightarrow{Z'} \in \Omega_{\varphi(I,q^I)}(x, X)$ such that $\forall i \in I$ $Z'_i = Z_i$, and $\forall j \in N \setminus I$ $Z'_j = X \setminus \{x\}$.

Proof. By definition of the rule $\varphi(I, q^I)$ the Basic list for it contains all sets $\widetilde{Z}_i$ such that $card(\bigcap_{i \in I} \widetilde{Z}_i) = q^I$, and $\forall j \in N \setminus I$ $\widetilde{Z}_i = X \setminus \{x\}$. Since the rule $\varphi(I, q^I)$ is neutral, and the intersection of sets $Z_i, i \in I$, according to which it is constructed contains exactly q^I elements, the list $\Omega_{\varphi(I,q^I)}(x, X)$ contains the ordered n-tuple $\overrightarrow{Z'}$ such that $\forall i \in I$ $Z'_i = Z_i$, where $Z_i \in \overrightarrow{Z} \in \Omega_F(x, X)$, and $\forall j \in N \setminus I$ $Z'_j = X \setminus \{x\}$. Lemma is proved.
To illustrate the statement of the Lemma consider the following example.
Example. Let $N = \{1, 2, 3\}$, $F \in \Lambda^C$ and $\overrightarrow{Z} \in \Omega(x; X)$ such that

$$\overrightarrow{Z} = (\{a\}, \{a, b\}, \{a\}).$$

Then for the coalition $I = \{1, 2\}$ we construct the rule $\varphi(\{1, 2\}, 1)$ since $(Z_1 = \{a\}) \cap (Z_2 = \{a, b\}) = \{a\}$; hence $q^{\{1,2\}} = 1$
Then the basic list $\Omega_{\varphi(\{1,2\},1)}(x, X)$ contains, in particular, the following ordered n-tuples

$$\begin{aligned}\overrightarrow{Z_1} &= (\{a\}, X \setminus \{x\}, X \setminus \{x\}), \\ \overrightarrow{Z_2} &= (\{b\}, X \setminus \{x\}, X \setminus \{x\}), \\ \overrightarrow{Z_3} &= (\{b\}, \{a,b\}, X \setminus \{x\}), \text{ etc.,}\end{aligned}$$

since all of these sets obey the condition

$$|Z_1^i \cap Z_2^i| = 1.$$

But due to the Neutrality of F, the list $\Omega_{\varphi(I,q^I)}(x, X)$ will contain n-tuple

$$\overrightarrow{Z} = (\{a\}, \{a,b\}, X \setminus \{x\}),$$

and due to Maskin's Monotonicity MM the n-tuple

$$\overrightarrow{Z'} = (\{a\}, \{a,b\}, \{a\})$$

as well.

Lemma 5.8 *Let $\Omega_{\psi(I,p^I)}(x, X)$ be the list of a rule $\psi(I, p^I)$ constructed according to (5.8) by $\{Z_i\}_{i \in I}$, $Z_i \in \overrightarrow{Z} \in \Omega_F(x, X)$. Then there exists $\overrightarrow{Z'} \in \Omega_{\psi(I,p^I)}(x, X)$ such that $\forall i \in I$ $Z_i' = Z_i$, and $\forall j \in N \setminus I$ $Z_j' = X \setminus \{x\}$.*

Proof is analogous to that of Lemma 5.7.
Consider now the following rule

$$\begin{aligned}\widetilde{F} = & \bigcup_{\overrightarrow{Z} \in \Omega} [(\bigcap_{i \in N} \varphi(\{i\}, q^i)) \bigcap (\bigcap_{I \in 2^N \setminus \{\emptyset\}} \varphi(I, q^I)) \bigcap \\ & \bigcap (\bigcap_{I \in 2^N \setminus \{\emptyset\}} \psi(I, p^I))].\end{aligned}$$

We prove now that $F = \tilde{F}$. Let $\vec{Z} \in \Omega_F$. We show that $\vec{Z} \in \Omega_{\tilde{F}}$, where $\Omega_{\tilde{F}}$ is the list for the rule $\tilde{F}$. Indeed, according to Lemmas 5.6-5.8 the list $\Omega_{\tilde{F}}$ contains $\vec{Z}'$ such that $\forall i$ $Z_i' \supseteq Z_i$, and $\exists i_0$ such that $Z_{i_0}' = Z_{i_0}$, where $Z_i \in \vec{Z} \in \Omega_F$.
Hence, by Lemma 5.4, $\Omega_{\tilde{F}}$ contains $\vec{Z}''$ such that $\forall i$ $Z_i'' = Z_i$, i.e., $\vec{Z} \in \Omega_{\tilde{F}}$. This immediately implies that if $x \in C(X)$, then $x \in \tilde{C}(X)$, where $\tilde{C}(\cdot) = \tilde{F}(\vec{P}, \cdot)$.
Let now $x \notin C(X)$. Assume that $x \in \tilde{C}(X)$. This means that the ordered n-tuple

$$\zeta = (X \cap \mathcal{D}_1(x), ..., X \cap \mathcal{D}_2(x)) \equiv (\zeta_1, ..., \zeta_n)$$

belongs to $\Omega_{\tilde{F}}$ and does not belong to Ω_F. Since $\zeta \in \Omega_{\tilde{F}}$, it follows from the construction of $\tilde{F}$ that there exist $\vec{Z} \in \Omega_{\tilde{F}}$ such that $\vec{Z} = (Z_1, ..., Z_n)$, and $|Z_1| =$

$|X \cap \mathcal{D}_1(x)|, ..., |Z_n| = |X \cap \mathcal{D}_n(x)|$. By Neutrality of F all n-tuples $\vec{Z}'$ which are obtained from $\vec{Z}$ by permutation of the set A belong to Ω_F.

Let us denote this class as $\widehat{Z}$, i.e.,

$$\widehat{Z} = \left\{ \vec{Z}' \mid \vec{Z} = \sigma(\vec{Z}) \text{ for all permutations } \sigma : A \to A \right\}$$

Then $\zeta \notin \Omega_F$ iff $\zeta \notin \widehat{Z}$. Consider now some element $\vec{Z}' = (\vec{Z}_1', ..., \vec{Z}_n') \in \widehat{Z}$ such that $\forall i = 1, ..., k$ $Z_i' = \zeta_i$.

Such element $\vec{Z}'$ exists since there exists $\vec{Z} = (Z_1, ..., Z_n)$ with $|Z_i| = |\zeta_i|$ for all $i = 1, \dots, n$ and due to Neutaralty of F.

Now, if $k = n$ then the statement of the Theorem holds. So, consider the case $1 < k < n$, i.e., $\forall i = 1, ..., k$ $Z_i' = \zeta_i$ and $Z_{k+1} \neq \zeta_{k+1.}$ It is obvious that there is no permutation $\sigma : A \to A$ such that $\sigma(Z_{k+1}') = \zeta_{k+1}$ for which

$$\sigma(Z_i') = \zeta_i, i = 1, ..., k,$$

holds as well. Indeed, if such permutation exists, then there is a $\vec{Z}''$ in $\widehat{Z}$ such that $\forall i = 1, ..., k+1$ $Z_i'' = \zeta_i$, and we can compare now $\vec{Z}''$ with ζ.

Let us study now the properties of the set ζ_{k+1}. The following relations should be studied:

1) $\zeta_{k+1} \subset Z_{k+1}'$;
2) $\zeta_{k+1} \supset Z_{k+1}'$;
3) $\zeta_{k+1} \cap Z_{k+1}' = \emptyset$;
4) $\zeta_{k+1} \cap Z_{k+1}' \neq \emptyset, \zeta_{k+1} \not\subset Z_{k+1}', \zeta_{k+1} \not\supset Z_{k+1}'$.

Case 1) is impossible due to the monotonicity of F - in this case as $\vec{Z}'$ we can consider

$$\vec{Z}' = (Z_1, ..., Z_k, \zeta_{k+1}, Z_{k+2}, ..., Z_n).$$

Case 2) It contradicts to the fact that $\vec{Z}' \in \widehat{Z}$ and $\forall i$ $|Z_i'| = |\zeta_i|$.

Case 3) It is divided to two cases:
3a) $\exists\, a \in \zeta_{k+1}, a \notin \zeta_i$ for any $i = 1, ..., k$;
3b) $\zeta_{k+1} \subseteq \bigcup_{i=1}^{k} \cup \zeta_i$.

For the case 3a) we obtain $\bigcup\limits_{i \in I} \zeta_i \supset \bigcup\limits_{i \in I} Z_i'$ for $I = \{1, ..., k\}$, i.e.,

$$\left| \bigcup_{i \in I} \zeta_i \right| > \left| \bigcup_{i \in I} Z_i' \right|.$$

It contradicts the construction of the component $\psi(I, q^I)$ in $\tilde{F}$.

Case 3b) . Since by assumption $Z_i = \zeta_i$ for all $i \leqslant k$, $\zeta_{k+1} \subseteq \bigcup\limits_{i=1}^{k} \zeta_i$, and $\zeta_{k+1} \cap Z_{k+1}' = \emptyset$, then there exists $b \in Z_{k+1}'$ such that $b \notin Z_i$ for all $i = 1, ..., k$.

Hence, $\bigcap_{i\in I} Z_i = \emptyset$ for $I = \{1, ..., k+1\}$, i.e.,

$$\left|\bigcap_{i\in I} Z_i\right| = 0.$$

On the other hand, $\bigcap_{i\in I} \zeta_i \neq \emptyset$ for the same I, i.e.,

$$\left|\bigcap_{i\in I} Z_i\right| > 0.$$

This contradicts the construction of the component $\pi(I, q^I)$ in $\tilde{F}$.

Case 4) can obviously be reduced to the case 3).

Thus, we have proved that $F = \tilde{F}$.

Let us show now how the rule $\tilde{F}$ can be reduced to the form (5.5). For this reason we use Lemma 5.5 in which we showed that the rule $\psi(I, p^I) = \bigcup_{\mathcal{K}} \bigcap_{i\in I} \pi(\{i\}, q^i)$, where $\mathcal{K}$ is the set of all n-tuples of integers $(p_1, ..., p_{|I|})$ such that $0 \leqslant p_i \leqslant p^I$, and

$$\sum_{i=1}^{|I|} p_i = p^I.$$

Thus, one can represent $\tilde{F}$ as

$$F = \bigcup_{\vec{Z}\in\Omega} \bigcap_{I\in 2^N\setminus\{\emptyset\}} \pi(I, q^I).$$

■

Stated differently, the above Theorem establishes that $\Lambda^C = \Lambda^{q\cup\cap}$.

At the end of this Section we study the following problem: what is the form of coalitional q-federation rule which satisfies No Veto Power (NVP) condition? NVP states that the unanimous decision of any $n-1$ agents concerning their best alternaive (top element in their linear orders) should be in the social decision. Consider the following rule

$$\Theta = \bigcup_{I,\, card(I)=n-1} \bigcap_{i\in I} \pi(\{i\}, 0).$$

This rule constructs social decision exactly as unanimous decision of any of $n-1$ agents about their top elements. Then, obviously, the coalitional q-federation rule which satisfies NVP can be written down as

$$F = \Theta \cup \Theta',$$

where Θ' is any rule from Central Class.

For instance, it can be the rule

$$\Theta' = \pi(\{i_0\}, q^{i_0}).$$

In this case, social decision consists of q^{i_0} top elements of agent i_0, and common top element of any of $n-1$ agents if such element does exist.

5.6 Rules from Central Class, II

In this Section we shall study different subclasses of the class $\Lambda^{q\cup\cap}$, i.e., we shall study special cases of the coalitional $q-$federation rule

$$F = \bigcup_{t=1}^{s} \bigcap_{I \in \mathcal{I}_t} \pi(I, q^I). \tag{5.9}$$

We introduce three special cases of the rule (5.9). The first one arises when for any I $q^I = 0$, i.e.,

$$F = \bigcup_{t=1}^{s} \bigcap_{I \in \mathcal{I}_t} \pi(I, 0). \tag{5.10}$$

The second one deals with the case when in (5.9) each coalition I in any family $\mathcal{I}_t$ contains only single index, i.e., I is a single agent coalition. Then, re-writing each $\mathcal{I}_t = (\{i_1\}, ..., \{i_l\})$ in the form $I_t = \{i_1, ..., i_l\}$ we obtain

$$F = \bigcup_{t=1}^{s} \bigcap_{i \in I_t} \pi(\{i\}, q^i). \tag{5.11}$$

Finally, let us consider the case when in (5.11) each $q^i = 0$. Then

$$F = \bigcup_{t=1}^{s} \bigcap_{i \in I_t} \pi(\{i\}, 0). \tag{5.12}$$

The classes of rules (5.10), (5.11), and (5.12) will be denoted as $\Lambda^{\cup\cap}$, $\Lambda^{q\cup\cap}_{(i)}$, and $\Lambda^{\cup\cap}_{(i)}$, respectively.
The rule (5.10) will be called as *'coalitional federation rule'*, the rule (5.11) will be called as *'q^i-federation'*, and the rule (5.12) will be called as *'federation rule'*.

Note that the rule Θ considered above is just federation rule with parameters $s = n$ and $|I_t| = n - 1$.

Remark. The federation rule is an exact couterpart of the federation rule in the space of functional aggregation rules Π_{II}. Indeed, define individual choice function $C_i(\cdot)$ as rationalizable via linear order P_i, i.e.,

$$C_i(X) = \{y \in X \mid \overline{\exists} x \in X \text{ such that } xP_iy\}.$$

Thus, $C_i(X)$ chooses maximal elements with respect to the linear order P_i. Such choice function as we know from Chapter 2 satisfies Arrow's Choice Axiom **ACA**. Then the rule (5.12) can be re-written as follows[37]: $\forall X$

$$C(X) = \bigcup_{t=1}^{s} \bigcap_{i \in I_t} C_i(X). \tag{5.13}$$

Moreover, one can re-write even the rule (5.11) in this form (5.13) if define $C_i(\cdot)$ in an appropriate way.

Consider the rule which is written as follows

$$F = \bigcap_{l=1}^{r} \bigcup_{J \in \mathcal{J}_l} \pi(J, q^J). \tag{5.14}$$

Note that the rule (5.14) is defined by r families of coalitions $\mathcal{J}_1, ..., \mathcal{J}_r$. In each coalition J from the family $\mathcal{J}_l$ we choose q^J- Pareto optimal alternatives, and unify these choices over coalitions from the family $\mathcal{J}_l$. Then we consider the intersection of choices which correspond to each family $\mathcal{J}_l$, i.e., our final decision contains alternatives which 'are accepted' by at least one coalition in each family of coalitions $\mathcal{J}_l$.

We will call this rule as *'$q-$representation' rule*. The class of these rules will be denoted as $\Lambda^{q\cap\cup}$.

Analogously to the coalitional $q-$federation rule one can introduce three special cases of the rule (5.14):

- *coalitional representation rule*

$$F = \bigcap_{l=1}^{r} \bigcup_{J \in \mathcal{J}_l} \pi(J, 0);$$

- *q^j-representation rule*

$$F = \bigcap_{l=1}^{r} \bigcup_{j \in J_l} \pi(\{j\}, q^j);$$

- *representation rule*

[37] It is important to note that in the case of functional aggregation rules we did not restrict individual choice functions to be somehow rationalizable.

$$F = \bigcap_{l=1}^{r} \bigcup_{j \in J_l} \pi(\{j\},0).$$

The classes of these rules will be denoted as $\Lambda^{q\cap\cup}$, $\Lambda^{q\cap\cup}_{(j)}$, and $\Lambda^{\cap\cup}_{(j)}$, respectively.

Let us study now special cases of the rules (5.9) and (5.14).

We will call the rule

$$F = \bigcap_{I \in \mathcal{I}} \pi(I, q^I) \tag{5.15}$$

a (generalized) *coalitional $q-$olygarchy rule*. It is obtained from (5.9) when $s = 1$, i.e., when there exists only one family of coalitions. Chosen alternatives are those which are q^I-Pareto optimal in each coalition $I \in \mathcal{I}$. If $q^I = 0$ for any coalition I, then the coalitional (0−) olygarchy rule chooses alternatives which are Pareto optimal for each coalition I. In this case we will call the rule as *coalitional olygarchy*. The class of coalitional $q-$olygarchy rules will be denoted as $\Lambda^{q\cap}$, and the class of coalitional olygarchy rules will be denoted as $\Lambda^{\cap}$.

Let each coalition in (5.15) satisfies condition $|I| = 1$. Then (5.15) can be re-written as follows

$$F = \bigcap_{i \in I} \pi(\{i\}, q^i). \tag{5.16}$$

Then it is natural to call the rule (5.16) as *'$q-$olygarchy'* rule. Indeed, according to this rule, if individual opinions are represented as linear orders every agent in I chooses q^i elements, and the social decision is defined as common opinion of those agents. Let us note that if it is restricted so that $q^i = 0$ for every agent i, then the *olygarchy rule* is defined as intersection of top elements of all agents in I.

The class of $q-$olygarchy rules will be denoted as $\Lambda^{q\cap}_{(i)}$, and the class of olygarchy rules will be denoted as $\Lambda^{\cap}_{(i)}$.

Consider now a special case of coalitional $q-$olygarchy rule when the family $\mathcal{I}$ contains only one coalition I, i.e.,

$$F = \pi(I, q^I) \tag{5.17}$$

Again, three more cases arise: a) when $q^I = 0$; b) $|I| = 1$; and c) $|I| = 1$ and $q^I = 0$. In case a)

$$F = \pi(I, 0), \tag{5.18}$$

i.e., the rule chooses alternatives which are Pareto optimal for coalition I.

In case b) we obtain

$$F = \pi(\{i\}, q^i), \tag{5.19}$$

i.e., it chooses those alternatives which have not more than q^i 'better' elements in the weak order P_i of agent i.

Finally, in case c) we have

$$F = \pi(\{i\}, 0), \tag{5.20}$$

since it chooses maximal elements of i-th preference (weak order) P_i irrespectively of opinions of other agents.
Last two rules can be called '*q–dictator*' and '*dictator*'. We will call the rule (5.17) as *coalitional q–Pareto rule*, and the rule (5.18) as *coalitional Pareto* one.

The class of rules (5.17) will be denoted as Λ^{qP}, the class of rules (5.18) will be denoted as Λ^P, finally, the class of q–dictatorial rules will be denoted as $\Lambda^{qd}_{(i)}$, and the class of dictatorial rules will be denoted as $\Lambda^d_{(i)}$.

Consider now special cases of the q–representation rule. First, we study this rule for the case when $r = 1$, i.e., the case when only one family of coalitions $\mathcal{J}$ does exist. Then the rule (5.14) can be re-written as

$$F = \bigcup_{J \in \mathcal{J}} \pi(J, q^J). \tag{5.21}$$

This rule chooses q^J–Pareto optimal alternatives for at least one coalition J. We can call it by analogy with social decision functions and functional aggregation rules as (generalized) *coalitional q–syndicate*. In case, when $q^J = 0$ for all J, the rule (5.21) chooses Pareto optimal alternatives in at least one coalition J. We wll call this rule as *coalitional syndicate*.
The class of the rules (5.21) will be denoted as $\Lambda^{q\cup}$, and the class of coalitional syndicate rules will be denoted as $\Lambda^{\cup}$

It follows from the definition of coalitional q–syndicate rule that it is coincide with the special case of coalitional q–federation rule when in the definition of the latter each family $\mathcal{I}_t$ contains only one coalition I.
The rule (5.21) in case when any coalition is a single agent coalition is transformed in the following way:

$$F = \bigcup_{j \in J} \pi(\{j\}, q^j).$$

According to this rule we just unify all q^j–Pareto optimal elements of preferences of agents which belong to the set J. This rule can be called as *q–syndicate rule*. The q–syndicate rule for the case when all $q^j = 0$ will be called '*syndicate rule*'. The class of $q-$syndicate rules will be denoted as $\Lambda^{q\cup}_{(j)}$, and the class of syndicate rules will be denoted as $\Lambda^{\cup}_{(j)}$.

Consider now the $q-$representation rule with the restriction that each family $\mathcal{J}_l$ contains only one coalition J. Then it is obvious that this special case of rule (5.14) coincides with the coalitional $q-$olygarchy.

Let us study the special cases of $q-$olygarchy and $q-$syndicate rules. For the $q-$olygarchy rule we constraint the family $\mathcal{I}$ in its definition in such a way that $\mathcal{I}$ contains all single element coalitions, i.e.,

$$\mathcal{I} = \{\{1\}, ..., \{n\}\}.$$

We can write then the rule as simple as

$$F = \bigcap_{i \in N} \pi(\{i\}, q^i).$$

Obviously, the rule can be called as q^i-*Unanimity rule*. The class of these rules arising due to different q^i, will be denoted as $q^i\mathcal{U}$.

Consider now the $q-$syndicate rule with the following restriction - the family $\mathcal{J}$ in its definition contains all single element coalitions. Then the corresponding rule can be re-written as

$$F = \bigcup_{j \in N} \pi(\{j\}, q^j).$$

This rule can be called as q^i-*One vote rule*. The class of these rules will be denoted as $q^j\mathcal{V}$.

Obviously, there are $m^n - 1$ q^i-Unanimity rules. Ideed, for each preference i the value of q^i maight be $0, 1, ..., m-1$, i.e., there are m possible values of q^i for any agent i. Hence, the total number of combinations for all agents is equal to m^n. The one case $\forall i\ q^i = m-1$ has to be excluded since in this case $F(X, \overrightarrow{P}) = X$ for any X and for any $\overrightarrow{P}$, i.e., the condition of Non-Imposition is violated.

5.7 Rules from Symmetrically Central Class

We will study in this Section the coalitional $q-$federation and $q-$representation rules and their special forms introduced above which satisfy the additional constraint of Anonimity (An). As usual in this Chapter, we begin with simple cases of rules and then generalize them.

A coalitional $q-$syndicate rule will be called 'a *weak $k-$majority $q-$Pareto rule*' if

$$F = \bigcup_{t=1}^{s} \pi(I_t, q), \tag{5.22}$$

where $|I_t| = k$, $s = \binom{n}{k}$ being all combinations from n to k.

A coalitional q–olygarchy rule will be called 'a *strong k–majority q–Pareto rule*' if

$$F = \bigcap_{l=1}^{r} \pi(J_l, q), \tag{5.23}$$

where $|J_l| = k$, $r = \binom{n}{k}$ being all combinations from n to k.

Let us discuss these rules. In both cases we consider all coalitions of size k, and in first case the social choice contains q–Pareto optimal alternatives in at least one such coalition. In case of the strong k–majority q–Pareto rule the social choice consists of alternatives which are q–Pareto optimal in each coalition of size k.

The class of weak k–majority q–Pareto rules will be denoted as $\Lambda_w^{q,k-maj}$, and the class of strong k–majority q–Pareto rules will be denoted as $\Lambda_s^{q,k-maj}$, the class of weak k–majority q–Pareto rules with $q = 0$ will be denoted as Λ_w^{k-maj}, and the class of strong k–majority q–Pareto rules with $q = 0$ will be denoted as Λ_s^{k-maj}.

Example. Consider the following profile shown at Figure 5-3

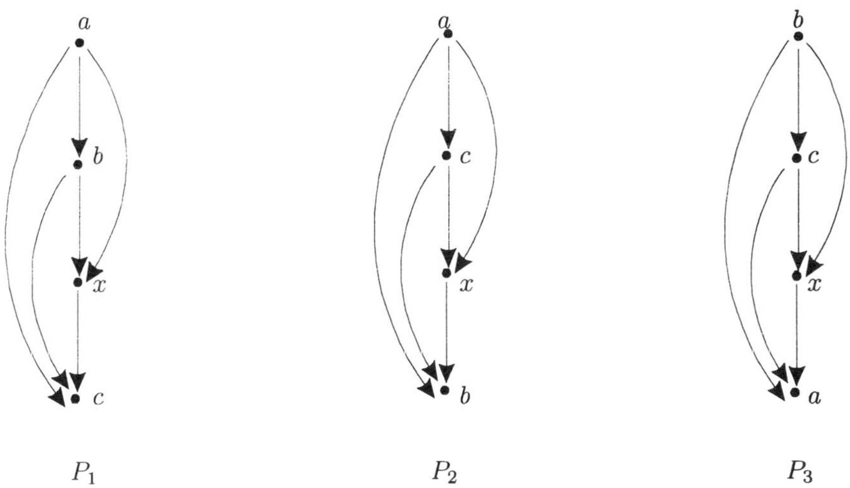

Figure 5-3

The alternative x is Pareto optimal on A when we consider grand coalition N. At the same time, x does not belong to the social choice made by strong 2-majority Pareto rule since it is not Pareto optimal for the coalition $I = \{1, 2\}$.

This example shows that strong k–majority Pareto rule with $k < n$ is stronger than usual Pareto rule.

Four special cases of these rules are of interest. Consider first the weak 1-majority

$q-$Pareto rule, i.e., the rule

$$F = \bigcup_{i \in N} \pi(\{i\}, q). \tag{5.24}$$

It is important to note that the parameter q is the same for each i. This rule will be called as $q-$*One vote rule*. Note also that 0–One vote rule is just One vote rule which chooses undominated alternatives in all ith preferences.
The class of $q-$One vote rules contain $m-1$ rules which correspond to different values of q, $q = 0, 1, ..., m-2$. This class of rules will be denoted as $q\mathcal{V}$, and One vote rule will be denoted as $\mathcal{V}$.

Let us study strong $n-$majority $q-$Pareto rule, i.e., the rule

$$F = \bigcap_{i \in N} f(\{i\}, q). \tag{5.25}$$

It will be called as $q-$*Unanimity rule* (but not q^i-Unanimity), and in case $q = 0$, it is called Unanimity rule. It chooses maximal elements common to all agents. Obviously, such alternatives may not exist.
The class of $q-$Unanimity rules contains $m-1$ rules for $q = 0, 1, ..., m-2$. This class will be denoted as $q\mathcal{U}$, and Unanimity rule will be denoted as $\mathcal{U}$.

Let us study now coalitional $q-$federation rule which satisfies the condition An as well. Let us remind that coalitional $q-$federation rule is defined as follows

$$F = \bigcup_{t=1}^{s} \bigcap_{I \in \mathcal{I}_t} \pi(I, q^I).$$

This rule satisfies the condition An if the families $\mathcal{I}_t$, $t = 1, .., s$, are formed in a special way. In contrast to social decision functions and functional aggregation rules in the case under study we have two 'degrees of freedom' - the size of coalition I (this was only one to be varied in previous cases), and the structure of the families $\mathcal{I}_t$. To illustrate this idea let us consider the following example.

Example. Let $N = \{1, 2, 3, 4\}$, $s = 5$, and

$$\begin{aligned}
\mathcal{I}_1 &= (\{1\}, \{2\}, \{3\}, \{4\}), \\
\mathcal{I}_2 &= (\{1,2,3\}, \{1,2,4\}, \{1,3,4\}) \\
\mathcal{I}_3 &= (\{1,2,3\}, \{1,2,4\}, \{2,3,4\}) \\
\mathcal{I}_4 &= (\{1,2,3\}, \{1,3,4\}, \{2,3,4\}) \\
\mathcal{I}_5 &= (\{1,2,4\}, \{1,3,4\}, \{2,3,4\})
\end{aligned}$$

Then

$$\begin{aligned} F(\overrightarrow{P}) &= (f(\{1\},q^1)\cap f(\{2\},q^1)\cap f(\{3\},q^1)\cap f(\{4\},q^1))\cup \\ &(f(\{1,2,3\},q^2)\cap f(\{1,2,4\},q^2)\cap f(\{1,3,4\},q^2))\cup \\ &(f(\{1,2,3\},q^2)\cap f(\{1,2,4\},q^2)\cap f(\{2,3,4\},q^2))\cup \\ &(f(\{1,2,3\},q^2)\cap f(\{1,3,4\},q^2)\cap f(\{2,3,4\},q^2))\cup \\ &(f(\{1,2,4\},q^2)\cap f(\{1,3,4\},q^2)\cap f(\{2,3,4\},q^2)). \end{aligned}$$

Thus, the rule consists of two kind of 'majorities' - the first one is $q-$Unanimity, and the second one is strong $3-$majority of $q-$Pareto rules which are defined on the coalitions of size 3. Below we will study such kind of rules in detail.

Consider a system of τ families of subsets of N

$$\widetilde{\mathcal{J}} = (\mathcal{J}_1, ..., \mathcal{J}_\tau)$$

such that $\mathcal{J}_j = (J_1^j, ..., J_{r_j}^j)$, where $\left|J_l^j\right| = k^j, l = 1, ..., r_j$, and $r_j = \binom{n}{k^j}$, i.e., each family $\mathcal{J}_j$ contains all coalitions of size k^j.
Consider now the set $\theta_j = \{1, ..., r_j\}$, and construct the family of sets

$$\mathfrak{J}(\theta_j) = (\mathfrak{J}_1, ..., \mathfrak{J}_{\rho(\theta_j)})$$

such that each $\mathfrak{J}_\sigma, \sigma = 1, ..., \rho(\theta_j)$, contains $t-$ majority families of indicies from θ_j, and $\rho(\theta_j) = \binom{r_j}{t}$.
Then we construct the rule as follows

$$F = \bigcup_{\sigma=1}^{\rho} \bigcap_{l\in\mathfrak{J}_\sigma} \pi(J_l^j, q^j). \tag{5.26}$$

We will call this rule as *$\tau-$system of $(t,k)-$majority families* of $q-$Pareto rules. The corresponding class of rules will be denoted as $\Lambda^{q,\tau-(t,k)M}$.

Let us illustrate the rule via three examples.

Example 1. Let $N = \{1,2,3\}$, $\widetilde{\mathcal{J}} = (\mathcal{J}_1)$, and $\mathcal{J}_1$ contains all single-valued coalitions $\mathcal{J}_1 = (\{1\},\{2\},\{3\})$. Construct now the set $\mathfrak{J}(\theta_1) = (\mathfrak{J}_1, ..., \mathfrak{J}_\rho)$ with $t(\theta_1) = 2$. Then $\rho = \binom{3}{2} = 3$, and

$$\mathfrak{J}(\theta_1) = (\{a1, a2\}, \{a1, a3\}, \{a2, a3\}),$$

where $a1 = \{1\}, a2 = \{2\}, a3 = \{3\}$.
The rule is written as follows

$$\begin{aligned} F &= (\pi(\{1\},q)\cap\pi(\{2\},q))\cup(\pi(\{1\},q)\cap\pi(\{3\},q))\cup \\ &(\pi(\{2\},q)\cap\pi(\{3\},q)) \end{aligned}$$

In words, this rule chooses common top $q+1$ alternatives of the first and second agents, or common top $q+1$ alternatives of the first and third agents, or common top $q+1$ alternatives of the second and third agents.

Example 2. Under the conditions of Example 1 let us put $t(\theta_1) = 3$. Then $\rho = \binom{3}{3} = 1$, and

$$\mathfrak{J}(\theta_1) = (\{a1, a2, a3\}).$$

The rule is written as follows

$$F = \pi(\{1\}, q) \cap \pi(\{2\}, q) \cap \pi(\{3\}, q),$$

i.e., the alternatives are chosen which are common to each agent from top $q+1$ alternatives in each i-th linear order. This rule is $q-$Unanimity rule.

Example 3. Let $N = \{1, 2, 3, 4\}$, $\widetilde{\mathcal{J}} = (\mathcal{J}_1, \mathcal{J}_2)$, and

$$\mathcal{J}_1 = (\{1,2\}, \{1,3\}, \{1,4\}, \{2,3\}, \{2,4\}, \{3,4\})$$

and

$$\mathcal{J}_2 = (\{1,2,3\}, \{1,2,4\}, \{1,3,4\}, \{2,3,4\}),$$

i.e., the family $\mathcal{J}_1$ contains all $2-$ majority sets, and $\mathcal{J}_2$ contains all $3-$majority sets. Let us construct now the sets $\mathfrak{J}(\theta_j) = (\mathfrak{J}_1, ..., \mathfrak{J}_{\rho(\theta_j)})$ for θ_1 and θ_2. Put $t(\theta_1) = 5$ and $t(\theta_2) = 2$. Then

$$\begin{aligned} \mathfrak{J}_1 \;\; = \;\; & (\{a1, a2, a3, a4, a5\}, \{a1, a2, a3, a4, a6\}, \{a1, a2, a4, a5, a6\}, \\ & \{a1, a3, a4, a5, a6\}, \{a1, a2, a3, a5, a6\}, \{a2, a3, a4, a5, a6\}. \end{aligned}$$

Here the elements in families of $\mathfrak{J}_1$ correspond to initial coalitions. In this way, $a1$ corresponds to the set $\{1,2\}$ in $\mathcal{J}_1$, $a2$ corresponds to $\{1,3\}$, $a3$ corresponds to $\{1,4\}$,etc. Analogously,

$$\mathfrak{J}_2 = (\{b1, b2\}, \{b1, b3\}, \{b1, b4\}, \{b2, b3\}, \{b2, b4\}, \{b3, b4\}),$$

where $b1 = \{1,2,3\}$, $b2 = \{1,2,4\}$, $b3 = \{1,3,4\}$, and $b4 = \{2,3,4\}$.

Now the rule is written as follows (we will give only the first two components which correspond to the first two sets $\{a1, a2, a3, a4, a5\}, \{a1, a2, a3, a4, a6\}$ in $\mathfrak{J}_1$, and the components which correspond to the third and fourth sets $\{b1, b4\}, \{b2, b3\}$ in $\mathfrak{J}_2$):

$$\begin{aligned} F \;\; = \;\; & (\pi(\{1,2\}, q^1) \cap \pi(\{1,3\}, q^1) \cap \pi(\{1,4\}, q^1) \cap \\ & \cap \pi(\{2,3\}, q^1) \cap \pi(\{2,4\}, q^1)) \cup \\ & \cup (\pi(\{1,2\}, q^1) \cap \pi(\{1,3\}, q^1) \cap \pi(\{1,4\}, q^1) \cap \\ & \pi(\{2,3\}, q^1) \cap \pi(\{3,4\}, q^1)) \cup ... \end{aligned}$$

$$\cup(\pi(\{1,2,3\},q^2)\cap\pi(\{2,3,4\},q^2))\cup$$
$$(\pi(\{1,2,4\},q^2)\cap\pi(\{1,3,4\},q^2))\cup...$$

It is worth mentioning here that for any component of $\mathfrak{J}_1$ the value of q has to be the same due to the condition An, and it is the case for any component of $\mathfrak{J}_2$, but for $\mathfrak{J}_2$ the value of q may be different of that for $\mathfrak{J}_1$.

The following Theorem holds:

Theorem 5.5 $\Lambda^{SC} = \Lambda^{q,\tau-(t,k)M}$, *i.e, Symmetrically Centarl Class coincides with the class of $\tau-$system of $(t,k)-$majority families of $q-$Pareto rules.*

Proof. It is obvious that the rule '$\tau-$system of $(t,k)-$majority families of $q-$Pareto rules' is just a coalitional q-federation rule written for the case when An condition holds. Hence, $\Lambda^{SC}\subset\Lambda^{q,\tau-(t,k)M}$. The inverse inclusion is also obvious ■

Now we study a special case of the $\tau-$system of $(t,k)-$majority families of $q-$Pareto rules, namely, the case when $k=1$. Then $\widetilde{\mathcal{J}}=(\mathcal{J}_1)$, and

$$\mathcal{J}_1 = (\{1\},...\{n\}).$$

In this case $\theta_1=(1,...,n)$, and we obtain $\binom{n}{t}$ sets $\mathfrak{J}_1,...,\mathfrak{J}_{\binom{n}{t}}$ each of which consists of one $t-$majority coalition. Then we can re-write the rule (5.26) as follows

$$F=\bigcup_{\substack{J,\\ |J|=t}}\bigcap_{i\in J}\pi(\{i\},q), \tag{5.27}$$

i.e., if individual opinions are represented as linear orders, the rule chooses common elements between $q+1$ top elements in any preference relation in at least one $t-$majority coalition. The rule will be called *$q,t-$majority rule*, and the corresponding class of rules will be denoted as $\Lambda^{q,t-maj}$.

Finally, if in (5.27) $q=0$, then we have just *$t-$majority rule* which chooses alternatives accepted as top elements by at least t agents, i.e.,

$$F=\bigcup_{J,|J|=t}\bigcap_{i\in J}\pi(\{i\},0). \tag{5.28}$$

The corresponding class will be denoted as Λ^{t-maj}.

Note that if in (5.28) $t=1$ we obtain the One vote rule $\mathcal{V}$, and if in (5.28) $t=n$ the Unanimity rule $\mathcal{U}$ is obtained.

At Figs. 5-4 and 5-5 the mutual relations of some of the classes introduced above are shown. These relations follow directly from the definitions of these classes. At Fig. 5-4 one can see the mutual relations of the classes $\Lambda^{q\cup\cap}$ and $\Lambda^{\cup\cap}$ and their subclasses, and at Fig. 5-5 the classes $\Lambda^{q\cup\cap}_{(i)}$ and $\Lambda^{\cup\cap}_{(i)}$ and their subclasses are shown.

One important comment is in order. In case of social decision functions and functional aggregation rules the intersection of olygarchy rules and syndicate rules consists of dictatorial rules. The same relation is shown at Figs. 5-4 and 5-5. However, there exists one more subclass in the intersection of $\Lambda^{q\cup}$ and $\Lambda^{q\cap}$. It is the class Λ^{qP} of coalitional $q-$Pareto rules. This class contains $(2^n-1)(m-1)$ rules since q may get values from 0 to $m-2$, and there are 2^n-1 non-empty coalitions.

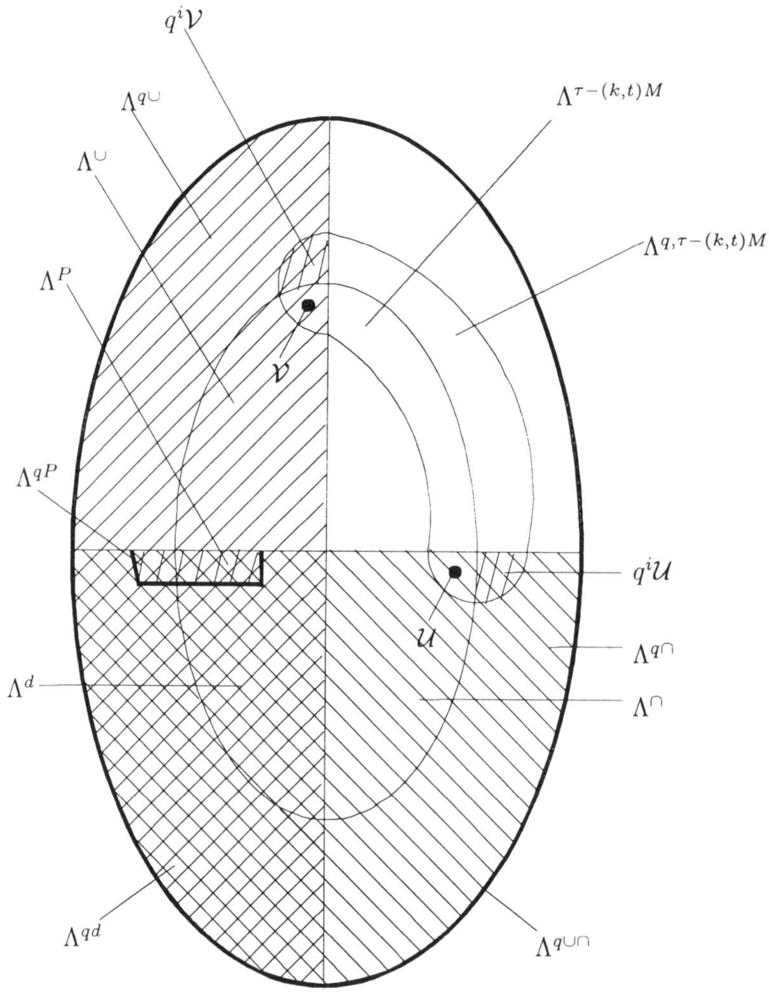

Figure 5-4

The subclass of Λ^{qP} is the class of coalitional Pareto rules which contains 2^n-1 rules.

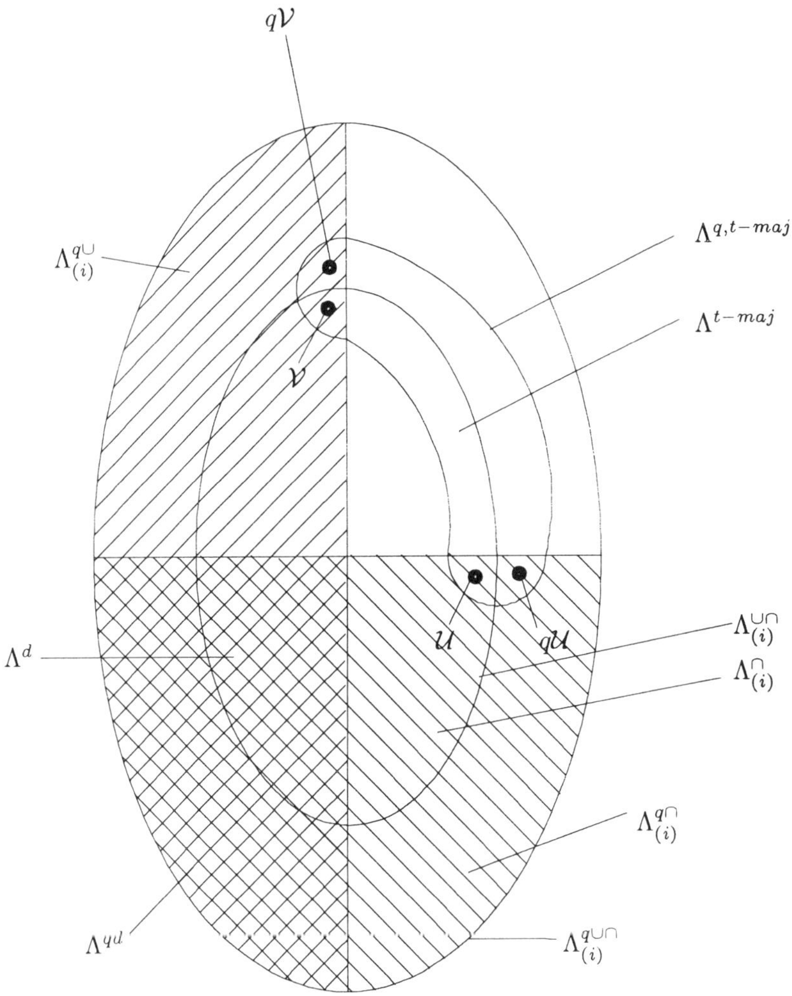

Figure 5-5

Two special rules shown at Fig. 5-4 in the class Λ^{qP} are $q-$Pareto rule when $I = N$, i.e., the rule

$$F = \pi(N, q),$$

and the Pareto rule

$$F_{Par} = \pi(N, 0).$$

It should be mentioned that both rules satisfy the Anonymity condition An.

It is worth mentioning here that in Fig. 5-4 the classes $q^i\mathcal{V}$ and $q^i\mathcal{U}$ are shown, and at the same intersections on Fig. 5-5 contain only one rule each - those of $q\mathcal{V}$ and $q\mathcal{U}$.

5.8 Rationality constraints: single-valuedness

Until now we did not restrict the range of Social Choice Correspondences under study, although the domain of the rule was fixed, i.e., the rule F was defined over the n–tuples of linear orders from $\mathcal{LO}$, and its values were the functions from $\mathcal{C}$, i.e., F was considered as the mapping $F : \mathcal{LO}^n \to \mathcal{C}$.

Definition 5.7 The set of choice functions $Q \subset \mathcal{C}$ will be called closed with respect to a rule $F \in \Pi_{III}$ if for any profile $\{P_i\}$ such that for all $i \in N$ $P_i \in \mathcal{LO}$, $F(\{P_i\}) = C(\cdot) \in Q$ holds.
The set $Q \subset \mathcal{C}$ will be called closed with respect to the class of rules $\mathcal{F}$ if Q is closed with respect to each rule $F \in \mathcal{F}$.
If $\mathcal{F}$ consists of all the rules with respect to which Q is closed, $\mathcal{F}$ will be called the *complete class of closedness* for the set Q and denoted by $\Lambda(Q)$.

Obviously, $\Lambda(Q)$ is the largest (in the sense of set theoretical inclusion) class with respect to which Q is closed.

Next, we study important rationality constraint on a social choice correspondences - single-valuedness of the social choice function.
The single valued social choice correspondences[38] were studied in the framework of manipulability problem [131,237]. The fundamental result for single-valued monotonic SCCs is Muller-Satterthwaite's Theorem [199] which we formulate and prove below. Let us remind that the class of single-valued choice functions is denoted as $\widehat{\mathcal{C}}$; hence the class of complete closedness for $\widehat{\mathcal{C}}$ is denoted as $\Lambda(\widehat{\mathcal{C}})$.

Theorem 5.6 *Let $card(A) \geq 3$, and $F : \mathcal{LO}^n \to \widehat{\mathcal{C}}$ be a single-valued SCC which satisfies Positive Non-Imposition and Maskin's Monotonicity. Then F is dictatorial, i.e.,*

$$\Lambda^{NI^+} \cap \Lambda^{MM} \cap \Lambda(\widehat{\mathcal{C}}) \subseteq \Lambda^d.$$

Proof of this Theorem is based on several lemmas.

Lemma 5.9 *Let F satisfies Maskin's Monotonicity and Positive Uminimity. Then F satisfies weak Pareto Optimality, i.e., $F \in \Lambda^{MM} \cap \Lambda^{U^+} \Rightarrow F \in \Lambda^{wPO}$.*

Proof. Let $F \in \Lambda^{MM} \cap \Lambda^{U^+}$. Assume $F \notin \Lambda^{wPO}$, i.e., there exist a profile $\overrightarrow{P}$ and x, y, X such that yP_ix for all $i \in N$, but $x \in C(X)$. Consider a profile $\overrightarrow{P'}$ such that

[38] In this case they are often called Social Choice Functions. However, we will not use this terminology since we call social choice function a function $C(\cdot)$ which represents social decision.

$$D'_i(y) = \emptyset\ ,\ D'_i(x) = \{y\},$$

and $\forall i$

$$P'_i/(A \setminus \{x,y\}) = P_i/(A \setminus \{x,y\}).$$

Then, by U^+, $F(\overrightarrow{P'}, X) = \{y\}$; on the other hand, since $D'_i(x) \subseteq D_i(x)$ by MM we have $F(\overrightarrow{P'}, X) = \{x\}$. Since $C(\cdot)$ is single-valued the contradiction is obtained which proves Lemma 5.9.

Note that the statement of Lemma 5.9 does not hold in the case of general social choice correspondences, i.e., when $C(\cdot)$ is not single-valued. Indeed, consider the rule $\pi(\overrightarrow{P}, A, q)$ which chooses q-Pareto-optimal elements on A, with $q > 0$, e.g., with $q = 1$. Then, obviously, F violates weak Pareto optimality.

Lemma 5.10 *Let F satisfies Positive Non-Imposition and Maskin's Monotonicity. Then F satisfies weak Pareto Optimality, i.e., $F \in \Lambda^{NI^+} \cap \Lambda^{MM} \Rightarrow F \in \Lambda^{wPO}$.*

Proof. Indeed, let $F \in \Lambda^{NI^+}$. Then for any given x, X there exists $\overrightarrow{P}$ such that $F(\overrightarrow{P}, X) = \{x\}$. Let $\overrightarrow{Z}$ be such that $\forall i$

$$D_i(x) \cap X = Z_i \text{ and } \overrightarrow{Z} \in \Omega(x, X).$$

By MM and Lemma 5.1 we immediately have

$$(\oslash, ..., \oslash) \in \Omega(x, X),$$

i.e., F satisfies U^+ , and from Lemma 5.9 $F \in \triangle^{wPO}$. Lemma is proved.

Let F be a rule which satisfies NI^+ and MM. Let a profile $\overrightarrow{P}$ be such that for any i from some coalition w

$$D_i(x) = \oslash,$$

and for any $i \in N \setminus w$

$$D_i(x) = A \setminus \{x\}.$$

In words, x is the top element of any agent from the coalition w, at the same time x is the worst alternative for all agents which do not belong to coalition w.

Coalition w will be called a winning one if $F(\overrightarrow{P}) = \{x\}$. Consider the set of all winning (for x) coalitions $W(x)$.

This set has the following properties
1. $N \in W(x)$ since by Lemma 5.9 $NI^+ \cap MM \Rightarrow U^+$.
2. $w \in W(x)$ and $w' \supseteq w \Rightarrow w' \in W(x)$, since $F \in \Lambda^{MM}$

Lemma 5.11 *Let $x, y \in A$, $x \neq y$. Then $w \in W(x)$ iff $N \setminus w \notin W(x)$.*

Proof. Let $w \in W(x)$ and $N \setminus w \in W(x)$, and consider a profile $\overrightarrow{P}$ such that

$$\forall i \in w \; D_i(x) = \emptyset, \; D_i(y) = A \setminus \{y\},$$
$$\forall i \in N \setminus w \; D_i(x) = A \setminus \{x\}, \; D_i(y) = \emptyset.$$

Then $F(\overrightarrow{P}) = \{x\}$ and $F(\overrightarrow{P}) = \{y\}$, which is contradicts the condition $F \in \Lambda(\widehat{C})$. Consider now the case when $w \notin W(x)$ and $N \setminus w \notin W(x)$, and consider a profile $\overrightarrow{P}$ such that

$$\forall i \in w \; D_i(x) = \emptyset, \; D_i(y) = \{x\},$$
$$\forall i \in N \setminus w \; D_i(x) = \{y\}, \; D_i(y) = \emptyset.$$

Since $F \in \Omega^{wPO}$, $F(\overrightarrow{P}) \in \{x, y\}$. By symmetry, we may assume that $F(\overrightarrow{P}) = \{x\}$. Then, consider a profile $\overrightarrow{P'}$ such that

$$\forall i \in w \; P_i = P_i'$$
$$\forall i \in N \setminus w \; D_i(x) = A \setminus \{x\}, \; D_i(y) = \emptyset.$$

Since $\forall i \; D_i(y) \supseteq D_i'(y)$, then $\{y\} \neq F(\overrightarrow{P'})$. By weak Pareto optimality $F(\overrightarrow{P'}) \in \{x, y\}$; hence $F(\overrightarrow{P'}) = \{x\}$, which contradicts the assumption that $w \notin W(x)$. Lemma is proved.

Consider a set W of coalitions w which satisfies the following properties

1. $N \in W$;
2. $w \in W$ and $w' \supseteq w \Rightarrow w' \in W$;
3. $w, w' \in W \Rightarrow w \cap w' \in W$;
4. $w \in W \Leftrightarrow \overline{w} \notin W$.

In Chapters 3 and 4 when study strougly local social decision rules and functional aggregation rules we already considered the sets of winning coalitions which obey properties 1-3 or 1-4. Let us remind that a set of coalitions which satisfy properties 1-3 is called a filter, and a set of coalitions which satisfy properties 1-4 is called ultrafilter.

Lemma 5.12 *If W satisfy the properties 1-4, then it is dictatorial.*

Proof. Since N is finite, $w_0 = \bigcap_{w \in W} w$ is not empty and belongs to W. Show that $|w_0| = 1$. Indeed, assume on the contrary that $w_0 = \{i, j\}$, and neither $\{i\}$ nor $\{j\}$ belong to W.

Since $\{i\} \notin W$, then by property 4, $N \setminus \{i\} \in W$, and by property 3 $w_0 \cap (N \setminus \{i\}) = \{j\} \in W$.
Lemma is proved.

Lemma 5.13 $F \in \Lambda^{NI^+} \cap \Lambda^{MM} \Rightarrow F \in \Lambda^{Ne}$, *i.e., a single valued SCC which satisfies Positive Non-Imposition and Maskin's Monotonicity is Neutral.*

Proof. Indeed, let $w \in W(x)$. Then by Lemma 5.11 $N \setminus w \notin W(z)$, and by the same Lemma $w \in W(y)$. We prove that $W(x) \subseteq W(y)$. By symmetry, $W(y) \subseteq W(x)$, i.e, $W(x) = W(y) = W$. Lemma is proved.

Lemma 5.14 *Let* $N = w_1 \cup w_2 \cup w_3$, *and* $w_i \cap w_j = \oslash$ *for* $i \neq j, i, j = 1, ..., 3$. *Then* w_i *for some* i *belongs to* W.

Proof. Consider three alternatives x, y, z and a profile $\overrightarrow{P}$ such that

$$\forall i \in w_1 \; xP_iyP_izP_i....$$
$$\forall i \in w_2 \; yP_izP_ixP_i....$$
$$\forall i \in w_3 \; zP_ixP_iyP_i....$$

By weak Pareto optimality $F(\overrightarrow{P}) \in \{x, y, z\}$. Assume that $F(\overrightarrow{P}) \in \{x\}$. Then show that $w_1 \in W$.
To this end consider the profile$\overrightarrow{P'}$ such that

$$\forall i \in w_1 \; xP'_iyP'_izP'_i....$$
$$\forall i \in w_2 \; zP'_iyP'_ixP'_i....$$
$$\forall i \in w_3 \; zP'_ixP'_iyP'_i....$$

Then, since $\forall i \in N \; D'_i(x) = D_i(x)$ and by MM $F(\overrightarrow{P'}) = \{x\}$. On the other hand, if $w_1 \notin W$, by Lemma 5.11 $N \setminus w_1 = w_2 \cup w_3 \in W$; hence , by Maskin's Monotonicity, $F(\overrightarrow{P'}) = \{z\}$. This contradiction proves that $w_1 \in W$. Lemma is proved.

Let us prove now the Theorem. Let w_0 be the minimal by set inclusion coalition in W, and let $i \in w_0$. Assume that $w_0 \neq \{i\}$. Then, since w_0 is minimal, $\{i\} \notin W$, $w_0 \setminus \{i\} \notin W$, and by Lemma 5.11 $N \setminus w_0 \notin W$. But $\{i\} \cup (w_0 \setminus \{i\}) \cup (N \setminus w_0) = N$, and these coalitions do not intersect. But this contradicts Lemma 5.14. Hence, $w_0 = \{i\}$.
If $i \in w$, then by monotonicity of W, $w \in W$. If $i \notin w$, then $i \in N \setminus w$, $N \setminus w \in W$ and $w \notin W$, i.e., W contains all coalitions which contain i. ■

Remark. The single-valuedness of F permits us to consider a set W of agents' coalitions, i.e., to use even in this third model 'an apparatus' of winning coalitions. This shows deep connections between all three models

- strogly local social decision functions when social decision is search for as linear orders. In this case, transitivity of social binary relation guarantees that the rule under study is neutral and that the property 3 obeys; linearity guarantees that property 4 is satisfied;

- functional aggregation rules when social decision is search for in the classes of choice functions satisfying Outcast ($\mathbf{O}$) and Concordance ($\mathbf{C}$) conditions. In this case, the fact that F belongs to $\Lambda(\mathbf{O})$ guarantees Neutrality of the rule as well as satisfaction of the property 4). When F belongs to $\Lambda(\mathbf{C})$ property 3 obeys; and

- single-valued social choice correspondences. In this case, as we could see above, neutrality of the rules are obtained (Lemma 5.13), and it is guaranteed that properties 3 and 4 satisfy.

5.9 Coalitional q-federation rules under rationality constraints

In this Section we study to which classes belong choice functions generated by the rules q-dictator $\pi(\{i\}, q^i)$, coalitional q-Pareto rule $\pi(I, q^I)$, q-olygarchy $\cap_{i \in I}\pi(\{i\}, q^i)$, coalitional q-olygarchy $\cap_{I \in \mathcal{I}}\pi(I, q^I)$, q-syndicate $\cup_{j \in J}\pi(\{j\}, q^j)$, coalitional q-syndicate $\cup_{J \in \mathcal{J}}\pi(J, q^J)$, and, eventually, q-federation rule $\cup_{t=1}^{s}\cap_{i \in I_t}\pi(\{i\}, q^i)$, and coalitional q-federation rule $\cup_{t=1}^{s}\cap_{I \in \mathcal{I}_t}\pi(I, q^I)$. In other words, we will analize to which condition of rationality satisfy choice function generated by the above rules from profiles of linear orders.

As range constraints we consider the classes of choice functions isolated by Expansion-Contraction Axioms - those of Heredity ($\mathbf{H}$), Concordance ($\mathbf{C}$), Outcast ($\mathbf{O}$), and Arrow's Choice Axiom ($\mathbf{ACA}$).

Theorem 5.7 *$\pi(\{i\}, q^i) \in \Lambda(\mathbf{H} \cap \mathbf{O})$ for $q^i > 0$, and $\pi(\{i\}, 0) \in \Lambda(\mathbf{ACA})$, i.e., q-dictator rule generates choice functions which belong to the domain $\mathbf{H} \cap \mathbf{O}$, and dictator rule generates choice functions which belong to the domain $\mathbf{ACA}$.*

Proof. The case of dictator rule, i.e., $\pi(\{i\}, 0)$, is just a re-formulation of Theorem 2.8.
Consider the case $q^i > 0$. Let $x \in C(X)$, $X' \subset X$, $x \in X'$. We show that $x \in C(X')$. Since $x \in C(X)$, $|X \cap \mathcal{D}_i(x)| \leq q^i$. Since $X' \subset X$, it follows that $|X' \cap \mathcal{D}_i(x)| \leq q^i$, hence $x \in C(X')$, i.e., condition $\mathbf{H}$ obeys.

Below we use the equivalent formulation of the condition $\mathbf{O}$ (see Section 2.4 or [6]): condition $\mathbf{O}$ is equivalent to the conjunction of the following two conditions:

$$1)\ x \in C(X),\ z \notin C(X) \Rightarrow x \in C(X \setminus \{z\});$$
$$2)\ y \notin C(X), z \notin C(X) \Rightarrow y \notin C(X \setminus \{z\}).$$

Let for some X, $x \in C(X), z \notin C(X)$. Then $|X \cap \mathcal{D}_i(x)| \leq q^i$, and $|X \cap \mathcal{D}_i(z)| > q^i$, and, obviously, $|(X \setminus \{z\}) \cap \mathcal{D}_i(x)| \leq q^i$, i.e., $x \in C(X \setminus \{z\})$. If $y \notin C(X)$, then there are two possibilities (remind that we consider the agents' preferences to be linear orders):

$$a)\ zP_iy;\ b)\ yP_iz.$$

In case b), exclusion z from X cannot change the dominant set of y; hence

$$|(X \setminus \{z\}) \cap \mathcal{D}_i(y)| > q^i,$$

i.e., $y \notin C(X \setminus \{z\})$. In case a) if $y \in C(X \setminus \{z\})$, then z must be chosen from X in contradiction with assumption above. Hence, $y \notin C(X \setminus \{z\})$ ■

Theorem 5.8 $\pi(I, q^I) \in \Lambda(\mathbf{H} \cap \mathbf{O})$ *for* $q^I > 0$, *and* $\pi(I, 0) \in \Lambda(\mathbf{H} \cap \mathbf{C} \cap \mathbf{O})$, *i.e., coalitional q-Pareto rule generates choice functions which belong to the domain* $\mathbf{H} \cap \mathbf{O}$, *and coalitional Pareto rule generates choice functions from the classic domain* $\mathbf{H} \cap \mathbf{C} \cap \mathbf{O}$.

Proof. For the case $q^I \equiv 0$, i.e., for the coalitional Pareto rule this statement is just a re-formulation of Theorem 2.8.
Consider general case $0 < q^I < m - 1$. Let $x \in C(X)$, $X' \subset X$, $x \in X'$. Then

$$q^I \geq \left|\bigcap\nolimits_{i\in I}(X \cap \mathcal{D}_i(x))\right| \geq \left|\bigcap\nolimits_{i\in I}(X \cap \mathcal{D}_i(x))\right|;$$

hence, $x \in C(X')$, and condition **H** is obeyed.
Consider condition **O**. Assume $x \in C(X)$; $y, z \notin C(X)$. This means that

$$\begin{aligned} |\cap_{i\in I}(X \cap \mathcal{D}_i(x))| &\leq q^I, \\ |\cap_{i\in I}(X \cap \mathcal{D}_i(y))| &> q^I, \end{aligned}$$

and

$$|\cap_{i\in I}(X \cap \mathcal{D}_i(z))| > q^I.$$

Show that $x \in C(X')$, $X' = X \setminus \{z\}$. Let on the contrary $x \notin C(X')$, i.e., $|\cap_{i\in I}(X' \cap \mathcal{D}_i(x))| > q^I$. Then, there exists $z' \notin \cap_{i\in I}(X \cap \mathcal{D}_i(x))$ and $z' \in \cap_{i\in I}(X' \cap \mathcal{D}_i(x))$. But this implies that there is i_0 such that $z' \notin X \cap \mathcal{D}_{i_0}(x)$; then exclusion from X the alternative z does not change the dominant set for x in X', i.e., $z' \notin \cap_{i\in I}(X' \cap \mathcal{D}_i(y))$. On the other hand, if $y \notin C(X)$ and $y \in C(X')$, this means that $|\cap_{i\in I}(X' \cap \mathcal{D}_i(y))| \leq q^I$, but $|\cap_{i\in I}(X \cap \mathcal{D}_i(y))| > q^I$. Hence, $z' \in \cap_{i\in I}(X \cap \mathcal{D}_i(y))$ but in this case $|\cap_{i\in I}(X \cap \mathcal{D}_i(z))| \leq q^I$, and $z \in C(X)$ on the contrast to the initial assumption. ■

Example below shows that coalitional q-Pareto rule in general does not satisfy the Concordance condition C.

Example. Consider two binary relations P_1 and P_2 shown at Figure 5-6, and the rule $\pi(\{1,2\},1)$. For this profile we obtain

$$|\cap_{i\in I}(\{x,z\}\cap\mathcal{D}_i(x))|\leq 1$$
$$|\cap_{i\in I}(\{x,y\}\cap\mathcal{D}_i(x))|=1,$$

so $x\in C(\{x,y\})\cap C(\{x,z\})$. But

$$|\cap_{i\in I}(A\cap\mathcal{D}_i(x))|=1,$$

hence $x\notin C(A)$.

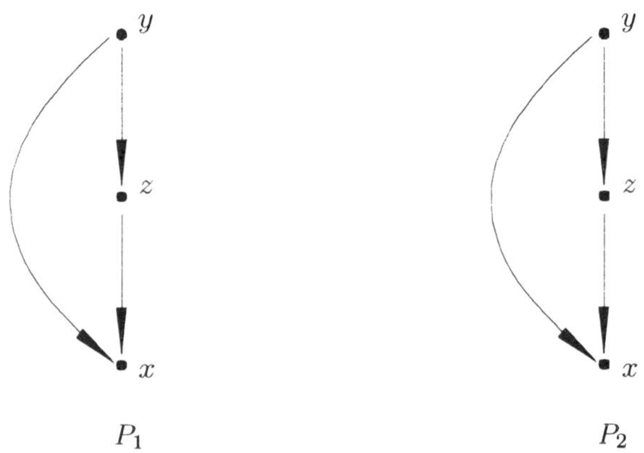

Figure 5-6

Consider now coalitional q-olygarchy rule. In Chapter 5 of [6] the following problem are studied: let Q be some domain in the space of choice functions; with respect to which set-theoretical operations $\cup$ and $\cap$ the domain Q is closed? Moreover, it was studied as well the problem in which domain Q_2 in $\mathcal{C}$ the n-tuples of choice functions each belonging to some Q_1 are transformed using operations $\cup$ and $\cap$. The answers to these questions are given in the following Table 5-2.

We will not prove these statements here (it is rather technical work; the interested reader is also referred to [6]). Using these results one can formulate the statements concerning the rules under study. These results are given below in Table 5-3.

It can be immediately derived from this Table 5-3 that all rules, even of the most general kind - coalitional q-federation, generate choice functions which belong to the domain **H**, or to one of its subdomains. The cause of this phenomenon is studied in the next Section.

Table 5-2

The domain in $\mathcal{C}$	$\cup$	$\cap$	$\cup\cap$
ACA	$\mathbf{H}\cap\mathbf{O}$	$\mathbf{H}\cap\mathbf{C}$	$\mathbf{H}$
$\mathbf{H}\cap\mathbf{C}\cap\mathbf{O}$	$\mathbf{H}\cap\mathbf{O}$	$\mathbf{H}\cap\mathbf{C}$	$\mathbf{H}$
$\mathbf{H}\cap\mathbf{C}$	$\mathbf{H}$	$\mathbf{H}\cap\mathbf{C}$	$\mathbf{H}$
$\mathbf{H}\cap\mathbf{O}$	$\mathbf{H}\cap\mathbf{O}$	$\mathbf{H}$	$\mathbf{H}$
$\mathbf{C}\cap\mathbf{O}$	$\mathbf{O}$	$\mathbf{C}$	$\mathcal{C}$
$\mathbf{H}$	$\mathbf{H}$	$\mathbf{H}$	$\mathbf{H}$
$\mathbf{C}$	$\mathcal{C}$	$\mathbf{C}$	$\mathcal{C}$
$\mathbf{O}$	$\mathbf{O}$	$\mathcal{C}$	$\mathcal{C}$

Table 5-3

Rule	$\pi(\{i\},q^i)$	$\pi(\{i\},0)$
Domain in $\mathcal{C}$	$\mathbf{H}\cap\mathbf{O}$	**ACA**
Rule	$\pi(I,q^I)$	$\pi(I,0)$
Domain in $\mathcal{C}$	$\mathbf{H}\cap\mathbf{O}$	$\mathbf{H}\cap\mathbf{C}\cap\mathbf{O}$
Rule	$\bigcap_{I\in\mathcal{I}}\pi(I,q^I)$	$\bigcap_{I\in\mathcal{I}}\pi(I,0)$
Domain in $\mathcal{C}$	$\mathbf{H}$	$\mathbf{H}\cap\mathbf{C}$
Rule	$\bigcap_{i\in I}\pi(\{i\},q^i)$	$\bigcap_{i\in I}\pi(\{i\},0)$
Domain in $\mathcal{C}$	$\mathbf{H}$	$\mathbf{H}\cap\mathbf{C}$
Rule	$\bigcup_{J\in\mathcal{J}}\pi(J,q^J)$	$\bigcup_{J\in\mathcal{J}}\pi(J,0)$
Domain in $\mathcal{C}$	$\mathbf{H}\cap\mathbf{O}$	$\mathbf{H}\cap\mathbf{O}$
Rule	$\bigcup_{j\in J}\pi(\{j\},q^j)$	$\bigcup_{j\in J}\pi(\{j\},0)$
Domain in $\mathcal{C}$	$\mathbf{H}\cap\mathbf{O}$	$\mathbf{H}\cap\mathbf{O}$
Rule	$\bigcup_{t=1}^{s}\bigcap_{I\in\mathcal{I}_t}\pi(I,q^I)$	$\bigcup_{t=1}^{s}\bigcap_{I\in\mathcal{I}_t}\pi(I,0)$
Domain in $\mathcal{C}$	$\mathbf{H}$	$\mathbf{H}$
Rule	$\bigcup_{t=1}^{s}\bigcap_{i\in I_t}\pi(\{i\},q^i)$	$\bigcup_{t=1}^{s}\bigcap_{i\in I_t}\pi(\{i\},0)$
Domain in $\mathcal{C}$	$\mathbf{H}$	$\mathbf{H}$

5.10 Rationality constraints: domains $\mathbf{H}, \mathbf{C}, \mathbf{O}$

Below several conditions are given each of which defines the property of the lists of the rules from the classes $\Lambda(\mathbf{H})$, $\Lambda(\mathbf{C})$ and $\Lambda(\mathbf{O})$.

(h) For any x, X, X' such that $x \in X' \subset X$, and any ordered n-tuple $\overrightarrow{Z} \in \Omega(x, X)$ follows $\overrightarrow{Z'} = \overrightarrow{Z} \cap X'$ belongs to $\Omega(x, X')$;

(c) For any X' and X'' and for any

$$\overrightarrow{Z'} = \{Z_1', ..., Z_n'\} \in \Omega(x, X'),$$
$$\overrightarrow{Z''} = \{Z_1'', ..., Z_n''\} \in \Omega(x, X'')$$

it follows that $\overrightarrow{Z^*} = \{Z_1^*, ..., Z_n^*\} \in \Omega(x, X' \cup X'')$, where $Z_i^* = Z_1' \cup Z_i''$ for any $i = 1, ..., n$;

(o) For any $\overrightarrow{Z'} \notin \Omega(t, X), \overrightarrow{Z''} \notin \Omega(y, X)$ such that $\overrightarrow{Z'} \subset \overrightarrow{Z''}$ follows $\overrightarrow{Z''} \notin \Omega(y, X \setminus \{t\})$.

The following theorem holds:

Theorem 5.9 *1) Condition (h) is necessary and sufficient for a local SCC F to belong to $\Lambda(\mathbf{H})$;*
2) Condition (c) is necessary and sufficient for a local SDF to belong to $\Lambda(\mathbf{C})$;
3) Let F be a monotone SCC, i.e., $F \in \Lambda^{MM}$. Then $F \in \Lambda(\mathbf{O})$ if condition (o) obeys.

Proof. 1) Let $F \in \Lambda(\mathbf{H})$. Show that condition (h) is obeyed. Assume on the contrary that (h) is violated, i.e., there are $x, X, X', \overrightarrow{Z}, \overrightarrow{Z'}$ such that $x \in X' \subset X$, and $\overrightarrow{Z} \in \Omega(x, X)$ but $\overrightarrow{Z'} = \overrightarrow{Z} \cap X'$ does not belong to $\Omega(x, X')$. But one can construct a profile such that $X \cap \mathcal{D}_i(x) = Z_i$ for any i, and in X' obviously $X' \cap \mathcal{D}_i(x) = Z_i'$. So, if $\overrightarrow{Z'} \notin \Omega(x, X)$, then $x \notin C(X)$ in contradiction with assumption that $F \in \Lambda(\mathbf{H})$.
Assume now that condition (h) holds. Then, if $x \in C(X)$, it is obvious that $x \in C(X')$ for any X', i.e., $F \in \Lambda(\mathbf{H})$.
2) Let $F \in \Lambda(\mathbf{C})$. Assume that (c) does not hold, i.e., there are X' and X'' such that $\overrightarrow{Z'} = \{Z_1', ..., Z_n'\} \in \Omega(x, X')$, and $\overrightarrow{Z''} = \{Z_1'', ..., Z_n''\} \in \Omega(x, X'')$, and $\overrightarrow{Z^*} = \{Z_1^*, ..., Z_n^*\}$ with $Z_i^* = Z_1' \cup Z_i''$ for any i, and $\overrightarrow{Z^*} \notin \Omega(x, X' \cup X'')$. Let us construct the profile $\overrightarrow{P}$ such that $\forall i \; X' \cap \mathcal{D}_i(x) = Z_i'$, $X'' \cap \mathcal{D}_i(x) = Z_i''$. Then, by list representation of F,

$$x \in F(X', \overrightarrow{P}) \cap F(X'', \overrightarrow{P}).$$

Since $P_i \in LO$, then

$$(X' \cup X'') \cap \mathcal{D}_i(x) = (X' \cap \mathcal{D}_i(x)) \cup$$
$$\cup (X'' \cap \mathcal{D}_i(x)) = Z_i' \cup Z_i'' = Z_i^*.$$

Since $\overrightarrow{Z^*} \notin \Omega(x, X' \cup X'')$, $x \notin F(X' \cup X'', \overrightarrow{P})$, i.e., $F \notin \Lambda(\mathbf{C})$.
Let now condition (c) holds. Then it is obvious that $F \in \Lambda(\mathbf{C})$.
3) Let $F \in \Lambda^{MM} \cap \Lambda(\mathbf{C})$, and assume that condition (o) does not hold. Then, there are $\overrightarrow{Z'} \notin \Omega(t, X), \overrightarrow{Z''} \notin \Omega(y, X)$ such that $\overrightarrow{Z'} \subset \overrightarrow{Z''}$, and $\overrightarrow{Z''} \in \Omega(y, X \setminus \{t\})$. Let us construct a profile $\overrightarrow{P}$ such that

$$\forall i \; X \cap \mathcal{D}_i(y) = Z_i'', \; X \cap \mathcal{D}_i(t) = Z_i'.$$

Then $y \notin F(X, \overrightarrow{P}), t \notin F(X, \overrightarrow{P})$.
Consider the set $X \setminus \{t\}$. Then

$$(X \setminus \{t\}) \cap \mathcal{D}_i(y) = Z_i'' \setminus \{t\}.$$

Now, if $\overrightarrow{Z''} \in \Omega(y, X \setminus \{t\})$ then by Maskin's Monotonicity

$$\overrightarrow{Z_t''} = (Z_1'' \setminus \{t\}, ..., Z_n'' \setminus \{t\}) \in \Omega(y, X \setminus \{t\}).$$

Hence, $y \in F(X \setminus \{t\}, \overrightarrow{P})$. Contradiction with **O** is obtained ■

Let us consider the rule the list representation of which is given in Table 5-1. It is obvious that this list satisfies condition (h) as well as condition (c). However, if one exclude the lists $(\emptyset, \{y, z\}, \{y, z\})$ from $\Omega(x, A)$, $(\emptyset, \{x, z\}, \{x, z\})$ from $\Omega(y, A)$, and $(\emptyset, \{x, y\}, \{x, y\})$ from $\Omega(z, A)$, the rule will satisfy the condition (h) but not (c). Thus, it will generate functions which satisfy the condition **H**, but not **C**.

The results of Theorem 5.9 concerning the domain **O** are much poor - only necessary condition has been obtained in this Theorem.

Our next Theorem is just a corollary from Theorem 5.9. It shows what kind of choice functions is generated by the rules from Central Class.

Theorem 5.10 $\Lambda^C \subset \Lambda(\mathbf{H})$, *i.e., any rule from Central Class generates choice functions which satisfy condition* **H**.

Proof. Condition (h) is obviously weaker than Maskin's Monotonicity and Neutrality conditions. When they hold, obviously condition (h) hold, which proves the statement of Theorem ■

This Theorem explains the results observed in the previous Section in Table 5-3, in which it was established that every rule from Central Class generates choice functions which belong to the domain **H** in $\mathcal{C}$, or to one of its subdomains $\mathbf{H} \cap \mathbf{C}$, $\mathbf{H} \cap \mathbf{O}$, $\mathbf{H} \cap \mathbf{C} \cap \mathbf{O}$, or **ACA**.

Remark. It is important to compare these result with results concerning rationality constraints for the functional aggregation rules. In that case, the class to which social choice function belongs depends on the class to which belong individual choice functions. For instance, if individual choice functions belong to the domain **O**, then using the federation rules one could get a social choice which does not, in general, satisfy any of rationality constraints.

In the case under study the situation is different. If we extend the class $\mathcal{LO}$ of binary relations used to represent individual opinions up to the class of weak orders $\mathcal{WO}$, or to strict partial orders $\mathcal{SPO}$, or up to even the class of arbitrary binary relations $\mathcal{B}$, the result of Theorem 5.10 will still hold, i.e., whichever class of individual binary relations is used to represent individual opinions, the social choice 'produced' by the rules from Central Class belongs to the domain **H**, or to one of its subdomains.

5.11 Comparing classes in Λ^C

In this Section the results are given which compare classes of rules isolated by rationality constraints, class of coalitional q-federation rules and its subclasses, and Central and Symmetrically Central Class. All these results are direct corollaries of the results obtained in previous Sections of this Chapter. First, we begin with the class $\Lambda(\mathbf{H})$.

Theorem 5.11 *The intersection of the Central Class with the complete class of closedness $\Lambda(\mathbf{H})$ coincide with the class of coalitional q-federation rules, i.e., $\Lambda^C \cap \Lambda(\mathbf{H}) = \Lambda^{q\cup\cap}$; the intersection of the Symmetrically Central Class with the complete class of closedness $\Lambda(\mathbf{H})$ coincide with the class of τ system of (t,k) majority families of q-Pareto rules, i.e., $\Lambda^C \cap \Lambda(\mathbf{H}) = \Lambda^{q,\tau-(t,k)M}$.*

Proof. In Theorem 5.4 it was proved that $\Lambda^C = \Lambda^{q\cup\cap}$. In Theorem 5.10 we found that $\Lambda^C \subset \Lambda(\mathbf{H})$. Using these two results we obtain the first statement of the Theorem. The second statement follows from Theorem 5.22 ($\Lambda^{SC} = \Lambda^{q,\tau-(t,k)M}$) and the fact that $\Lambda^{SC} \subset \Lambda^C \subset \Lambda(\mathbf{H})$
■

Theorem 5.12 *1) $\Lambda^C \cap \Lambda(\mathbf{H} \cap \mathbf{C}) = \mathbf{\Lambda}^{\cap}$, i.e., the intersection of Central Class with the class of complete closedness for the domain $\mathbf{H} \cap \mathbf{C}$ contains the class of colitional olygarchy rules, i.e.,*

$$\Lambda^{\cap} \subset \Lambda^C \cap \Lambda(\mathbf{H} \cap \mathbf{C} \cap \mathbf{O});$$

2) The intersection of Central Class with complete class of closedness for the domain $\mathbf{H} \cap \mathbf{C} \cap \mathbf{O}$ contains the class of partial Pareto rules, i.e.,

$$\Lambda^P \subset \Lambda^C \cap \Lambda(\mathbf{H} \cap \mathbf{C} \cap \mathbf{O});$$

3) The intersection of Central Class with complete class of closedness for the domain $\mathbf{ACA}$ contains the class of dictator rules, i.e.,

$$\Lambda^d \subset \Lambda^C \cap \Lambda(\mathbf{ACA}).$$

Proof. These statements are just corollaries from the results given in Table 5-3 ■

Since any choice function from $\mathbf{H} \cap \mathbf{C} \cap \mathbf{O}$ is rationalizable via strict partial order, and any choice function from $\mathbf{ACA}$ is rationalizable via weak order (see Chapter 2, Section 2.5), the following corollaries from Theorem 5.12 can be obtained

Corollary 5.1 *Social choice function constructed by a rule from Central Class in Π_{III} is rationalizable via strict partial order if the correponding rule is partial Pareto one.*

Corollary 5.2 *Social choice function constructed by a rule from Central Class in Π_{III} is rationalizable via weak order if the correponding rule is dictator one.*

5.12 Concluding remarks and guide to the literature

Remark 1. In contrast to the rules from Π_I and Π_{II} no attention has been given in Chapter 5 to the non-monotonic neutral rules, and to non-neutral monotonic rules. Using the boolean representation of local social choice correspondences one can study such cases.

Remark 2. There are no so many publications concerning the rules from the space Π_{III} although indirectly these rules were intensively studied in the framework of the implementation theory. Following [178] let us describe briefly the main notions of that theory.

A game form is a pair (S, g), where $S = \prod_{i \in N} S_i$, and

$$g : S \to A.$$

Elements of S are written as $s = (s_1, ..., s_n)$. For any $s \in S$ and $i \in N$ the totality $s_{-i} = (s_1, ..., s_{i-1}, s_{i+1}, ..., s_n)$ denotes the strategies of all agents but ith. We denote $g(S_i, s_{-i}) = a' \in A$ such that $a' = g(s'_i, s_{-i})$ for some $s'_i \in S_i$.

A strategy (n-tuple) $s \in S$ is said to be a Nash equilibrium for g under the profile $\overrightarrow{P}$ if for no i $g(S_i, s_{-i})P_i g(s)$. The set of all Nash equilibria for g under profile $\overrightarrow{P}$ will be denoted as $N(g, \overrightarrow{P})$. The SCC F is said to be Nash implementable if there exists a game form (S, g) such that for all profiles $\overrightarrow{P}$

$$F(\overrightarrow{P}) = g(N(g, \overrightarrow{P}));$$

in this case it is said that g implements SCC F.

The concept of Nash implementability of SCCs was first introduced by E.Maskin in his pioneering paper [180] . In this framework the rules themselves are not described - the problem is to find the conditions to which the rules should satisfy to be Nash implementable. In [180] (see also [181] , [182]) E.Maskin introduced the Monotonicity condition[39] (which we, following many authors, called Maskin's Monotonicity MM), and the condition of No Veto Power NVP. He showed that MM is necessary, and both these two conditions are sufficient for a SCC to be Nash implementable.

Next important step in the implementation theory was made in [196] by introducing the notion of implementation in strong equilibria. In this case, not only a single agent has no incentives to deviate from her sincere preference, but also no coalition can be better of as a result of unanimous deviation of its members. Again, Maskin's Monotonicity turns out to be sufficient condition for the implementability of social choice correspondence in strong equilibria.

In all publications in this field no attention has been drawn to the problem of representation of procedures implementable via Nash or strong equilibria. Rather, the conditions were established to which the implementable procedures should satisfy.

In construction of space S it is usually assumed that this space contains all binary relations R_i, i.e., any agent knows the sincere relations of all other agents. This assumption seems rather artificial and not applicable to real problems. Since, we know what kind of rules satisfy Maskin's Monotonicity, it will be interesting to construct the pace S minimal in some sense. However, these topics go far beyond the scope of this monograph. The interested reader is referred to [91, 92, 181, 182, 216] .

It looks like that from that period, i.e., from 1977 when E.Maskin formulated the problem of implementation in Nash equilibria, studies on these two important problems - an axiomatic synthesis of SCCs and implementability problem - have been developed in parallel and no intersection between them have been established.

It seems that first and unique attempt to connect implementation theory with the problem of axiomatic synthesis of Arrovian rules was made by C.Plott [222] . In that work, the Independence of Irrelevant Alternatives condition had been discussed in general form, and it was found that any implementable SCC should satisfy the IIA condition.

The model of local social choice correspondences considered above was first formulated in [13] in the framework of multicriterial choice, or, strictly speaking, in the case when instead of binary relations P_i ordinal utility functions are considered. In that work condition of strong locality was formulated but attention was given only to the rules from Symmetrically Central Class.

In [15] strongly local SCCs were studied further. Practically all main results obtained above can be found in [17] , in Chapter 5 we give a more detailed study of the rules from Λ^C (see also [19]). In [17] the main representation Theorem 5.4 was formulated using the rules $\pi_\cup(I, p^I)$ together with the rules $\pi(I, q^I)$. In the unpublished manuscript [18] (available, nevertheless, in the State Library of Russian Federation and in the library of the Institute of Control Sciences) further generalizations of the results dealing with local rules from Π_{III} are obtained.

Theorem 5.6 was first proved in [199] , we use the prove given in [91] . The results about the relations between the rules $\pi(I, q^I)$ and $\pi_\cup(I, q^I)$ were obtained in master's

[39] It is worth emphasizing here that in the formulation of Monotonicity condition E.Maskin used lower contour sets. It is a tradition of all publications in that field to use the definition of monotonicity in that form.

thesis by Arnaud Taddei from l'Ecole Superior des Telecommunicationnes made under my supervision in the Institute of Control Sciences in 1992.

In publications dealing with the third aggregation model, i.e., with the rules from Π_{III}, there are several studies in which locality of rules is understood as satisfaction of Independence of Irrelevant Alternatives in general form. At the same time, the social choice function is restricted by some additional condition, e.g., by Arrow's Choice Axiom **ACA**, however, social choice correspondence is defined not on all set A but on subsets of fixed cardinality. Nevertheless, the existence of dictator are obtained (see, e.g., [120, 135, 139, 219, 221]).

In [52] the condition of locality for the third model was formalized in a pair-wise form, i.e., if $\forall x, y$ and any two profiles $\overrightarrow{P}$ and $\overrightarrow{P'}$ the following relation holds

$$\forall i \; P_i/\{x.y\} = P_i'/\{x,y\}$$

then

$$C(\{x,y\}) = C'(\{x,y\}).$$

Function $C(\cdot)$ was restricted then by different rationality restrictions, e.g., by path independence, the the existence of dictator in some form was established.

V.Denicolo [95] , [96] constructed 'a bridge' between local social decision rules and independent (local in a special sense) social choice correspondences. It is worth describing here using the notation of this monograph his definition of Independence for SCCs.

Definition 5.8 An SCC is called to satisfy The Independence condition if for all $x, y \in A$ and for all $\overrightarrow{P}, \overrightarrow{P'}$ in $\mathcal{WO}^n$ the following holds: if $x \in F(A, \overrightarrow{P}), y \notin F(A, \overrightarrow{P})$ and $\forall i \; P_i/\{x,y\} = P_i'/\{x,y\}$, then $y \notin F(A, \overrightarrow{P'})$.

As usual, $P_i/\{x,y\}$ means the contraction of P_i on the set $\{x,y\}$, i.e., $P_i/\{x,y\} = P_i \cap (\{x,y\} \times \{x,y\})$.

In this definition the rationalizability of social choice function is not assumed. However, to check the fact that y is not included in the social choice on A one should check pair-wize relations between x and y in both profiles $\overrightarrow{P}$ and $\overrightarrow{P'}$.

Let us give here two of the theorems obtained in [96] which connect those two models mentioned above.

Theorem 5.13 *A SCC satisfying Independence and Weak Pareto Optimality exists iff there exists SDR which satisfies Locality and Positive Unanimity.*

To formulate next Theorem we need to define the 'dictator' rule in Denicolo's model. Namely, an SCC F is dictatorial if there exists $d \in N$ such that xP_dy implies $y \notin F(A, \overrightarrow{P})$.

Theorem 5.14 *If SCC satisfies Independence and Weak Pareto Optimality then it is dictatorial.*

For other results on this model the reader is reffered to [217] , [236] .

BIBLIOGRAPHY

[1] Agaev RP, Aleskerov FT. Interval choice - classic and general cases. Mathematical Social Sciences 1993; 26 (3): 249-272

[2] Aizerman MA, Aleskerov FT. Local operators in models of social choice. Systems and Control Letters 1983; 3: 1-6

[3] Aizerman MA, Aleskerov FT. Arrow's problem in the theory of social choice. Automation and Remote Control 1983; 9: 127-151

[4] Aizerman MA, Aleskerov FT. Voting operators in the space of choice functions. Mathematical Social Sciences 1986; 11 (3): 201-242

[5] Aizerman MA, Aleskerov FT. Structural properties of voting systems.- In *Topics of General Theory of Structures,* M.Aizerman and E.Caianiello, eds. D.Reidel Publishing Company, 1987.

[6] Aizerman M, Aleskerov F. *Theory of Choice.* North-Holland, Elsevier Science B.V., 1995

[7] Aizerman MA, Malishevski AV. Some aspects of general theory of the choice of best alternatives. Automation and Remote Control 1981; 2: 65-83

[8] Aizerman MA, Zavalishin NV, Pyatnitski ES. Global set functions in the theory of alternatives' choice: I. Automation and Remote Control 1977; 3: 111-125

[9] Aizerman MA, Zavalishin NV, Pyatnitski ES. Global set functions in the theory of alternatives' choice: II. Automation and Remote Control 1977; 5: 103-113

[10] Aleskerov FT. Principles of mutually exclusive neutralities in Arrow's social choice problem. Preprints of IX All-Union Congress on Control Sciences, Moscow: VINITI, 1983 (in Russian).

[11] Aleskerov FT. Formal methods of constructing collective decisions. Proceedings of 2d All-Union Conference on Statistical and Discrete Analysis of Ordinal Data, Moscow: VINITI, 1984 (in Russian)

[12] Aleskerov FT. Decision making procedures making use of voting procedures. Proceedings of the Conference of Complex Control Systems. Varna, Bulgaria: 1985

[13] Aleskerov FT. Procedures of multicriterial choice. Preprints of the IFAC/IFORS Conference on Control Science and Technology for Development; China, Beijing: 1985.

[14] Aleskerov FT. Local collective decision making procedures in different classes of the space of choice functions. Proceedings of the Institute of Control Sciences 'Data Analysis in Control Systems', Moscow: 1985 (in Russian).

[15] Aleskerov FT. Qualitative models of multicriterial choice. In *Methods of Collecting and Analyzing of Complex-Organized Data,* A.Dorofeyuk, ed. Moscow: IPU, 1991 (in Russian)

[16] Aleskerov FT. Binary relations, numerical comparisons with errors and rationality conditions for choice. Social Science Working Paper 812, California Institute of Technology, Pasadena, CA, USA, 1992.

[17] Aleskerov FT. Relational-functional voting operators. Social Science Working Paper 818, California Institute of Technology, Pasadena, CA, USA, 1992.

[18] Aleskerov FT. *Local Models of Voting.* Unpublished manuscript. Institute of Control Sciences, Moscow: 1993 (in Russian).

[19] Aleskerov FT. Multicriterial interval choice models. Information Sciences 1994; 80 (1 and 2): 25-41

[20] Aleskerov FT, Duggan J. Functional voting operators: the non-monotonic case. Mathematical Social Sciences 1993; 26 (2): 175-201

[21] Aleskerov F, Kurbanov E. A degree of manipulability of known social choice procedures. Automation and Remote Control 1998 (forthcoming)

[22] Aleskerov FT, Vladimirov AV. Hierarchical voting. Information Science 1986; 39 (1): 41-86

[23] Aleskerov FT, Vol'skiy VI. Analysis of procedures in collective and multi-criteria decision making. Preprints of 9th World Congress of International Federation of Automatic Control. Budapest, Hungary: 1984.

[24] Aleskerov FT, Vol'skiy VI. Choice of the best variants on binary relations and the extremizational choice. Preprints of 10th World Congress on Automatic Control, v.5, FRG, Munich: 1987

[25] Armstrong TE. Hierarchical Arrow social welfare functions. Economic Theory 1992; 2, 1: 27-47

[26] Arrow KJ. A difficulty in the concept of social welfare. Journal of Political Economy 1950; 58 (4): 328-346

[27] Arrow KJ. *Social Choice and Individual Values*. Wiley, 1951.

[28] Arrow KJ. Rational choice functions and orderings. Econometrica 1959; 26: 121-127

[29] Arrow KJ. *Social Choice and Individual Values*. Yale University Press, 1963, 2d ed.

[30] Arrow KJ. The place of moral obligation in preference systems.- In *Human Values and Economic Policy*, Sidney Hook, ed. New York: New York University Press, 1967.

[31] Arrow KJ. Current developments in the theory of social choice. Social Research 1977; 44: 607-622

[32] Arrow KJ. Extended sympathy and the possibility of social choice. American Economic Review 1977; 67: 219-225

[33] d'Aspremont C, Gevers L. Equity and the informational basis of collective choice. Review of Economic Studies 1977; 44: 199-209

[34] Aumann RJ. Rationality and bounded rationality.- Nancy L.Schwartz Memorial Lecture, J.L.Kellogg School of Management, Northwestern University, 1986

[35] Baigent N, Xu Y. Independent necessary and sufficient conditions for approval voting. Mathematical Social Sciences 1991; 21 (1): 21-29

[36] Bandyopadhyay T. Rationality, path independence and the power structure. Journal of Economic Theory 1986; 40: 338-348

[37] Banerji D. Choice and order, or, first things first. Economica 1964; 31: 158-167

[38] Banks J. Acyclic social choice functions from finite sets. Social Choice and Welfare 1995; 12 (3): 293-310

[39] Barbera S. Majority and positional voting in a probabilistic framework. Review of Economic Studies 1979; 66, 143 : 389-397

[40] Barbera S. Pivotal voters: a new proof of Arrow's theorem. Economic Letters December, 1980; 6: 13-16

[41] Barbera S, Sonnenschein H, Zhou L. Voting by committees. Econometrica 1991; 59 (3): 595-609

[42] Barbera S, Masso J, Neme A. Voting under constraints. Journal of Economic Theory 1997; 76 (2): 298-321

[43] Barthelemy JP. Arrow's theorem, unusual domains and extended co-domains. Mathematical Social Sciences 1982; 3 (1): 79-89

[44] Barthelemy JP, McMorris FR, Powers RC. Dictatorial consensus functions on n-trees. Mathematical Social Science 1992; 25 (1): 59-64

[45] Batra R.N., Pattanaik P. On some suggestions on having non-binary social choice. Theory and Decision 1972; 3 (1): 1-11

[46] Berezovskiy B, Borzenko V, Kempner L. *Binary relations in multicriterial optimization.* Moscow: Nauka, 1981 (in Russian)

[47] Binmore K. Social choice and parties. Review of Economic Studies 1976; 43: 21-37

[48] Black D. *The theory of committees and elections.* Cambridge, England: Cambridge University Press, 1958.

[49] Black D. On Arrow's impossibility theorem. Journal of Law and Economics 1969; 12 (2): 227-248

[50] Black D, Newing RA. *Committee Decisions with Complementary Valuation.* London: William Hodge, 1951.

[51] Blair DH. Path-independent social choice functions: a further result. Econometrica 1975; 43: 173-174

[52] Blair D, Bordes G, Kelly J, Suzumura K. Impossibility theorems without collective rationality. Journal of Economic Theory 1976; 13 (3): 361-379

[53] Blair D, Miller E. Essential aggregation procedures on restricted domains of preferences. Journal of Economic Theory 1983; 30, 1:34-53

[54] Blair D, Pollack R. Collective rationality and dictatorship: the scope of the Arrow theorem. Journal of Economic Theory 1979; 21: 186-194

[55] Blair D, Pollack R. Acyclic collective choice rules. Econometrica 1982; 50 : 931-934

[56] Blau JH. The existence of social welfare functions. Econometrica 1957; 25 (2): 302-313

[57] Blau JH. Arrow's theorem with weak independence. Economica 1971; 38 (152): 413-420

[58] Blau JH. A direct proof of Arrow's theorem. Econometrica 1972; 40 (1): 61-67

[59] Blau JH. Liberal values and independence. Review of Economic Studies 1975; 42 (3): 395-403

[60] Blau JH. Neutrality, monotonicity, and the right of veto: a comment. Econometrica 1976; 44 (3): 603

[61] Blau JH. Semiorders and collective choice. Journal of Economic Theory 1979; 21 (1): 195-206

[62] Blau JH, Deb R. Social decision functions and the veto. Econometrica 1977; 45 : 871-879

[63] Blydenberg JC. The closed rule and the paradox of voting. Journal of Politics 1971; 33 (1): 51-71

[64] Bongard M. *The Problem of Recognition.* Moscow: Nauka, 1967 (in Russian)

[65] Borda JC. Memoire sur les Elections au Scrutin. Histoire de l'Academie Royale des Sciences, Paris, 1781.

[66] Border K. Social welfare functions for economic environments with and without Pareto principle Journal of Economic Theory 1983; 29: 205-16

[67] Bordes G. Consistency, rationality and collective choice. Review of Economic Studies 1976; 43 (3): 447-457

[68] Bordes G. Some more results on consistency, rationality and collective choice. In *Aggregation and Revelation of Preferences*, J.J.Laffond, ed. Amsterdam: North Holland, 1979

[69] Bordes G. On the possibility of reasonable consistent majoritement. Universite de Bordeaux, Faculte des sciences economiques, 1981.

[70] Bordes G, Le Breton M. Arrovian theorems for economic domains: the case when there are simultaneously private and public goods. Social Choice and Welfare 1990; 7: 1-18

[71] Bordes G, Tideman N. Independence of irrelevant alternatives in the theory of voting. Theory and Decision 1991; 30 (2): 163-186

[72] Brams SJ, Fishburn PC. *Approval Voting.* Boston: Birkhaeser, 1982.

[73] Brams SJ, Fishburn PC. Yes-No voting. Social Choice and Welfare 1993; 10 (1): 35-50

[74] Le Breton M, Uriarte JR. On the robastness of the impossibility result in the topological approach to social choice. Social Choice and Welfare 1990; 7: 131-40

[75] Le Breton M, Truchon M. Acyclicity and dispersion of the veto power. Social Choice and Welfare 1995; 12 (1): 43-58

[76] Brown DJ. Aggregation of Preferences. Quaterly Journal of Economics 1975; 89: 456-469

[77] Buchanan JM. Individual choice in voting and the market. Journal of Political Economy 1954; 62 (4): 334-343

[78] Campbell DE. Arrow's theorem for economic environments and effective social preferences. Social Choice and Welfare 1989; 6: 325-329

[79] Campbell DE. *Equity, Efficiency, and Social Choice.* Oxford: Clarendon Press, 1992

[80] Chernoff H. Rational selection of decision functions. Econometrica 1954; 22 : 422-443

[81] Chichilnisky G. Social choice and the topology of spaces of preferences. Advances in Mathematics 1980; 37: 165-76

[82] Chichilnisky G. Social aggregation rules and continuity. Quaterly Journal of Economics 1982; 97: 337-52

[83] Coleman JS. The possibility of a social welfare function. American Economic Review 1966; 56 (5): 1105-1122

[84] Condorcet Marquis de. Essai sur l'application de l'analyse a la probabilite des decisions rendues a la pluralite des voix. Paris: 1785.

[85] Copeland AH. A 'reasonable' social welfare function. Mimeo,. University of Michigan, Seminar on Applications of Mathematics to the Social Scienses, Ann Arbor: 1951.

[86] Cramer-Benjamin R, Crown G, Janowitz M. Permutation invariant consensus methods. Presented at the IV International Meeting of the Society for Social Choice and Welfare 1998; Vancouver, Canada.

[87] Danilov VI. Algebraic aspects of the theory of social choice. In 'Categories of social utility: problems of methodology and structurization'; Moscow: CEMI, 1982 (in Russian)

[88] Danilov VI. Aggregation of tolerant preferences. In 'Categories of social utility: problems of methodology and structurization'; Moscow: CEMI, 1982 (in Russian)

[89] Danilov V.I. Models of group choice. Tekhnicheskaya Kibernetika 1983; 1: 143-164 (in Russian)

[90] Danilov VI. The structure of binary rules for aggregating preferences . Matecon 1985; 21 (4): 44-65

[91] Danilov V, Sotskov A. *Mechnisms of Group Choice.* Moscow: Nauka, CEMI, 1991

[92] Dasgupta P, Hammond P, Maskin E. The implementation of social choice rules. Reviw of Economic Studies 1979; 46, 1: 185-216

[93] Davies OA, DeGroot MH. and Hinich MJ. Social preference orderings and majority rule. Econometrica 1972; 40 (1): 147-157

[94] Deb R. Binariness and rational choice. Mathematical Social Science 1983; 5 (1): 97-106

[95] Denicolo V. Some further results on nonbinary social choice. Social Choice and Welfare 1987; 4 (4): 227-285

[96] Denicolo V. Fixed agenda social choice theory: correspondence and impossibility theorems for social choice correspondences and social decision functions. Journal of Economic Theory 1993; 59 (2): 324-332

[97] Demange G. Single peaked orders on a tree. Mathematical Social Sciences 1982; 3 (4): 201-212

[98] Dobra JL. An approach to empirical studies of voting paradoxes: an update and extension. Public Choice; 1983; 41 (2): 241-250

[99] Dodgson CL. A discussion of various methods of procedure in conducting elections. Oxford: 1873

[100] Dodgson CL. Suggestions as to the best method of taking votes when more than two issues are to be voted on. Oxford: 1874

[101] Donaldson D, Weymark J. Social choice in economic environments. Journal of Economic Theory 1988; 46: 291-308

[102] Downs A. *An Economic Theory of Democracy*. New York: Harper and Row, 1957.

[103] Duggan J. Axioms for Committee Design.- unpublished, 1993.

[104] Dummet M. *Voting Procedures*. Oxford: Clarendon Press, 1984

[105] Dushnik B, Miller W. Partially ordered sets. American Journal of Mathematics 1941; 63, 5: 600-610

[106] Dutta B. On the possibility of consistent voting procedures. Review of Economic Studies 1980; 47: 603-616

[107] Emel'yanov SV, Nappelbaum EL. Metods of control of complex systems: principles of rationality of social choice. Moscow: Tekhnicheskaya Kibernetika, Itogi nauki i tekhniki 1978; 10 (in Russian)

[108] Enelow J, Hinich M. (eds) *Advances in the Spatial Theory of Voting*. Cambridge University Press, 1990

[109] Farquharson R. *Theory of Voting*. New Haven: Yale University Press, 1968

[110] Feldman A. *Welfare Economics and Social Choice Theory*. Boston: Kluwer, Nijhoff, 1980

[111] Ferejohn JA. Decisive coalitions in the theory of social choice. Journal of Economic Theory 1977; 15 (2): 301-306

[112] Ferejohn J, Fishburn PC. Representation of binary decision rules by generalized decisiveness structures. Journal of Economic Theory 1979; 21 (1): 28-45

[113] Ferejohn JA, Grether DM. On a class of rational social decision procedures. Journal of Economic Theory 1974; 8 (4): 471-482

[114] Ferejohn JA, Grether DM. Some new impossibility theorems. Public Choice 1977; 30: 35-42

[115] Ferejohn JA, Grether DM.Weak path independence. Journal of Economic Theory 1977; 14(1): 9-31

[116] Fine K. Conditions for the existence of cycles under majority and non-minority rule. Econometrica 1973; 41 (5): 888-899

[117] Fishburn PC. Arrow's impossibility theorem: concise proof and infinite voters. Journal of Economic Theory 1970; 2 (1): 103-106

[118] Fishburn PC. The irrationality of transitivity in social choice. Behavioral Science 1970; 15 (2): 119-123

[119] Fishburn PC. Should social choice be based on binary comparisons?- Journal of Mathematical Sociology 1971; 1 (1): 133-142

[120] Fishburn PC. *The Theory of Social Choice*. Princeton: Princeton University Press, 1973

[121] Fishburn PC. Choice function on finite sets. International Economic Review 1974; 15 (3): 729-749

[122] Fishburn PC. On collective rationality and a generalised impossibility theorem. Review of Economic Studies 1974; 41 (4): 445-457

[123] Fishburn PC. Paradoxes of voting. American Political Science Review 1974; 68 (2): 537-548

[124] Fishburn PC. Social choice functions. SIAM Review 1974; 16 (1): 63-90

[125] Fishburn PC. Axioms for lexicografic preferences. Review of Economic Studies 1975; 42 (1): 19-35

[126] Fishburn PC. Dictators on blocks: generalisations of social choice impossibility theorems. Journal of Combinatorial Theory B 1976; 20 (2): 153-170

[127] Fountain J, Suzumura K. Collective choice rules without Pareto principles. International Economic Review 1982; 32 (2): 299-308

[128] Gaertner W. An analysis and comparison of several necessary and sufficient conditions for transitivity under the majority rule. In *Aggregation and Revelation of Preferences*, J.J.Laffont ed. Amsterdam: North Holland, 1979

[129] Gärdenforce P. Positionalist voting functions. Theory and Decision 1973; 4 (1): 1-24

[130] Gibbard A. Social choice and Arrow condition. Mimeo, 1969.

[131] Gibbard A. Manipulation of voting schemes: a general result. Econometrica 1973; 41: 587-601

[132] Gibbard A, Hylland A, Weymark A. Arrow's theorem with a fixed feasible alternative. Social Choice and Welfare 1987; 4 (2): 105-115

[133] Gorgescu-Roegen N. The relation between binary and multiple choices: some comments and further results. Econometrica 1969; 37 (4): 728-730

[134] Green D, Shapiro I. *Pathologies of Rational Choice Theory: A Critique of Applications in Political Science.* New Haven: Yale University Press, 1994

[135] Grether DM, Plott CR. Nonbinary social choice: an impossibility theorem. Review of Economic Studies 1982; 49, 2

[136] Guha AS. Neutrality, monotonicity and the right of veto. Econometrica 1972; 40 : 821-826

[137] Guilbaud GT. *Elements de la theorie mathematique des jeux*. Paris: Dunod, 1968.

[138] Hansson B. Choice structures and preference relations. Synthese 1968; 18 (4): 423-442

[139] Hansson B. Voting and group decision functions. Synthese, 1969; 20 (4): 526-537

[140] Hansson B. The independence condition in the theory of social choice. Theory and Decision 1973; 4 (1): 25-49

[141] Hansson B. The existence of group preference function. Public Choice, 1976; 28: 89-98

[142] Hansson S. Social choice with procedural preferences. Social Choice and Welfare 1996; 13 (2): 215-230

[143] Herzberger HG. Ordinal preference and rational choice. Econometrica, 1973; 41: 187-237

[144] Houthakker HS. Revealed preference and the utility function. Economica 1950; 7: 159-174

[145] Houthakker HS. On the logic of preference and choice.- In *Contribution to Logic and Methodology*, A.T.Tyminienicka, ed. Amsterdam: North Holland, 1965.

[146] Jacquet-Lagrèze E. L'aggregation des opinions individuelles. Informatique et Sciences Humaines, 1969; 4: 1-21

[147] Johnson M. Information, assotiativity, and choice requirements. Journal of Economic Theory 1990; 52: 440-452

[148] Ilyunin O, Popov B, El'kin L. Functional majority operators in voting theory. Automation and Remote Control 1988; 7

[149] Inada K. The simple majority decision rule. Econometrica 1969; 32, 3: 490-506

[150] Inada KI. Majority rule and rationality. Journal of Economic Theory 1970; 2: 27-40

[151] Kalai E, Megiddo N. Path independent choices. Econometrica 1980; 48: 781-784

[152] Kalai E, Muller E, Satterthwaite E. Social welfare functions when preferences are convex, strictly monotonic, and continuous. Public Choice 1979; 34: 87-97

[153] Kanai Y, Peleg B. A note on the extension of an order on a set to the power set. Journal of Economic Theory 1984; 32: 172-175

[154] Kelly JS. *Arrow Impossibility Theorems.* New York: Academic Press, 1978.

[155] Kelly JS. *Social Choice Theory: An Introduction.* Berlin: Springer-Verlag, 1987

[156] Kelly JS. Social choice bibliography. Social Choice and Welfare, 1991; 8 (2): 97-169

[157] Kelly JS. Abelian symmetry groups in social choice. Mathematical Social Science, 1992; 25 (1): 15-25

[158] Kelly JS. Almost all social choice rules are highly manipulable, but few aren't. Social Choice and Welfare 1993; 10 (2): 161-175

[159] Kim KH, Roush FW. *Introduction to Mathematical Consensus Theory*. New York: Marcel Decker, 1980.

[160] Kirman AP, Sondermann D. Arrow's theorem, many agents and invisible dictators. Journal of Economic Theory 1972; 5: 267-77

[161] Laslier J-F. *Tournament solutions and majority voting*. Berlin, Heidelberg: Springer Verlag, 1997

[162] Levchenkov V. Theory of group choice: algebraic approach. Moscow, Preprints of VNIISI, 1985 (in Russian)

[163] Levchenkov V. Theory of group choice: general form of aggregation functions. Moscow, Preprints of VNIISI, 1985 (in Russian)

[164] Levchenkov V. Algebraic representation of group choice. Doklady Akademii Nauk SSSR 1987; 293(6): 1324-1329

[165] Lezina Z. Procedures of social choice. Automation and Remote Control 1987; 8: 3-35

[166] Libkin L. Algebraic methods of construction and analysis of choice function classes. In *Problem of choice and fuzzy sets*, Moscow: VNIISI, 1987

[167] Little IMD. Social choice and individual values. Journal of Political Economy 1952; 60 (4): 422-432

[168] Luce RD. Semi-orders and a theory of utility discrimination. Econometrica 1956; 24: 178-191

[169] Luce RD, Raiffa H. *Games and Decisions*. New York: Wiley, 1957

[170] Makarov I, Vinogradskaya T, Rubchinskiy A, Sokolov V. *Theory of Choice and Decision Making*. Moscow: Nauka, 1982. (in Russian)

[171] Malishevski A. Path independence in serial-parallel data processing. Mathematical Social Sciences 1994; 27: 335-367.

[172] Matsumoto Y. Nonbinary social choice: revealed preferential interpretation. Economica 1985; 52 (206): 121-162

[173] May KO. A set of independent, necessary and sufficient conditions for simple majority decision. Econometrica 1952; 20 (4): 680-684

[174] May RM. Some mathematical remarks on the paradox of voting. Behavioral Science 1971; 16 (2): 143-151

[175] Mayston D. *The Idea of Social Choice*. New York: St Martin's Press, 1975.

[176] McGarvey DC. A theorem on the construction of voting paradoxes. Econometrica 1953; 21: 608-610

[177] McKay AF. *Arrow's Theorem: The Paradox of Social Choice*. New Haven: Yale University Press, 1980.

[178] McKelvey RD. Game forms for Nash implementation of general social choice correspondences. Social Choice and Welfare 1989; 6: 139-156

[179] Mas-Colell A, Sonnenshein H. General possibility theorems for group decisions. Review of Economic Studies 1972; 39 (2): 185-192

[180] Maskin E. Nash Equilibrium and Welfare Optimality. Mimeo, MIT, 1977

[181] Maskin E. The theory of implementation of Nash equilibria: a survey. Cambridge: Cambridge University Press, 1986.

[182] Maskin E. Implementation and strong Nash equilibrium. In *Aggregation and Revelation of Preferences*, J.J.Laffont ed. Amsterdam: North Holland, 1979.

[183] Mendelson E. *Introduction to Mathematical Logic*. New Jersey: D.Van Nostrand Co, 1968.

[184] Mihara H. Anonimity and neutrality in Arrow's theorem with restricted coalition algebras. Social Choice and Welfare, 1997; 14 (4): 503-512

[185] Miller N. Pluralism and social choice. American Political Review 1983; 77 : 734-735

[186] Mirkin B. *Theory of group choice*. Moscow: Nauka, 1974. (in Russian)

[187] Mirkin B. Federations and transitivity of social choice. In *Models of socio-economic processes and social planning*, Moscow: Nauka, 1979 (in Russian)

[188] Monjardet B. An axiomatic theory of tournament aggregation. Mathematics and Operation Research 1978; 3 (4): 334-351

[189] Monjardet B. On the use of ultrafilters in social choice theory. In *Social Choice and Welfare*, P.Pattanaik and M.Salles eds. Amsterdam: North Holland, 1983.

[190] Monjardet B. Arrowian characterization of latticial federation consensus functions. Preprint, University Paris V and C.A.M.S., 1988.

[191] Moulin H. *The Strategy of Social Choice*. Amsterdam: North Holland, 1983.

[192] Moulin H. Choice functions over a finite set: a summary. Social Choice and Welfare 1985; 2 (2): 147-160

[193] Moulin H. From social welfare orderings to acyclic aggregation of preferences. Mathematical Social Sciences 1985 :1-17

[194] Moulin H. *Axioms of Cooperative Decision Making*. Cambridge: Cambridge University Press, 1988

[195] Moulin H. Social choice. In *Handbook of Game Theory*, v.2, R.Aumann and S.Hart (eds.) Elsevier Science B.V., 1994

[196] Moulin H, Peleg B. Cores of effectivity functions and implementation theory. Journal of Mathematical Economics, 1982; 10 (1): 115-145

[197] Mueller D. Voting by veto. Journal of Public Economics 1978; 10, 1: 57-75

[198] Mueller D. *Public Choice*. Cambridge: Cambridge University Press, 1979.

[199] Muller E, Satterthwaite M. The equivalence of strong positive assosiation and stategy-proofness. Journal of Economic Theory, 1977; 14, 4: 412-418

[200] Murakami Y. *Logic and Social Choice*. New York: Dover, 1968.

[201] Naiton W, Watanabe T. An extended formulation of Arrows theorem for $k-$social welfare function. Social Choice and Welfare 1995, 12 (3): 215-224

[202] Nakamura K. The core of a simple game without ordinal preferences. International Journal of Game Theory, 1975; 4, 1: 95-104

[203] Nanson EJ. Methods of election. Transactions and Proceedings of the Royal Society of Victoria, 1882; 18

[204] Nehring K. Rational choice and revealed preference without binariness. Social Choice and Welfare 1997; 14, 3

[205] Nurmi H. *Comparing Voting Systems*. Dordrecht: D.Reidel Publishing Comp, 1987.

[206] Ore O. *Theory of Graphs*. American Mathematical Society, Colloquium Publication, v.XXXVIII, 1962.

[207] Osborne DK. Irrelevant alternatives and social welfare. Econometrica 1976; 44 (5): 1001-1015

[208] Packard DJ. Social choice theory and sitizens' intransitive weak preference. Public Choice 1975; 22: 107-111

[209] Panda SC. On nonbinary social choice. Mathematical Social Sciences, 1983; 4 (1): 73-78

[210] Pareto V. *Cours d'Economie Politique*. Lausanne: Rouge, 1889.

[211] Parks RP. Further results on path independence, quasi-transitivity and social choice. Public Choice, 1976; 26: 75-87

[212] Pattanaik PK. *Voting and Collective Choice.* London: Cambridge University Press, 1971.

[213] Pattanaik PK. *Strategy and Group Choice.* Amsterdam: North-Holland, 1979.

[214] Pattanaik PK, Salles M. *Social Choice and Welfare.* Amsterdam: North-Holland, 1983.

[215] Peleg B. Consistent voting systems. Econometrica, 1978; 46 : 153-161

[216] Peleg B. *Game Theoretic Analysis of Voting in Committees.* London: Cambridge University Press, 1984.

[217] Peris JE, Carmen-Sanchez M. Fixed agenda social choice correspondences. Social Choice and Welfare (forthcoming)

[218] Peters H, Wakker P. Independence of irrelevant alternatives and revealed group preferences. Mimeo, Limburg Rijksuniversiteit, 1987.

[219] Plott CR. Recent results on the theory of voting. In *Frontiers of Quantitative Economics*, Michel Intrilligator ed. Amsterdam: North-Holland, 1971.

[220] Plott CR. Path independence, rationality and social choice. Econometrica 1973; 41:1075-1091

[221] Plott CR. Axiomatic social choice theory: an overview and interpretation. American Journal of Political Sciences 1976; 20, 3

[222] Plott CR. A relationship between independence of irrelevant alternatives, game theory, and implementability. Mimeo, California Institute of Technology, Pasadena, California, 1984

[223] Popov B, L.El'kin Functional local operators of non-complete and non-empty choice of options. Automation and Remote Control 1989; 7: 987-992

[224] Ray P. Independence of irrelevant alternatives. Econometrica, 1973; 41 (5): 978-991

[225] Richelson JT. A comparative analysis of social choice functions I. Behavioral Sciences 1975; 20 (5): 331-337

[226] Richelson JT. A comparative analysis of social choice functions II. Behavioral Sciences 1975; 23 (1): 38-44

[227] Richelson JT. A comparative analysis of social choice functions III. Behavioral Sciences 1975; 23 (3): 169-176

[228] Richelson JT. Majority rule and collective choice. California Institute of Technology, Mimeo, 1980.

[229] Riker W. *Liberalism Against Populism.* San Francisco: Freeman, 1982.

[230] Roberts F. Interpersonal comparability and social choice theory. Review of Economic Studies 1980; 47: 421-439

[231] Saari D. *Basic Geometry of Voting.* Berlin: Springer, 1995.

[232] Saari D. Connecting and resolving Sen's and Arrow's theorems. Social Choice and Welfare 1998; 15 (2): 239-261

[233] Salles M. A general possibility theorem for group decision rules with Pareto transitivity. Journal of Economic Theory 1975; 21 (1): 110-118

[234] Samuelson PA. A note on the pure theory of consumers behavior. Economica 1938; 5: 61-71: 353-354

[235] Samuelson PA. Arrow's mathematical politics.- In *Human Values and Economic Policy*, Sidney Hood, ed. New York: New York University Press, 1967.

[236] Sanchez M, Peris JE. Veto in fixed agenda social choice correspondences. Social Choice and Welfare (forthcoming)

[237] Satterthwaite MA. Strategy-proofness and Arrow's conditions: existence and correspondence theorems for voting procedures and social welfare functions. Journal of Economic Theory 1975; 10: 198-217

[238] Schick F. Arrow's proof and the logic of preference. Philosophy of Science 1969; 36 (2): 127-144

[239] Schmitz N. A further note on Arrow's impossibility theorem. Journal of Mathematical Economics 1977; 4 (2): 189-196

[240] Schofield N. *Social Choice and Democracy*. Berlin: Springer Verlag, 1985.

[241] Schwartz T. *The Logic of Collective Choice*. Los Angeles: University of California Press, 1980.

[242] Seidl C. The impossibility of nondictatorial tolerance. Zeitschrift für Nationalökonomie 1986; 46 (Supplementum 5): 211-225

[243] Sen AK. *Collective Choice and Social Welfare*. San-Francisco: Holden Day, 1970.

[244] Sen AK. Choice functions and revealed preferences. Review of Economic Studies 1971; 38 : 307-317

[245] Sen AK. Social choice theory: a re-examination. Econometrica 1973; 45, 1: 53-89

[246] Sen AK. Social choice theory.- In *Handbook of Mathematical Economics*, Kenneth J. Arrow and Michael D. Intriligator, eds. Amsterdam: North-Holland, v.3, 1983.

[247] Sen AK. Internal consistency of choice. Econometrica 1993; 61 (3): 495-521

[248] Sen AK. Rationality and Social Choice. American Economic Review 1995; 85 (1): 1-24

[249] Sen AK. How to Judge Voting Schemes. The Journal of Economic Perspectives 1995; 9 (1): 91-98

[250] Sen AK. Maximization and the act of choice. Econometrica 1997; 65 (4): 745-779

[251] Sen AK, Pattanaik PK. Necessary and sufficient conditions for rational choice under majority decision. Journal of Economic Theory 1969; 1, 1

[252] Sertel M, Kalaycioglu E. *On The Road To Designing The New Electoral System For Turkey*. Istanbul: TUSIAD, 1995. (in Turkish)

[253] Sholomov L. Logic methods in the problems of consistent choice. Moscow, Preprints of VNIISI, 1978 (in Russian)

[254] Sholomov L. Application of logic methods in the problems of sequential choice. Moscow, Preprints of VNIISI, 1980 (in Russian)

[255] Sholomov L. *Logic methods of study of discrete choice models*. Moscow: Nauka, 1989 (in Russian)

[256] Sholomov L. Logic methods of study of relations in criterial spaces: classes of relations and aggregation. Moscow, Preprints of VNIISI, 1990 (in Russian)

[257] Sholomov L. Synthesis of social decision rules. Mathematical Social Sciences (forthcoming)

[258] Sholomov L, Yudin D. Synthesis of multi-step schemes of choice. Automation and Remote Control 1986; 10

[259] Smith J. Aggregation of preferences with variable electorate. Econometrica 1973; 41, 6: 1027-1041

[260] Stearns R. The voting problem. American Mathematical Monthly, 1959; 66 :761-763

[261] Stefanescu A. Impossibility results for choice correspondences. Mathematical Social Sciences 1997; 33(2): 129-148.

[262] Straffin PD. *Topics In The Theory of Voting*. The UMAP Expository Monograph Series, Boston: Birkhaueser, 1980.

[263] Suzumura K. Rational Choice and Revealed Preferences. Review of Economic Studies 1974; 44 (1): 38-47

[264] Suzumura K. *Rational Choice, Collective Decisions and Social Welfare*. Cambridge: Cambridge University Press, 1983.

[265] Szpilrajn E. Sur l'extension de l'ordre partiel. Fund.Math., 1930; 16 : 386-389

[266] Tanguiane AS. Hierarchical model of group choice. Economica i Matematicheskiye Metody, 1980; 16, 3 (in Russian)

[267] Tanguiane AS. *Aggregation and Representation of Preferences: Introduction to Mathematical Theory of Democracy*. Berlin: Springer, 1991.

[268] Tversky A, Kahneman D. Rational choice and framing of decisions. In *Decision Making: Normative and Prescriptive Interactions*, D.Bell, H.Raiffa, and A.Tversky eds., 1988

[269] Tullock G. *Toward a Mathematics of Politics*. Ann Arbor: University of Michigan Press, 1967.

[270] Vinogradskaya T, Rubchinskiy A. Logic forms of binary relations in criterial space. DAN SSSR, 1980; 251, 2

[271] Vladimirov A. Neutrality conditions of voting operators isolated by structural constraints. In *Analysis of Problems of Alternatives Formation and Choice*, Moscow: VNIISI, v.10, 1986 (in Russian)

[272] Vladimirov A. Functions of algebra of logic in the theory of social choice. In Preprints 'Control of complex technical systems', Moscow, Institut Problem Upravleniya, 1987 (in Russian)

[273] Vol'skiy V. Tournament functions in the theory of social and multicriterial choice. In *Topics of General Theory of Structures*, M.Aizerman and E.Caianiello, eds. D.Reidel Publishing Company, 1987.

[274] Vol'skiy V, Lezina Z. *Voting in Small Groups*. Moscow: Nauka, 1991 (in Russian)

[275] Ward B. Majority rule and allocation. Journal of Conflict Resolution 1960; 5

[276] Wilson RB. The finer structure of revealed preferences. Journal of Economic Theory 1970; 2, 4: 348-353

[277] Wilson RB. Social choice theory without the Pareto principle. Journal of Economic Theory 1972; 5, 3: 476-486

[278] Wilson RB. On the theory of aggregation. Journal of Economic Theory 1975; 10 (1): 89-99

[279] Young H.P. An axiomatization of Borda's rule. Journal of Economic Theory 1974; 9: 43-52

INDEX

THEORY AND DECISION LIBRARY

SERIES B: MATHEMATICAL AND STATISTICAL METHODS

Editor: H. J. Skala, *University of Paderborn, Germany*

1. D. Rasch and M.L. Tiku (eds.): *Robustness of Statistical Methods and Nonparametric Statistics*. 1984 ISBN 90-277-2076-2
2. J.K. Sengupta: *Stochastic Optimization and Economic Models*. 1986 ISBN 90-277-2301-X
3. J. Aczél: *A Short Course on Functional Equations*. Based upon Recent Applications to the Social Behavioral Sciences. 1987 ISBN Hb 90-277-2376-1; Pb 90-277-2377-X
4. J. Kacprzyk and S.A. Orlovski (eds.): *Optimization Models Using Fuzzy Sets and Possibility Theory*. 1987 ISBN 90-277-2492-X
5. A.K. Gupta (ed.): *Advances in Multivariate Statistical Analysis*. Pillai Memorial Volume. 1987 ISBN 90-277-2531-4
6. R. Kruse and K.D. Meyer: *Statistics with Vague Data*. 1987 ISBN 90-277-2562-4
7. J.K. Sengupta: *Applied Mathematics for Economics*. 1987 ISBN 90-277-2588-8
8. H. Bozdogan and A.K. Gupta (eds.): *Multivariate Statistical Modeling and Data Analysis*. 1987 ISBN 90-277-2592-6
9. B.R. Munier (ed.): *Risk, Decision and Rationality*. 1988 ISBN 90-277-2624-8
10. F. Seo and M. Sakawa: *Multiple Criteria Decision Analysis in Regional Planning*. Concepts, Methods and Applications. 1988 ISBN 90-277-2641-8
11. I. Vajda: *Theory of Statistical Inference and Information*. 1989 ISBN 90-277-2781-3
12. J.K. Sengupta: *Efficiency Analysis by Production Frontiers*. The Nonparametric Approach. 1989 ISBN 0-7923-0028-9
13. A. Chikán (ed.): *Progress in Decision, Utility and Risk Theory*. 1991 ISBN 0-7923-1211-2
14. S.E. Rodabaugh, E.P. Klement and U. Höhle (eds.): *Applications of Category Theory to Fuzzy Subsets*. 1992 ISBN 0-7923-1511-1
15. A. Rapoport: *Decision Theory and Decision Behaviour*. Normative and Descriptive Approaches. 1989 ISBN 0-7923-0297-4
16. A. Chikán (ed.): *Inventory Models*. 1990 ISBN 0-7923-0494-2
17. T. Bromek and E. Pleszczyńska (eds.): *Statistical Inference*. Theory and Practice. 1991 ISBN 0-7923-0718-6
18. J. Kacprzyk and M. Fedrizzi (eds.): *Multiperson Decision Making Models Using Fuzzy Sets and Possibility Theory*. 1990 ISBN 0-7923-0884-0
19. G.L. Gómez M.: *Dynamic Probabilistic Models and Social Structure*. Essays on Socioeconomic Continuity. 1992 ISBN 0-7923-1713-0

20. H. Bandemer and W. Näther: *Fuzzy Data Analysis*. 1992 ISBN 0-7923-1772-6
21. A.G. Sukharev: *Minimax Models in the Theory of Numerical Methods*. 1992 ISBN 0-7923-1821-8
22. J. Geweke (ed.): *Decision Making under Risk and Uncertainty*. New Models and Empirical Findings. 1992 ISBN 0-7923-1904-4
23. T. Kariya: *Quantitative Methods for Portfolio Analysis*. MTV Model Approach. 1993 ISBN 0-7923-2254-1
24. M.J. Panik: *Fundamentals of Convex Analysis*. Duality, Separation, Representation, and Resolution. 1993 ISBN 0-7923-2279-7
25. J.K. Sengupta: *Econometrics of Information and Efficiency*. 1993 ISBN 0-7923-2353-X
26. B.R. Munier (ed.): *Markets, Risk and Money*. Essays in Honor of Maurice Allais. 1995 ISBN 0-7923-2578-8
27. D. Denneberg: *Non-Additive Measure and Integral*. 1994 ISBN 0-7923-2840-X
28. V.L. Girko, *Statistical Analysis of Observations of Increasing Dimension*. 1995 ISBN 0-7923-2886-8
29. B.R. Munier and M.J. Machina (eds.): *Models and Experiments in Risk and Rationality*. 1994 ISBN 0-7923-3031-5
30. M. Grabisch, H.T. Nguyen and E.A. Walker: *Fundamentals of Uncertainty Calculi with Applications to Fuzzy Inference*. 1995 ISBN 0-7923-3175-3
31. D. Helbing: *Quantitative Sociodynamics*. Stochastic Methods and Models of Social Interaction Processes. 1995 ISBN 0-7923-3192-3
32. U. Höhle and E.P. Klement (eds.): *Non-Classical Logics and Their Applications to Fuzzy Subsets*. A Handbook of the Mathematical Foundations of Fuzzy Set Theory. 1995 ISBN 0-7923-3194-X
33. M. Wygralak: *Vaguely Defined Objects*. Representations, Fuzzy Sets and Nonclassical Cardinality Theory. 1996 ISBN 0-7923-3850-2
34. D. Bosq and H.T. Nguyen: *A Course in Stochastic Processes*. Stochastic Models and Statistical Inference. 1996 ISBN 0-7923-4087-6
35. R. Nau, E. Grønn, M. Machina and O. Bergland (eds.): *Economic and Environmental Risk and Uncertainty*. New Models and Methods. 1997 ISBN 0-7923-4556-8
36. M. Pirlot and Ph. Vincke: *Semiorders*. Properties, Representations, Applications. 1997 ISBN 0-7923-4617-3
37. I.R. Goodman, R.P.S. Mahler and H.T. Nguyen: *Mathematics of Data Fusion*. 1997 ISBN 0-7923-4674-2
38. H.T. Nguyen and V. Kreinovich: *Applications of Continuous Mathematics to Computer Science*. 1997 ISBN 0-7923-4722-6
39. F. Aleskerov: *Arrovian Aggregation Models*. 1999 ISBN 0-7923-8451-2

KLUWER ACADEMIC PUBLISHERS – DORDRECHT / BOSTON / LONDON